WITHDRAWN FROM
TSC LIBRARY

W9-DAM-785

LIBRARY
COMMUNITY COLLEGE

A History of
Eastern Europe
1740–1918

A History of
Eastern Europe
1740–1918

IAN D. ARMOUR

History Instructor, Grant MacEwan College

Hodder Arnold

A MEMBER OF THE HODDER HEADLINE GROUP

First published in Great Britain in 2006 by
Hodder Education, a member of the Hodder Headline Group,
338 Euston Road, London NW1 3BH

www.hoddereducation.com

Distributed in the United States of America by
Oxford University Press Inc.
198 Madison Avenue, New York, NY10016

© 2006 Ian Armour

All rights reserved. No part of this publication may be reproduced or
transmitted in any form or by any means, electronically or mechanically,
including photocopying, recording or any information storage or retrieval
system, without either prior permission in writing from the publisher or a
licence permitting restricted copying. In the United Kingdom such licences
are issued by the Copyright Licensing Agency: Saffron House, 6–10 Kirby
Street, London EC1N 8TS.

The advice and information in this book are believed to be true and accurate
at the date of going to press, but neither the authors nor the publisher can
accept any legal responsibility or liability for any errors or omissions.

Every effort has been made to trace and acknowledge ownership of
copyright. The publishers will be glad to make suitable arrangements with
any copyright holders whom it has not been possible to contact.

British Library Cataloguing in Publication Data
A catalogue record for this book is available from the British Library

Library of Congress Cataloging-in-Publication Data
A catalog record for this book is available from the Library of Congress

ISBN-10 0 340-76040 0
ISBN-13 978-0 340-76040 6

1 2 3 4 5 6 7 8 9 10

Typeset in 10.5 on 12.5pt Apollo by Phoenix Photosetting, Chatham, Kent
Printed and bound in Great Britain by CPI Bath.

What do you think about this book? Or any other
Hodder Education title? Please send your comments to
the feedback section on www.hoddereducation.com.

CONTENTS

LIST OF MAPS

PREFACE

Writing a general textbook of this nature is a sure-fire antidote to academic hubris. While the freedom to range far and wide, rummaging about in other people's specialisms, is in many respects liberating, the further one goes down this route, the more obvious it becomes how limited is one's own knowledge and understanding. At the end of several years' labour on this inherently impossible packaging exercise, I can only hope that readers will bear in mind the difficulties of the genre and that students in particular will find the book of use.

This project had its origins in my experience teaching the survey course 'Quest for Modernity', on Eastern Europe since 1740, at the School of Slavonic and East European Studies (SSEES) in London between 1993 and 1996. I shall always be grateful to Dr Mark Wheeler, who initially asked me to help with the teaching of the course, and to Professor Lindsey Hughes, then head of department, who gave me the opportunity to continue teaching it on my own when Mark Wheeler left SSEES. At the time it struck both me and my students that while twentieth-century Eastern Europe was already well served by a number of texts, the preceding, but crucially formative, century and a half or so was less adequately covered. The present text is the result.

Rather against the wise advice of one of Hodder Arnold's readers of the original proposal, who commented that a thematic or conceptual approach would have made the task easier, I have opted for an essentially narrative structure, dealing with individual empires or regions in turn, in the belief that a textbook must fulfil certain practical and informative functions, and that a primarily undergraduate readership will profit from this most.

Many people have assisted in translating the original idea into publishable form. I am grateful to Christopher Wheeler, commissioning editor for what was then Edward Arnold, for positively inviting me to undertake the project, and to a succession of editors for their indulgence since, notably Jamilah Ahmed, Tiara Misquitta and Liz Wilson. Former colleagues at Staffordshire University, especially Martin Brown and Don MacIver, have been generous with constructive criticisms; and I am indebted to the History team at SSEES for providing a temporary but extremely congenial academic home during 2005–6. Thanks also go to Esther MacKay for repeatedly putting up with me on research trips to London. Finally, my wife Jane Leaper has been a constant intellectual companion as well as a searching critic of successive chapters;

her patent scepticism as to whether I would ever finish has been a major stimulus to doing so. Can-Can, Kissy, Spud and Small all helped by leaving their paw-prints all over the manuscript.

Ian D. Armour
Wetley Rocks, Staffs
15 May 2006

Introduction

DEFINITION

Where is Eastern Europe? Does the term have any meaning at all, now that the cold war has ended and the literally physical division of Europe between East and West has disappeared? The premise of this book is that the answer to the latter question must still be 'yes'. Why that is so, however, depends on how one answers the first question, on the definition of Eastern Europe.

For the purposes of this book, Eastern Europe is defined as the area stretching from the present-day Baltic states of Estonia, Latvia and Lithuania south to Greece. This includes, on an east–west axis, present-day Poland, Belarus and Ukraine; Austria, the Czech Republic, Slovakia, Hungary and Romania; and the states of the former Yugoslavia, Albania and Bulgaria.

In terms of today's political boundaries, the above definition is a geographical one only. The governments of some of the states listed above, not to mention their inhabitants, would object bitterly to being classified as part of Eastern Europe. Put differently, therefore, the present work is a 'prehistory' of those states which emerged in this region by, or since, 1918, and of their peoples.

It was only in the twentieth century that the concept of Eastern Europe was formulated, when it was generally perceived that this area was different from Western, and to some extent Central, Europe. This was not just because of the foundation or expansion of states on territory formerly subsumed within the much larger empires of Germany, Austria–Hungary, Russia and the Ottoman Empire. It was also because, in economic and social terms, Eastern Europe was increasingly perceived as backward, less industrialised and hence less modern than much of Western and Central Europe. In strategic and political terms, Eastern Europe in the twentieth century was an area no longer belonging formally to any regional great power, whatever the fluctuating hegemony of Germany, the Soviet Union or the West. In the phrase used by one scholar for a title, Eastern Europe has been, and remains, 'the lands between'.[1]

The rationale for the present work is that this East European difference was forged in the century and a half preceding 1918, in a period when,

1

conceptually at least, Eastern Europe did not exist. Instead, the area was originally divided between conglomerate, multinational empires. Yet throughout the period in question, all these empires – and the nation-states and nationalities which with time emerged from them – had to come to terms with their backwardness as powers, as well as their own rivalries and the way in which the nationalism of their constituent peoples complicated both internal affairs and international relations.

It is perfectly reasonable to point out that this perception of Eastern Europe as backward was to some extent the 'invention' of West Europeans who, from the eighteenth century, were happy to see the region as the 'complementary other half' of their own 'enlightened' civilisation.[2] Nevertheless, it was a perception endorsed by an increasing number of East Europeans themselves. Long before the idea of Eastern Europe became common, in other words, Eastern Europe had a certain historical reality as a region with certain shared characteristics. It is the identifiability of those characteristics which sets Eastern Europe apart in the period from the mid-eighteenth century to the end of the First World War, just as it sets the region apart in the main twentieth century.

THEMES

Such a claim might seem far-fetched, given the vast diversity of Eastern Europe's peoples, economic and social conditions, political systems and so on. Yet the things that East European states and societies had in common, for all their differences, offer a thematic unity which this introduction aims to emphasise. A summary of these main themes will also serve to explain the chronological span chosen for this history.

The first main theme and in some respects the dominant one is that of *modernisation* or, conversely, backwardness and the stratagems chosen to overcome it. Throughout the period in question, starting with the initial attempts at reform in the Habsburg Monarchy, rulers and leaders of all descriptions in Eastern Europe were aware that their states compared increasingly ill with certain competitors.[3] Early in the eighteenth century the perceived disparities were not all that great. Prussia's superiority over Austria in the 1740s, for instance, was more a matter of organisational flair, concentrated military power and individual genius than one of an innately better socio-economic or political 'system'. In the same way, the enlightened reforms of the last Polish king later in the century were a response to the obvious threat posed by huge standing armies on Poland's borders; in other respects Poland was not markedly inferior to its predators.

In this initial stage, modernisation was essentially about becoming more efficient, about rationalising the financial resources of government and in other ways making polities 'enlightened'. By the end of the century, however, modernity was acquiring other attributes. The French Revolution spread the concepts of individual liberty and civil rights, giving rise to the conviction, on the part of some, that the truly modern state was also a liberal, constitutional one. Even more explosive a legacy of the French Revolution was the ideology known as nationalism, to which further space will be devoted shortly. Later still, the gradual spread of industrialisation from Britain to the European continent, in the nineteenth century, created the ultimate template for modernity, against which Eastern Europe has been measured ever since. Modernisation now meant an industrialised economy, an efficient bureaucratic structure for managing the fruits of that economy and, if not a liberal, then at the very least a constitutional political system, which was able to maintain order within society and ensure that its energies could be directed at goals deemed appropriate by the country's political leadership.

The efforts to modernise made by rulers and elites in Eastern Europe ran into increasing difficulties as the societies in question became more complex. At the outset of our period the assumption of the so-called enlightened absolutist rulers was that modernisation could be ordained. Precisely because it was so rational an agenda, modernisation did not require the consent of the governed, and indeed might have to be imposed against their will. Yet even in the eighteenth century a moderniser like Joseph II encountered the vested interests of historic classes such as the Hungarian nobility. The effect of the French Revolution was to complicate this picture by introducing demands for political representation which went far beyond those of the earlier period. In addition, what modernisation was achieved in Eastern Europe, in economic terms, gradually contributed to a greater social diversity in the areas affected. The rise of a native merchant class and the slow growth of towns made possible in turn the emergence of political opposition to East European rulers. It is characteristic of the gap between Eastern and Western Europe that this potential liberal class was everywhere tiny. Nevertheless it constituted both an impediment to and an argument for further modernisation.

The second major theme in Eastern Europe is the phenomenon of *nationalism*. It would be fair to say that this concept, which most historians agree emerged only in the late eighteenth century, played as little a role in the history of Eastern Europe, in this early period, as it did elsewhere. Nevertheless, the eighteenth century is very much the period of incubation for the idea of the nation, an idea which takes shape, in the writings of some European thinkers, with specific reference to the peoples of Eastern Europe. Once formulated, nationalism in the nineteenth century increasingly took centre stage in the affairs of East European states and societies, to the point where the unwary student might be pardoned for thinking that the whole of this period can be explained as the story of successive 'national' uprisings, 'national' struggles for recognition and 'national liberations' achieved through the formation of 'nation-states', a process broadly completed, according to this scenario, by 1918. No such interpretation could be less satisfactory as an account of historical events, yet there can be no denying that the nineteenth century was a period of increasingly visible nationalism.[4]

If we define nationalism, with some crudity, as loyalty to one's nation, and the strongly held conviction that membership in one's nation is a fundamental aspect of human identity, we are still left with the crucial question of what constitutes a nation. It is essential to the understanding of nationalism that the answer to this question is to be found to a large extent in artificial factors and depends on a good deal of subjectivity. In other words, nations have been identified according to a variety of criteria, and the decision as to whether a nation exists has always depended on how many people subscribe to the view that it exists.

Thus, in Western Europe from about 1500, it was relatively easy for the view to emerge that the peoples living in the unitary, centralised monarchies of this region – states with on the whole stable territorial boundaries like England, Scotland, Portugal, Spain and France – could be identified as nations. 'Nation' in this context meant the people living within a particular state; in short, it was a political definition. As a concept to which people expressed loyalty, however, the nation in this early modern period is still hard to identify. People's allegiance was still primarily to their monarch, or their religion, or to some narrower, more regional definition of identity than the nation. It was only in the late eighteenth century that the first conscious appeals are made for loyalty to the *idea* of the nation. One sees this most strikingly in two commonly cited examples of early nationalism. One is the formation of the United States of America: a new, entirely artificial state, to which the inhabitants of the former British colonies agreed to owe allegiance. The other is the French Republic which emerged from the French Revolution by 1792. For the first time in Europe, a deliberate attempt was made by the leaders of the new Republic to mobilise the entire population of France, all citizens of the Republic, in defence of the *nation* against foreign invaders. This was still a political definition of the nation, in that it equated the nation with the state: all loyal inhabitants of France were deemed members of the French nation.[5]

The applicability of this political definition of the word 'nation' to Eastern Europe, and indeed to many other parts of the world, is much more difficult. What constituted a nation in the East European context had no obvious political units of reference, in other words states, by which nations could be identified. The peoples of Eastern Europe were scattered across, and among, the huge dynastic empires into which the region was divided: the Polish–Lithuanian Commonwealth, the Russian Empire, the Habsburg Monarchy, the Ottoman Empire. None of these institutions was clearly identified with a single people, even if the Polish–Lithuanian Commonwealth, at least, was often wrongly referred to even in the eighteenth century as being exclusively 'Polish'. Within the Habsburg Monarchy, it is true, the formerly independent Kingdom of Hungary, and within it the sub-kingdom of Croatia, retained a separate constitutional identity, and the representatives of these units undoubtedly thought of themselves as Hungarians and Croatians. This, however, was a national consciousness almost entirely confined to a single social class, the nobility. In most of Eastern Europe, by contrast, nations could not be equated with states as they were in Western Europe, because any such potential nation-states had been extinguished in previous centuries or had never existed.

Yet the peoples of Eastern Europe were clearly many and varied, even to the most superficial observer; the multiplicity of spoken languages alone was ample testimony to this diversity. As a consequence, the first attempts to categorise the inhabitants of the region were made according to cultural criteria, like language, rather than political criteria. The most renowned exponent of this cultural definition of the nation was the German philosopher Johann Gottfried Herder who, precisely because he was German, was aware that the sources of a specific German identity were not to be sought in political terms, since Germans lived in a wide variety of states. For Herder, language was the most important identifier of nationality: it was something that made all speakers of that language different from other peoples, and because language itself went back to the earliest origins of a community, it was also inextricably bound up with that people's history.[6] Herder, one of the first systematic linguistic philosophers, was an enthusiastic collector of German folk songs, as proof of this historical cultural identity of the German nation. He also, however, extended his principle of linguistic cultural identity to the other peoples of Eastern Europe. On the basis of language alone, Eastern Europe could no longer be seen as simply the territory of four huge states; it was also a kaleidoscope of nations.

The implications of this central insight – the multinational nature of Eastern Europe – were explosive, even if they were long term. For clearly, if the members of individual nations were encouraged to see themselves as separate, even in a purely cultural sense, then this self-perception was likely to have political consequences, and not just in the internal affairs of the multinational states of the region. Herder was in fact the first person to use the term 'nationalism', in 1774, to describe the concept of loyalty to the nation, the 'conscious cherishing' of the nation's language, its cultural roots, its 'soul'.[7] With time, nationalism came to mean something else: the right of the nation to self-determination, in other words to a state of its own. The world, but especially Eastern Europe, is still living with the murderous fall-out from this ideology.

How nationalism developed in Eastern Europe will be charted below. Here it is enough merely to foreshadow this process, but with the important caveat that nationalism as an ideology, the idea of the nation in our modern sense, is not even thought of at the beginning of our period. Even in the late eighteenth century, after a decade of upheaval caused by the French Revolutionary Wars, nationalism in Eastern Europe was very much a minority preoccupation. It was a phenomenon observable, in the main, among some members of the educated elite of individual peoples – Hungarians,

Poles, some scattered thinkers among the other Slav peoples and the Greeks – but it was not a mass movement. Nor could it be, given the economic and hence social condition of the vast majority of people in the region.[8]

The third main theme of this study is directly related to the question of nationalism and could be regarded as nationalism's antithesis. This is the persistence throughout the whole period of *multinational states*. The Polish–Lithuanian Commonwealth disappeared before the end of the eighteenth century, partitioned among its neighbours Russia, Prussia and Austria. The other conglomerate empires, however, survived right down to 1918; indeed, most of them augmented their territory in Eastern Europe. Only the Ottoman Empire suffered a progressive rolling back of its territory in the Balkans and even this process was not completed until the Balkan Wars of 1912–13.

Apart from their mere physical survival, however, there are other considerations which make the continued existence of such empires a matter of thematic importance. These were hardly moribund concerns. Whatever the internal problems and international weaknesses of both Russia and the Habsburg Monarchy – and these were often severe – both states continued to play the role of great powers and were regarded by most of their subjects as permanent and solidly established authorities. Prussia's control over its Polish population was made all the more secure by its development into the German Empire in 1871. The Ottoman Empire was frequently referred to as 'the sick man' of Europe, where throughout the nineteenth century at least a series of revolts and break-aways succeeded in whittling down Ottoman sovereignty in the Balkans.[9] But even here the 'sick man' epithet was misleading: not only was the Ottoman imperium a long time dying, but repeated efforts were made to reform it and gave it a vitality which continued to take its foes by surprise.

The tendency to see the nineteenth century as an 'age of nationalism' has perhaps obscured this persistence of multinational empires and reinforced the view of them as ramshackle, unviable and doomed to disintegration, history's losers. Without in any way succumbing to an unhistorical nostalgia for such states, however, we should accept that it took the cataclysm of the First World War to overthrow them entirely. Moreover, until the war, which not only strained the resources of these states to the utmost but also opened up the hitherto almost unimaginable prospect of their possible destruction, very few inhabitants of Eastern Europe, with the exception of the Ottoman Empire's Christian subjects, thought in such apocalyptic terms. On the contrary, most people in the Habsburg Monarchy, the German Empire and Russia were resigned to living in them, indeed could probably imagine no alternative. Nationalism by the end of the nineteenth century was undoubtedly a greater force than ever before, but most peoples were not striving for independence from the empire in which they found themselves. Rather, their political aspirations, where they existed at all, were committed to achieving autonomy or some other form of self-determination within the framework of the existing state. Only a very few uncompromising nationalists were dedicated to what they fondly referred to as 'national' revolution and complete independence.

Not only was the degree of popular discontent with multinational empires relative, but the rulers of these empires, and the political and social elites whom the rulers increasingly co-opted to advise them, did what they could to reinforce loyalty to the state. Often this did not amount to much and we should not exaggerate its effects. A good deal depended on the will of rulers and elites to promote such loyalty, or even to admit that there was a problem. When Emperor Francis I of Austria was told that a certain individual was an Austrian patriot, he allegedly replied, 'But is he a patriot for *me*?' Francis felt he should be able to take his subjects' loyalty for granted; it was the first duty of any subject.[10] Other dynasts, however, were not so egotistic, and in their attempts to bind together their diverse realms they deployed a number of stratagems.

The most obvious of these was to inculcate loyalty, to the dynasty personally but also, by implication, to the concept of empire itself. This had mixed results and was arguably most successful in the Habsburg Monarchy, where *Habsburgtreue*, or loyalty to the Habsburgs, was not confined to Austrian Germans (the original base of the dynasty) but was also discernible in other nationalities, at least among certain classes and professions, such as the military and the bureaucracy. In the Russian Empire and in Prussia dynastic loyalty was much less likely among non-Russian or non-German minorities, although Baltic Germans at least were traditionally loyal subjects of the tsar. In the Balkan provinces of the Ottoman Empire fealty to the sultan could not be taken for granted even in Muslims, whether of Turkish or non-Turkish ethnic origin, and was even more problematical among Christians.

Towards the end of the nineteenth century we can see the development of what has been termed 'official nationalism'. This was the attempt by the empires to promote loyalty specifically to the state, regardless of the subject's nationality. The most ambitious example of this state nationalism is the so-called 'Russification' campaign of the tsarist government in Russia. Similar attempts were made by the Prussian government and by Hungarian governments after 1867, and by the reformist but also incipiently Turkish nationalist Young Turk movement in the Ottoman Empire after 1908. By and large this coercive approach was a failure and merely stirred up nationalist resentment among the subject peoples against whom it was directed. A notable side effect, however, was the creation of a modern nationalism among Russians, Germans, Hungarians and Turks.

The final stratagem to which the rulers of multinational empires resorted was to promote economic development. This was generally undertaken for the primary purpose of strengthening the state, and only secondarily, if at all, with an eye to averting social or nationalist unrest. Nevertheless, where modernisation was even partially achieved it had two seemingly contradictory effects. On the one hand, the greater social variegation which came in the wake of economic development made the emergence of nationalism all the more likely. On the other hand, greater prosperity gave all those classes, and nationalities, who shared in it a greater reason for regarding the status quo, in other words the preservation of the multinational state, as acceptable, not to say inevitable. Which of the two, nationalism or loyalty to the state, was likely, if at all, to come out uppermost remained a moot point short of some geopolitical upheaval, but, on balance, circumstances favoured the status quo.

ORGANISATION

With these three themes in mind, then – modernisation, nationalism and the multinational state – the organisation of this book will become clear. The overall structure of the three main parts is chronological, but within each of these parts subject matter is necessarily broken down into chapters on specific areas and states. Each part is introduced by a thematic chapter which sets the scene and describes particular developments which span the whole or much of the period in question.

Part One covers the eighteenth-century background. This is an essential part of the story, since the conditions and events of this period not only help explain subsequent developments but also illustrate each of the key themes of the book. As far as modernisation is concerned, the eighteenth century saw the first serious attempts made outside Peter the Great's Russia to improve state efficiency, with the specific aim of closing a perceived gap between East European regimes and more modern competitors. The would-be modernisers here were Maria Theresa of Austria and her even more determinedly modernising sons, Joseph II and Leopold II. Some attention will also be paid to the comparable effort made in the final decades of the Polish–Lithuanian Commonwealth, even though, in the end, this effort was frustrated by partition. In this respect Poland offered a cautionary illustration to other states, such as the Ottoman Empire, of the potential penalty for failure to modernise.

The eighteenth century is also important, as already suggested, for an understanding of the origins and nature of nationalism, even if its full force was not felt until later. Some of the earliest expressions of East European nationalism will be described, together with an explanation of the narrower, gentry-based nationalism that distinguishes the Hungarian and Polish variants. The incendiary potential of nationalism, as demonstrated by the French Revolution, can also be said to be among the reasons for East European rulers' deliberate abandonment of modernisation, typified by the reaction of Francis I of Austria.

Finally, the eighteenth century was the first point at which all the major multinational empires of Eastern Europe came into direct conflict with one

another. Russian encroachment on the Ottoman Empire began in earnest in this period; the Habsburg Monarchy was in conflict with the Ottomans, but also became aware of the new Russian power; Austro-Prussian rivalry became a byword; and Poland–Lithuania was ground to pieces between its predatory neighbours.

In *Part Two*, the full impact of the eighteenth-century legacy in the period between 1804 and 1867 is discussed. This impact is broadly summarised as one of nationalism, revolution and state formation. The importance of the Napoleonic Empire in transmitting this impact is undeniable, since the conquests of Napoleon I, brief though they were, succeeded in turning much of Eastern Europe upside down and had an effect long after Napoleon's fall in 1815.[11] Although the following period was one of political reaction, it was clear from the revolutions of 1848 that the genie of change could not be stuffed back into its bottle. By 1867, when the Habsburg Monarchy adopted certain wide-ranging constitutional changes, Eastern Europe as a whole had also been transformed by the emergence of nationalism, social as well as political revolution, and the appearance of entirely new states.

Nationalism, from being the preoccupation of the few, was by the end of this period increasingly seen as a mass motivator, an irresistible force of the age. This, it should be remembered, was the perception above all of committed nationalists, who tended everywhere to project their enthusiasm onto the whole of society; among those peoples whose population remained largely peasant, nationalism was still embryonic. Nevertheless, wars had been fought in Eastern Europe, and blood spilt, in the name of the nation, and the more this happened, the greater the number of people aware of their nationality. This had implications for the nature of political change within existing states and even greater implications for the viability of the international state system.

In terms of other political changes the period through to 1867 saw the long-term effects of the French Revolution itself rippling through Eastern Europe like the aftershocks of an earthquake. The concepts of political rights, equality, constitutionality and even social justice became issues among at least some classes of East Europeans. By the end of this period the form, if not the reality, of liberal constitutionalism was more common in Eastern Europe. In addition to political revolution, some societies of Eastern Europe were also beginning to be exposed to the effects of economic and social change. The fundamental precondition for this was the freeing of peasant labour from serfdom, in the Habsburg Monarchy by 1848, in Russia by 1861 and in the Ottoman Empire through the establishment of autonomous nation-states. This made possible in turn the beginnings of genuine modernisation, albeit with the gap between Eastern and Western Europe even greater than it had been in the eighteenth century.

The final feature of this period, the emergence of nation-states, was a phenomenon confined to the Ottoman Empire. This entailed a succession of

international crises, and was indeed accomplished in each case only as a result of great power intervention, but was important for the intensification of nationalism and the creation of fresh sources of international conflict.

Part Three is about nationalism, independence and modernisation through to the end of the First World War. Put differently, this part can be seen as taking each of our three main themes to a sort of culmination, or climactic point. Nationalism plays an increasingly eye-catching role in this third period. This is nowhere more so than in the Habsburg Monarchy, which became a byword for nationality disputes, and whose very existence as a great power came into question by 1914 as a result of the fatal symbiosis between the Monarchy's internal problems and its foreign relations. Nationalism also put paid to the Ottoman Empire, at least that portion of it in South-Eastern Europe. A less well-known aspect of nationalism in this period was its effect on the German and Russian empires. In the case of Germany this was exclusively a Polish problem; in the case of Russia, Poles were only one of a multitude of subject nationalities increasingly unhappy with the tsarist regime.

Several states formally achieved independence in this period well before 1914. The First World War, however, brought formal independence for even more states, or rather peoples, and in the process transformed the political map of Eastern Europe into more or less the outlines it has today. The great multinational empires disappeared, with the exception of the Soviet Union, the revolutionary Communist regime which took over the Russian Empire. The emergence of the so-called successor states in Eastern Europe and the establishment of the Soviet Union were the dominant features of the political landscape throughout most of the twentieth century.

As for modernisation, this is a part of the story which perhaps ought to be termed anticlimactic, for the societies of Eastern Europe in this third period remained backward by comparison with the rest of Europe. It is true that much of Eastern Europe experienced an accelerating industrialisation and consequently considerable social change. The vast majority of East Europeans, however, continued to live in an agrarian economy, even if one increasingly influenced (often negatively) by outside forces. Independence as a sovereign state, for instance, did not necessarily avert economic dependence. In a political sense, too, Eastern Europe remained backward. Despite the formal existence of constitutional government in most states (even Russia had a constitution after 1905) and the spread of political parties, governments and political institutions were on the whole authoritarian and in many ways unrepresentative and unresponsive to the needs of ordinary people. The catastrophe of the First World War added widespread physical destruction, loss of life and psychological traumatisation to the factors keeping Eastern Europe behind.

PART ONE

THE EIGHTEENTH-CENTURY BACKGROUND
1740–1804

1   Languages of Eastern Europe. Source: (p. 437) Languages of Europe, *A History of the Modern World*, 3rd edn, by R. R. Palmer and Joel Colton (Alfred A. Knopf, 1965)

1

PEOPLES, STATES AND SOCIETIES

The purpose of this chapter is to describe eighteenth-century Eastern Europe in general terms at the outset of our period. This involves first of all the human geography of the region, the peoples inhabiting it. Second is a summary of the political geography: the states of Eastern Europe, including their historical evolution and the changing nature of their relationships with each other in this period. Third is a survey of economic and social conditions, and the way in which these determined political systems within individual states.

PEOPLES AND LANGUAGES

The sheer multiplicity of peoples in Eastern Europe is at first sight bewildering. Altogether there were eight major ethnic groups settled by the eighteenth century, speaking some two dozen languages and practising half a dozen religions. (See Map 1.)

One of the most important points to make about the ethnography of Eastern Europe (as of Western Europe) is that the region was settled for the most part by successive waves of peoples arriving from outside. For centuries Eastern Europe was used as a sort of doormat by Germanic, Slavic, Turkic and other peoples, all seeking entry to the region, fighting, conquering or expelling each other. Indigenous peoples, like the Greeks and Albanians, were either conquered or pressed to the mountainous margins of the region; sometimes territory could be reclaimed, sometimes the newcomers were assimilated by the conquered population, as happened with the Turkic Bulgars and their Slav subjects. The last major influx of people was the invasion of the Magyars in the ninth century, but recurrent wars and conquests ensured that the ethnographic balance was constantly being altered.

The results of this process were twofold. First, the peoples of the region were, by the eighteenth century, highly intermixed, in the sense that many areas contained numerous ethnic groups. Second, the centuries-long process of settlement and resettlement meant that very few peoples, let alone individuals, could claim any sort of direct, unbroken lineal descent from their ancient ancestors. The very languages that the inhabitants of the region spoke betrayed a complex, multi-ethnic inheritance. In Eastern Europe, as elsewhere, everyone was a mongrel.

Apart from Celtic and other early inhabitants of whom only archaeological traces remain, the *Greeks* were among the longest-established peoples. The degree to which eighteenth-century Greeks, and the language they spoke, were descended from the ancient Greeks has been contested; what cannot be denied is that a belief in this link with the Hellenic past was to prove a powerful element in modern Greek nationalism. More important in the context of the eighteenth century was the fact that the Greek world was a far-flung one: Greek settlements were to be found across the region and the largest of these were in Constantinople and Smyrna, not in the Greek Peninsula.

Equally long established were the *Albanians*, an indigenous people originally inhabiting the Roman province of Illyria, but gradually crowded into the mountains of the western Balkans by the arrival of new peoples. Converted in large numbers to Islam following the Ottoman conquest, Albanians became a favoured people in the Ottoman Balkans, and the area of Albanian settlement slowly spread into areas bordering on present-day Albania.

On the south-eastern shores of the Baltic, the peoples collectively known as *Balts* were one of the first groups of Indo-European language-speakers to arrive in Europe, around 2000 BC. Two of these peoples, the Prussians and the Curonians, had been assimilated following the conquest of the Baltic shore by the Teutonic Knights in the Middle Ages; they left behind their names in the shape of the (German) Duchy of Prussia and the coastal area known as Courland. The other two peoples, Letts or Latvians, and Lithuanians, survived, the Letts as a subject people of the Teutonic Knights and then Russia, the Lithuanians by uniting with Poland in the fourteenth century.

Two peoples, widely separated, represented the *Romance*, or Latin-based, group of languages. In the Istrian Peninsula and along the Adriatic coast lived substantial numbers of Italians, most of them still subjects of the Venetian Republic. On the other side of the Balkan Peninsula, the inhabitants of what was to become today's Romania claimed descent from the ancient Roman colonists of Dacia. Romanian is undoubtedly a Latinate language, though one showing heavy traces of Slavic, Turkic and other tongues.

The most numerous language group in Eastern Europe is that of the *Slavonic*-speaking peoples. Originating in the area between the Dniester and Vistula rivers, the Slavs were to begin with an undifferentiated mass of tribes, all of whom spoke essentially the same language. From the first to the sixth century onwards, however, the Slavs began to fan out in different directions, settling in what is now Russia proper, in the lands further to the west, and in the Balkans. The longer they remained settled in their respective new homelands, the further apart grew their languages, to the point where philologists nowadays distinguish between three main sub-groups. The East Slavs speak Russian, Ukrainian and Byelorussian or White Russian. The West Slavs are the Czechs, Slovaks and Poles. The South Slavs include Slovenes, Croats, Serbs and Bulgarians. Croats, Serbs and Bulgarians all take their names from Iranian or Turkic peoples who imposed themselves on the Slavs already settled in the Balkans and were then assimilated by them.

One group of peoples who have nothing in common, linguistically, with their Indo-European neighbours are the *Finno-Ugrians*. This includes the Estonians, who had arrived on the north-east coast of the Baltic with their close relatives, the Finns, by Roman times; another related people, the Livs, left their name to the coastal area of Livonia after conquest by the Teutonic Knights. Much later, in the ninth century, the Magyars, or ethnic Hungarians, burst upon the European world from the east. They rampaged as far afield as Burgundy and northern Italy before settling down in the Pannonian Plain, which forms today's Hungary. In doing so, the Magyars drove a permanent wedge between the West and South Slavs, over several of whom they gradually established a dominion in the early Middle Ages.

A special role had been played in Eastern Europe, for centuries, by the *Germans*. The various Germanic peoples had been knocking at the doors of the Roman Empire long before the Slavs, and by the end of the first millennium Germanic kingdoms, including the vast domain founded by Charles the Great (Charlemagne) in AD 800, which came to be known as the Holy Roman Empire, were part of the state structure of medieval Europe. The first German outpost in Eastern Europe was the Duchy of Austria, the 'eastern realm' (*Österreich*), created in the ninth century by Charlemagne as a buffer zone against barbarians from the east. Then, in the early Middle Ages, German influence was extended along the Baltic littoral when the Teutonic Knights undertook the 'northern crusades' against the pagan peoples of the region, exterminating some like the Prussians, subjugating and Christianising others. The final extension of German influence in Eastern Europe was more peaceful: throughout the late Middle Ages, there was a steady influx of German artisans and tradesmen, clerics and artists, many invited into kingdoms whose rulers were acutely conscious that their realms lacked such specialists. As a result German settlements could be found the length and breadth of Eastern Europe, from the Baltic ports to Transylvania, from western Bohemia to St Petersburg. Ethnic Germans were above all an urban class, although the oldest communities, such as the Saxons of Transylvania, were also agriculturists.

Among the latest entrants into the Balkans were the *Ottoman Turks*. This was a consequence of the conquest, by the late sixteenth century, of southeastern Europe as far north as central Hungary by the Ottoman sultans, even though Hungary at least had been reclaimed for Christendom by 1699. Apart from the religious divide created by this subjection of the Balkans to an Islamic power, the dominance of the Ottomans for so long meant that by the start of our period a sizeable proportion of the population was ethnically different as well. The term 'Ottoman' denotes the Muslim ruling class rather than a single ethnic group; but in so far as the Ottoman conquest brought in its wake large numbers of ethnic Turks in the form of administrators, soldiers and their hangers-on, it altered the demographic balance of the Balkans substantially.

As a result of their dispersion across the Mediterranean and European world since Roman times, *Jews* by the eighteenth century were to be found in many parts of Eastern Europe, and in several cases had been there for centuries. Virtually everywhere, however, Jewish communities were at best a tolerated minority within their 'host' society, at worst subject to appalling and repeated indignities and persecution. Jews' retention of a distinctive religious rite and customs meant that they remained a class apart, repeatedly subjected to restrictions on their faith, where they lived, what occupations they could pursue. These very restrictions ensured that Jews, wherever they settled in Eastern Europe, tended to establish themselves as a commercial class. They made their often highly precarious livings as merchants, as craftsmen, as bailiffs for the landowner class and, above all, as moneylenders to rich and poor alike, and in the case of a select few lending millions to European princes.

Suffering an even worse plight than the Jews were Eastern Europe's *Gypsies* or Roma, an Indo-European people from India who had arrived in the Balkans via the Byzantine Empire by the eleventh century or even earlier. Gypsy communities spread across Eastern Europe in the Middle Ages, working as metal craftsmen, musicians, even soldiers; but everywhere they were treated as aliens, the lowest of the low, and persecution forced on them a wandering, unsettled way of life. This in turn confirmed the Gypsies' image as rootless and they remained trapped between the popular prejudice which excluded them and the inveterate desire of local rulers to regulate them and, by forcing them to settle, to make them taxable. In the Romanian principalities of the Ottoman Empire, Gypsies had for a long time been treated virtually as slaves; and although this was exceptional, the position of Gypsies elsewhere was generally invidious.

STATES

The political geography of Eastern Europe in 1740 did not reflect the ethnic diversity outlined above. Instead, the region was divided between seven sovereign states, all multinational, all the product of complex historical developments. (See Map 2.)

Least significant was the city-state of *Ragusa* (today's Dubrovnik). Though overshadowed throughout its long history by more powerful neighbours,

Ragusa had profited from its strategic position at the southern end of the Adriatic and as the western end of major trade routes across the Balkans. The Ottoman conquest of the peninsula, while it spelt economic decline for the Venetian Republic and for much of the eastern Mediterranean, was by

2   States of Eastern Europe in 1740. Source: (pp. 304–5) Europe 1740, *A History of the Modern World*, 3rd edn, by R. R. Palmer and Joel Colton (Alfred A. Knopf, 1965)

contrast an opportunity for Ragusa, which benefited from the fact that it posed no threat to Ottoman power and was at the same time a valuable conduit for trade and diplomacy. Largely populated by Croatian Slavs, in cultural character Ragusa had more in common with its fellow city-states in Italy. Politically it was a republic, dominated in the eighteenth century by an oligarchy of leading merchant families.

The Republic of *Venice*, which still ruled over most of the Dalmatian coast to the north of Ragusa, was also a city-state in decline, though more sizeable and a former regional great power. Much of its energies had been devoted to combating Ottoman encroachments on its very doorstep. Venice retained its grip on the Istrian Peninsula and the Dalmatian coast until the Ottoman threat was past; but by the eighteenth century it too was decrepit, its commerce evaporated and its foothold on the eastern Adriatic dependent on the goodwill of the much more powerful Habsburg Monarchy.

Of the remaining five states in Eastern Europe, two, the Ottoman Empire and the Polish–Lithuanian Commonwealth, can be characterised as states on the defensive, if not positively in decline. Both these powers, for varying reasons, had ceased to expand in terms of territory and were in fact seen as fields for expansion by their more predatory neighbours.

The *Ottoman Empire* was for centuries the terror of Christian Europe and, despite its manifold problems, was still a formidable military power in the eighteenth century. This absolute, military monarchy, whose ruler, the sultan, was regarded by his Muslim subjects as God's vassal on earth, had been a presence in the Balkan Peninsula since 1345. At its zenith, in the mid-sixteenth century, the Ottoman imperium stretched from Arabia to northern Hungary, and as late as 1683 the sultan's armies unsuccessfully besieged Vienna. In a series of stubborn campaigns thereafter, the Habsburg Monarchy had wrested Hungary from Ottoman control; later, the Habsburgs briefly held the core of modern-day Serbia (1718–39). In a sign that Ottoman power was not quite moribund, however, the sultan actually regained Serbia in 1739. The Ottoman dominions still covered the whole of the Balkan Peninsula south of Croatia and Hungary and west of Venetian Dalmatia and Ragusa; they included the vassal principalities of Moldavia and Wallachia, and the Black Sea, despite Russian advances from the north-east, was still a Turkish lake.

One of the largest states in Europe in 1740, reaching from the Baltic almost to the Black Sea, was the '*Polish Commonwealth of the Kingdom of Poland and the Grand Duchy of Lithuania*'. This union of two medieval states dated from 1386, although it was not formalised until 1569, and included in the Commonwealth's borders not only Poles and Lithuanians but Germans, Jews, Ukrainians and White Russians. By the early eighteenth century the balance of power had altered drastically in Poland–Lithuania's disfavour and this, combined with its internal weaknesses, had already made it the plaything of its neighbours.

The *Habsburg Monarchy* was in many respects a more dynamic state than either Poland–Lithuania or the Ottoman Empire; nevertheless, the very nature of the Monarchy's historical development meant that it too was vulnerable. Its starting point was the Duchy of Austria, originally founded by the Holy Roman Empire as a defensive outpost against eastern barbarians. Ruled from the thirteenth century by the family of Habsburg, who also held the elective dignity of Holy Roman Emperor almost continuously from the fifteenth century, Austria became the nucleus of a vast agglomeration of principalities and kingdoms, most acquired through dynastic alliance rather than war. The Habsburg realm embraced the kingdoms of Hungary (including Croatia) and Bohemia and was a classic case of imperial 'overstretch', with territory and pretensions to hegemony in the Netherlands, Germany and Italy, as well as an uneasy relationship with its East European neighbours.

A state just beginning to play a more forceful role in Eastern Europe, despite being part of it for centuries, was the Kingdom of *Prussia*, an amalgam of the Margravate of Brandenburg and the Duchy of Prussia. Brandenburg had also been formed as a border territory of the Holy Roman Empire and was from an early point an entirely German principality, ruled from 1411 by the Hohenzollern dynasty. It was Prussia, however, as the original conquest of the crusading Teutonic Knights, which had made the greatest impact on Eastern Europe in the Middle Ages. At its greatest extent, the 'State of the Order' (*Ordenstaat*) had occupied the whole of the Baltic coast and its hinterland, from Danzig to present-day Estonia. The area known as 'East Prussia' became Germanised, whereas 'West Prussia' was lost to Poland in the fifteenth century. In the Baltic provinces to the north, also lost to neighbouring states from the fifteenth century, the legacy of the Order's rule was more complex: colonisation by the Teutonic Knights created urban centres and a landowning class, which were largely German; but the peasant mass of the population remained Lithuanian, Latvian and Estonian. Prussia itself came under the rule of the Hohenzollerns in 1511, and the modern Kingdom of Prussia, proclaimed in 1701, was thus a state in two halves, divided by Polish territory. Prussia was ruled by a dynasty which saw military strength, founded on the economic exploitation of the resources of the state, as the sole security of the state itself. This preoccupation had ominous implications for Prussia's neighbours in the region.

Finally, the *Russian Empire* was by 1740 firmly established as a regional great power. The earliest Slav state on the Russian Plain was formed in the ninth century, but was overwhelmed by the Mongol invasion of the thirteenth century. For the next two and a half centuries the eastern Slavs lived under Mongol domination, a period which saw the emergence of Russian, White Russian and Ukrainian as separate languages. In the fifteenth century the Principality of Muscovy, centred on Moscow, struggled free of the Mongol yoke and by 1584 had expanded north to the Arctic Ocean, east into Siberia and south-east as far as the Caspian Sea. In the seventeenth century, the tsars of the Romanov dynasty began to make inroads into the territory of the Polish–Lithuanian Commonwealth to the west; this included most of what is today Belarus and the area of the Ukraine east of the Dnieper. It was under tsar Peter I (1682–1725) that Russia became a force to be feared in Eastern Europe. In a series of wars owing their success to Peter's determined modernisation of Russian arms and administration, Russia defeated the regional great power of the day, Sweden, and seized control of the Baltic coast from Riga to the Gulf of Finland. Russian interference in the affairs of the weakened Polish–Lithuanian Commonwealth steadily increased; and Russia acquired its first permanent port on the Black Sea when it took Azov from the Ottoman Empire in 1696. The enlargement of this already huge, autocratically ruled state, at the expense of Poland–Lithuania and the Ottomans, looked set to continue.

SOCIETIES

The handiest method for understanding East European societies in the eighteenth century is to explain the different classes into which they were divided; to grasp the profound gulf between urban and agrarian life; and to appreciate the importance of religious identities.

The last of these, *religion*, deserves mention first, as a factor which had shaped societies in the region since antiquity. The Roman Empire officially adopted Christianity in the fourth century, but even before that the Emperor Constantine moved the imperial capital from Rome to Byzantium, henceforth Constantinople, at the junction of Europe and Asia. The move to what was in the main a Greek-speaking, Hellenised environment meant, with time, an increasing divergence between an eastern, Greek-based Church and the original, Latin-based Church of Rome, a gap widened by the barbarian invasions of Europe and the breakdown of imperial control in the west. By 1071 the differences in liturgy, ritual and certain aspects of religious belief itself were such that a formal schism occurred between the Roman papacy and adherents of the Greek rite.

This split between *Roman Catholicism*, as we know it today, in the west, and *Greek Orthodoxy*, in the east, has shaped Eastern Europe ever since. For the pagan peoples who arrived in Eastern Europe over the centuries and were converted to Christianity found themselves the objects of a competition between east and west to retain their religious loyalty. Broadly speaking, those converted from the direction of Rome stayed with the Latin rite, while those who owed their conversion to Byzantium followed Orthodoxy. This religious, and hence cultural, fault-line runs in an arc from the Adriatic to the Russo-Finnish border to this day. Croats, some Albanians, Hungarians, Czechs, Slovaks, Poles and Baltic peoples all belonged, at least initially, to the Catholic world and, when they developed a literary language, used a Latin-based alphabet. The peoples of the Balkans, together with the Slav inhabitants of Russia, were Greek Orthodox in religion and, with the exception of the Romanians and Albanians, eventually developed literary languages using a Cyrillic or Greek-based alphabet.

The Ottoman invasions introduced a new religion, *Islam*. This was the faith of the new Ottoman overlords; but its establishment did not herald the forcible conversion of the Christian population. On the contrary, the Ottomans by medieval standards were remarkably tolerant of other religions. As long as non-Muslims acknowledged the sultan's suzerainty, they were free to practise their faith and even allowed autonomy in running their own churches. This was convenient for the Ottoman government, which preferred to tax the non-Muslim rather than the Muslim population. Despite the material advantages of conversion, the majority of Ottoman Christians remained true to their faith. Only in parts of Bosnia, and in the Albanian-inhabited parts of the Empire, did substantial numbers convert to Islam, a process which has left Muslim populations in these areas to the present. In addition, the Jewish population of the Ottoman Empire gradually rose as Jews were lured there by the promise of a religious toleration not extended to them in Christian Europe.

In the sixteenth century *Protestantism* further divided the Christians of Eastern Europe. The teachings of Martin Luther proved popular among the German population of Prussia, the Polish–Lithuanian Commonwealth and the Baltic coast, as well as in Bohemia and Moravia; as an essentially German import, however, Lutheranism made rather fewer converts among Poles, Czechs and Hungarians. Calvinism, by contrast, was initially quite success-ful among the Polish and Hungarian gentry, largely for political and social reasons: it was associated with freedom of conscience and hence political liberty, but also with a sense of being the elect or chosen by God. By the early eighteenth century, however, the Catholic 'counter-reformation' had won back many in both countries, although a substantial minority of the Hungarian gentry, at least, stayed Calvinist. The religious situation was more complicated in the Bohemian lands, where the proto-Protestant heresy of Hussitism had already taken root before the Reformation; Czech Protestants then suffered persecution and exile at the hands of the Catholic Habsburgs in the seventeenth century and by 1740 very few of them were left.

Apart from Eastern Europe's scattered Jewish communities, the last major religious grouping was the *Uniate* Church. This consisted of all those who accepted the so-called 'Union of Brest' of 1596, a device whereby the Catholic Church of the Polish–Lithuanian Commonwealth persuaded the country's Orthodox population, most of them Ukrainian, to acknowledge the supremacy of the Pope, in return for the right to practise the traditional rites and customs of Orthodoxy, such as priestly marriage. Uniates, it was reasoned, would thus be less likely to succumb to the blandishments of Orthodox Russia, Poland's increasingly threatening neighbour. At the outset of the eighteenth century Uniates made up 33 per cent of the Common-wealth's population.

No attempt to explain the class structure of Eastern Europe in this period would make sense without an appreciation of the overwhelmingly *agrarian* nature of the societies in question. Towns in this environment were small islands in a sea of countryside. This was not unique to Eastern Europe: across the continent it was rare for any urban centre to exceed a population of 100,000, and London and Paris, with 675,000 and 500,000 in 1750, were giants.[1] It was rather the pattern and speed of urbanisation, and the relatively greater number of towns in Western and especially north-western Europe, which made Eastern Europe seem backward by comparison. In England by 1750 17 per cent of the population was urban.[2] In the Habsburg Monarchy of 1700, by contrast, only 2 per cent of the population was urban.[3] Vienna, capital of the Habsburgs, had a mere 120,000 inhabitants in 1750; Prague, 50,000; Warsaw, 30,000.[4] The exceptional size of Constantinople, with over 400,000 people in the mid-century, was due to its long history as an imperial capital, at the crossroads of two continents.[5]

Populations in Eastern Europe continued to increase throughout the eighteenth century and this was reflected in the growth of some towns: Vienna by the 1790s had 200,000 inhabitants, Warsaw had 150,000 and St Petersburg, founded in 1703, had 191,000.[6] But the majority of towns remained stagnant economically, for reasons which were largely negative. Historians are still debating why modern, industrialised society should have emerged first in north-western Europe, but among the long-term causes were the breakdown of feudalism, the intensification of commerce, the accumulation of capital and 'the uniquely flexible parliamentary system that allowed capitalism to flourish'.[7] Towns were at the heart of this politico-economic culture and 'the combination of strong towns and the absence of strong imperial and Church rule' released powerful forces in society.[8] Eastern Europe lacked these advantages. Not only were its political institutions authoritarian but its social structures were both a consequence and a reinforcement of the existing political order.

At the top of the social tree, in the Christian societies of Eastern Europe, were the *magnate* class, or titled aristocracy, the feudal origins of whose status lay in the lands granted to them by the monarch in exchange for military or bureaucratic service. Few in numbers, magnates were distinguished from the rest of the landowning or noble class by the sheer size of their estates, their fabulous wealth and their near-monopoly, at least in the Habsburg Monarchy, of the high offices of state, at court, in government and in the military, as well as in the hierarchy of the Catholic Church. This was a class most visible in the Austrian and Bohemian crownlands, the Kingdom of Hungary (including Croatia) and the Polish–Lithuanian Commonwealth. In this context, it is worth noting that monarchs themselves were also great landowners, as were the Catholic Church and the Russian Orthodox Church.

An entirely different class was the lesser nobility, or *gentry* class. This distinction is important for two reasons. Firstly, in Poland–Lithuania, and in

Hungary, the gentry were numerous: the Polish *szlachta*, as the nobility was called, amounted to some 10 per cent of the population, while in Hungary the nobility generally (including magnates) made up about 5 per cent.[9] Many Polish and Hungarian nobles were wealthy, but many were not; indeed, at the lower end of the scale the 'sandalled nobility', so called because they could not afford leather boots, lived a life little different from that of peasants. Rich or poor, however, the nobility in Poland–Lithuania was the only class entitled to vote and to sit in the *Sejm* (the Polish parliament), while in the Hungarian Diet, nobles had an overwhelming predominance over townspeople; when Poles or Hungarians referred to the 'nation' in the eighteenth century, they meant this gentry class, not all Poles or Hungarians. And the Polish *szlachta* exercised real power, as we shall see, while containing the turbulent Hungarian gentry was a recurrent headache for the Habsburgs.

The second reason for singling out the lesser nobility is that, in Russia most of all, but also in Prussia, nobles functioned as an arm of the state. This *service nobility* held their estates and their privileges explicitly on condition that they rendered service to the monarch, whether in the bureaucracy or the military. In autocratic Russia, this was a method by which successive tsars tightened their control over the potentially rebellious landowning class. A partial exception to this pattern, in the recently acquired Baltic provinces of the Russian Empire, was represented by the German landowners there, who retained ancient privileges of local assembly and self-regulation. In Prussia, the *Junkers*, as the landowning class was called, had been more recently subordinated to the monarch's supervision in this fashion, but were fast acquiring a reputation for blind loyalty and pride in military service.

Town dwellers, in this top-heavy social order, played a much less significant role than their counterparts in Western Europe. The economic stagnation alluded to above was part consequence and part cause of the fact that towns in Eastern Europe did not enjoy an independent existence. In the lands that came to make up the Habsburg Monarchy, as in Prussia and the Polish–Lithuanian Commonwealth, some towns emerged in the Middle Ages as royal boroughs, obliged to submit to the authority of the crown in return for protection in an uncertain world. This subordinate status, as a source of taxable revenue for the monarch rather than an urban power, was still a characteristic of the royal towns of these kingdoms. In addition, in all these states there were private as opposed to royal towns, built on the estates of noble landowners or the Church, and even less encouraged to develop a separate corporate identity. In the Russian Empire, again with the partial exception of the Baltic provinces, towns were if anything even less regarded, having virtually no municipal autonomy. In the rest of Eastern Europe, towns might be represented as a separate estate in provincial or national diets, but as one historian has said in relation to the Habsburg Monarchy, they 'never developed a legal or constitutional base to match their commercial advance from the later Middle Ages'.[10] Only the city-states of Venice and Ragusa, by definition merchant oligarchies, stood out against this rule.

At the bottom of the heap suffered the most numerous but the most powerless class of all, the *peasantry*. Here one must distinguish between those peasants who at the start of the eighteenth century were still free and the vast majority who were decidedly unfree. On the whole, peasants whose economy revolved around transhumance, or the seasonal herding of livestock, such as the Alpine farmers of the Austrian crownlands, retained their personal freedom, however hard their lives. But for tillers of the soil the picture was far grimmer. In contrast to the trend in Western Europe, peasants in this category from the fifteenth century had been increasingly subjected to what has been called the 'second serfdom'. Originally tenant farmers or even freeholders, dependent on noble or royal protection but otherwise free, peasants were the victims of a complex series of economic changes which impelled nobles, or monarchs, to impose even more tax or labour obligations on peasants, while at the same time restricting their personal freedom of movement. In Russia this process of enserfment, whereby the service nobility were granted absolute ownership of their peasants by the autocracy in return for service, was complete by 1649. In Poland–Lithuania, Prussia and the Habsburg Monarchy, economic downturn, often due to war, depopulation and the drying up of monetary rents, drove landowners to create trade monopolies, take over common land, insist on payment of rents in kind and above all demand unpaid labour services and bind the peasant legally to the land. Often landowners were the sole judicial authority over peasants.

Here, in the condition of the peasantry, was one of the central reasons for the continuing backwardness of Eastern Europe throughout the eighteenth century. Serfdom was an inherently inefficient system, with the added disadvantage that the peasants periodically erupted in savage revolt. Rulers and nobles alike recognised its inefficiency, and in some cases its injustice, but were locked into it by economic interest and fear of the consequences of relaxation.

In contrast to Christian Eastern Europe, the social order in the European provinces of the Ottoman Empire was much simpler. In a society where the ultimate authority was God, ruling through the absolute intermediary of the sultan and his vassals, the fundamental distinction was between the Ottoman Muslim ruling class and all non-Muslims, whether Christian or Jewish, Catholic or Orthodox. The gradation of the Ottoman class will be dealt with below, as will the complexities of Christian societies. Here it is enough to say that the sultan's provincial administrators, his army and the landowning class throughout the Balkans, with the exception of the Romanian principalities, were Muslim. By the eighteenth century some officials of the imperial bureaucracy, notably that part of it which handled diplomacy, were by tradition Greeks, among whom education and knowledge of foreign languages was not uncommon. Greeks also functioned throughout European Turkey not only as Orthodox clergy but also as a ubiquitous merchant class. For the Christian population as a whole, however, second-class status was the norm. The majority of non-Muslim inhabitants of the Ottoman Balkans lived the life of peasants, free to practise their religion but heavily taxed and subject to a whole range of galling restrictions.

2

WAR, ENLIGHTENMENT AND NATIONALISM

We can now turn to those general developments which effected the most striking change during the eighteenth century.

The most obvious motors of change throughout the century were war and the underlying shifts in the state system which brought war about. Down to the 1790s, conflict in Eastern Europe occurred for reasons not perceptibly different from those which had occasioned it in the past: dynastic ambition, territorial aggrandisement and the economic self-interest of states.

A general development more difficult to assess was what is called, for want of a better term, the Enlightenment. In its most widely accepted usage, Enlightenment has been taken to mean the spread of a more rational way of thinking, to begin with in the sciences and other scholarly fields but gradually extending to all spheres of human endeavour, including the organisation of government and the beginnings of social reform. In Eastern Europe as elsewhere, it is important to distinguish between the efforts of rulers and public figures to promote more rational and hence more efficient government – efforts which were not necessarily dependent on enlightened thinking – and the spread of ideas and attitudes later in the century, which clearly *did* derive from an accepted model of Enlightenment.

A third development which was in part a product of the Enlightenment, but also a reaction to it, was nationalism. Nationalism as an ideology was very clearly imported into Eastern Europe from the West and it was not consciously adopted by more than a handful of people in the region until late in the century. However, the nature of nationalism in Eastern Europe was quite distinct from that of Western Europe, and national consciousness expressed itself in cultural rather than political forms in most cases.

Finally, both Enlightenment thinking and nationalism culminated at the end of the century in the French Revolution, which marked a radical departure from everything which went before it. The revolutionary wars of the 1790s not only caused a major upheaval in the international order but introduced the disruptive new element of ideological conflict and political radicalism, even in far-off Eastern Europe. Even more explosively, the example of the French nation in arms gave a long-term impetus to East European nationalism, which is impossible to underestimate, even if its immediate effects must not be exaggerated.

EAST EUROPEAN WAR AND DIPLOMACY

Relations between states in this period continued to be violently self-regulatory. That is, the rulers of individual states judged their interests as they saw fit, untrammelled by any higher authority, and pursued those interests by means of war if they thought they could or should do so. This calculation of a state's vital interest by a monarch and his personal council of ministers was known as 'cabinet policy' (*Kabinettspolitik*) and a war waged in such a cause was a 'cabinet war'. In contrast to the sixteenth and seventeenth centuries, rulers were increasingly uninfluenced by religious feelings, and in contrast to the period following the French Revolution, they could still afford to be indifferent to political ideology.

East European rulers of the eighteenth century were no different from any others in this respect; indeed, several of them became famous paradigms of *Kabinettspolitik*. Religion, for instance, was unlikely to shape the foreign policy of Frederick II of Prussia, who had abandoned all religious belief by the age of fifteen; or Catherine II of Russia, a German princess who upon her arrival in Russia converted effortlessly from Lutheranism to Orthodoxy. Maria Theresa of Austria, and her son and successor Joseph II, were devout Catholics, but did not let this interfere with matters of international import. Even the perennial conflict between the Ottoman Empire and the Christian states of Eastern Europe was by the eighteenth century dictated less by religious animosities than by the clash of vital state interests.

State interest was defined in a number of ways. In the first place, the fact that most of the states in the region were monarchies meant that their foreign policy was in a very literal sense dynastic. Monarchs for the most part conducted their own foreign policy, usually through the intermediary of a foreign minister but at times on a monarch-to-monarch basis. Monarchs equated the state, or rather the agglomeration of territories over which they ruled, with their own persons and dynasties; and the territorial extent of the state could be, and was, determined by the marriage and other personal fortunes of the monarch and his family. Allied to this was the widespread perception that the strength of the state, or rather the dynasty, was in direct relation to the size of the state and, just as important, its territorial cohesion. Territorial aggrandisement was thus seen as a desirable thing in itself, for only in this way could the dynasty assure itself of the number of subjects and material resources for the perpetuation of its house and the maintenance of its prestige. The role that considerations of economic gain played in such thinking is debatable. On the one hand, monarchs of the period and their advisers were scarcely blind to the economic advantages of seizing, or retaining, territory; on the other hand, the prodigal expenditure of accumulated wealth in the pursuit of territorial claims suggests that economic rationality was never uppermost.

In one important respect the economic strength or weakness of states did begin to affect international relations in this period, in that for the first time we can see a serious differential between states. Economic stagnation, or decline, or inefficiency meant that the Ottoman Empire, the Polish–Lithuanian Commonwealth and the Habsburg Monarchy were more likely to be preyed upon by their neighbours. The margin of superiority was narrow: Prussia's edge over Austria lay initially more in the concentration of its military resources than in anything else; and Russia's victories over Sweden and the Ottomans owed much to the sheer vastness of its manpower. The spur to reform, however, both economic and administrative, was clear, and from the early eighteenth century on much of the international scene was shaped by the pace of modernisation. It is unnecessary to rehearse the conflicts of this period in detail here, when they form an important part of the story in subsequent chapters. More instructive is to see the principal wars in Eastern Europe as a reflection of underlying conflicts of interest, which waxed and waned depending on the changing strengths of individual states or combinations of states.

The longest-lasting conflict was undoubtedly that between *Venice* and the *Ottoman Empire*, but by the eighteenth century Venice was dependent on an alliance with the more powerful Habsburg Monarchy for the preservation of its overseas territories. The Treaty of Passarowitz (1718) confirmed Venice in its possession of Dalmatia and the Ionian Islands, but it was obliged to renounce its title to parts of the Greek Peloponnesus. Thereafter Venice was lucky to be able to avoid war; its legacy was something to be squabbled over by others.

Of far greater importance was the *Habsburg–Ottoman* rivalry. The Habsburgs' military effort against this traditional enemy had by the late seventeenth century taken on a much more aggressive character. The wars of this period culminated in the Treaty of Carlowitz (1699), whereby the Habsburgs wrested most of Hungary from the Ottomans. In the war of 1714–18, the Monarchy encroached even further, conquering Serbia, the Banat and western or Little Wallachia; but at the end of a disastrous war in 1737–9, Serbia and Wallachia had to be handed back to the Ottomans by the Treaty of Belgrade (1739). The changing nature of the Habsburg–Ottoman conflict is of interest, in that by the 1730s the Monarchy's own poor leadership contrived to lose it the war of 1737–9 despite winning the battles, thus creating an impression of weakness in the eyes of other powers like Prussia. Significantly, too, Austria's involvement in that war was as much due to fear of being left out of an already existing war between the Ottomans and Russia. By the late eighteenth century, it is clear that the genuine conflict of interests between Habsburg and Ottoman was a thing of the past.

Both these empires were instead discovering a mutual interest in preserving the status quo in south-eastern Europe, an interest inspired by their shared mutual fear of Russia's growing power.

The *Russo-Ottoman* antagonism, by contrast, not only intensified throughout the eighteenth century but was to dominate the nineteenth century as well. This reflected the much greater energies of Russia, not only in terms of its manpower but also in the strategic logic of its drive west and south to the sea. Russia waged in total four wars against the Ottomans in the eighteenth century. The first was a disaster and lost Russia its hard-won outlet to the Black Sea at Azov. The war of 1735–9 regained Azov, as well as a strip of steppeland between the Donets and the Bug; it also won Russia the right to trade on the Sea of Azov, although only in Turkish vessels. Catherine II's war of 1768–74 revealed even more clearly how formidable a regional power Russia now was. For the first time Russian armies advanced into the Balkans, occupying Moldavia and Wallachia; an appeal was made to the Balkan Christians to rise up in Russia's aid; and the Baltic fleet sailed around Europe to appear in the Mediterranean. By the Treaty of Küçük Kaynarci in 1774 Russia obtained a Black Sea coast from the mouth of the Dnieper to the east side of the Sea of Azov, the right to trade freely in Ottoman waters, including passage of the Straits, and, most controversially, the right to 'make ... representations' to the Ottoman government on behalf not only of the autonomous principalities of Moldavia and Wallachia but also of Orthodox Christians throughout the Ottoman domains.[1] It was Russia's outright annexation of the Crimea in 1783, and its opening two years later of a naval base at Sevastopol, which led to the fourth Turkish war in 1788–92; the Turks were forced to cede a further strip of Black Sea coast as far as the Dniester.

Russia's expansion was also made at the expense of two old enemies to its west, Sweden and Poland–Lithuania. Of the two, *Sweden* posed more of an active threat, in that on two occasions it tried to regain the Baltic territories it had lost to Russia in the Great Northern War. By 1741, however, when the first of these attempts was made, the positions of the two powers were clearly reversed, and by the Treaty of Åbo (1743) Sweden was obliged to cede a further slice of Finnish territory to Russia. In 1788, Gustavus III of Sweden took advantage of Russia's Turkish war to mount yet another attack, but even with the diplomatic support of Prussia the Swedes could not break Russia's naval power in the Baltic and this war ended in stalemate in 1790.

The *Polish–Lithuanian Commonwealth* was no threat to anyone, least of all Russia, by the early eighteenth century. Instead it acted as a huge buffer zone between other states. Hard to defend physically, Poland's chief internal weakness was the strength of its nobility, which had the right to elect the king. Royal elections were consequently contested not only by domestic factions but by foreign powers. In essence, the 'Polish question' of the eighteenth century was whether Poland would continue to be manipulated in this fashion by its neighbours or whether international fears would lead to its partition.

Russia had most at stake in the Polish question, having suffered invasion and devastation at Polish hands in the past. By the turn of the century the tables were turning: it was Russian power which ensured the election in 1697 of the Elector of Saxony, as Augustus II, and on the latter's death in 1733, the succession of his son as Augustus III. Poland was in effect a Russian protectorate, which Russian governments preferred to keep in a state of internal weakness. When Augustus III died in 1763, Catherine II had little difficulty in getting one of her numerous lovers, the Polish noble Stanisław Poniatowski, elected as King Stanisław August in 1764.

Stanisław August, however, proved more of an enlightened reformer than Catherine had bargained for, while at the same time his dependency on Russian power aroused the hostility of the *szlachta*. A noble insurrection against Stanisław August provided the pretext for the First Partition of 1772, suggested to Russia and Austria by Frederick II as a means of alleviating tensions between Russia and Prussia itself. This was the paradox of the Polish question: up to a point the Commonwealth's neighbours could see the advantage of keeping it weak and easily manipulated, but the fear that it might be too exclusively dominated by one power made the others anxious to stake a claim to it. The First Partition saw Poland lose over a quarter of its territory and more than a third of its population. Spurred on by this proof of the Commonwealth's weakness, Stanisław August carried on with his reforms, yet it was these, culminating in the constitution of 1791, which prompted further intervention. In the climate following the French Revolution of 1789, neither Russia nor Prussia was minded to tolerate so radical a departure as the Polish constitution, and it was these two powers which forced the abolition of the constitution and a Second Partition in 1793. The revolt against this, in 1794–5, simply provoked the final, Third Partition of 1795, in which Austria joined Russia and Prussia. Poland disappeared from the map. For the next century and a quarter, the three conservative empires of Eastern Europe would have a common interest in repressing any signs of a Polish revival, but they also acquired common boundaries with each other, a new source of friction.

The final cause of conflict was the rise of *Prussian power*. This was founded on Prussia's internal strengths in an economic and hence military sense; it was also driven by a conscious ambition to expand and round out the territory of the Prussian state. Expansion implied designs against the Polish–Lithuanian Commonwealth; it was also directed against the Habsburg Monarchy and ultimately it assumed a greater role for Prussia within the Holy Roman Empire. In pursuit of these aims, Frederick II invaded Austrian Silesia in 1740 and held it in the face of all the Monarchy's efforts to regain it. The century was dominated, therefore, by a bitter Austro-Prussian antagonism, but also by increasing tension between Prussia and Russia, driven into the background only by the urgency of agreeing a coordinated response to the threat of the French Revolution.

ENLIGHTENED ABSOLUTISM

The term 'Enlightenment', which originated in the mid-eighteenth century, is associated with the spread of a more rational, 'scientific' approach to the world as opposed to the presumed ignorance and superstition of preceding ages. Building on the genuine advances in scientific understanding since the seventeenth century, this concept of rational, empirical enquiry came to be applied to the analysis of society and systems of government, as well as the physical universe. With this went a heightened interest in the collection of verifiable knowledge, typified by the famous *Encyclopédie* of the French scholar Diderot, a hostility to religion coupled with a commitment to religious toleration and freedom of thought, and the advocacy of a more rational organisation of social and political institutions. In this last respect the Enlightenment in Western Europe gave a powerful impetus to political liberalism, in that it encouraged demands for more accountable and representative government, such as those voiced in the American and French revolutions.

In considering the phenomenon of the Enlightenment in Eastern Europe, we are immediately confronted with the twin problems of sequence and instrumentality. First of all, many of the government-led changes, or attempts at change, in the region preceded by a long chalk any sign of enlightened thinking penetrating the countries in question. In other words, the need for reform had practical, local inspiration, which has to be accounted for with reference to local conditions. Secondly, the intentions of those most closely associated with change were not necessarily enlightened in the sense accepted by those who later consciously promoted enlightenment. Rather, the East European rulers who first undertook reform were motivated by basic needs such as survival against foreign aggression, maximisation of revenue and control over their subjects. Only later did theory catch up with practice.

The name given to this rational approach to government in most of eighteenth-century Europe, however, and which in Eastern Europe we associate with the process of modernisation, is *enlightened absolutism*. This is because the changes being attempted were on the whole ordained by rulers, without reference to any popular, representative institutions. At the same time the underlying assumption behind such changes was that they were in fact rational, that they would benefit not only the ruler but also his subjects. The overriding aim, in all cases, was nevertheless to enhance the efficiency of government and hence the viability of the state itself.

Part of the difficulty in linking the Enlightenment to what was going on in Eastern Europe in this period, as well as in determining whether East European rulers were enlightened absolutists, is that there were different types of Enlightenment. The French variant was more explicitly based on the cult of rationality, on scientific empiricism and on the belief in rational, and hence more liberal, government. The more moderate, or conservative thinkers of the German Enlightenment showed less interest in empiricism and the physical sciences, and a greater reliance on metaphysical philosophy and intuition. Most importantly, it was German philosophers like Samuel von Pufendorf and Christian Wolff who evolved the concept of natural law. According to these thinkers, there was a 'natural' contract in societies between rulers and ruled: in return for physical protection and just government, a monarch's subjects implicitly accepted his absolute title to govern. Widely disseminated among the educated elite in the German states by the mid-eighteenth century (Frederick II was an outstanding advocate), natural law theory constituted 'an important source of enlightened absolutism throughout Germany'.[2] As a consequence it had more of an impact on Eastern Europe, especially Russia, than did the writings of the French Enlightenment, even if the latter were well enough known to East European rulers by the mid-century.

In addition to the question of which strand of the Enlightenment was most influential, there is the problem of explaining practical reforms in Eastern Europe which preceded the very concept of Enlightenment. Many of these, in several parts of the region, were inspired by the body of economic thought referred to as *cameralism*, which had its origins in the seventeenth century. Cameralists, several of whom were influential in the Habsburg Monarchy of Leopold I (1657–1705), taught that the strength and security of the state stood in direct relation to the well-being and prosperity of its subjects. The greater the population and the more wealth they produced, the greater would be the tax revenue available to the monarch and hence his ability to maintain a standing army. It was thus in the self-interest of rulers, as well as their duty, to promote economic development. They could do this, according to the cameralists, by lifting economic restrictions such as the labour service obligations of the peasantry, the monopoly rights of artisans' guilds and the commercial privileges of the nobility. They could free their subjects from social restrictions and attract immigrants from other realms by proclaiming religious toleration, maintaining domestic order and furthering education. They could encourage industry and trade by paying for the training of artisans and the founding of merchant companies.

Rulers could do all this, but they did not necessarily succeed, even where they made the attempt. The record of cameralism in the Habsburg Monarchy down to 1740 was one of failure: recurrent wars, the limited scope of the reforms attempted and the sheer strength of vested interests ensured that little in the way of fundamental change occurred. In Russia, where the modernising energy of Peter the Great owed much to that ruler's perception of the nexus between prosperity and the strength of the state, the impetus behind modernisation fell away after his death in 1725. The Saxon kings of

Poland–Lithuania held their throne on the specific condition that they did not interfere with the 'golden liberties' of the Polish nobility. The furthest the Ottoman sultans got to remedying their increasingly obvious disadvantage *vis-à-vis* the Christian powers was to appoint a French military adviser, the Comte de Bonneval, in 1729. Only Prussia, under Frederick William I (1713–40), can be said to have successfully implemented cameralist policies. Through strict economy, the reform of the tax system, a tightly controlled bureaucracy, the subordination of both landowners and peasantry to the needs of the army and the encouragement of industry, much of it state-run, this single-minded monarch transformed his kingdom into the most formidable military power in Europe.

Events in Eastern Europe from 1740 increasingly showed the necessity of modernisation. The Habsburg Monarchy's loss of Silesia, Poland–Lithuania's powerlessness to resist Russian domination, the Ottoman Empire's erosion at the hands of Russian armies, suggested that all three might cease to exist if they failed to adapt. And by mid-century the thinking of the Enlightenment was beginning to reinforce this purely practical impetus, in that individual rulers, ministers and other influential figures were appearing who were clearly inspired by its ideals.

Frederick the Great, for example, famously considered himself 'the first servant of the [Prussian] state'.[3] Not only did he see himself, in accordance with natural law theory, as contractually bound to govern justly and rationally; not only did he pour large sums of money into the promotion of industry, on good cameralist lines; but he described himself at the age of sixteen as '*Frédéric le philosophe*' (Frederick the philosopher) and cultivated personal ties with the great intellectuals of the Enlightenment, such as Voltaire, whom Frederick invited to stay in Berlin, and Christian Wolff, whose teaching he prized. True, Frederick's practice as a ruler did not live up to his professions as a philosopher, but there can be no doubt that throughout his life the ultimate touchstone for his actions, whether in foreign policy or in domestic policies like religious toleration, legal reform and economic development, was whether they were rational. In this he was a genuinely enlightened monarch.

In similar ways we can see the effect of the Enlightenment on other rulers in Eastern Europe. Catherine II of Russia was an omnivorous reader of Enlightenment thinkers such as Montesquieu on principles of government, Beccaria on penal reform and the English jurist Blackstone. She corresponded with Voltaire and, in 1773, invited Diderot to St Petersburg and offered him a pension. In the Habsburg Monarchy Maria Theresa, though less well read than Catherine, surrounded herself with advisers steeped in Enlightenment thinking; the rationalist and hence reform-minded strand of Catholicism known as Jansenism was especially well represented at the Viennese court. Senior ministers were free-thinkers; and both Joseph II and Leopold II were literally products of Enlightenment teaching, educated by such luminaries as the jurist Karl Anton von Martini. In Poland–Lithuania, Stanisław August was a consciously enlightened king, determined to reform the Commonwealth in order to forestall its further decline.

All these rulers, in their different ways, pursued a more rational, efficient administration, based on clearly codified legal systems. They strove for economic rationalisation and development as the basis for this, as well as the indispensable precondition for financing a strong standing army. They saw education and cultural advance as essential for training the bureaucracy required for this more complicated state and society. They uniformly saw some measure of land reform as desirable, in the interests of productivity and social stability if not natural justice. Their overall aim, it should be stressed, was not a liberal society but a strong state.

Between the aspiration of enlightened absolutism and its implementation, however, there was a wide gap. None of the rulers of Eastern Europe ever attained literally absolute rule, either because of the entrenched opposition of historic classes and interests or because of the sheer scale of the problems facing them. However sweeping the changes attempted, in the end genuine modernisation proved beyond all of Eastern Europe's rulers. The consequences of this failure, particularly the inability to abolish serfdom, were to be profound.

THE ROOTS OF NATIONALISM

Some of the basic features of nationalism in its East European context have already been touched on. It is time to indicate some of the factors which enabled nationalism to develop in this period.

Nationalism was obviously rooted in Eastern Europe's ethnic complexity and yet on its own this is an inadequate explanation. Before the eighteenth century the number of different peoples and languages had not posed an especial administrative problem. In an age where literacy was confined to a small social elite, it was still possible to operate a rudimentary tax collection and legal system by means of traditional customs and a traditionally accepted *lingua franca*.

The Enlightenment changed all this. The diversity of peoples in each of Eastern Europe's states was on its own an obstacle to their rulers' attempts at enlightened reform. A more complicated and rationalised administration presupposed a common language. The expansion of education, to create a bureaucratic class capable of implementing enlightened reforms, also demanded a common language, since the alternative was a multiplicity of education systems in different languages. By the time serious efforts were being made to impose enlightened reform, however, the consciousness of possessing a different culture, rooted in one's own language, was more widely distributed among some East European peoples, or at least among their elites. Thus Enlightenment itself helped stimulate national consciousness by provoking a reaction against its homogenising aspects; the uproar in

Hungary in the 1780s when Joseph II imposed German as the language of state is the clearest example of this.

What national consciousness meant in the eighteenth century, however, needs careful qualification, and especially in Eastern Europe. Firstly, it is important to bear in mind that the cultural definition of a nation, in Eastern Europe, quite quickly assumed political overtones. Secondly, what passed for nationalism, to begin with, rested on an extremely narrow definition of what the nation was, or rather who belonged to it.

The German philosopher Herder, already mentioned, whose writings on the subject of nationality were widely read in Eastern Europe, was much influenced by Jean-Jacques Rousseau and other representatives of what has been called Romanticism. Such thinking constituted a reaction to the rationalism of the Enlightenment, stressing instead the diversity, the mystery, the irrationality even, of nature, including human nature.

Herder's interest in the origins of human societies, and especially their language, led him to define a people (in German: *Volk*) in terms of its language, customs and history. For Herder nationality was a cultural quality possessed by each people as a result of its natural historical evolution; the term for him did not have political connotations. A nation (*Nation*), by contrast, in Herder's terminology was something quite different: the totality of people living within a particular state, in other words a political concept. It is significant that Herder used the French word for this equation of 'nation' with 'state'; in doing so he was employing a usage of 'nation' no different from that current in Western Europe by the 1780s. Herder regarded nations (or states) as responsible for much of the unhappiness in human history. Nationality, however, was a positive thing, the natural expression of a people's inner 'soul' and mankind would be at peace only if all nationalities were free to cultivate their cultural identity. Each nationality should be free and none should have dominion over another.

Herder's emphasis on the historical origins of language, culture and the national (*völkisch*) identity of peoples was to give a powerful impetus to the development of nationalism, although Herder himself was hardly a nationalist but rather a humanitarian idealist. In particular Herder's condemnation of multinational states as 'patched-up contraptions' and 'lifeless monstrosities'[4] which stifled the cultural development of their constituent peoples was to resonate throughout the nineteenth century. Herder was one of the first to single out the Slavs as a group of distinct peoples, whose history and culture deserved to be studied and preserved.

The early reception of Herder's thinking, however, was a rather garbled one. Many of those who took up his ideas in the German lands and Eastern Europe failed to maintain his distinction between people, or nationality, and 'nation'. Instead the two terms with time became virtually interchangeable, to the point where the use of either 'nation' or 'nationality' was synonymous with the idea of a cultural community, identified primarily by language. This was largely a nineteenth-century development; yet clearly the identification of peoples such as the Slovaks or the Serbs as nations, despite their statelessness, originated in Herderian ideas. From the discovery that nations had a cultural uniqueness, it was but a short step to demanding that they should also enjoy a political autonomy.

In the meantime, however, the mantra of the nation had been adopted by certain classes of people in Eastern Europe in an equally political but much more exclusive sense. This was the class-based nationalism of the Hungarian and Polish nobility. In both the Kingdom of Hungary (including Croatia) and the Polish–Lithuanian Commonwealth political rights had long been exercised solely by this relatively numerous section of society. Nobles were happy to appropriate the new language of nationalism as an additional weapon in the defence of their traditional privileges against monarchical power. Yet for many years, well into the nineteenth and even into the twentieth century, this noble nationalism was to pose as representative of society as a whole. Because nobles referred to themselves as the 'nation', they were not only accepted as such by outside observers but their values tended to be absorbed also by those few members of the middle class who were eventually allowed to play a political role. Certainly in the eighteenth century nationalism in these lands remained very much a gentry-led affair.

We can nevertheless see, by the late eighteenth century, a series of cultural awakenings which, however varied their origins, can be said to have laid the foundations for nineteenth-century nationalism. Indeed, nationalists have tended ever since to refer to these phenomena as 'national revivals', as a 'renascence', as if the nation had been there, dormant, all along. What all these awakenings involved, in reality, was the gradual application of Herder's insights to the study of the language and history of individual peoples, many of whom before this had no agreed, written language and very little in the way of recorded history. Everywhere, from the Baltic to the Greek world, the new interest in the historical roots of human societies began to prompt research into where Eastern Europe's peoples had come from, how their languages were spoken and how they were to be classified. The first dictionaries, grammars and in some cases alphabets were produced, followed by the first collections of oral poetry and folk tales and the first literary works.

This process of awakening depended heavily on the socio-economic development of individual societies and above all on the existence of an educated class. In the cases of Hungary and Poland–Lithuania, the nobility, as a class wealthy enough to command a private education, filled this role to some extent. Even here, however, the education of nobles was by no means uniform; and the establishment of schools for nobles was an important milestone in the creation of an educated class. Even more important was the establishment of universal educational systems in the Polish–Lithuanian Commonwealth from 1773 and the Habsburg Monarchy between 1774 and 1777. The aim of such reform was of course to maximise the efficiency of the state; but since the language of instruction at primary level was necessarily in the native tongue of the pupils, the result was to create for the first time a mass base of literacy, which was crucial to the spread of nationalism. Where no such educational system was in place, in Russia and the Ottoman Empire, the spread of nationalism was correspondingly delayed. In these parts of Eastern Europe, the principal source of any sense of cultural identity at first could be only the various sub-divisions of Orthodoxy: the Greek and Romanian and Serb Orthodox churches. These organisations, tolerated on both sides of the Ottoman–Habsburg border, constituted for most of the eighteenth century the only educated class of their respective peoples. The great exception, in the Ottoman domains, was the omnipresent Greek merchant class, a class which, because of its foreign contacts, language skills and growing wealth was uniquely equipped to act as an importer of ideas from the outside world, as well as to finance Greek-language schools and publications.

Before the turn of the century this tiny new class of educated East Europeans, whether nobles or clerics or the still minuscule urban middle class, had begun the process of self-discovery which was to make the cult of the nation a dominant one in the next century.

IMPACT OF THE FRENCH REVOLUTION

The political earthquake of the French Revolution affected the whole of Europe. Its impact on Eastern Europe can be measured both physically and in ideological terms.

The wars waged by the French Republic against its monarchical enemies began in 1792 and after several different instalments ended in defeat for each of the powers ranged against France.[5] The rise to power of Napoleon Bonaparte as first consul in 1799 and emperor in 1804 only confirmed this French ascendancy. Even in Eastern Europe there was territorial upheaval. Russia and Prussia took advantage of the war in Western Europe to seize yet more territory from Poland in the Second Partition of 1793; two years later the Habsburg Monarchy joined them in the Third and final Partition. At the same time Prussia backed out of the war against the French. In 1797 the Habsburg Monarchy was forced to come to terms with France; by the Treaty of Campo Formio it lost its possessions in the Low Countries and most of northern Italy, and accepted French gains at the expense of the Holy Roman Empire, but was compensated with the territory of the Venetian Republic. Renewed war led to renewed defeat and in 1801 the Habsburgs conceded an even greater French presence within the Holy Roman Empire. The news that Napoleon was set to crown himself emperor of the French prompted Francis II to proclaim himself the first emperor of Austria in 1804.

Far more fateful than these changes in the international balance of power was the French Revolution's ideological challenge to the rulers and peoples of Eastern Europe. In opposing the principles of political rights and popular sovereignty to the established, monarchical order, the Revolution sparked a war of ideologies as well as states. The monarchies of Eastern Europe could not ignore this challenge. Although the number of people in Eastern Europe who responded positively to revolutionary ideas was never very great, the effect of what little agitation there was on their rulers was to confirm in their minds the dangers, rather than the necessity, of further enlightened reform. The process of modernisation, where it had been undertaken at all, was abandoned for many years to come.

Most explosive of all was the force of the French Republic's example as the first explicitly mobilised nation, whose citizen armies rolled irresistibly across Europe, toppling monarchies and making the old regime everywhere tremble. The Republic's conquests set in motion the gradual amalgamation of territories that, in the mid-nineteenth century, was to culminate in Italian and German 'unification', an attractive template for nationalists throughout Eastern Europe. Just as crucial, the language of nationalism was increasingly adopted after 1790, at first by the leaders of noble rebellion against Habsburg absolutism, or noble resistance to partition in Poland–Lithuania, but thereafter, in increasing numbers, by the second generation of nationalists, the cultural awakeners who were finding their voice by the turn of the century. In both the following it attracted and in the reaction it met with among Eastern Europe's rulers, this incipient nationalism was among the most important long-term effects of the revolutionary period.

3

THE HABSBURG MONARCHY'S ATTEMPT AT MODERNISATION

The Habsburg Monarchy has already been described as an essentially dynastic state. Indeed, some historians deny that this assortment of territories merits the title of 'state' at all.[1]

Maria Theresa, who became Archduchess of Austria in 1740, was also the sovereign of a number of other 'hereditary lands' in what are today's Slovenia and northern Italy, as well as queen of Hungary and Bohemia. Her father had been Emperor Charles VI of the Holy Roman Empire, one title which his daughter, as a woman, could not inherit. Instead, after a disputed interlude, the imperial dignity was conferred on Maria Theresa's husband in 1745 and remained with the Habsburgs until 1806. Finally, the dynasty ruled the Austrian Netherlands (today's Belgium) and the north Italian duchies of Milan, Mantua and Parma. The total population of the Monarchy, in 1740, was less than 14 million.[2]

The problem in ruling this hotchpotch was that the machinery of government was replicated many times over. Each *Land* or realm had its own laws and institutions, and above all its own diet, in which the estates, or prominent social classes, were represented. Such basic functions of government as the maintenance of order, the administration of justice and the collection of revenue were performed at this local level; there was no central government in this sense. The Monarchy had an 'ordinary' income derived from its own landed property, from indirect taxes on consumption and from customs. Money for an army, and for waging war, counted as 'extraordinary' income and had to be voted by the diet of each *Land* as a 'contribution'. In the reign of Charles VI both the Bohemian and Hungarian diets, whose taxable wealth was the most substantial, had agreed to fix the amount of their contributions, thereby guaranteeing the Monarchy something like a regular income. Anything beyond that still had literally to be negotiated between monarch and diet; and in the other hereditary lands the contribution was not even fixed.

In such circumstances the Monarchy's ability to play the role of a great power had always been subject to serious limitations. Habsburg rulers sought to obviate their dependence on the diets by increasing 'ordinary' revenue. Previous reigns had been notable for a conscious effort to implement the principles of cameralism, encouraging industry and foreign trade, and promoting the repopulation of Hungary, devastated by the Turkish wars. Charles VI made appreciable improvements in infrastructure, with the building of roads linking the interior with the Adriatic.

Yet there was a point beyond which the Monarchy seemed unable or even unwilling to go in modernising its diverse realms. Despite cameralist reforms there was little large-scale industry, agriculture remained primitive and the revenue base problematic. The Habsburgs themselves accepted the decentralised structure of the Monarchy. Charles VI is famous for spending much of his reign negotiating the Pragmatic Sanction, a recognition of his daughter's right to succeed him, with each of the diets, in tacit recognition of their separate status. With Charles's death in October 1740, however, the Monarchy received the clearest possible warning of the consequences of a failure to modernise. Maria Theresa's succession was the signal for an assault on its very existence.

THE FIRST THERESIAN REFORMS 1740-60

Charles VI's efforts to win acceptance of the Pragmatic Sanction, which by recognising Maria Theresa's right to succeed also asserted the indivisibility of the Habsburg realms, had been directed abroad as well as at home. By 1740 most European governments had recognised the Sanction in principle, but in practice this proved no security. The accession of Maria Theresa, with as yet no male heir, meant that the elective dignity of Holy Roman Emperor was contested. Charles Albert of Bavaria immediately put forward a claim to be emperor and was supported by France and Spain. He also claimed, with less justification, the succession to the Austrian hereditary lands. It was in response to this that Frederick II of Prussia offered to 'defend' the Habsburg Monarchy in return for the wealthy duchy of Lower Silesia. When Maria Theresa rejected this transparent blackmail, Frederick marched his troops into the duchy in December 1740. Despite bitter fighting the Monarchy failed to dislodge the Prussians and by the summer of 1741 an anti-Austrian coalition had been formed, consisting of Bavaria, France, Spain, Prussia and Saxony–Poland. Only Russia offered assistance, but was promptly distracted by a French-inspired attack from Sweden. The coalition's forces invaded Upper Austria in October and had taken Prague by December; in January 1742 Charles Albert was crowned Holy Roman Emperor as Charles VII. The Monarchy appeared to be facing partition.

The Habsburg who met this catastrophe was a heavily pregnant 23-year-old, indifferently educated and previously excluded from affairs of state, whose husband was generally deemed incompetent and whose fractious ministers were for the most part decrepit. Yet Maria Theresa was also stubborn, strong-willed, pragmatic and a shrewd judge of people. Although the first years of her reign were necessarily devoted to the task of ensuring the Monarchy's simple survival, Maria Theresa made a crucial contribution to that survival by signalling so clearly her determination to resist.

In terms of immediate response there was little Maria Theresa could do to reverse the seizure of Lower Silesia. At 80,000 men each the Austrian and Prussian armies were of equal size; but the Monarchy had its enemies in the west to consider too. With the Franco-Bavarian army on her doorstep in the summer of 1741, Maria Theresa chose to concentrate on the more pressing threat. Armed with her six-month-old son Joseph and the allure of a female in distress, she appeared before the Hungarian Diet at Pressburg in September and extracted from the traditionally recalcitrant Magyar nobles a commitment to raise 55,000 troops for the defence of the Monarchy. In reality the number raised did not exceed 10,000, and that at the price of reconfirming the nobles' tax exemption. Yet the political importance of the Hungarians' support was immense: it convinced Frederick II that the Monarchy was likely to survive and led him to seek an armistice with Maria Theresa in October.

As a result the Monarchy was able to go on the offensive in 1742. Not only was Upper Austria retaken, but Habsburg forces went on to conquer Bavaria, occupying Munich. When Charles VII died in January 1745, his successor was only too glad to negotiate the return of Bavaria, in exchange for supporting the election of Maria Theresa's husband to the imperial throne as Francis I (1745–65). Silesia, however, remained irrecoverable, and the bloody, second Silesian War was finally concluded in December 1745, leaving the Monarchy only a modest corner of what had been its wealthiest province. War with France and Spain dragged on until 1748.

Long before the conclusion of this 'War of the Austrian Succession', Maria Theresa had embraced change. In a series of reforms she and her ministers for the first time gave the Monarchy something like the trappings of a modern state. In administrative terms, centralised institutions brought some coherence into the key areas of foreign policy, the army and domestic affairs. A State Chancellery, in 1742, superseded a bewildering array of bodies hitherto involved in foreign policy. A General War Commissary, from 1746, assumed many of the functions of a war ministry. And in 1749 the creation of the Directory of Administration and Finance meant that, for the first time, there was a single governing body for the Austrian and Bohemian crown-lands. Hungary, whose support had been so vital for Maria Theresa in 1741, was tactfully left untouched by this last reform.

The guiding intelligence behind these changes was Count Friedrich Wilhelm von Haugwitz, a refugee from Prussian Silesia strongly influenced by cameralist thinking. Haugwitz soon applied his financial genius to the Monarchy's chronic cash-flow problems. In 1747 he pushed through the crucial reform of persuading the diets to double their contributions and extracted from most of them a fixed contribution. Equally innovative was the imposition of taxation on the nobility and clergy of the Austrian and Bohemian crownlands, a reform Haugwitz argued was essential if the peasantry were not to be driven to revolt. Finally, regularity of income was ensured by appointing court deputations, in 1748, to take charge of the money raised; increasingly the officials responsible for collection were royal appointees. Hungary, again, was unaffected by this reform and the Hungarian nobility remained exempt from taxation. Nevertheless the Hungarian Diet, which already paid a fixed contribution, continued to do so and in 1751 increased the amount.

Other reforms undertaken in this early period show a concern with social and economic change altogether more radical than anything contemplated before. In economic terms Maria Theresa undoubtedly continued cameralist policies pursued by her predecessors. Native manufacturers received subsidies, and were protected from outside competition by successive tariff increases in the 1750s. Over land reform, Maria Theresa showed even in the 1740s a concern for protecting the peasantry from the worst excesses of serfdom, which reflected not so much philanthropy as a cameralist view that an oppressed peasantry meant an inefficient economy and hence a weak state. Accordingly, the new tax regime levied half from the 'dominical' land reserved for the nobles' own use and half from the 'rustical' land which peasants farmed for themselves. Nobles were not supposed to shift their share of the tax onto their peasants, nor were they allowed simply to take over rustical holdings to lighten their own tax burden, which lessened tax revenue from peasants. Well-intentioned though these rules were, they proved difficult to enforce.

It was in cultural and educational matters that the Theresian break with the past was most obvious. This was due less to Maria Theresa herself who, though anxious to modernise the machinery of state, was socially conservative, than to the advisers around her from an early stage. Several members of the new State Chancellery had been educated at north German universities and were ardent cameralists. Equally influential were the writings of Italian reformers, who shaped the thinking of a generation of Austrian clergymen and criticised the obscurantism of the Church and above all the powerful Society of Jesus, the Jesuits, for their backward and unscientific approach to education.

A decisive shift occurred in the early 1740s, when control of censorship was taken away from the Jesuits, signalling that there should be a freer flow of ideas into the Monarchy. New faculties of history, philosophy, geography and 'cameral science' were founded at the universities, and the number of Jesuits in faculties was gradually whittled down. The *Theresianum* school was founded in 1746 to impart a modern education to the Monarchy's civil servants; in 1751 followed the Military Academy for army officers; and in

1754 the Oriental Academy for diplomats, with a speciality in teaching languages. The cumulative effect, traceable within the next few decades, was to create an educated elite capable of carrying the modernisation agenda even further.

The results were remarkable. From a total revenue in 1744 of some 20 million florins (about £2 million), the proceeds of the new system reached twice that by 1754. The taxes raised from the Austrian crownlands alone, by the early 1760s, were over three times those received at the start of the reign. Increased revenue, moreover, enabled the arm of the state bureaucracy to reach further: whereas there were only 6000 state officials in 1740, by 1762 their number was 10,000 and by 1782 20,000.[3] Most impressively, the Monarchy's military strength was enhanced in the most convincing way possible: by 1756 it was able to field a standing army of 180,000 men and at the height of the Seven Years' War, in 1760, the total reached 250,000.[4]

Renewal of war with Prussia and the reconquest of Silesia were, of course, the ultimate aims of this administrative rationalisation. Diplomacy effected a 'diplomatic revolution' in the Monarchy's traditional alliances, with France and Russia as allies. The Monarchy entered the Seven Years' War in 1756 rich both in cash and in allies; yet the outcome of this conflict was a bitter disappointment. Prussia's military superiority, and Frederick's own skill as a commander, made it a tough nut to crack, despite being vastly outnumbered. The alliance, by contrast, was a shambles: France, heavily defeated by Prussia at the outset, was preoccupied with its colonial war with Britain, and the Monarchy's own military leaders proved no more than competent, for all the improvements in the size and quality of Habsburg forces. The withdrawal of the Monarchy's allies by 1763 meant there was no option but to conclude peace with Prussia and concede Silesia for good; the entire conflict had been for nothing.

THE SECOND PHASE OF REFORMS 1760-80

The phenomenal cost of the Seven Years' War, at some 40 million florins annually, far exceeded even the improved revenue-raising capacities of the Haugwitz system. Well before the conclusion of hostilities, therefore, Maria Theresa agreed to the creation of a new central advisory body, the Council of State. This six-member body had no formal administrative role, and its competence was in theory confined to the Austrian and Bohemian lands; in practice, however, the Council of State advised on the affairs of the entire Monarchy. In the various lands the Representations and Chambers were renamed governorships (*Gubernien*) in 1763, but continued to be the main arm of government at provincial level. Most local diets had little function after 1763, although their estates continued to approve taxation. By the 1760s, the increase in the number of centrally appointed provincial officials was becoming a significant factor in itself: the state was gradually equipping itself with a bureaucracy responsive to its own demands, not those of local elites.

After 1760 Maria Theresa embarked on a second wave of reforms, which focused more on fundamental changes in the Monarchy's social and economic life. These reforms clearly owed more to the spread of Enlightenment thinking on such issues than the pragmatic, necessity-driven reforms of the 1740s. Ministers by the 1760s were all products of an enlightened education. Above all, these progressive-minded men were joined in 1765 by the new emperor, Maria Theresa's son and heir Joseph, whom she designated as co-regent and who was, unlike his mother, a genuine child of the Enlightenment in both education and temperament.

Mother and son had a famously difficult relationship: whereas Maria Theresa was all caution and pragmatism, Joseph was impatient, doctrinaire and convinced of his rightness. He was also, however, personally tutored by leading exponents of cameralism, grew up in the company of the enlightened, and was widely read in the works of the French *philosophes*. Maria Theresa mistrusted his judgement and withheld effective power from him, which was one reason why Joseph became one of the best-travelled Habsburgs, visiting every corner of the Monarchy over the years and returning to Vienna every time bristling with facts and figures, petitions for reform from his mother's subjects and ever more urgent ideas of his own for change. Partly driven thus from behind, partly of her own volition, in the second half of her reign Maria Theresa undertook reforms which struck at the very root of the Monarchy's backwardness, by addressing the conditions in which the vast majority of Habsburg subjects lived.

The most pressing area of concern by the 1760s was land reform. In common with the rest of Eastern Europe, by the mid-century the Monarchy's peasants lived in conditions which had been worsening for generations. Peasants in the Austrian hereditary lands were legally free men; but in the lands of the Bohemian and Hungarian crowns they existed in a state of 'hereditary subjection', or serfdom. Everywhere in the Monarchy, with the exception of the Tyrol, peasants were obliged to perform unpaid labour services, or *Robot*, on their lords' land as opposed to that they farmed themselves. The number of days' *Robot* had increased steadily since the sixteenth century, to the point where in some lands of the Monarchy it stood at four days a week, even though the official norm was supposed to be no more than two. Hated by peasants, *Robot* not only limited the labour they could devote to farming their own plots but ensured that they worked the lord's land with minimum efficiency. Yet the danger inherent in serfdom was increasingly obvious: there were peasant revolts in 1751, 1753, 1755 and 1759. Serfdom was not only inefficient, it threatened the stability of society itself.

In response to renewed peasant unrest in the mid-1760s, Maria Theresa and her ministers sought to regulate the landlord–peasant relationship through a series of edicts, known as *Robotpatente* in the Austrian and Bohemian lands and *urbaria* in Hungary and Croatia. The principal aim was to reform inefficient usages which so obviously limited the productivity of the Monarchy's population. But Maria Theresa was also motivated by a genuine sense of outrage at rural conditions and a pious determination to do right. The *urbarium* of 1767 for Hungary prohibited any further enclosure of rustical land and fixed *Robot* at a maximum of 52 days a year. In 1769 a separate decree was issued for Transylvania: there *Robot* had been among the highest in the Monarchy at four days a week and was accordingly reduced to three. At the start of the 1770s the government was spurred to renewed action in the western lands by the devastating famine in Bohemia, where an estimated 250,000 people died.[5] The *Robotpatent* for Silesia in 1771, and those for Bohemia and Moravia in 1774 and 1775, limited *Robot* to three days a week, but not before a revolt had broken out in Bohemia in 1775, which was swiftly put down. Throughout the 1770s further *Robotpatente* were issued for the Austrian crownlands, with *Robot* levels varying from none in the Tyrol to four days in Carniola, a reflection of the resistance to the reforms in different provincial diets.

Maria Theresa stopped short of outright abolition of serfdom, which she herself favoured at the time of the Bohemian revolt. The only exception was on royal estates where, beginning in 1775, a reform advocated by Franz Anton von Raab was adopted. The 'Raab system' abolished serfdom and *Robot* on two Bohemian estates, and parcelled the demesne land out among the peasants, in return for cash rents. So successful was the scheme in raising productivity that by 1777 Maria Theresa authorised its extension to other crown estates. She was dissuaded from imposing the Raab system on private landowners by the counter-arguments of Joseph and her ministers, most of whom baulked at the cost of compensating nobles for the free labour services they would lose.

The second area of reform was education and here the changes wrought were profound. Maria Theresa's own reasons for deploying the state in educational matters were essentially religious: herself no advocate of religious toleration, she was concerned that the Church, still the main provider of education, was not doing enough to maintain the faith and hence the loyalty of subjects to the Monarchy. In addition, however, Maria Theresa was surrounded by enlightened intellectuals who saw the issue of Church, especially Jesuit, control of education as one affecting the efficiency of society as a whole. In 1770 it was specifically proposed to phase out Jesuit teachers and replace them with state-funded lay teachers. Initially shelved because of the sheer lack of qualified teachers, this plan was revived when, in 1773, the Papacy itself abolished the Society of Jesus in response to pressure from other Catholic monarchs. Overnight, the Jesuits ceased to exist as an educational organisation and the sale of their property in the Habsburg lands made it possible to fund an alternative system. Her hand forced, Maria Theresa issued a General School Ordinance for the Austrian and Bohemian lands in 1774, and for the Kingdom of Hungary in 1777.

The purpose of the ordinances was to create a universal, state-run system of education, by which the Monarchy would ensure the maintenance of

Catholicism, but also the inculcation of loyalty to the dynasty and the heightened economic efficiency of the population. Maria Theresa set up three tiers of schooling. There was compulsory primary education for all, with the main stress on religious instruction and vocational skills, but with numeracy and literacy an intrinsic part of the curriculum, especially among the urban population. Middle schools would prepare mainly urban children for either vocational or academic study and at secondary level the *Gymnasium* continued as preparation for university. To raise the requisite number of lay teachers, special teacher training schools were established in each provincial capital, with the curriculum prescribed for both teachers and taught highly centralised, both as to methods and textbooks.

In practical terms the Theresian school reforms were probably the single greatest stride towards modernity made anywhere in Eastern Europe in the eighteenth century. By 1780 some 500 schools had been founded in the Austrian and Bohemian lands, and even more in Hungary, and the number increased the more teachers were produced by the training schools. By the end of the reign the Monarchy had 6000 schools, teaching 200,000 pupils.

This represented a socio-economic change with important consequences. An entirely new class of literate subjects was being created, which made social and hence economic diversification, urban growth and political ferment all more likely. Just as significant was the impetus given to nationalism, even if the results were fully evident only in the nineteenth century. Primary education, after all, was necessarily in the local language, whether German, Czech or Hungarian, but where the necessary teachers in that language were not available, the question immediately arose: in what language should elementary education be conducted? The very fact that there were no dictionaries or grammars in certain languages, that they did not even exist in literary form, prompted a growing awareness of the need to formalise them. Herder's insistence that language reflected the 'spirit' of a people meant that the 'revival' of language became an overriding preoccupation for some. In the meantime the logic of existing conditions determined that elementary education among the rural masses was perforce conducted in the vernacular, or not at all.

Maria Theresa's reign saw three territorial additions to the Monarchy, one of which had major implications for the future. The annexation of Galicia from the Polish–Lithuanian Commonwealth, in 1772, was in cameralist terms a valuable acquisition, with 83,000 square kilometres, 2.5 million inhabitants, vast mineral resources and fertile land.[6] Yet Galicia was economically backward: Polish landowners, bitterly resentful of the Partition, lorded it over a peasantry which, whether Catholic Polish in the west and north or Uniate Ruthene in the east, was among the most oppressed in the Monarchy, with five days *Robot* per week. Galicia also contained a Jewish population of over 200,000, far in excess of the 30–40,000 in each of Bohemia and Hungary.[7] The takeover of this largely Slav province represented a considerable shift in the Monarchy's ethnic balance. Of similar significance was the annexation of the Bukovina from the Ottoman Empire in 1775; this was another ethnic kaleidoscope of Romanians, Ruthenes and Jews. Finally, as a result of the largely bloodless but enormously expensive Austro-Prussian War of the Bavarian Succession, in 1778–9, the Monarchy was awarded the *Innviertel*, a strip of Bavarian territory on the right bank of the River Inn.

JOSEPH II: THE 'REVOLUTIONARY EMPEROR'

Although the reign of Maria Theresa saw the most sustained attempt at modernisation of the century, effecting more fundamental change than anything which came after, historians have until recently tended to devote more attention to the dramatic escalation of reform under Joseph II. It is not hard to see why. Joseph's ten-year reign seems a whirlwind of purposeful activity, at its centre the restless, ultimately tragic personality of the man one of his biographers called 'the revolutionary emperor'.[8] Maria Theresa in the 15 years of the co-regency issued 700 edicts; Joseph churned out that many every year of his reign, at a rate of about two a day, until by his death he had issued over 6,000.[9] And yet, as Joseph lay dying, he offered up his own bitter epitaph for his tombstone: 'Here lies Joseph II, who was unfortunate in all his enterprises.'[10]

Joseph was literally educated to be an enlightened ruler, and central to his outlook was the concept of the rationally ordered, efficient state. A genuine idealist, he saw himself as the 'first servant' of the state and believed, as he put it in 1785, that 'no constitution should exist if it is contrary to the principles of natural and social justice'.[11] The rub was that, since the state was the only guarantor of such ideals, it followed that the good of the state transcended all other considerations: 'Every member of a specific community must contribute to the general good in proportion to his property, to his abilities and to the benefit which he himself derives from his membership of that community.'[12] As T.C.W. Blanning points out, 'Joseph's state religion' amounted to a radical break with the historical development of the Habsburg Monarchy; it assumed that the Monarchy could be reformed centrally by decree, without regard for the institutional accretions of past centuries.[13] This determination to rule absolutely was characteristic of Joseph's temperament. Intelligent and well meaning, he was also an obstinate, inflexible prig, notorious for his obsession with petty detail and his 'hands-on' approach to government. This ruler of a vast empire would drop in unannounced on his officials and time the speed with which they made decisions. He issued minute instructions to local officials, demanding to know whether the houses in towns and villages were individually numbered. He took a personal interest in the suppression of masturbation among military cadets. Apart from his hankering to emulate his role model, Frederick II, by military conquest, which led to disastrous foreign complications, Joseph's temperamental defects can also be said to have undermined most of his domestic reforms. His methods stirred up opposition in crucial quarters and in the process the cause of modernisation was dealt a fatal blow.

Joseph's reforming zeal extended to every facet of life in every corner of the Monarchy. His main reforms were in the realm of civil liberties, Church–state relations, agrarian conditions and administration. None of the changes that Joseph attempted can be understood without grasping that their central thrust was the creation of a unitary state.

Joseph, although a devout Catholic, was, unlike his mother, a believer in religious toleration. This was in part genuine humanitarianism, but it was also because Joseph shared the view of other enlightened monarchs that discrimination on religious grounds was economically irrational and impeded the efficiency of the state. One of his first acts as sole ruler was to start lifting the humiliating restrictions imposed on the Monarchy's Jews: in a series of edicts in 1781–2 Jews were allowed greater educational and occupational opportunities, freedom of movement and worship, and were no longer required to wear the yellow Star of David on their clothing. In a similar vein was the Toleration Patent of October 1781, which accorded freedom of worship to Lutherans, Calvinists and Orthodox Christians. With this, for the first time, went formal civil equality: members of all these tolerated denominations could own property, enter higher education and join guilds and government employ. There were limits to Joseph's concept of toleration, however: groups falling outside the designated faiths did not qualify and the clear aim of tolerating the Jews was to facilitate their assimilation.

The relaxation of censorship in 1781 was another eye-catching innovation. In reality complete freedom of expression was not on offer: the prudish emperor was still prepared to ban pornography, violently anti-clerical material and much else, on the ground that none of this contributed to the well-being of the state. Not all Joseph's subjects agreed with him, and despite the controls, the first half of the 1780s saw an astonishing proliferation of publishing. In the latter half of the reign the censor's pen was wielded with increasing frequency, but the important thing was that the freedom to publish, while it lasted, played a major role in politicising the Habsburg Monarchy.

An essential prerequisite of state-building, in Joseph's eyes, was the rationalisation of the legal system and criminal law, but he was also motivated by the spirit of the age. To this end he had already prevailed on Maria Theresa to abolish torture in the Austrian and Bohemian lands in 1776 and this was extended to the rest of the Monarchy when Joseph became sole ruler. Similarly enlightened, on the face of it, was the abolition of the death penalty, of mutilation as a punishment, and of trying witchcraft and magic as capital offences. Joseph was a sincere egalitarian, who denounced the privileges of the nobility, proclaimed the principle of equality before the law, and opened the imperial parks of Vienna to the public. Yet his idea of a just punishment left much to be desired by modern standards: offenders formally spared the death penalty could still suffer it in the end in being condemned to tow barges on the Danube. As an adviser chillingly put it, this was 'punishment useful to the state', a phrase with a ring of the twentieth-century Gulag to it.[14] The fact that members of the nobility could be, and were, punished in this way, like any commoner, sent shock waves through the whole of society, but alienated many of the traditional elites.

At the heart of Joseph's agenda was his conviction that it was essential to reshape the role of the Church in society. Under Maria Theresa what has misleadingly been called 'Josephism' had already got under way, with the recognition that the Church must contribute to the costs of the state through taxation of Church lands, and proceeds from the sale of religious institutions closed down after the dissolution of the Jesuits in 1773 were being used to bankroll the new school system. Joseph went even further than his mother, brusquely rejecting the authority of the Pope in the Monarchy, continuing with the work of secularising monasteries, insisting on state-run training of clergymen, creating 600 new parishes, and permitting civil marriage for the first time. In the course of Joseph's reign some 700 monasteries out of 1700 were appropriated by the state, and the Religious Fund set up to administer the profits resulted in the building of more schools, and charitable institutions like the huge General Hospital in Vienna.

Land reform dominated Joseph's reign, as it had Maria Theresa's. Although Joseph had opposed outright abolition of serfdom in the 1770s, by the time of his succession he was convinced that hereditary subjection was not only an affront to natural law and the equality of man but an ever more obvious impediment to the efficiency of the state and a growing threat to social stability. Most annoying of all, the private nature of the landlord–peasant relationship meant that the noble, not the state, drew what meagre profit there was to be had from serfdom, while the unfreedom of the peasant tied up vast reserves of labour, which would otherwise be available to trade and industry.

In 1781 a series of decrees further regulated the peasant's status. The Penal Patent defined the judicial procedure to be followed by manorial courts against peasants in their jurisdiction and limited the punishments which could be meted out. The Subjects' Patent gave the peasant legal redress against his lord, albeit through a very complicated system, and provided for an appeals procedure to the local administrative authorities. The Buying-In Patent gave peasants the right to buy the holdings they farmed from their lord, although the practical obstacles to such a move remained enormous. Most important of all, the Serfdom Patent abolished 'the servile status of subjects', that is peasants, wherever it still existed in the Austrian and Bohemian crownlands; it also abolished the obligation to perform domestic service.[15] In addition peasants were now legally free to marry, to take up a trade or train for an occupation, to migrate and to own property. The Serfdom Patent did not abolish *Robot*, nor manorial jurisdiction over peasants, but it limited the peasant's obligations to the performance of stipulated *Robot* and any other payments in cash or in kind already agreed on.

Later decrees abolished the nobles' monopolies on milling, brewing and distilling, and limited the nobles' right to hunt over the peasants' crops. The Directive Regulation of March 1783 finally ended *Robot* on royal estates; it also aimed to extend the Raab system to private estates everywhere except Galicia. In 1784, a separate patent for Galicia finally limited *Robot* there to three days per week rather than five. A separate Serfdom Patent was issued for Hungary in 1785.

Joseph had no intention of stopping there. In 1783 he initiated a survey of all land in the Monarchy, on the assumption that since all wealth derived from land, so it was essential for the state to tax it equally. None of the preparations for instituting a general land tax was necessarily likely to improve the peasants' conditions. Yet the mere fact that peasants had been granted rights and freedoms gave rise to powerful social tensions, like the lifting of the lid on a cauldron. In Hungary, where the Serfdom Patent had not yet been promulgated, peasant discontent escalated. A rebellion in Transylvania in the winter of 1784–5, led by the Romanian peasants Vasile Horea and Ioan Cloşca, rapidly attracted 36,000 supporters, who went on a violent rampage against noble landowners and their families, slaughtering thousands. Horea's rebellion was put down with even greater brutality by the army and the Transylvanian nobility, and Horea and Cloşca were executed. Tellingly, however, Horea had raised the following he did on the strength of his false claim to be acting on Joseph's authority. The landowning elite across the Monarchy noted this in horror, even though the uprising gave Joseph all the justification he needed for issuing the Hungarian Serfdom Patent the following year.

Undaunted, Joseph forged ahead with his general land tax, issuing the Taxation and Urbarial Patent in February 1789. The essence of the Taxation Patent was that it required all 'feudal' obligations of the peasants, including *Robot*, to be commuted into cash, thus making such payments liable to taxation. On the basis of the completed land survey, the peasant was to receive 70 per cent of the gross produce, while 12.5 per cent went to the state and 17.5 per cent to the landowner.[16] This amounted to nothing less than the introduction of a money economy. If implemented, it would have revolutionised the various peasant-based societies of the Monarchy in much the same way as the renunciation of 'feudalism' in France, later that year, transformed French society.

One of the reasons why this most fundamental of Joseph II's reforms remained stillborn was the way in which he approached the administration of the Monarchy. Joseph took the absolutist element of enlightened absolutism seriously. To him it was axiomatic that the Monarchy could be ruled efficiently only if it were centrally organised and controlled; the historic institutions and customs of its different provinces were mere annoying baubles. Accordingly Joseph not only refused a formal coronation as king of Hungary, as the coronation oath would have obliged him to uphold Hungary's laws and constitution; he also refused to convene the Hungarian

Diet, which had not met since 1764. With even more offensive symbolism, signifying his centralising intent, he then had the Crown of St Stephen brought from Pressburg, the Hungarian capital, to Vienna, and consigned it to the imperial treasury chamber; a similar fate befell the Bohemian Crown of St Wenceslas.

In practical terms the main agents of Joseph's absolute will were the imperial bureaucracy and the army, the principal unifying elements in the Monarchy. Certainly the increased training and professionalism of the army owed much to Joseph's personal interest. The problem with the bureaucracy, however, was that trained officials, whose first loyalty was to the state, were few in number even in the 1780s; it took time to create a class of dedicated bureaucrats. Joseph can also claim to be one of the godfathers of the modern police state: in the latter part of his reign especially, as his difficulties multiplied, he proved more willing to resort to surveillance and denunciations as a means of controlling his subjects. A secret police was established in Lower Austria in 1782, was centralised in 1786 and finally applied to the whole Monarchy in 1789. Originally for supervising the bureaucracy, this police network was gradually extended to watching the general public and foreigners.

Most explosive were Joseph's attempts to refashion the civil administration generally, which brought him into head-on collision with the Hungarian nobility. In 1784 he decreed that German was to be the language of state and administration in Hungary forthwith; officials throughout the Monarchy, with the exception of Belgium, the Italian provinces and Galicia, would be given three years to become proficient in this language, or lose their positions. For Joseph this was only rational. As he replied to the protest of the Hungarian chancellor, 'You can easily work out for yourself just how advantageous it will be when there is only one language for written communications in the Monarchy and how conducive that will be to binding all the different parts to the whole and to creating a sense of fraternity among all the inhabitants.'[17] The likelihood that peoples across the Monarchy, in an age of dawning national consciousness, might resent this logical proposition was, for Joseph, hardly worth consideration. On the contrary, he sought to expedite this transition by decreeing that German would also become the language of instruction in all educational institutions above elementary level, in all parts of the Monarchy.

At the same time Joseph took the decisive step towards a truly central government. Beginning in Transylvania in 1784, and ignoring historic county boundaries, he redivided the province into 11 new districts, headed by officials directly responsible to Vienna. In 1785 it was the turn of Hungary, divided into ten similar units. The crucial provocation here (the language issue aside) was that these changes bypassed the 52 Hungarian counties and two 'free districts'. Each of these sent two of their representatives to the Diet, if it met; more importantly, they elected their own officials every three years, who formed the real administrative backbone of the kingdom. It was the county officials, nobles all, who still carried out government decrees, collected taxes, administered justice and raised recruits. To the Hungarian nobility, Hungary's separate status as a kingdom, governed by its own laws and constitution, and agreed by successive pacts with the dynasty, was sacrosanct; sidestepping the fundamental laws in this fashion not only broke the compact between crown and nation but entitled the nation, that is the nobility, to resist. In reality there was little sign of insurrection in Hungary in the first years of Joseph's reign, but resentment was high after 1784, compounded by Joseph's urbarial decrees and the land tax of 1789. The real danger would come if Hungary's nobles received encouragement and support from a foreign power.

In 1789 this is precisely what happened, as Joseph II's involvement in foreign affairs rendered him vulnerable to pressure both foreign and domestic. The unravelling began when Austria joined Russia in its war against the Ottoman Empire in 1788, more for the purpose of limiting Russian expansion in the Balkans than for any specific territorial ambitions on Joseph's part. The Turkish war was unsuccessful to start with, with Austria's formidable army ill deployed and hindered, rather than helped, by Joseph's personal command at the front in the first campaign. At the same time, a full-scale revolt was brewing in the Austrian Netherlands against Joseph's abolition of ancient laws, and when violence did break out in the course of 1789, with much of the army tied down in the Balkans, there was little Joseph could do to counter it. In Hungary, emboldened by the sudden increase in Joseph's financial needs, the nobles refused to cooperate with revenue collection and clamoured for the Diet to be called. Worst of all, the Prussian government in 1789 established contact with the forces of opposition in both Belgium and Hungary, and at the start of 1790 concluded an alliance with the Ottomans.

Faced with the threat of Prussian invasion, Joseph caved in. Mortally ill with tuberculosis, he first revoked his edicts concerning the Austrian Netherlands in November 1789. In January 1790 the emperor conceded defeat in Hungary, agreeing to convene the Diet and revoking all his decrees for Hungary except the Toleration Patent, the Serfdom Patent of 1785 and some of his ecclesiastical decrees. Joseph died on 20 February 1790, embittered by the lack of understanding which had greeted his reforms and blind to the way in which his own obstinacy had imperilled them.

FROM LEOPOLD II TO THE CONSERVATIVE REACTION

Joseph's brother and successor, Leopold II (1790–2), bade fair to continue the modernisation agenda by subtler means. As Grand Duke of Tuscany Leopold had practised an enlightened rule the equal of Joseph's but, unlike his brother, Leopold was a genuine believer in constitutional rule as well. He was both astute and pragmatic, and his brief reign as emperor is one of the great might-have-beens of East European history. In short order the new ruler displayed all the political skills which Joseph had lacked. He suspended the land tax within weeks of his accession; signified his willingness to accept that landowners had the right to refuse commutation of *Robot*; convened not only the Hungarian Diet but all the others as well; ostentatiously went to Hungary to be crowned king and swear the coronation oath; cut a diplomatic deal with Prussia agreeing the re-imposition of Austrian rule in Belgium, subject to the restoration of Belgian liberties and an end to the Turkish war; reoccupied Belgium with minimum resistance in December 1790; and in August 1791 concluded the Peace of Sistova with the Ottomans. Leopold's readiness to make such concessions was rooted in conviction as much as necessity. He simply did not agree with Joseph's project of the unitary state and could see virtue in the Monarchy's diversity. At the same time he clearly wished to continue modernisation, but within the context of existing laws and institutions, modified if possible through negotiation.

There is no denying the skill with which Leopold confronted the witches' brew of discontent stirred up by Joseph. The Hungarian Diet, when it met in September 1790, voiced quite novel demands for a separate Hungarian army and administration, for annual diets, for the reincorporation into Hungary of Transylvania and the Military Frontier and, ominously, for Hungarian, not Latin (let alone German), to be the language of state. In response to this, other nationalities within Hungary for the first time voiced counter-demands. The Croatian *Sabor* (diet) denounced the proposal to make Hungarian the language of state and protested that neither diet should be able to enact laws for the other. A congress of Hungarian Serbs, which Leopold cannily permitted to convene at Sremski Karlovci in September 1790 and to call itself a 'diet', demanded a separate national territory within Hungary and vilified the Hungarians as 'orang-utans whom Vienna has turned into men'.[18] In Transylvania there were similar demands, led by the Romanian Orthodox hierarchy, for recognition of the Romanians as the 'fourth nation' of the province, in addition to the Hungarians, Szeklers and German 'Saxons'.[19] Leopold exploited this subsidiary unrest to negotiate a deal with the Hungarian Diet that restored stability. In addition to his coronation, he recognised Hungary as a separate state with its own constitution and confirmed the non-taxation of nobles and abandonment of the land tax. In return the Diet formally accepted as Hungarian law the Toleration Patent and the *urbarium* of 1767.

In foreign affairs, Leopold was less successful after Sistova, in that he was unable to avert a declaration of war by France on Austria and Prussia in April 1792. Leopold had not wanted war; on the contrary he welcomed the French Revolution, urged his brother-in-law Louis XVI to accept constitutional rule, and refused to support French *émigré* efforts to stir up reaction abroad, replying to one such appeal that he was 'neither a democrat nor an aristocrat'.[20] His alliance with Prussia, however, and a joint declaration to the effect that the two states were ready to intervene in France to protect the royal family, provoked the hostility of the French National Assembly. Shortly before the outbreak of war, Leopold died suddenly on 1 March 1792. His passing was a demonstration of the importance of the individual in history, for under his son and successor, Francis II (1792–1835), the half-century of modernisation in the Habsburg Monarchy faltered and ground to a halt.

There is not much point in dwelling on the decade and a half of conflict with revolutionary France which followed. Suffice it to say that, in the words of Charles Ingrao, 'the French Revolution was nothing short of a catastrophe for the monarchy'.[21] This was not just because the Monarchy went from one humiliating lost war to another, culminating in defeat at Austerlitz in 1805 and the abolition of the Holy Roman Empire in 1806. These reverses were compensated for only partially by territorial gains, in the shape of 'New' Galicia, the Habsburg share of the Third Partition of Poland in 1795, and the former Venetian Republic, awarded to the Monarchy by the victorious General Bonaparte in 1797 and including Venetia, the west coast of Istria and Dalmatia. Both acquisitions increased the Monarchy's Slav and Italian populations still further. The revolutionary period was equally catastrophic, however, because it entrenched reaction in Habsburg government, in the person of Francis II and the conservative ministers he chose. Personally likeable if unimaginative, Francis was 24 at his accession, and through youth and inexperience was disinclined to continue with the grand reshaping of his realms prosecuted, in their very different ways, by his two predecessors. He was even less inclined to experiment while waging a war of survival against the French Republic and then Napoleon, who claimed to be the heir and executor of the Republic's principles. Economically, socially and politically the Monarchy remained frozen in time for the next two generations.

This reactionary trend was only reinforced by the discovery, in 1794, of the so-called 'Jacobin conspiracy' led by the Hungarian academic Ignác Martinovics. Recent scholarship has played down the significance of this phenomenon, and certainly Martinovics and his handful of associates were guilty of no more than sympathising not only with the ideals of the French Revolution but with the enlightened agenda of Joseph II and Leopold II. Martinovics, a translator of Tom Paine and Rousseau (into Latin), was actually on the payroll of Leopold's police minister until 1792, and the republic he then started advocating was one where nobles would still be politically dominant and receive their dues from peasants. The 'Jacobins' paid for their somewhat confused radicalism on the scaffold in 1795. Their real importance lay in the impetus their apprehension gave to even fiercer censorship and political repression on the part of Francis II's government.

NATIONAL STIRRINGS

Nowhere were the first, confused stirrings of nationalism more numerous than in the Habsburg Monarchy. At the same time the order and intensity of these early nationalisms depended on the different levels of economic and social development of individual peoples. Where some sort of educated elite existed, nationalism could be voiced; where a people remained largely peasant, nationalism is hard to discern. Everywhere the number of people capable of articulating something like nationalist sentiments was, to begin with, tiny.

This is especially true of the front runners, the 'gentry nationalists' among Hungarian and Polish nobles. In Hungary the nobility was effectively the only class to exercise political rights and dominated both the county assemblies and the Diet. When Hungarians referred to the 'Hungarian nation' they meant the nobles; lesser social classes scarcely existed in the constitutional sense. It was thus among the nobility, the only educated class, that the first expressions of nationalism were made. A pioneer in this respect was György Bessenyei, one of the first generation of young Hungarian nobles to profit from service in Maria Theresa's Royal Hungarian Bodyguard, stationed in Vienna and exposed to the full force of the Enlightenment. Bessenyei, who published the first anthology of Hungarian poetry in 1777, was also one of the first to advocate the use of Hungarian as a literary language and to promote means of improving it, such as teaching it at the revived University of Buda, compiling a dictionary and founding a learned society for the furtherance of good writing.

A much greater stimulus to nationalism was provided by Joseph II's language decree of 1784, ordaining German as the language of administration throughout Hungary, and extended to Galicia in 1785. Some of the most well-known literary works of the late eighteenth century were written as furious diatribes against all foreign influence, or as a celebration of the Magyars' ancient origins. Such works were only a fraction of the pamphlet literature provoked among educated Hungarians generally by Joseph's reign, culminating in the ferment surrounding the Diet of 1790–1. By the late 1780s a second generation of writers was appearing. Ferenc Kazinczy founded the critical periodical *Magyar Múzeum* (Hungarian Museum) in 1787; this succumbed to government censorship in 1792, but while it lasted it was 'the centre of Hungarian literary activity'.[22] Kazinczy devoted himself increasingly to the job of setting standards of expression in Hungarian and raising it to the status of a genuinely national language.

Among the Polish *szlachta* of Galicia, Old and New, the concept of the nation was a similarly exclusive one. Given the backwardness of the south Polish lands, even nobles who could boast an education were few; the masses of Polish and Ruthene peasants, despite the School Ordinance of 1774, remained untouched by education and hence oblivious to national consciousness. For the *szlachta*, nevertheless, the consciousness of membership in the 'republic of nobles' was a powerful cause of resentment against Habsburg rule, as was the flooding of Galicia with Czech-speaking officials after 1772, and the language decree of 1784. Even after 1795, when Poland disappeared from the map, the idea of Poland persisted among Polish nobles everywhere, whether clinging to their estates under foreign rule or in the widely scattered Polish diaspora.

Among the other nationalities of the Monarchy nationalism was far more obviously tied to socio-economic development and the emergence of an educated class, because there was no gentry elite to speak for all. In the case of the Czechs it is striking how much the 'national awakening' owed to Germans initially, many of them scholars intent on following up Herder's injunction to trace the historical origins of all peoples and languages, including the Slavs. The Czechs had a long history and a literary language, but following the reconquest of Bohemia in the early seventeenth century Czechs had been relegated to subordinate status and German had taken over as the dominant culture. It was thus German scholars who first troubled to learn the Czech language and studied the history of their Slav neighbours. The study of Czech had been given a big boost by Joseph II, who in 1784 permitted the formation of a Learned Society, later the Czech Society of Sciences. Most influential was the philologist Josef Dobrovský, professor of philology in Prague from 1791, author of a *History of the Czech Language and Literature* (1792) and teacher of an entire generation of national awakeners.

The Slovaks, though closely related to the Czechs, were slower to manifest signs of nationalism because of the almost entirely peasant nature of their society within the Kingdom of Hungary. Accordingly the foundation by Joseph II of a general seminary at Pressburg, in 1784, made a crucial contribution towards producing a first generation of literate Slovaks. Anton Bernolák, a graduate of the Pressburg seminary, went on to publish his *Grammatica slavica* in 1790, and was the first to identify Slovak as a distinct West Slavonic language. For some time after the turn of the century, however, many of the few educated Slovaks continued to write in Czech, a medium with a greater audience.

The case of the Transylvanian Romanians is an example of a national awakening led by clerics, since the Uniate or Greek Catholic priesthood was virtually the only educated class among the Monarchy's Romanians. The overwhelmingly peasant Romanian population remained firmly frozen out of the political picture in Transylvania. First to protest against this situation was the Uniate Bishop, Ion Inochentie Klein, who argued that the Romanians, having embraced the Union, ought to be accorded the same status as the Hungarians, Szeklers and Saxons. This religion-based identification of the Romanians as a people apart was perhaps the beginning of national feeling.

More obviously nationalist was the later activity of the 'Transylvanian School' among the Uniate clergy. This was a group of Vienna-educated, enlightened figures, led by Ion Inochentie's nephew, Samuil Klein, who in the 1770s started investigating the early history of the Romanians, tracing their origins to the ancient Roman colony of Dacia. In 1780, with Gheorghe

Şincai, Klein produced the first grammar of the Romanian language and, before his death, a dictionary. In March 1791 Klein, Şincai and two other leading Uniate intellectuals, Petru Maior and Ion Budai-Deleanu, helped frame a petition to Leopold II, the *Supplex libellus Valachorum*. This unprecedented document made an historic claim for the Romanians to be granted equality with other nations in Transylvania, on the basis of their longstanding presence in the region; it also claimed a natural right to be represented in the province's institutions on the basis of numbers. Even more significant, the *Supplex* defined the nation as all persons of the same origin and speaking the same language. The petition failed in its object, but disappointment did nothing to dampen a growing sense of identity among educated Romanians and a growing tension between them and the Hungarians.

The South Slavs varied widely in their receptivity to national consciousness. Among the Croatian nobility a class-based national sentiment already existed, similar to that in Hungary itself. There was no denying the novel nature of the dispute which broke out between the Hungarian Diet and Croatian *Sabor* in 1790–1 over the language of state. During Joseph II's reign both Croats and Hungarians made common cause in defence of Latin, as opposed to German, but after Joseph's death Hungarian motions to substitute Magyar provoked bitter opposition from Croatian deputies. The built-in majority of the Hungarians, however, coupled with a shared conservative interest in cooperating against 'Jacobinism', induced the Croats to accept Hungarian as an optional language in schools in 1791. As yet there was still no agreement as to what form the Croatian language should take, nor as to how much, if anything, Croats had in common with other South Slavs.

The Slovenes, a largely peasant people concentrated in the southern Austrian hereditary lands, had even fewer spokesmen. The first history of the Slovenes, or rather of Carniola and other provinces populated by them, was written in German by Anton Linhart in 1791. Slovene national consciousness, however, also suffered from confusion as to what exactly 'Slovene' meant, not to mention the absence of a literary language.

Finally, the Serbs of the Monarchy, scattered as they were across the southern borderlands of Hungary and Croatia, with a few also in Dalmatia and a long-established community on the Danube north of Buda, were a mixed lot. The majority, like the Croats, were peasants or, in the so-called Military Border extending along the frontier with the Ottoman Empire, border guards. Yet the number of urban Serbs was higher in the Monarchy than in the neighbouring Ottoman Empire. Conscious of their separate if rather ill-defined status as refugees from the Ottoman world, the Serbs' self-consciousness was also preserved by the Orthodox Church, which played a cultural role as educator and publisher. As a consequence there was a small but interesting Serb elite. The most striking representative of this class was Dositej Obradović, a lapsed monk who served as a sort of one-man Enlightenment. Educated in Germany, Obradović travelled extensively and acquired a wide range of languages. From the early 1780s he was an industrious translator of European literature into Serbian and a prolific writer on his own account. The significance of Obradović's activity was his choice of the Serbian vernacular as a medium, rather than the antique Church Slavonic favoured by the Orthodox hierarchy. In this way Obradović struck a powerful blow for a popular language, an essential prerequisite for Serb nationalism in the Monarchy.

Two observations on these 'national awakenings' seem apposite, in view of the tendency of nationalists to treat them as both inevitable and autonomous phenomena. One is the fact that all this ferment of philological, historical and literary endeavour was dependent on the multilingual and international cross-fertilisation of ideas produced by the Enlightenment. 'Nationalism', in Robin Okey's words, 'was an international movement arising from a common grounding in classical and European culture'.[23] Czechs studied and wrote about their language and history in German; Serbs and Romanians and Slovaks published some of their first works via the presses of the University of Buda; the first translation in Hungary of the French revolutionary anthem, the 'Marseillaise', was not into Magyar but Latin. Secondly, given that literacy was the essential prerequisite for nationalism, it is clear that the Theresian school legislation of the 1770s was decisive in unwittingly promoting the new concept of the nation. An enlightened reform, introduced to facilitate the conversion of the Habsburg Monarchy into a state, made possible the dissemination of the ideology which was eventually to tear the Monarchy apart.

4

THE POLISH–LITHUANIAN COMMONWEALTH

The partition of the Polish–Lithuanian Commonwealth has been described above (p. 31). It is impossible to understand the disappearance of this second-largest European state, however, without some knowledge of its internal history. Poland–Lithuania also offers a fascinating variation on each of the three main themes of this book. It was a multinational and multiconfessional society. It attempted modernisation, not through enlightened absolutism but through political reforms enacted by a representative assembly (of sorts). And it exhibited, in the Polish nobility, a strain of class-based nationalism which both drove the modernisation experiment and hindered it fatally, but which in the end made it possible for a modern Polish nationalism to emerge.

THE REPUBLIC OF NOBLES

The 'Commonwealth of the Two Nations, the Polish and the Lithuanian', as it was formally known after 1569, was not only one of the largest states in Europe in 1740 but also one of the strangest.[1] It was the result of a union in the 1380s between the Kingdom of Poland (often referred to simply as the *Korona* or Crown) and the Grand Duchy of Lithuania. The 1569 Act of Lublin formalised this partnership, in that for the first time it established a unitary *Sejm*, or representative assembly. The Polish lands and the Grand Duchy, however, continued to have separate administrative structures, whose ministers answered technically to the king. Poland–Lithuania was thus unique in Eastern Europe, not so much for its dual structure as for the fact that it was a constitutional monarchy, with restrictions on the power of the crown going back centuries.

The human geography of the Commonwealth was even more complicated. Of its estimated 12–13 million inhabitants at the time of the First Partition (1772), fewer than half were Polish speakers and about a million were Lithuanian speakers. There were 5 million Ukrainians and Belorussians, more of them in the *Korona* than in the Grand Duchy, while in the vassal Duchy of Courland to the north (only nominally subject to the Commonwealth by the early eighteenth century), a German-speaking nobility ruled over some 300,000 Latvian peasants.[2] Germans formed a substantial portion of the urban population, especially in the three great trading towns of northern Poland, Gdańsk, Toruń and Elbląg. Finally the Commonwealth was home to one of the largest Jewish minorities in Europe, between 750,000 and 900,000 strong, as well as small pockets of Greeks, Armenians and Tartars.[3]

The Commonwealth also exhibited considerable religious diversity and had in fact been famous for its willingness to tolerate different faiths. Although Protestantism had made substantial gains during the Reformation, by the eighteenth century the majority of Polish speakers were once again Catholic, as were most Lithuanians. Most Ukrainians and White Russians, by contrast, were Orthodox, yet of the Uniate or 'Greek Catholic' variety, in other words practising the Orthodox rite while acknowledging the leadership of the Pope in Rome. The resulting tensions between the Uniates and the remaining Orthodox community, who numbered only half a million by the mid-century, were a fruitful source of excuses for Russian intervention in Polish affairs. Among Germans, Lutheranism was the dominant religion, especially in the commercial centres of the north. The few Polish Protestant nobles, whether Lutheran or Calvinist, were banned from serving in the *Sejm* from the 1730s, but otherwise were free to participate in political life. Jews were also free to practise their religion, but were still required to live apart from the Christian community.

Poland–Lithuania, like every other East European society, was overwhelmingly agrarian, but it was unusual in the size and undisputed dominance of its noble class. The Polish *szlachta* in the pre-Partition era, on a conservative estimate, numbered 120,000 adult males who, together with their families, made up 6 per cent or more of the population, or 720,000 out of 12 million; in the period 1772–93 the proportion rose to between 7.0 and 7.5 per cent.[4] The *szlachta*, moreover, was Polish in language and culture; the nobility of Lithuania had long become polonised, and with the exception of a few German families in the north, to be noble was to be Polish.

The other outstanding fact about the Polish nobility was that it was the only class which counted in the Commonwealth, because it was the only class with effective political rights. The 'Two Nations' referred to in the state's title did not mean all inhabitants of the *Korona* and the Grand Duchy, but rather all members of the nobility. The nobility, as in Hungary, *were* the 'Polish nation', and when they spoke of the 'nation' they meant themselves, not townspeople or peasants. As Jean-Jacques Rousseau put it in 1771, in a perceptive essay on the government of Poland, burghers were 'nothing' and the peasantry 'less than nothing'.[5]

Rousseau might have lumped the kings of Poland–Lithuania in with these latter categories of the sidelined and powerless. For the practical result of noble numbers and noble determination over the centuries was a constitutional monarchy where the monarch was elected, and elected by the nobles, and where the tendency towards royal absolutism, so prevalent elsewhere, had been effectively blocked. Because Polish kings were elected, and because their election was conditional upon promising to uphold the so-called 'golden liberties' of the nobles, no Polish ruler, even a militarily successful one like Jan III Sobieski (1674–96), was ever able to achieve greater executive power. Yet the nobles themselves did not step into the constitutional vacuum this created, nor did the *Sejm* evolve into the engine of government that Parliament became in contemporary England. 'Privilege', according to Jerzy Lukowski, 'made the *szlachta* free and Poland ungovernable.'[6]

Nobles could not be arrested without due process, were exempt from taxation, were the undisputed masters of their estates and exercised judicial authority over the wretched peasants who farmed them. All nobles, even the substantial number who were landless, were entitled to vote in the elections to the *sejmiki* or local diets, which in turn sent their delegates to the *Sejm*. As in Hungary, the fifty-odd *sejmiki* were the real instruments of power in Polish–Lithuanian society: they elected local officials and the judiciary (invariably fellow nobles) and collected taxes from the non-noble (and non-enfranchised) population. Beyond this, every noble had the right personally to vote in the election of the king, a right many continued to exercise, travelling with great show to Warsaw and assembling in their thousands in a field outside the city.

At the pinnacle of noble privilege was the notorious *liberum veto*, the right of every noble to block legislation in the *Sejm* simply by voicing his disagreement. Once used, this 'free veto' annulled not only the legislation under discussion but every single act of that particular *Sejm*. Dating from 1505, the *liberum veto* had its origins in the theoretically laudable desire for consensus, in an age when the very concept of a binding majority vote was still a novelty. The veto was first used in earnest in 1652 and thereafter was invoked all too often to paralyse the business of state. Not only could individual deputies in the pay of the wealthiest nobles bring proceedings to a halt, but the *Sejm* was by the early eighteenth century literally a marketplace for foreign diplomats, whether lobbying for the election as king of their country's candidate or buying votes for the obstruction of much-needed reforms. Despite the obvious consequences of the veto for the stability, and even the survival, of the Commonwealth, no *Sejm* could be brought to abolish it. The only circumstance in which majority voting could be followed was when, in response to some emergency, a group of nobles, in or out of the *Sejm*, exercised their right of 'confederation'. Confederation, however, was a dubious political tool at the best of times: most often it was used by individual great nobles or groups of nobles to obstruct some measure the *Sejm* had actually agreed upon, and it was equally liable to manipulation by foreign powers.

Mention of the great nobles, or magnates, brings us to the real source of power in the Commonwealth. Although every Polish noble was in theory the equal of every other, the reality was otherwise. Roughly half of the *szlachta* owned no land, or farmed plots so small as to make them in economic terms hardly distinguishable from peasants; such nobles could be seen ploughing their own fields, with their swords, symbol of noble status, hanging from a tree behind them. Above this class were the middle ranks of the nobility, whose estates were big enough to assure them a reasonable income. Perhaps 300 families owned estates equal to the biggest imaginable in Western Europe. At the top, however, 20–30 families disposed of wealth – and status – that even by modern standards is mind-boggling. A single family, the Potockis, were the owners of an estate half the size of the Dutch Republic, with revenues of 3 million florins a year, a third that of the king. Karol Radziwiłł, who maintained a private army of 6000 men, when told that he lived like a king, retorted: 'I live like a Radziwiłł – the king can do what he likes.'[7] One noble, bored with the gamebirds of northern Europe, 'imported parakeets by the shipload from Africa' to brighten up his hunting.[8]

Such fantastic wealth enabled magnates literally to buy power. They monopolised the highest offices of state and controlled entire provinces as both officials and landowners. They provided employment to hundreds, in some cases thousands, of landless or otherwise needy nobles, who could be trusted to turn out in force at elections to the *sejmiki*, to serve as deputies in the *Sejm* and to vote the desired way at coronation *Sejms*. On two occasions in the eighteenth century, candidates from magnate families wore the crown itself. What the magnates could not or would not do, however, was to fill the vacuum at the centre of the Polish–Lithuanian state. They were, in fact, part of the problem, in that their economic and political clout, coupled with the seeming impossibility of reforming the *Sejm*, ensured that power remained decentralised and hence liable to infinite manipulation.

The political debility of the Commonwealth was compounded by economic weakness, which prevented the emergence of an urban class capable of challenging the nobility's stranglehold on public affairs. In the early modern period, Poland–Lithuania was one of the principal granaries of Europe, and the steady rise of prices ensured that Polish landowners grew fabulously wealthy. This prosperity, though it benefited the great commercial *entrepôts* of the Baltic coast, did not lead to a sustained growth of towns. On the contrary: legislation passed by the *Sejm* specifically excluded non-noble town dwellers not only from owning landed estates but from participating in the grain trade itself. If we add to this the increasing restrictions imposed by the nobles on their peasantry, which meant the pool of labour available for urban work remained limited, and the catastrophic effect of warfare in the late seventeenth and early eighteenth centuries, which saw the urban population drop by 70 per cent, the feebleness of towns is unsurprising. In addition, by 1700 65 per cent of towns were private in any case, as opposed to royal; in other words they had been established to meet the needs of individual noble landowners. Private towns catered only to the requirements of their locality and were unlikely to act as centres of capital accumulation, or indeed any economic activity not directly related to their noble owners. The eighteenth century, though it saw a gradual rise in the urban population, was nevertheless a period of general urban stagnation.

Long before 1740 this much-vaunted 'noble democracy' was the plaything of its more powerful neighbours, and Russia was the principal kingmaker, intervening not once but twice to ensure the election of the Elector of Saxony as king. Augustus III (1735–63) was an indolent drunkard who during his reign spent a total of 24 months in Poland; but in any case, like his father before him, he was forbidden by treaty with Russia to maintain more than 1200 Saxon troops in the country. At the insistence of the Polish nobility, supported by Russia, the administration of the Commonwealth was kept strictly separate from that of Saxony and the standing army, in the period after 1717, never rose above 24,000, a ludicrously small number for the second-largest state in Europe.[9] Russian troops were the real guarantors of order, and the great magnate families' control of the *Sejm* saw to it that political paralysis remained the order of the day. The election in 1764 of Stanisław Poniatowski, Catherine II's ex-lover, seemed to be the final confirmation that the Commonwealth was a Russian province in all but name.

THE STIRRINGS OF REFORM 1740–72

Despite or rather because of the Commonwealth's abysmal situation, something like a reform movement was emerging in the 1740s and 1750s. The very powerlessness of the state in the War of the Polish Succession of 1733–5, when the election of a Polish noble, Stanisław Leszczyński, was set aside by foreign intervention, was seen by some nobles as a humiliation, not to mention a harbinger of partition. Under Augustus III, an absentee king if ever there was one, Poland–Lithuania had in effect no government at all. For all the collusion by Poland's nobles in this anarchy, a few voices began to consider the alternatives.

Some of these reformers grouped at first around Leszczyński who, in 1735, as father-in-law to Louis XV of France, was compensated for his dethronement with the Duchy of Lorraine. Stanisław's court at Lunéville, near Nancy, became not only a beacon for Polish *émigrés* but a model of enlightened government in its own right. Stanisław himself published a tract in 1749, probably ghost-written, entitled 'A Voice Ensuring Freedom', which restated the basic principle 'that the Commonwealth was a political fatherland, defined neither by its ruler nor its ethnic distinction nor its geographical frontiers'.[10] This restatement of the original idea of the 'commonwealth' as all politically active inhabitants of the state had an unquantifiable effect on the thinking of French political philosophers like Rousseau, in particular their changing interpretation of the term 'nation'.

In the Commonwealth, it is significant that the first serious calls for reform started to appear in the wake of the war of 1733–5. Historians are still divided as to when the thinking of the Enlightenment can be said to have had an influence. What is undisputed is that the number of the 'enlightened' in Polish society was small, probably never more than 2000 individuals at any one point.[11] Ironically, too, such reforming spirits could emerge only from the class responsible for the Commonwealth's decline, the nobility.

As in the Habsburg Monarchy, an important initial contribution was made by reformist Catholic clerics, who argued that the dead hand of the Church in educational and intellectual matters was as much a factor in Poland's decline as its economic underdevelopment and the dominance of the nobility. A central figure in educational reform was the Piarist priest Stanisław Konarski, who received his education abroad and spent time at Lunéville, before returning to Poland in the 1730s. Konarski was supported in his vision of the need literally to educate nobles into a more public-spirited and enlightened attitude by the brother-bishops Andrzej and Józef Załuski, enthusiastic bibliophiles and disseminators of enlightened ideas. Together the three men published not only legal texts but works of political philosophy and literature and in 1747 the Załuski brothers merged their personal libraries into a single collection of 180,000 books, housed them in a Warsaw palace and donated this 'first public reference library on the European mainland' to the Commonwealth.[12]

Konarski and the Załuskis also modernised the school system. Konarski's *Collegium Nobilium*, opened in 1740, aimed to give the sons of nobles a truly modern education. Even more radical was the transition effected by Konarski, in the Commonwealth's 28 Piarist schools, from Latin to Polish as the language of instruction, and the introduction of such subjects as political philosophy, modern languages and philosophy. The rival Jesuit schools copied Konarski's methods and much of his curriculum in their own 66 institutions. Although confined exclusively to the noble class, this change in the pattern of education not only produced a generation of relatively modern-minded Poles by the 1750s but, by opting for Polish as the medium, laid the foundations of a more broadly based conception of the Polish nation.

The relative dearth of such forward thinking helps account for the failure, in 1744, of the first serious attempt at political reform. This centred on the faction in the *Sejm* led by one of the wealthiest magnate families, the Czartoryskis, and their allies. The Czartoryski *'Familia'* proposed sweeping changes: a larger army, to be financed by improvements in revenue collection; the lifting of economic restrictions on non-nobles; the limitation of the *liberum veto*; and the payment of salaries to *Sejm* deputies. Despite support for this programme among other factions, there was also opposition; the matter was settled when it became clear that the king of Prussia, in particular, wished that 'matters should remain in a state of some confusion in Poland'.[13] As usual, a deputy was induced to apply the veto and the *Sejm* was dissolved.

Two decades on, when the death of Augustus III required a royal election, the pressure for reform was harder to deny and the Czartoryski *Familia*'s candidate, Stanisław Poniatowski, enjoyed a unique advantage. As the former lover of Catherine II of Russia, Poniatowski was deemed to be a pliant instrument of Russian policy and was backed by Russian troops. This, together with the exhaustion of the great powers at the close of the Seven Years' War, was decisive in ensuring that the Polish succession did not unleash fresh conflict. The young king, however, was no cipher, but a committed adherent of enlightened thought, shaped by an intensive education, widely travelled and even more widely read, and an admirer of the more advanced political systems of Western Europe, especially Britain's. The very title he assumed at his election in September 1764, Stanisław II August, indicated his ambition to reform the Commonwealth as Caesar Augustus had reformed Rome.

Stanisław August was aware of the almost insuperable obstacles to change. A start was nevertheless immediately made in the Convocation *Sejm* of 1764, which was formally 'confederated' and hence legally free to adopt legislation by majority vote, unhindered by the veto. The new king won approval for measures originally proposed in 1744. In 1766, the government grasped the prickliest nettle of all, the abolition of the *liberum veto*. The response of Poland–Lithuania's neighbours was unambiguous. Prussia had already, in 1765, made impossible the operation of the Commonwealth's new customs regime by blockading the River Vistula where it passed East Prussian territory. Now, both Russia and Prussia demanded the retention of the veto; otherwise, as the Russian ambassador put it, he would see to it that Warsaw was torn down 'stone by stone'.[14] Stanisław August had little option but to dissolve the *Sejm*; but this was only the beginning. For some time the Russian and Prussian governments had been using the issue of religious toleration, for Orthodox and Lutherans respectively, as an excuse for interference in the Commonwealth's affairs. On this pretext, and profiting from the resistance to toleration from the almost exclusively Catholic *Sejm*, the two powers insisted on the calling of another confederated *Sejm* in the winter of 1767–8, during which Russian bullying reached new heights. Russian troops occupied Warsaw, the Russian ambassador kept careful watch over the proceedings and prominent opponents were temporarily deported to Russian territory. In the end the deputies reluctantly approved a series of laws which the Empress Catherine undertook to 'guarantee'. These enshrined yet again the elective kingship, the *liberum veto*, the right of noble insurrection against royal power, the exclusion of non-nobles from land ownership and public office, and the continuation of serfdom. The Commonwealth's 'golden liberty' did not, it seemed, include the liberty to modernise.

The enforced settlement of 1768 produced a number of reactions welcome to neither Stanisław nor Catherine. Before the *Sejm* had even risen a group of disaffected nobles and clergymen, who objected to both religious toleration and Russian interference, formed the Confederation of Bar in the south-east of the country; the aim of this ill-led but persistent insurrection was to depose Stanisław August and somehow repudiate Russian tutelage. Almost immediately after, in April 1768, a savage uprising broke out among the Orthodox Ukrainian peasantry, enraged by the failure to address the question of serfdom as well as the threatening stance on toleration assumed by the Barists. Before the revolt was stamped out, with the help of Russian forces, in mid-1769, an untold number of people had been massacred: Poles, Ukrainian peasants and Jews. Finally, the continuing presence of Russian troops in south-eastern Poland, and the suspicion that Russia intended using the Commonwealth as a mustering post for invasion, led the Ottoman sultan to declare war on Russia in October 1768. This meant that Catherine could spare few troops for the suppression of disorder in Poland and the Confederation of Bar maintained a low-level guerrilla war against those Russians in the Commonwealth for the next four years. To Catherine's exasperation, the Polish–Lithuanian government made little contribution to the campaign against the Barists, for fear of being seen to be fighting Poles.

The chaos in the Commonwealth gave Frederick II of Prussia all the justification he desired for territorial aggrandisement. Frederick actively sought to acquire Polish or Royal Prussia, the territory separating Brandenburg from East Prussia. This would not only unify the Prussian lands but would give Prussia additional rich agricultural land and control of the lucrative trade on the River Vistula. It was only when the Russo-Turkish War threatened to touch off hostilities between Russia, Prussia's only ally, and the Habsburg Monarchy that Frederick put forward concrete proposals for a tripartite partition of Poland–Lithuania. This would compensate Russia for renouncing the Ottoman principalities of Moldavia and Wallachia, whose mooted annexation was risking war with the Monarchy. It also forced a reluctant Maria Theresa to join in, for fear of being overshadowed by the territorial aggrandisement of its rivals. Agreement in principle on the territories to be annexed was reached in February 1772. It remained only to force the settlement on the Commonwealth, whose government, Frederick argued, had long since forfeited any right to be taken seriously as the guarantor of Polish liberties, not to mention Poland's internal stability. The Commonwealth, that 'land of fools, madmen and war', did not deserve to survive, a dismissive verdict which has tended to affect the judgement of historians ever since.[15] In reality the Commonwealth did not have much choice in the matter. Stanisław August, with tiny forces at his disposal and much of the country either loyal to the Barists or already under foreign occupation, was in no position to resist the demand by the three powers to call a *Sejm* to ratify a done deal.

Once assembled, the *Sejm* was immediately forced to devolve the 'debate' on the partition treaties to a Delegation of its members, most of whom were in the pay of the powers. It was the Delegation which approved the treaties of cession, in August and September 1773, and which finally swallowed a constitutional reordering of the Commonwealth itself cooked up by the Russians. According to this, not only were the free veto and the elective kingship reaffirmed, but what little powers Stanisław August had left were effectively abolished by the creation of a Permanent Council. This was to be composed of 36 members of the *Sejm* and answerable to that body; but it was in no sense a government and had no legislative powers as such. In theory, this represented the apogee of noble democracy, since not only the king but the Council was accountable to the *Sejm*. In fact, the ultimate arbiter of what happened remained the Russian government.

By the terms of the First Partition (see Map 3), the Commonwealth lost more than a quarter of its territory, as well as something like a third of its population. Russia was the largest gainer in terms of territory, while the Habsburg Monarchy took over the largest number of inhabitants. In economic terms, the annexed lands were among the most valuable in the Commonwealth. In addition, the rump Polish state was choked off from the outside world through

3 The three Partitions of the Polish-Lithuanian Commonwealth. Redrawn from The Russo-Polish Borderlands to 1795 (p. 772) from *The Russian Empire 1801-1917* by Hugh Seton-Watson, (Oxford University Press, 1967)

the loss of control over river routes and ports; Prussia in particular held the Polish economy in a vice. Neutered both physically and politically, Poland–Lithuania's prospects for any sort of regeneration looked minimal. In the next two decades, however, a brave attempt was made to modernise, fascinating precisely because the odds against its success seemed so long.

THE FINAL ATTEMPTS AT REFORM 1772-95

It would be an exaggeration to say that the First Partition's effect on Polish society was comparable to that produced in the Habsburg Monarchy by the seizure of Silesia. An increasing but still small number of Poles could see that the costs of not modernising might include the destruction of the state itself. Nevertheless, the vast majority of nobles do not seem to have made this connection. Most nobles bewailed the Partition but could envisage no constructive response, least of all one that involved the curtailment of their own privileges. In the annexed territories, as if to highlight the dangers, thousands of Polish nobles faced the choice of accepting a new allegiance or losing their land; most yielded to obvious self-interest and chose the first. For the millions of peasants involved, the change of regime arguably made no difference in their condition.

Poland–Lithuania's Enlightenment thus flourished in paradoxical conditions: the growing intelligentsia, actively encouraged by Stanisław August, were free to debate the Commonwealth's problems endlessly, but there was little they could do about them. Nevertheless, Stanisław August's reign saw, before and after the First Partition, a broadening and deepening of discussion which served only to increase the temptation to attempt further reform.

Right from the start of his reign the young king was determined that, however limited his political powers, he would use the social prestige and capacity for patronage of his position to further culture and the arts. Himself a connoisseur and collector, Stanisław August imported noted painters and architects from abroad, as well as promoting the careers of native Poles. In the year of his election the king founded the first formal association of writers in the Polish language; he patronised one of the first Polish periodicals, the *Monitor*, a weekly and later bi-weekly started in 1765 for the discussion of social and political issues. Another weekly literary journal, *Useful and Pleasant Pastimes*, ran from 1770 to 1777 and 'became the king's literary platform and an expression of his aesthetic ideas.'[16] In 1765 Stanisław August created the Commonwealth's first theatre company; he was responsible for the introduction of Polish translations of works such as *Julius Caesar*, as well as commissioning plays by Polish writers. He encouraged some of the first serious Polish historians, notably Adam Naruszewicz, who in the early 1770s began his *History of the Polish Nation*, a timely plea for, among other things, the restoration of hereditary monarchy. Finally, Stanisław August acted as a personal facilitator of cultural and intellectual exchange through his Thursday evening dinners. Taking his cue from his 'spiritual *maman*', the famous Parisian *salonnière* Madame Geoffrin, through-out the 1770s and early 1780s the king held these regular meetings, where guests from all walks of intellectual life – poets, architects, scientists, artists, *litterateurs* – were encouraged to exchange ideas. In the last decade of the reign the example of salons was copied throughout Warsaw society.

In the aftermath of the Partition certain institutional changes, which even the Russians accepted were necessary, further deepened the impact of the Enlightenment. The most famous was the Commission for National Education, created in October 1773 as the result of a personal deal between Stanisław August and the Russian ambassador, which was the only govern-ment department not directly subordinate to the toothless Permanent Council. Taking advantage of the fact that, as in the Habsburg Monarchy, the abolition of the Jesuits put their property at his disposal, the king set up what was in effect the first ministry of education in Europe, designed, as one of his supporters put it, to 'turn people into Poles, and Poles into citizens'.[17] The Commission's regulations removed Latin from the curriculum and scaled down religious instruction. In their place came Polish literature and history, the natural sciences, mathematics, geography and foreign languages. A separate curriculum for girls was introduced the following year. There was a general shortage of textbooks, so in 1775 a sub-committee was set up, which invited tenders for such texts from across Europe. As a result the Commonwealth's schools soon boasted primers written by the best minds of the eighteenth century, including a textbook on logic by the French *philosophe*, the Abbé de Condillac. Resistance to the new schools among the *szlachta*, it has to be said, was high – only 15 per cent of the noble youths sent to them ever completed the course – and the secular emphasis and abandonment of Latin were denounced as godless. Nevertheless a genuinely modern education system had been instituted, the long-term effects of which on the next couple of generations can only be guessed at.

Circumstances in the 1780s conspired to heighten both the pressure for reform and the hope that the Commonwealth might actually be allowed to undertake it. A new generation of Polish intellectuals was coming of age, whose systematic analysis of Polish backwardness impelled them towards increasingly radical solutions. One such was the noble and cleric Hugo Kołłątaj, whose prescription was partly economic: he argued for a rational tax system as the indispensable precondition for modernisation, which would depend on a bureaucracy and an army. Kołłątaj and the circle around him, the 'Forge', also pressed for political modernisation; Kołłątaj himself was realist enough to see that only very gradual change was likely, whereas some of his younger followers were more inclined to forget the international restraints on Polish action. The most systematic critique of the Commonwealth's predicament came from Stanisław Staszic, a former priest and non-noble who stressed the need for greater economic development, in particular the lifting of restrictions on the still tiny middle class. Staszic also brought out, in 1787, an ostensible work of history, his *Reflections on the Life of Jan Zamoyski*, which argued that the only way to break the Commonwealth's political deadlock was to make the monarchy hereditary, give the *Sejm* full legislative and executive authority, abolish the *liberum veto*, raise taxes, increase the army and emancipate the serfs. The only subject on which Staszic was silent, predictably, was Russia's own veto on such a programme.

Jerzy Lukowski has rightly criticised Poland–Lithuania's last generation of reformers as high-minded but unrealistic, living 'in an enlightened universe of their own'.[18] Yet the international situation itself seemed, in the late 1780s, to provide an irresistible opportunity. Not only did the American Revolution, and the deliberations on the American constitution in 1787, offer a distant but inspiring example of rational state-building, but in France there was political ferment surrounding the Assembly of Notables that year, followed in 1788 by the decision to convene the Estates-General. Most tantalising, however, was the outbreak of war between the Ottoman Empire and Russia in October 1787. This entailed a physical diversion of Russian power, in that Catherine was forced to withdraw all but a token force from Polish–Lithuanian territory. Austria, which joined the conflict in February 1788, already had its hands full dealing with the consequences of Joseph II's reforms in the Netherlands and Hungary. In Prussia, Frederick the Great had died in 1786.

Even before the start of the Russo-Turkish War, Stanisław August conceived the idea of joining it on Russia's side. By his proposed treaty of alliance, the Commonwealth would be permitted to raise its army to 45,000 men, which would make its support in the field worth having. In return, Stanisław August asked for greater leeway in domestic affairs. Catherine, however, turned down the offer; despite the difficulties of the Turkish war she had no intention of giving Poland the means of self-defence.

It was characteristic of the fractiousness of the Polish *szlachta* that Stanisław August was furiously denounced as a tool of Russian despotism for his project. Its failure prompted several leading magnates to initiate secret negotiations with the Prussian court. Their aim, in defiance of any dispassionate analysis of Prussian policy, was to secure Prussia's support against Russia. Frederick William II of Prussia was happy to encourage this trend, suggesting in October 1788 that an alliance with Prussia would secure the Commonwealth territorial compensation; equally arresting, he intimated that Prussia, hitherto one of the 'guarantors' of the constitutional strait-jacket imposed on Poland in the 1770s, henceforth considered internal reform to be the Poles' own business.

The *Sejm* which met in October 1788, and which because of its prolongation became known as the *Four Years' Sejm*, accordingly met in an atmosphere of unprecedented tension and anticipation. Prussian intrigues ensured that the *Sejm* was vehemently anti-Russian, and for the first time there was widespread if not unanimous agreement that the entire settlement of the early 1770s had to be revised, an ambition strengthened by the exciting news from France in the summer of 1789. Emboldened by the Prussian alliance offer, the *Sejm* immediately confederated itself, thus enabling votes by simple majority, and then voted an increase in the army from 18,000 to 100,000 men, though without much thought to how this was to be financed. The deputies followed this up with a demand that all Russian troops be withdrawn from the Commonwealth, an ultimatum with which the embattled Russians, in the circumstances, had no choice but to comply. Throughout 1789 the spate of legislative reform continued: the abolition of the Permanent Council in January and the indefinite prolongation of the *Sejm* itself; in March the first ever tax on noble and Church lands; in September the appointment of a commission to draft a constitution; and in December the presentation of a petition, masterminded by Kołłątaj, appealing for parliamentary representation of towns. In explicit allusion to events in France, this petition warned: 'The slave will violently tear his bonds asunder if his ruler stifles all the Rights of Man and of the Citizen.'[19] Fears of a violent revolution *à la française* were undoubtedly exaggerated, but there was clearly great popular (that is, non-noble) interest in the *Sejm*'s activities and something like mass politicisation was taking place.

In the course of 1790, however, the limitations of noble democracy became increasingly apparent. In particular, the resistance of many of the *szlachta* to serious social change, such as the representation of towns, let alone the abolition of serfdom, was such that a gap opened between them and more radical reformers like Staszic. Most strikingly, Staszic argued that Poland was a 'moral entity', in other words a society comprising all classes, not just nobles. This was not a view easily accepted by noble deputies. It was not until December 1790 that the reformers managed to pass a law banning landless nobles from taking part in *sejmiki* elections, a measure aimed at the power of the magnates; and in April 1791 the 'Statute of the Cities' finally granted 22 seats in the *Sejm* to towns, a step many nobles bitterly opposed.

In the meantime, the king enlisted other reformers like Kołłątaj to help draft a constitution to resolve these issues. Because of the uncertainty of opinion in the *Sejm*, however, Stanisław August and his advisers decided to present their draft to the *Sejm* when many of the deputies were still absent after the Easter recess of 1791. The constitution of 3 May was accordingly passed as a surprise measure by 100 out of 182 members.

The 1791 constitution has been termed then and since a 'Polish revolution', although Stanisław August and his helpers, mindful of moderate opinion at home and abroad, were anxious to repudiate this label. The constitution resolved the succession (Stanisław August was childless) by proclaiming the Elector of Saxony the next king and the Wettin dynasty henceforth hereditary, not elective. The *Sejm* was confirmed as the supreme legislative body, but with voting to be by majority; the *liberum veto* and the right of confederation were abolished. The king would rule through a royal council of five ministers and the Catholic Primate, who were to be answerable to the *Sejm*. The representation of towns already agreed on was confirmed. If there was anything revolutionary about the constitution it was this admission that non-nobles had a role to play in affairs of state. Commissions were set up to draft further reforms affecting the economy, notably the conversion of peasant labour services into money payments, and plans were drawn up for lifting some of the restrictions affecting Polish Jews, although none of this got very far. The constitution's real significance was the possibilities it opened up for continuing, moderate change.

What is indisputable is that the mere passing of the constitution of 3 May 'sealed Poland's fate'.[20] The reaction in the courts of the Commonwealth's two most dangerous neighbours was consternation. Prussia's foreign minister called the constitution 'a mortal blow' to Prussia: 'Because of this Poland will become dangerous to Prussia . . . How are we to defend our state . . . against a numerous and well-governed nation?'[21] The Empress Catherine preserved a chilly silence for months, but as soon as a Russo-Turkish peace was concluded in January 1792 it became apparent that she regarded the idea of a regenerated Poland as intolerable and was preparing troops on the frontier. Only Leopold II of Austria approved of the Commonwealth's experiment in enlightenment – but Leopold died in March and the French declaration of war on both Austria and Prussia in April made any practical support from the Habsburgs unlikely. Catherine had no difficulty in finding Polish magnates willing to lead the so-called Confederation of Targowica, proclaimed just inside Polish–Lithuanian territory in May but hatched in St Petersburg, and which declared its opposition to the constitution. The Russo-Polish war which followed was mercifully brief. Faced with Catherine's demand that Stanisław August renounce the constitution and himself adhere to the Targowica Confederation, the Polish government had little choice but to yield. Kołłątaj and other reformers went into exile in Saxony; the more radical among them, like the army general Tadeusz Kościuszko, wound up lobbying the new republican regime in Paris for support.

The Second Partition, agreed by Russia and a Prussia eager for 'compensation' in January 1793, reduced the Commonwealth to a powerless buffer state of 4 million people. Russia sheared off an immense territory in the east comprising 250,000 square kilometres; Prussia annexed the triangle comprising Poznań, Toruń and Kalisz. Stanisław August was left to reign over what was clearly intended to be a Russian puppet state. Tragically for Poland the brutal circumstances of the Second Partition helped to conjure up a resistance which, however noble, was too little, too late, and which only convinced the conservative monarchies surrounding the Commonwealth that they were confronting revolutionary 'Jacobinism'.[22] Exiles like Kołłątaj and Kościuszko hatched various improbable plots for raising an insurrection and entertained high hopes that the new French Republic's declaration of support for fraternal nations everywhere would translate into concrete assistance. Yet the vital precondition for a mass uprising, the explicit abandonment of noble privilege and emancipation of serfs, was something that very few of the *szlachta* could contemplate. Only in Warsaw, where the years of political reform had involved an increasing number of townspeople and urban poor, and in the Commonwealth's expanded army, was there anything like a genuine popular radicalism.

It was the army which acted as the catalyst for rebellion because of plans announced by the government in February 1794, on Russian orders, for inducting most of the Polish troops into the Russian army. A detachment of cavalry refused to accept this fate and in March joined up in Kraków with Kościuszko, who proclaimed an insurrection on 24 March. Despite the hopeless long-term prospects, Kościuszko, an experienced soldier who had fought on behalf of American independence, won an initial encounter with the Russians at Racławice in April. The news of this had an electrifying effect on the populace and army units of Warsaw and Wilno, who rose against the Russian forces in occupation there and expelled them with heavy loss of life on both sides.

Famously, Kościuszko's victory at Racławice was secured with the help of 2000 scythe-wielding peasants. They, and the artisans and other townspeople who rose in Warsaw and Wilno, were clearly responding to Kościuszko's known position of favouring the abolition of serfdom and equal political rights for all Poles, regardless of class. It was in recognition of the need to generate a genuinely mass following that on 7 May Kościuszko, with the assistance of Kołłątaj, issued the Declaration of Połaniec. This proclaimed all serfs to be free, and free to move as long as their existing obligations were commuted; but it did not abolish labour services, merely reducing the levels. The reason was that Kościuszko was also acutely aware of the *szlachta*'s reluctance to relinquish serf labour. The Polish insurrection was the victim of a fatal dilemma: it needed both the nobles, as the class of traditional leadership, and the broad masses, whose sheer numbers were essential. Kościuszko never bridged this gap. Many nobles preferred not to risk their estates by participating in resistance; the vast majority of peasants saw no reason for sacrificing themselves to a cause which they did not see as their own.

The very prolongation of Polish resistance, however, and the language of equality used if never wholly implemented by its leaders, helped lay the foundations for modern Polish nationalism, not least the myth that 1794 was a 'national' uprising. In the end it was the overwhelming might of Russia which settled the matter. Kościuszko was defeated and captured in October; in November Russian troops stormed the Warsaw suburb of Praga, slaughtering 10,000 people in an exemplary terror which brought the capital's speedy surrender. Many leaders of the insurrection, like Kościuszko and Kołłątaj, languished in tsarist prisons for years; many others fled abroad, initiating a century-long Polish diaspora.

Catherine II now had all the excuse she needed for a final partition of Poland–Lithuania. This time her principal partner was the Habsburg Monarchy, excluded from the Second Partition but determined to be in on the Third, especially if it meant thwarting Prussia, whose abandonment of the war against France had led to the loss of the Austrian Netherlands. Catherine, too, was exasperated by Prussian duplicity and cupidity over Poland; it was only on the basis of an initial Austro-Russian understanding, reached in January 1795, that Prussia was later suffered to join in dismembering the Commonwealth. Russia took over another huge strip of territory, from Courland on the Baltic south to Austrian Galicia; Austria received a central wedge including Kraków and Lublin; while Prussia was allotted Warsaw as well as territory further to the east and south. Stanisław August was forced to abdicate in November 1795 and spent the remaining three years of his life in enforced if comfortable captivity in Russia. The Commonwealth ceased to exist even in name: by the final Convention of St Petersburg, of 26 January 1797, the three partitioning powers agreed on 'the need to abolish everything which can recall the memory of the existence of the kingdom of Poland'.[23]

Poland–Lithuania's experiment in modernisation had failed, in part, as some historians rightly remind us, because the Commonwealth was brutally subverted and attacked by its neighbours, but in part also because of the incurable backwardness and selfishness of its own traditional elite, the nobility. Yet the attempt at modernisation itself, followed by the physical conflict in which the Commonwealth was extinguished, had done more to create a sense of being Polish among a wider cross-section of the population than ever before. The majority of Poles, Lithuanians, Ukrainians, White Russians, Germans and Jews were henceforth subsumed in the much greater, but equally backward, partitioning empires. The tiny urban class, however, and even some peasants, retained memories of the ferment of the 1790s, and of iconic leaders like Kościuszko. Most of all, the principal guardians of this flame of nationhood were the Polish nobility, whether in the lands of the Partition or further afield. Most Polish *émigrés* gravitated to revolutionary France, as the one European power likely to assist the resurrection of the Polish state. In the course of 1797–1800 no fewer than three Polish legions were formed in northern Italy, mainly from captured or deserted Austrian Polish troops, and under the command of exiles like Jan Henryk Dąbrowski and Józef Wybicki. The 'Dąbrowski march', composed by Wybicki, became the national anthem in the twentieth century. At the close of the eighteenth, however, Polish soldiers perished liberally in other people's wars. Notoriously, 6000 members of the Polish legions were sent by Napoleon in an attempt to suppress the black slave revolt in French Haiti; barely 300 returned alive. The representatives abroad of the Polish–Lithuanian Commonwealth, whose centrepiece had always been the liberty of nobles, seemed apt to get their priorities wrong. In the meantime, their compatriots in the partitions dreamed of a Polish rebirth.

5

THE OTTOMAN EMPIRE

The Ottoman Empire in 1740 embraced a vast array of territories and peoples, from Bosnia to the Persian Gulf, although the concern of this chapter is principally with its provinces in south-eastern Europe. (See Map 2.) It illustrates each of the three themes of this study: modernisation, nationalism and the nature of multinational states. Firstly, the Empire in the eighteenth century offers a conspicuous example of failure to modernise, despite fitful attempts in that direction and despite having every incentive to reform in the threat of partition. Secondly, although nationalism was barely discernible among most of the sultan's Balkan Christian subjects, we can see some of the essential preconditions falling into place, to the point where open revolt against Ottoman rule was imminent by the turn of the century. Finally, the very nature of the Ottoman imperium meant that the Empire was by definition supranational and opposed to any accommodation with nationalism. In addition, the Empire was weakened in the Balkans not only by the fundamental division between Muslims and Christians but by conflict between its own Muslim subjects and the central authority in Constantinople.[1]

To make sense of what one historian has called 'an enormous and intricate mosaic of social subsystems', we need first to understand the nature of the Ottoman state and why it appeared to be breaking apart in the eighteenth century.[2] Only in this way can the reactions of individual peoples and classes, whether Christian or Muslim, be explained, or the increasing liability of the Empire to be attacked by its rivals be understood. The inability of the Ottoman government either to reform, or to maintain order in its Balkan provinces, ultimately led to territorial losses, internal revolt and that long nineteenth-century career as the 'sick man' of Europe.

THE OTTOMAN STATE AND SOCIETY

Mention has been made of the Ottoman Empire's expansion and contraction prior to 1740, as well as the range of peoples conquered by it. It is important to remember the Empire's origins as an engine of militant, Islamic conquest, in which the world was divided into the 'realm of the faithful' (*dar ül-Islam*) and the 'realm of war' (*dar ül-harb*), in other words all those who resisted Islam. The Ottoman sultans regarded themselves as God's vassals on earth, whose sacred duty was to expand the realm ruled by the faithful, and to whom all earthly inhabitants, not just Muslims, owed an absolute duty of submission.[3] The Empire had long since reached the limits of its expansion, but the pretension to universal dominion remained, as did the mutual fear and detestation between the Ottoman-led Islamic world and Christian Europe. This great religious and cultural division was one that also separated the Ottomans from their Balkan Christian subjects.

'Ottoman' (in Turkish *Osmanli*) meant 'those who are with Osman', the founder of the dynasty, but the term connoted far more than that.[4] Above all, 'Ottoman' did not, and could not, mean simply 'Turkish'. Since the expansion of Islam was the *raison d'être* of the Empire, the latter must be seen as a Muslim empire rather than a Turkish one. Anyone Muslim was, by definition, capable of rising through the ranks of the sultan's service and becoming part of the Ottoman elite. This naturally included the Turks who had founded the Empire and remained at its core, but it also came to include individuals of the most diverse ethnic origins: Albanians, Serbs, Greeks, Arabs and many others. In some parts of the Balkans, notably in Bosnia and among the Albanians, substantial numbers of people converted to Islam for the advantages it conferred, although the majority of indigenous peoples across the Balkans remained Christian. Over the centuries of Ottoman rule, ethnic Turks and others entered the Balkans and settled throughout the peninsula. The fundamental division, however, was between Muslim and non-Muslim. To be Muslim meant to be, potentially, part of the Ottoman elite, and to be Ottoman was to be part of the Empire's ruling class, wherever the Empire reached. To be non-Muslim, for the most part, was to belong to a largely peasant underclass, given the extermination, flight or conversion of the original Christian nobility. The only exception was in the Romanian principalities of Moldavia and Wallachia, whose rulers and noble class, or *boyars*, in the fourteenth century had opted for vassalage under the sultan, and where there thus remained the only body of Christian landowners under Ottoman rule.

The sultan was in theory an absolute ruler, although this must always be seen in the context of his own obligation to observe the precepts of Islam and *sharia* law as laid down in the Koran and other sacred texts. The sultan's chief minister was the *grand vezir* and the business of government was conducted through the *divan* or imperial council. The seat of government in Constantinople, because it was approached through an ornate gate known in French as the *Porte Sublime*, was habitually referred to in diplomacy as 'the Porte'. At provincial level the Empire was divided into *vilayets* or *paşalıks*, which were administered by governors known as *pashas* (Turkish *paşa*).

In practice by the eighteenth century the centre of power had shifted from the person of the sultan to the Ottoman administrative elite grouped around him. In part this was because of the lack of clarity concerning the succession: any male member of the house of Osman was eligible to be sultan, a circumstance complicated by polygamy and the fact that a sultan might have many sons by different wives. This meant that factions could form around individual claimants while they were still in infancy. The successful heir, and his supporters, were often so fearful of sibling rivalry that many sultans routinely executed their brothers and even sisters upon accession. The wives and mothers of sultans, though technically slaves of the harem, were influential players in this murderous competition and on occasion exercised real power. Crucially, potential sultans were kept in seclusion within the harem, deprived of administrative or military experience, until their faction was able to summon them to the throne. The result was a succession of weak and incompetent sultans, leading to the gradual assumption of effective power by the high officials of the court, notably the grand vezir and other officials of the rank of pasha.

The Empire in its expansionist phase was an efficient military machine and the immediate instruments of control at the local level, in the conquered Balkan provinces, were the feudal cavalry, the *sipahi*. To begin with, *sipahi* were granted lands known as *timar* (fief) for their personal maintenance until the next year's campaign, and such land grants, as in any feudal system were held conditionally in return for military service. By the eighteenth century, however, the cessation of Ottoman expansion meant that most *sipahi* had long ceased to move from one part of the Empire to another and many had acquired *de facto* hereditary possession of land, known as *çiftlik*. Many more *çiftlik* estates were acquired by Ottoman officials, local Muslim notables and others. This shift from *timar* to *çiftlik* was not universal throughout the Balkans, but was most concentrated in the 'core' provinces nearest to the capital. Wherever *çiftlik* was introduced, the lot of the Christian peasantry who tilled the land was noticeably harsher in terms of payments to the landowner and labour services. With the exception again of Moldavia and Wallachia, where peasants had the dubious comfort of being oppressed by Christian *boyars*, the landowning class throughout the peninsula was Muslim.

The other pillar of the Ottoman imperium was the famous corps of janissaries (in Turkish *yeni çeri* or 'new troops'), the musketeers who had provided the shock troops of the Empire at the height of its power. Originally recruited from the *devşirme* or 'child levy', by which the children of Balkan Christians were taken from their families and brought up as Muslims, the janissaries had in the course of the seventeenth century become more of a threat than an asset to the state. They acquired the right to hold property, to marry and to enrol their offspring in the corps. By the eighteenth century the *devşirme* was no longer needed because so many

Muslims wanted to be janissaries, but as the numbers swelled the government found it more difficult to keep paying them and the corps became an element of political instability. Increasingly used not on campaign but as a praetorian guard for the sultan, the janissaries became crucial in determining the succession, leading revolts against vezirs who tried to limit their privileges and deposing or murdering sultans they disapproved of. Because of the chronic arrears in their pay, janissaries were granted the right to engage in trade and handicrafts, but this merely increased their financial independence of the sultan while failing to end their political power. The consequences of this development for the Balkan provinces will shortly become apparent.

The position of the sultan's non-Muslim subjects in the Balkans was in many respects invidious, though it must be stressed that until the eighteenth century it was not intolerable. In particular the Ottoman conquest had not meant forcible conversion, far less extermination, of Balkan Christians. In comparison with Christian Europe the Ottoman Empire was tolerant when it came to religion; indeed, the Koran laid a specific obligation on Muslim rulers to respect and protect the other monotheistic 'people of the Book', Christians and Jews. Freedom of worship was assured to all subjects of the sultan, as long as they submitted to his authority; in the centuries following the Ottoman conquest this was the principal reason for the influx of substantial numbers of West European Jews. Even the *devşirme*, traditionally seen by Balkan nationalists as a cruel imposition, was held by at least some Christian families as a positive avenue of advancement for their sons.

The basis of Ottoman rule in the Balkans by the eighteenth century, if not earlier, was the *millet* system, whereby the subject population was divided for administrative purposes, not according to nationality but religion. Each *millet* or religious community was the responsibility of its respective Church hierarchy, so that in addition to the Muslim *millet* there was an Orthodox *millet* under the Greek Patriarch in Constantinople, and Armenian, Catholic and Jewish *millets*. The Orthodox *millet* alone, the largest after the Muslim, embraced not only Greeks but Serbs, Bulgars, Romanians and Vlachs, as well as some Albanians. The *millet* system enabled the sultan to run the Empire on the cheap, by entrusting religious leaders with the collection of taxes, maintenance of order and judicial functions where Muslims were not involved. In return for a wide-ranging autonomy in religious matters and local affairs, the *millet* leaders were obliged to enjoin obedience to Ottoman authority among their flocks. This included payment of taxes to the state, to landlords and to one's own church; for non-Muslims, who were deemed unsuitable for military service, there was a special head-tax, the *cizye*, in lieu. Despite the exemption from the army it was not uncommon for local armed militias, or *armatoles*, to be formed from the Christian population.

A recent history of the Ottoman Empire has made the reasonable point that, at least to begin with, Ottoman rule 'rested lightly' on its Christian subjects: taxation was often less than under former Christian rulers, the position of the peasantry was in some respects freer, and there was religious toleration and local autonomy.[5] At the same time, to describe the Empire as 'a multi-ethnic, multi-religious enterprise that relied on inclusion for its success' overstates the case.[6] Religious leaders may have been trusted as intermediaries between the state and the non-Muslim subject, and the opportunities for wealth creation, largely through trade, may have led to the emergence of a class of non-Muslim notables, but non-Muslims remained decidedly second-class subjects, more highly taxed than Muslims and subject to a number of humiliating restrictions on dress, deportment and status.

More importantly, and whatever the virtues of the Ottoman state in the sixteenth century, by the eighteenth its decline in effectiveness was having serious consequences for its Balkan peoples. The Empire's long economic decline, with the attendant difficulty of financing military expenditure, spurred the transition to *çiftlik* land tenure and increased the burden on peasants. Generally disastrous military fortunes from the late seventeenth century increased the level of taxation, especially in time of war; the wars themselves devastated the Balkan provinces; and the progressive loss of terri-tory to the Habsburg Monarchy and Russia reduced revenues further, flooded the remaining Ottoman provinces with Muslim refugees and height-ened the financial burden yet again.

Above all, the imperial government's control of its outlying provinces became increasingly weak as the eighteenth century wore on. Rebellious janissaries were deported from the capital to the Balkans in a vain attempt to break their stranglehold on imperial politics; this meant that Balkan Christians were increasingly at the mercy of freebooting Muslims intent on extorting as much profit out of their new underlings as possible and unwill-ing to brook any interference in their activities by imperial officials. At the same time, Muslim notables in the Balkans found it all too easy to set themselves up as regional warlords, effectively independent of the sultan's authority and capable of levying crushing exactions on the Christian popula-tion. It was in these circumstances that the autonomy allowed Balkan Christians under the *millet* system, which had permitted through the centuries a separate religio-cultural consciousness to survive, became the kernel of modern Balkan nationalism.

THE PEOPLES OF THE OTTOMAN BALKANS

Given the diversity of the peoples inhabiting the Ottoman Balkans it is impossible to generalise about their condition and development in this period. The picture is also complicated by the fact that the landowning class everywhere except the Romanian principalities, and substantial numbers of the town-dwelling and administrative classes throughout the region, were Muslim and hence, with significant exceptions, of a different ethnicity than the surrounding population. Nevertheless certain shared factors shaped the lives of all the Balkan peoples.

The centuries of Ottoman rule had, firstly, increased the ethnic and confessional intermixture of the region. Christians had fled, occasionally *en masse*, to the more mountainous areas of the Balkan Peninsula or to the Habsburg Monarchy, and in their place the Ottoman authorities encouraged Muslims or more reliable peoples to settle. Secondly, the entire region was affected by the economic backwardness of the Empire: despite a gradual increase in trade with the outside world, and the emergence of limited handicraft-based manufacturing in the areas closest to Constantinople, the Balkans continued to be an economic backwater in comparison with Western and even Central Europe, not least because of the almost total absence of a transport infrastructure. Thirdly, and despite the survival of a native landowning class in the Romanian lands and the emergence of local Christian notables through commerce, the need for abject submission to Ottoman authority arguably bred in the sultan's non-Muslim subjects a form of political backwardness.

The *Greeks* present perhaps the most complicated and diverse picture, scattered as they were across the Empire. The Greek diaspora included not only present-day Greece but sizeable communities in the capital, Constantinople, as well as western Anatolia, the Romanian principalities and the rest of the Black Sea littoral. In addition the Orthodox clergy almost everywhere in the Balkans, with some exceptions, tended to be Greek, a fact resented by non-Greek communicants. Despite their own low level of education these clerics constituted what little there was of an educated elite in many areas. The offices of the Patriarchy and provincial bishoprics had to be bought from the sultan, with the incumbents expected to recoup the expense through their control of taxation and the judicial system; the Orthodox hierarchy thus became a byword for rapaciousness and corruption.

The Phanariots, a select group of families from the Phanar or lighthouse quarter of Constantinople, played a special role in the Greek world. They came to prominence towards the end of the seventeenth century, when the Ottomans' military reverses necessitated an increasing use of diplomacy, which in turn required language skills only Phanariots tended to possess. Such was the Phanariots' usefulness that they virtually monopolised the office of grand dragoman (interpreter), effectively the sultan's foreign minister, as well as key administrative posts in the Ottoman navy. Phanariots were also chosen, after 1714, as the *hospodars* or governors of the Romanian principalities, and this period of Phanariot rule in Moldavia and Wallachia became notorious for its venality, despite the fact that Phanariot wealth was an important source of patronage for Greek culture.

Between this cosmopolitan, wealthy but corrupt elite and the overwhelming majority of Greeks there was a vast gulf. In mountain valleys and coastal hamlets most Greeks scraped a living as peasants and fishermen; some became *klephts* (bandits), preying on Muslim and Christian alike, but frequently invested in the eyes of their fellow Greeks, as elsewhere in the Balkans, with the status of rebels if not freedom fighters. Equally important in fostering a national consciousness, however, were the activities of Greek traders and seafarers. Greeks had always had links with other lands and in the eighteenth century 'the conquering Balkan Orthodox merchant' formed the nucleus of a wealthy and increasingly educated elite. After 1774, when Ottoman Greeks were free to trade under the Russian flag, trade with Western Europe not only made some Greeks extremely wealthy,[7] it also exposed them to western ideas and influence, and their wealth enabled them to sponsor the education of other Greeks, in some cases at western universities. The number of books printed in Greek between 1775 and 1800, for instance, was seven times the number printed in the preceding 75 years.[8] One of the first leaders of this new intelligentsia was Adamantios Korais, an indefatigable classicist and publisher of ancient Greek texts, but aimed at a modern audience, that it might ponder the connection with its Hellenic past. By the 1790s some Greeks had identified liberation from the Ottoman yoke and the revival of a Byzantine Greek empire as the ultimate goals of the Greek nation. One such was Rigas Velestinlis, who was inspired by the French Revolution to publish a constitution for the projected new state and who was executed by the Ottoman authorities at Belgrade when, in 1798, he attempted to foment a Balkan uprising.

Among *Albanians* it is more difficult to discern anything like a common identity for much of the eighteenth century. Albanian speakers divide into two major dialects, Ghegs in the mountainous north of present-day Albania and Kosovo, and Tosks in the southern lowlands. Ghegs still lived in an essentially tribal society and these clans spent much time fighting one another, with the Ottoman authorities content to exact tribute from them in return for local autonomy. The Tosks by contrast were absorbed as peasants into the Ottoman feudal system. Confessionally Albanians were split between the majority Muslims, a small number of Catholics around Shkodër and an Orthodox minority in the south-east. To complicate matters Catholics used a Latin script, Orthodox a Greek one and Muslims an Arabic script. Albanians' conversion to Islam appears frequently to have been for purely tactical reasons, to avoid the child levy or to secure the privileges of being Ottoman; certainly Muslim Albanians played an important role in the Ottoman period as soldiers and administrators and were among those encouraged to take the place of Orthodox Serb emigrants from neighbouring Kosovo.

In the Albanian heartlands, however, tribal feuding was the bane of what little economic and cultural life there was, and in the second half of the century it produced two powerful local warlords. Mehmet Bey Bushati seized control of the *paşalık* of Shkodër in 1757. His son, Kara Mahmud, fought off the sultan's armies in the 1780s with Habsburg support and was finally recognised as governor of Shkodër in 1788; on Kara Mahmud's death in 1796 power in northern Albania was held by his younger brother Ibrahim Pasha until 1810. Even more successful was Ali Pasha, a bandit turned bandit hunter who in 1788 was appointed governor of Ioannina in Epirus and who used this strategic crossroads to extend his power over much of the western Balkans. Exploiting the rivalry of the great powers in the region, and increasingly dismissive of the sultan's authority, Ali Pasha and his sons after 1810 controlled southern Albania and the whole of western Greece including the Peloponnesus. If only fortuitously, this ruthless warlord provided the first focus for an Albanian national identity.

The *Romanian* principalities of Moldavia and Wallachia were unique, in that they had an autonomy of sorts, although in the eighteenth century this meant less than hitherto. Since medieval times the princes had been vassals of the sultan, to whom a yearly tribute was due; in return the *boyars* remained dominant in each principality, electing their prince from their own ranks, exempting themselves from taxation and loading it all onto the peasantry. Over the centuries there was a steady increase in the tribute and other contributions exacted by the Porte, including levies of foodstuffs for Constantinople. By the early eighteenth century up to five-sixths of each principality's revenue went to the sultan.[9] Phanariot Greeks, increasingly influential at Constantinople, started settling in the principalities as merchants and ecclesiastics. By the turn of the century the shifting balance of power between the Ottoman Empire and its rivals placed the Romanian princes in a dilemma; and when Moldavia sided with Russia in the war of 1711, the Ottoman response was to replace the native rulers with Phanariot *hospodars* (literally governors) who would ensure the loyalty of these lucrative frontier provinces.

The Phanariot period, in Moldavia from 1711 and Wallachia from 1715, lasted until the 1820s and was one of unbridled corruption, which spelt misery for the majority of Romanians. Phanariot rule was seen as alien, although by the eighteenth century many Phanariot families had Romanianised through intermarriage, while the native *boyars* adopted the notoriously luxurious Phanariot lifestyle. The *hospodars*, like the Greek Patriarch, had to purchase their office, usually with borrowed money, and expected to recover their costs, with profit, as did all those whom they appointed to subordinate offices. Competition for these posts among Phanariot families was fierce, with the result that the average 'reign' of a *hospodar* was two and a half years, although several individuals held office repeatedly. While office was seen as a path to enrichment, the *hospodars* were nevertheless expected, on pain of death, to ensure the flow of wealth and supplies to Constantinople, so, with the *boyars* determined to avoid any taxation, the burden on the peasantry increased. By mid-century, however, the flight of Romanian peasants to neighbouring lands had become so widespread that even the Phanariot rulers felt obliged to tackle the issue of land reform. The solutions adopted were more efficient tax collection and the regulation of labour dues, usually upwards. This did little for the peasants while exacerbating relations with the *boyars*, who consistently obstructed such reforms as the taxation of the minor nobility. The *boyars'* political aspirations by the late eighteenth century centred increasingly on the restoration of genuine autonomy, if not full independence, and they had every reason to hope for outside support. The Treaty of Küçük Kajnarcı, in 1774, formalised Russia's interest in the principalities: henceforth Russia had a right to advise on their governance, and the amount of tribute, as well as the prices for Romanian supplies, was supposed to be regulated. In practice it proved difficult to hold the Ottoman government to these terms and in the war of 1787–92 Russia aimed to detach the principalities entirely from Ottoman rule. The distractions of the French wars, however, meant the postponement of this agenda.

Among the *South Slavs* an important minority were *Muslim*. In the *vilayet* of Bosnia Muslims had long constituted the majority, a situation which appears to have been more the result of mass conversions rather than an influx of Ottoman Muslims. The landowning class generally in Bosnia, as well as many of the officials, the urban merchants and even some peasants, were Muslim Slavs. Only in the eighteenth century did the demographic balance start swinging towards the Christians, until by the end of the century Muslims accounted for 33 per cent of the population, Orthodox Serbs 43 per cent and Catholic Croats 20 per cent.[10] Bosnia's Muslims enjoyed an unusual degree of autonomy: nominally the sultan's pasha was in charge, but in practice the 39 *kapetans* or district military administrators were the real power in the province. In addition Bosnia was host to large numbers of janissaries, 20,000 in Sarajevo alone, and their economic independence made them, as in Constantinople, unruly. For much of the century Bosnia was wracked by open conflict between *kapetans* and janissaries, with the pasha only intermittently in control.

The position of Christian South Slavs was generally grimmer. Catholic *Croats*, most of them peasants, were concentrated in Bosnia, where their potential as supporters of the Habsburg enemy made them objects of suspicion. The Habsburg Monarchy indeed claimed the right to protect the Catholic population, financed the education of some of them in Croatia and called on Christians to revolt when it went to war against the Ottomans in 1788. Although some Croats joined the invaders, others fought on the Ottoman side, suggesting that the Porte's mistrust of the Croats was misplaced.

By the late eighteenth century Orthodox *Serbs*, whether in Bosnia or the neighbouring *paşalık* of Belgrade (the core of what became Serbia), more probably merited the suspicion of being potential rebels. In previous centuries Serbs, as members of the Orthodox *millet*, had been regarded as more reliable than Croats, which was why many of them were settled on the Bosnian frontier.[11] Serb Orthodoxy had its own Patriarch at Peć in Kosovo.

But by the 1700s Serb dissatisfaction with Ottoman rule was a matter of record: substantial numbers had risen in support of the Habsburgs in the 1680s and again in 1737; many migrated north to Habsburg territory; and among those who remained, disaffection continued to be high, even surviving the negative experience of Austrian rule in 1718–39, when Serbs found themselves subjected to the proselytising attentions of the Catholic Church. Ottoman attitudes in turn were affected by the Serbs' stance and in particular by the unremitting hostility of the Serb Patriarchs, to the extent that in 1766 the Patriarchate was formally abolished. Henceforth what cultural and educational opportunities were available to Serbs were provided by the Metropolitanate at Sremska Karlovci, in Habsburg territory. Ottoman Serbs remained a largely peasant people.

Yet the Ottoman system, even after the reacquisition of Serbia in 1739, allowed Serbs some elements of self-administration. Land tenure was still largely *timar*, not *çiftlik*, so that the Serb peasant had some property rights and freedom of movement. As in the Greek lands, local government was mediated through councils of notables for each *knežina* or district, who elected the *knez* or headman. The *knezes* were responsible for tax collection, law and order and judicial functions affecting Christians only. Although the majority of Serb notables were illiterate, they were able to amass considerable wealth as merchants, especially livestock traders; they were thus the natural leadership of the Serb community. Relations with the Ottomans remained relatively stable until the war of 1788–91, when once again the Austrians recruited Serb units, operating behind Ottoman lines. Yet again, the Habsburgs' defeat and withdrawal led to mass flight and Ottoman reprisals. In the end, the Ottoman government offered an amnesty and 50,000 Serbs returned to the *paşalık*; but in the process many had become proficient in arms.

Montenegrins deserve special mention because their development in the Ottoman period set them apart from their fellow Orthodox Serb brethren. The forbidding terrain of the 'Black Mountain' made its subjugation even by the Ottomans problematical, even though the Montenegrins, like their Albanian neighbours, retained a tribal system which ensured that they spent as much energy fighting one another as they did repelling outsiders. No Ottoman system of land tenure was ever imposed on Montenegro, nor was it ever easy to collect taxes. Instead, the only authority acknowledged by Montenegrin tribesmen was the bishop of Cetinje monastery; from the eighteenth century this office of prince-bishop, or *Vladika*, was held hereditarily by the Petrović family. The *Vladikas* profited from their access to the Adriatic to secure support against the Ottomans, first from Venice and then increasingly from Russia; Bishop Vasilije was a frequent visitor to St Petersburg and, in 1754, published a *History of Montenegro* in Moscow. Relations were spoiled only when, in 1766, an impostor claiming to be the murdered Tsar Peter III turned up in Cetinje and managed to oust the

Vladika; only 15 years after 'Stephen the Small' was assassinated by an Ottoman agent in 1773 was Montenegro again courted by Catherine the Great for its support against the Porte. The Montenegrins remained largely isolated, however, and it was thanks to their own efforts that the pasha of Shkodër, Kara Mahmud, was beaten back and, on his second foray into Montenegro, captured and beheaded in 1796.

Finally, the lot of the *Bulgarians* was determined largely by their proximity to the Ottoman capital. Spread across several provinces today divided between Bulgaria, Macedonia and Greece, they remained an Orthodox peasant underclass, with few notables, because the concentration of *çiftlik* land was highest in these areas and because there was a much higher population of Muslims, including ethnic Turks, in addition to the minority of Bulgarian-speaking Muslims, the *Pomaks*. Towns remained almost exclusively Muslim, with the exception of the ubiquitous Greek merchants and a few Bulgarians; only towards the end of the eighteenth century did Bulgarians start entering trade guilds in numbers. The abolition in 1767 of the Archbishopric of Ohrid, the only autonomous Bulgarian religious institution, meant that the priesthood was mainly Greek and what little schooling was available to Bulgarians was in Greek. Although the Bulgarian population had the same degree of local self-administration as other Christian peoples, the benefit of this was vitiated by the high degree of public insecurity, not only because of banditry and marauding soldiery but, increasingly, because of the same breakdown of Ottoman official control over local Muslim notables that afflicted other provinces.

IMPULSES TO REFORM AND THE BREAKDOWN OF CONTROL

The Ottoman Empire at the height of its power was in no sense backward by comparison with its European enemies, but by the mid-eighteenth century this was clearly no longer true. Economically and militarily the Ottomans appeared to have fallen behind and the consequences well before 1740 were military defeat and loss of territory, most of it never to be regained. Just as ominously, the costs of political debility at the centre were evident in the spread of lawlessness and warlordism in the periphery, especially the Balkans. It was this breakdown of central control, rather than the fact of Ottoman rule itself, which led to the Christian revolts of the early nineteenth century.

Long before this, some perception of the need for change had been dawning at Constantinople; the question as to precisely what sort of change was needed, however, was not so easily answered. The strength of religious tradition in the Ottoman elite meant that the need for modernisation was actively denied; instead, traditionalists argued, only a return to the 'purer' ways of the early Empire could save things. But successive defeats suggested that military reform was essential and that this in turn was dependent on an overhaul of revenue collection and corrupt administration.

The sultans of the early century, themselves in thrall to the janissaries, could do little to alter things. Under Ahmed III (1703–30) envoys were sent to Western Europe, especially France, to study conditions there; but when Ahmed's grand vezir tried to collect taxes more efficiently he was executed for his pains and the sultan deposed. Mahmud I (1730–54) got as far as appointing a French artillery officer, the Count de Bonneval, to train troops and establish modern armaments factories, but once de Bonneval died in 1747 the training was discontinued. Little more was done until the catastrophic defeat of 1774. Abdül Hamid III (1774–89) appointed as grand vezir Halil Hamid, who brought in yet more French advisers, dared to dismiss large numbers of janissaries and drafted plans for new training and new weapons. The Ottoman navy in particular, with both British and French advice, was modernised by 1784. The conservative opposition aroused by Halil Hamid's reforms was such, however, that the sultan was forced to execute him in 1785. The culmination of these efforts came under Selim III (1789–1807), but it was the misfortune of this reforming sultan that his reign coincided with a radical breakdown in the centre's control of the periphery.

The janissary problem was central to Selim's dilemma. Some 50,000 served in military units no longer considered reliable enough for anything more demanding than garrison duty, but beyond this, by Selim's reign there was a total membership of 400,000, attracted by the pay and privileges, especially tax exemption.[12] Because of their drift towards trade and handicrafts it is true to say that the janissaries 'came to represent the interests of the urban productive classes', but given their role in destabilising the Ottoman government and Ottoman rule in the Balkans it seems unduly idealising to call them a 'popular militia'.[13] They could be relied upon to resist reforms, especially of themselves; because they were armed and urban their ability to terrorise the sultan and his officials was very real; and worst of all, their dispersal as garrison troops across the Balkan provinces, in an attempt to export the problem from Constantinople itself, simply produced chaos elsewhere. Janissaries and their hangers-on became a terror to Muslim notables and Christian peasants alike, roaming the land in armed bands, seizing land or property forcibly, levying illegal 'taxes' on the local population and murdering any who resisted them. Most Ottoman provincial officials, if they were not in collusion with the janissaries, were powerless to oppose them, although the majority saw it as their duty to protect the tax-paying Christian population.

Matters were complicated by the emergence of warlords as regional, effectively independent, powers. Figures like Ali Pasha of Ioannina, mentioned above, while their ascent was often in defiance of central authority, could act as a stabilising force locally once they had consolidated power. Others, like Kara Mahmud Bushati of Shkodër, destabilised entire regions. The most formidable warlord was Pasvanoğlu Osman Pasha. A bandit turned soldier, he then returned to the renegade life, proving particularly adept at recruiting janissary bands; in 1795, having established a power base at Vidin in north-western Bulgaria, he proclaimed himself independent of the sultan's authority. Pasvanoğlu's forces went on numerous pillaging expeditions into Serbia and Wallachia; they were briefly driven back to Vidin by Ali Pasha, acting on the sultan's behalf. But the French attack on the Ottoman Empire in 1798 forced Selim III to divert attention from the Balkans to Egypt, and in the absence of serious opposition Pasvanoğlu continued to rule in Vidin and harry his neighbours, inflicting a notable defeat on Ottoman forces in 1801.

Before the French invasion of Egypt, Selim had attempted to sidestep the janissary problem by creating a 'New Model' army, largely from the Turkish peasantry of Anatolia and trained on European lines by French advisers. Although the advisers were dispensed with in 1798, the New Model continued to expand until by 1806 it totalled 22,000.[14] By that point, however, even this modest reform was threatened by the explosion of revolt in Serbia.

The janissaries in the *paşalık* of Belgrade, encouraged by Pasvanoğlu Osman Pasha, were especially lawless and violent. Expelled from the *paşalık* during the Austrian occupation of 1788–91, their return had been forbidden by Selim III and for a time was opposed by the loyal Ottoman pasha, Hadji Mustafa. In 1797 the janissaries launched an attack on Belgrade. Hadji Mustafa, significantly, was helped to defend the town by an armed militia of Serbs; only the withdrawal of Ottoman troops in 1798 forced him to readmit the janissaries. The latter soon proved just how dangerous they were to Ottoman authority: in 1801 they murdered Hadji Mustafa, and security of life and property in Serbia continued to deteriorate. The difference, by the early years of the new century, was that the Serbs were not only armed but increasingly determined to seize control of their own destinies. The revolt which broke out in 1804 was initially against the janissaries, not the Ottomans, but the patent inability of the Ottoman state to protect its subjects was to change the course of the fighting almost immediately. And revolt, once successful, had a habit of spreading.

6

RUSSIA AND PRUSSIA AS REGIONAL POWERS

Russia's conflicts with the Ottoman Empire in the eighteenth century, and the role of both Russia and Prussia in the partitions of Poland–Lithuania, have already been outlined. The expansion of these two powers meant that many of Eastern Europe's peoples were Romanov or Hohenzollern subjects by the century's end; but the Russian Empire was already a multinational state at the outset.

There were striking parallels between Russia and Prussia, which justify considering them in tandem. Both were in theory absolute monarchies, with few if any institutional trammels on the ruler. Both sought in their different ways to modernise and, in the relative absence of intermediaries, did so from the top down. Both were hindered in the drive to modernise by the backwardness of their societies, in particular the persistence of serfdom or its near equivalent, and the vested interest of the nobility in retaining serfdom. Both were expansionist, with a dynastic and cameralist disregard for the fact that this entailed dominion over alien peoples. And both were to discover the paradox that empire was the source of both great power status and weakness, as more and more unwilling subjects were acquired.

THE RUSSIAN EMPIRE

Peter the Great assumed the title of *Imperator* (emperor) in 1721, but as Tsar (Caesar) of Muscovy he already ruled over a state which had begun its conquest of non-Russian peoples as far back as the 1550s. By 1740 Russia was the largest state in Europe, claiming dominion over Siberia as far as the Pacific, but also possessing a Baltic coastline since 1710, the so-called Hetmanate of Ukraine or left-bank Ukraine, including Kiev, and a toehold on the Black Sea at Azov. Of an estimated total population in 1719 of 15.7 million, 70 per cent were ethnic Russians, 13 per cent were Ukrainian and about 3 per cent were Belorussians. The remaining 14 per cent comprised

Estonians and Latvians, Tartars and other nomadic steppe peoples. By 1795, however, the balance had shifted radically against the ethnic Russians, who now constituted only 53 per cent of a population of 37 million. Nearly half the Empire's peoples were non-Russian.[1]

In the eighteenth century neither the tsars nor the vast majority of their subjects were concerned about this. The Romanov dynasty saw the expansion of the state as necessary for its own sake, given Russia's vulnerability to foreign invasion in the past; the more territory and population the Empire could accrue, the safer and more powerful it would be. Among the peoples conquered, local elites in some cases acquiesced, and in others resisted, for reasons which occasionally had their origins in a dawning national consciousness, but which generally had more to do with how far Russian rule either preserved or undermined their own position. The peasant majority were oblivious to such a consideration as nationality: for them the only issue that mattered was whether their conditions of service were bettered or worsened.

It is impossible to understand Russia's role in Eastern Europe since the eighteenth century without appreciating what Geoffrey Hosking has called 'its hybrid position as Asiatic empire and European great power'.[2] A legatee of three centuries of Mongol domination, and the conqueror of diverse agrarian and nomadic peoples, Russia was a genuine autocracy, with a wide gap between ruler and ruled. As an emerging European power, however, Russia was entering a world where states were becoming synonymous with nationhood and hence cultural homogeneity. Down to the present day Russia has arguably never overcome this internal tension between empire and nation-state.

In Russia, autocracy had real meaning, in that all subjects, including nobles, were 'in complete subjection to the Tsar'; there was nothing comparable to the feudal relationship of mutual obligation between monarch and noble that had obtained in Western European societies.[3] Instead, Russian nobles constituted a 'service nobility': all their status and privileges, including land tenure, derived from the service, military or bureaucratic, which they rendered the state. Individual nobles or noble families could wax powerful, but this was more the result of temporary weakness in the autocracy, or the autocrat's favour, than proof of the strength of the nobility as a class.

Under Peter the despotic nature of the Russian state was if anything intensified; however, the programme of modernisation he embarked on had profound consequences. It was Peter who acquired Russia's 'window on the West' by conquering territory at the head of the Gulf of Finland and then Estland and Livland (most of today's Estonia and northern Latvia) from Sweden. This in turn was possible only because of the modernisation, or rather westernisation, of Russia's military. Peter both prized the contribution foreigners could make to Russian modernisation and copied the principle that the state must patronise the arts and sciences in order to create its own skilled workers and intellectuals. He tirelessly promoted industry, and in St Petersburg, founded in 1703 on a Baltic swamp, he created a European-style capital through the labour of conscripted serfs, thousands of whom died in the process.

Peter saw himself as a servant of the state, but by extension so was everyone else. In particular Peter tightened the conditions of noble service, which had implications for the rest of Russian society. In a state where the nobility were virtually the only instrument of control at local level, Peter was determined to make them the shock troops of modernisation, but this was to be an elite based entirely on service and merit, not birth. Service meant that Russia's nobility were utterly dependent on the tsar for status as well as employment. They were expected to serve years in the army or navy, or the imperial bureaucracy, without sight of their own estates; they were expected to supply recruits for the armed forces from their own serfs. Small wonder that Peter's successors found it increasingly difficult to enforce such strict conditions, although the fundamental subjection of nobles to the autocrat's will remained.

The *quid pro quo* for noble service was ever tighter subjection of Russia's peasant population. Russian peasants were already effectively the chattels of their landlords; this was to ensure a supply of cheap labour on noble estates and thereby safeguard the nobles' ability to render service. Peter's reign only increased the burdens on the serfs. From 1723 peasants were liable to the hated poll tax, as well as forced labour in state mines, factories and construction sites, not to mention conscription.

The increasing miseries of serfdom resulted in two phenomena characteristic of eighteenth-century Russia: serfs sought refuge in flight, or they revolted in terrifying, elemental bloodbaths like the Pugachev rebellion of 1773–4. Much of the territory eventually taken over by the Empire to the south and south-east, in the Ukraine and the Volga basin, was the refuge of escaped peasants; and where Russian rule was established and land parcelled out to new noble owners, the peasant population frequently proved recalcitrant. The expansion of Russia in the eighteenth century, which increased the wealth and resources of the state and facilitated great-power status, thus rested on a paradox: because it also entailed the extension of serfdom, expansion perpetuated Russia's backwardness. Modernisation was the driving motive behind the policy of every Russian ruler from Peter the Great on, but no society based on serfdom could modernise beyond a certain point.

A final legacy of Peter's obsession with modernisation was the further division of Russian society. By importing not just western technology but western fashions, dress and manners, the tsar drove a wedge between his westernised, cosmopolitan noble elite and the mass of Russian, and other, peasants. The Empire's enlargement did little to bridge this gap between the 'two Russias'. Although some local elites, such as the Polish *szlachta* or the Baltic German nobility, had something socially at least in common with their Russian counterparts, to the majority of peasants, of whatever nationality, the state and nobility were seen as an alien, godless culture. The Pugachev revolt in the 1770s, for instance, specifically appealed to the Cossacks' hatred of the secular, westernised, centralising state; it 'showed how wafer-thin was the loyalty of some of the non-Russians, and above all of the Russian peasants, to the regime'.[4]

Russia after Peter continued to expand. Under Peter's niece Anna (1730–40), who was also duchess of the Polish fiefdom of Courland, the sole territorial acquisition was the recapture of Azov from the Ottomans in 1739. Peter's daughter Elizabeth (1741–61) annexed a further slice of Finnish territory from Sweden in 1743. But it was in the reign of Catherine II (1762–96) that the most significant expansion took place. The First Partition of Poland was in 1772. Russian domination of the Black Sea, including an 'independent' Crimea, naval bases and the right of merchant ships to sail in and out, was secured in 1774. In 1783 the Crimea was formally annexed; in 1791 more Ottoman territory north-west of the Black Sea was added; and the dismemberment of Poland–Lithuania was completed in 1793–5.

This access of territory and population made Russia feared among European powers, and Catherine and her advisers were in no doubt that this was desirable in itself. Nor was there much concern about the takeover of huge non-Russian populations. Nevertheless towards the end of Catherine's reign a debate was stirring as to whether expansion was either necessary or desirable, as well as how to deal with the people thus conquered. This debate was possible only because something like a Russian nationalism was beginning to emerge, a product of the elite's westernisation.

Historians are still arguing as to whether Russian nationalism could exist even in the nineteenth century, let alone the eighteenth, given the impossibility of identifying the Empire with any one nationality. However, if there was such a beast it had to start with the nobility. Under Anna nobles had won the freedom to travel abroad. Peter III (January–July 1762), before his murder by the noble conspirators who put his consort Catherine on the throne, issued a series of edicts which effectively emancipated the nobility, making their service to the state voluntary. Catherine's reign saw a proliferation of Enlightenment high culture, the importation of foreign learning and even more extensive travel. The result, well before the turn of the century, was a genuinely cosmopolitan aristocracy, many of whose members spoke better French than Russian. Nevertheless, this was also the period in which Russian itself became a literary language, an amalgam of the old Church Slavonic and the spoken tongue, and it was the literary language which facilitated nationalism.

A key figure in shaping modern Russian was the polymath Mikhail Lomonosov, who was influential in founding Moscow University in 1755 and also produced the first Russian grammar in 1757. Lomonosov's historical work was pathbreaking because it took issue with the view, current among the largely German scholars of the Academy of Sciences, that the founders of the Russian state were Vikings, invited to rule Russia by its Slav inhabitants. To Lomonosov such a version of events, which suggested that Russians were dependent on outsiders to build a state, was a denial of Russian character tantamount to 'political subversion'.[5] An emerging generation of ethnic Russian scholars saw it as their task to emphasise the essentially Russian origins of the state and the strength of Russian culture, and to downplay the role of foreigners in Russian greatness.

The implications of this for the Empire's non-Russian subjects were problematic. Russian intellectuals increasingly tended to equate the state with being Russian and especially to assume that all East Slavs, in other words Russians, Ukrainians and Belorussians, were one people. Such an assumption was facilitated by the common Orthodox faith of all three peoples, although the persistence of the Uniate confession among Ukrainians remained a problem. The language used by Russian governments from Catherine on reflects this, speaking of 'Russian' in the sense of 'inhabitants of the state'. Even with peoples such as Tartars, Poles and Balts, the assumption was that Russian culture would eventually assimilate them. In the words of one scholar, 'the uniformity of state organization wisely helps to bring this along by leading our rude peoples by giant steps toward the common goal of general enlightenment in Russia, of a wonderful fusion of all into a single body and soul'.[6] The apotheosis of this glorification of the Russian Empire as a nation-state in the making was provided by Ivan Boltin, who first advanced the dubious argument that Russian expansion had been largely peaceful and that peoples like the Ukrainians and Belorussians had requested inclusion. However much violence this interpretation did the facts, Boltin's vision of an Empire of voluntary subjects proved a powerful one among Russian thinkers in the nineteenth century.

In the eighteenth century it is true to say that some of the peoples in tsarist Russia were more voluntary than others. A special and privileged position was occupied by the *Baltic German* nobility of Estland, Livland and the Duchy of Courland. The latter, although formally a vassal-state of Poland–Lithuania, was effectively ruled from St Petersburg, especially once its Duchess Anna became tsarina in 1730. These provinces had been ruled for centuries, at local level, by associations of nobles, or *Ritterschaften*, descendants of the medieval crusaders, and in the German-speaking towns corporations of burghers existed. Peter the Great guaranteed these elements of self-government, together with the free exercise of the Lutheran faith, precisely because he could see the utility of the Baltic Germans.

Self-governing, educated at German universities, productive landowners and prosperous traders, the Germans were just the sort of subjects Peter wanted. Baltic German nobles rapidly established themselves throughout the imperial bureaucracy, in the armed forces and in the diplomatic service: Russia's subsequent foreign policy is littered with names like Nesselrode, Benckendorff and Lieven. By the reign of Anna some 30 per cent of Russian officials were non-Russian, most of them German.[7] Anna herself brought her Baltic German lover, Count Ernst Johann von Bühren, with her to St Petersburg and then in 1737 made him Duke of Courland, where he commissioned a magnificent palace at Mitau.

Such ubiquity on the part of Germans was a major factor in the development of a Russian national consciousness. Yet the Baltic Germans were in fact the ideal servants of empire. They were loyal, identifying their own interests with those of the dynasty and state, and regarding their privileged position as a safeguard against their own Estonian or Latvian peasantry. Even here the Baltic German role was arguably a progressive one: not only did the Lutheran faith enjoin on its practicants a duty to provide an education for all, including peasants, that they might seek religious improvement, but the Baltic provinces were the only part of the Empire, starting in 1785, where a 'limited regulation of peasant services' was enacted.[8] In this way the traditional German elite in these lands paved the way not only for Russia's painful nineteenth-century modernisation but also for the eventual development of Estonian and Latvian nationalism.

The *Estonian* and *Latvian* peasants of the Baltic provinces were largely passive subjects of the tsars in this period, tied to their German lords' estates like serfs elsewhere in the Empire. Estonians and Latvians were unusual, however, in that the beginnings of their literary languages went back to the Reformation, when conscientious German Lutherans had troubled to print prayer books and the like in the languages of their flocks. In 1803 the University of Dorpat in Livland was refounded and, although the language of instruction was German, it rapidly became a beacon of Enlightenment, where the history and folk culture of the Baltic peoples were studied, offering the possibility at least of an education to the sons of Estonian and Latvian peasants.

Any description of the medley of peoples inhabiting, in the eighteenth century, what is present-day *Ukraine* calls for careful qualification. The vacuum to the south of Muscovy was first filled by the Grand Duchy of Lithuania, which in the late Middle Ages expanded into virtually all of today's Belarus and most of Ukraine. Matters were further complicated by the union of Poland and Lithuania and the transfer to the Polish *Korona*, in 1569, of Lithuania's Ukrainian lands. Finally, the great rebellion in the Ukraine against Polish–Lithuanian rule, in the 1640s and 1650s, meant the division of Ukraine and the establishment, in the eastern half, of an autonomous Ukrainian Hetmanate, under Russian protection. The fact that this Hetmanate sided with Sweden against Russia was one of several reasons for the gradual restriction and eventual abolition of Ukrainian autonomy in the eighteenth century.

From an ethno-linguistic viewpoint, even the term 'Ukrainian' is problematic in the eighteenth century. 'Ukraine' means literally 'on the border', in short a frontierland, but in the eighteenth century the area was generally referred to as *Malorossiia* or Little Russia. The Slavic-speaking population of the region customarily called themselves *Rus*; but in ecclesiastical circles the convention had gradually arisen of referring to Muscovy, seat of the Russian Orthodox Patriarchy, as 'Great Russia' and the Ukrainian lands as 'Little Russia'. The common people undoubtedly spoke the variant of East Slavonic known today as Ukrainian, but the literary language until the nineteenth century was the ecclesiastical Church Slavonic. The nobility consisted in part of the old Polonised *szlachta* from Polish–Lithuanian times, but the majority of the social elite were Cossacks.

The *Cossacks* were a group almost impossible to assign to any ethnic or linguistic category, but who played a major role in both the establishment of the Hetmanate and the expansion of Russia. The term 'cossack' means 'nomad soldier' or 'freebooter' and was applied to the Tatar horsemen who occasionally went over to the Slav, Christian side in the shifting border warfare with the Tartar khanates. With time, Christians adopted the same mobile marauding tactics and came to be called Cossacks too. Cossacks were thus a defence force against the Islamic enemies to the south; but they were also, increasingly in Russian history, escapees from the servile conditions of labour in Muscovy, who sought land and freedom in Siberia, in the steppelands north of the Black Sea and the dangerous borderlands of the Don basin. In the Polish–Lithuanian Commonwealth, similarly, the Orthodox Slavs sought refuge from the onerous manorial system in the lands 'beyond the rapids' of the River Dnieper (in Ukrainian: *za porohamy*) and hence became known as the Zaporozhian Cossacks, to distinguish them from the Don Cossacks and others.

Cossack society was warlike, jealous of its independence and essentially egalitarian, although the Cossacks accepted the authority of their leader or *Hetman*, elected by a council of officers. By the seventeenth century this officer class had become the social elite of Ukrainian society. In the early eighteenth century this Cossack nobility retained its special status and identity. The Cossack-led Hetmanate was thus an important stage in defining what it meant to be Ukrainian; it was the potential nucleus of the modern Ukrainian nation-state. The Cossack elite, moreover, were the first to articulate a separate sense of Ukrainian identity, although in the eighteenth century their most common term for this was 'Little Russian'. Their sense of themselves as a nation, however, had more in common with the gentry nationalism of the Polish *szlachta* or the Hungarian nobility. This put the Ukrainian elite on a collision course with Catherine II, who saw the unruly Cossacks as an obstacle to modernisation and abolished Ukrainian autonomy in 1782–6, despite passionate Ukrainian protests. Nevertheless, incorporation in the main body of the Russian Empire offered certain advantages to the Ukrainian elite: most of them received the right to full noble status, they were allowed to enserf their peasants completely and they had careers in the imperial service open to them.

By the reign of Paul I (1796–1801), the traditional elite of the Ukraine had become indistinguishable from the Russian nobility, speaking Russian instead of colloquial Ukrainian. As such they were now an alien presence among the mass of Ukrainian peasants and townspeople; one noble went so far as to argue in print, early in the new century, that Ukrainians were in fact Russians. At most the Ukrainian nobility confined themselves to a romanticisation of the past glories of the Hetmanate, but otherwise their identification with the Russian state was complete by the turn of the century. The Russification of the Ukrainian nobility thus delayed the emergence of an ethnic Ukrainian nationalism by several generations; it was only later in the nineteenth century that enough of a Ukrainian middle class existed to support a modern sense of nationhood.

The Polish Partitions brought yet more Ukrainians, Latvians and Germans into the Russian Empire, but also *Belorussians, Lithuanians, Poles* and some 400,000 *Jews* – 'the largest Jewish community in Europe'.[9] Altogether more than 7 million people were added to Catherine the Great's domains, but in addition to the problem of nationality there was a confessional obstacle to assimilation, in that most of the Belorussians and Ukrainians were Uniate, while Lithuanians, Latvians and Poles were Catholic, and Germans Lutheran. Socially the new subjects were mostly peasants, but Polish and German nobles, and German, Jewish and Polish burghers complicated the task of integration.

From the point of view of securing physical control, a prime object of the tsarist government was to co-opt local elites where possible. In Courland the *de facto* Russian hegemony exercised through the German nobility continued. Although the Polish lands were immediately incorporated into the Russian system of provinces, at a local level there was no practical alternative to relying on the Polish nobility. This applied even in the easternmost areas annexed in 1772. Here Russian became the language of administration and the courts, but Polish nobles still filled the local administrative jobs. In the territories annexed in the 1790s, consolidation was disrupted by the uncertainties of the French Revolutionary period. Here, in Lithuania and the Polish *Korona*, including right-bank Ukraine, most administrators at all levels were Polish and the language of administration and justice was Polish.[10]

The Polish *szlachta*'s response to Russian rule varied. Some resisted and fled into exile or refused to cooperate with Russian authorities. The majority, conscious of the need to preserve their privileged status and lands, preferred to work with the regime, some reluctantly, others in a spirit of constructive, if self-interested, resignation. Their willingness was doubtless expedited by the determination of the Russian government to whittle down the number of Polish nobles, which in comparison with the Russian nobility was huge. Despite the culling of landless nobles, Polish nobles continued to constitute a majority of the nobility in the Empire as a whole for generations: 66 per cent in 1795.[11] The *szlachta* even profited, after years of economic blockade by Prussia before the final Partitions, from the ability to export grain via Russia's Black Sea ports.

The Russian government practised toleration vis-à-vis the Catholic Poles and Lithuanians, as well as the Baltic German Lutherans, but towards the Uniate Ukrainians and Belorussians, regarded as renegade Orthodox, its attitude was frankly hostile. Uniate bishoprics were abolished, and as early as 1796 1.8 million Uniates had been 'converted' to Orthodoxy.[12] The Jews were an unprecedented problem, in that Russia had not had any before 1772. Catherine II's government took an initially enlightened approach, hoping to utilise alleged Jewish economic skills for the good of the Empire. All freedoms enjoyed in the old Commonwealth were guaranteed, although the Jews' separate legal status was abolished, and the specifically Jewish organ of local self-government, the *kahal*, was continued. However, the government soon ran into the entrenched prejudices of the Christian population, Catholic and Orthodox, over the economic role especially of rural Jews. A policy was adopted in the 1780s of moving Jews to urban areas, sometimes forcibly. The prejudice against Jews in towns proved no less, nor were most Jews keen on assimilating. In the end, in 1804 the government of Alexander I (1801–25), created the Pale of Settlement: Jews were banned from living outside the former Polish lands, left-bank Ukraine and the 'New Russian' territories down to the Black Sea. They were also required to abandon Jewish dress and to keep their business accounts in Russian, Polish or German rather than Yiddish. In return, the Jews' freedom of worship was again confirmed, as was their access, in theory, to state education and their right to maintain their own schools. In practice, many of the 1804 statute's liberal provisions remained a dead letter, while the visible restrictions on Jewish freedom of movement, as well as the prejudice against them, remained.

Polish culture continued to be dominant in the annexed territories. Alexander I, in drafting his own educational reforms, even relied on the Polish experience in setting up the 1773 Commission of National Education and on enlightened Polish aristocrats like Prince Adam Jerzy Czartoryski. The six school regions created for the Empire in 1802 were modelled on the 1773 legislation. The University of Wilno, founded in 1803, became the first serious institute of higher education in this part of the Empire, and although the language of instruction was Polish it did much to promote the discovery of the Lithuanian language as well. The collaboration with the imperial regime of nobles like Czartoryski, who briefly rose to be Alexander's foreign minister (1804–6), reflects the dilemma most patriotic Poles found themselves in: only by helping to modernise and liberalise Russia itself, so they reasoned, could Poland hope for its own eventual liberation.

Beneath the level of the nobility few inhabitants of the Russian Partition could expect much improvement in their circumstances. Baltic German ports and cities like Riga and Mitau experienced a trade-related prosperity and there was a certain agricultural revival in the Polish grain-growing regions. But urban centres in most of the Russian Partition languished, affected by increased taxation and the general inefficiency of the Russian economy; what meagre manufacturing had arisen in the old Commonwealth, cut off from its original sources of raw materials, withered. For the mass of peasants, whether Polish, Lithuanian, Ukrainian or Belorussian, Russian rule arguably made things worse: labour service was increased almost everywhere, peasants were treated more as transferable property than hitherto, they paid more tax and they were now liable to 25 years' service in the army.

In conclusion, Russia succeeded in imposing a uniform administrative structure on its new East European territories, although anomalies like the Baltic Germans' privileges survived. It was also on the whole successful in co-opting local elites into the task of running the Empire, at the minor expense of conceding the privileged position, socially and economically, which they had hitherto occupied. With regard to the peoples of the new territories, Russian governments were not militantly assimilationist; Russian rulers and ministers assumed that the chief duty of the conquered peoples was to be obedient and productive subjects. The difficulties of ruling, and if need be repressing, recalcitrant non-Russians were to become apparent only in the new century.

PRUSSIA

The Kingdom of Prussia was in one important respect already part of Eastern Europe, through its possession of the Duchy of Prussia, which most textbooks refer to as East Prussia. The former state of the Teutonic Knights apart, the expansion of Prussia in the eighteenth century consisted of Silesia, taken from the Habsburg Monarchy, and Prussia's share of the Polish Partitions: 'West Prussia' (1772), 'South Prussia' (1793) and 'New East Prussia' (1795).[13] Most of the latter and about half of South Prussia were subsequently lost by Prussia in 1806 during the Napoleonic Wars and not restored in 1815. Prussian rule was thus limited to a mere decade in some areas, whereas in West Prussia and what became known as Posen (Polish: Poznań) it persisted down to 1918.

The people who came with the Polish territories were for the most part Polish speakers or Polish Jews, but there were also substantial numbers of German speakers. In West Prussia some of this German population could be traced back to the Middle Ages. A second wave of German immigration, however, had taken place in the seventeenth and eighteenth centuries, encouraged by the Polish–Lithuanian authorities. The result was a sizeable minority of Germans across western and northern Poland, especially in towns. On the other side of the 'nationality frontier', East Prussia had a minority of Polish-speaking, but Lutheran, peasants in its southern and eastern districts, and in Upper Silesia there was still a large Polish-speaking peasantry as well as Polish townspeople. Finally, to the west and north-west of Danzig lived the Kashubians, a Slavic minority of peasants and fishermen speaking a language akin to Polish.

Prussia at the start of our period might best be described as aspirationally absolutist: the king was undoubtedly the 'focal point of government' and aimed for as much control as possible, but was constantly being brought up short by reality.[14] Only later in the century did Frederick II exercise effectively absolute power, within certain self-imposed limits.

Prussian policy was governed by certain geopolitical factors. With a population in 1740 of 2.25 million and meagre natural resources, it seemed negligible beside giants like Russia and Austria, and this vulnerability was heightened by the scattered and divided character of its territories, some two dozen parcels of land from the Rhine to East Prussia, covering a span of 800 miles. These territories moreover all had their own institutions, legal systems, traditional elites and customs, in particular their own estates or local representative bodies, which usually consisted of nobles and important townspeople. The king of Prussia, like the Habsburg monarch, had either to negotiate with these traditional institutions or somehow steer around them.

Frederick William I (1713–40) did much to build up the centralised, quasi-absolutist state inherited by his famous son Frederick the Great. A centralisation of state administration, especially revenue collection, facilitated increased spending on the army, which more than doubled in size between 1713 and 1740 to 81,000 men.[15] In addition, Frederick William won the agreement of the Prussian nobility, the *Junkers*, to a reorganisation of the army, in return for the crown's undertaking not to interfere with serfdom as an institution.

Frederick II (1740–86) thus inherited a formidable army, but equally a well-ordered, cameralist administration with carefully husbanded resources. Unlike his devout father, however, Frederick was a free thinker, utterly contemptuous of religion and unrestrained by considerations of morality in his pursuit of *raison d'état*, given Prussia's exposed position. Throughout his reign Frederick explicitly sought absolute power, gathering the direction of foreign policy, for instance, into his hands right from the outset, and after the last of his wars in 1763 increasingly directing all governmental affairs in person. Yet the philosopher king, who prided himself on his enlightened thinking and his personal contacts with the leading minds of the age, did not consider himself a despot, nor would many of his subjects have accepted the charge. The tradition of natural law, after all, was strong in German and Prussian thinking by the eighteenth century: according to Frederick's somewhat selective understanding of this a monarch's subjects owed him absolute obedience, in return for which he was obligated to govern rationally and justly. But above all, in a hostile world Prussia had to be strong or it would go to the wall like the Poles, and the safeguards against this were a strong government and an army second to none.

In accordance with this concept of enlightenment, religious toleration meant something in Frederician Prussia. Not only did Prussia continue to attract immigrants fleeing persecution elsewhere, but (with the significant exception of the Jews) whatever other disadvantages Frederick's new Polish subjects laboured under, religious discrimination was not one of them. In like fashion, enlightened absolutism meant the rule of law, which indeed was the only surety against abuse of power. Frederick abolished torture and reduced the number of capital offences. Prussia was thus, like the Habsburg Monarchy and unlike Russia, a *Rechtsstaat* or state where the rule of law applied, and the values displayed by the monarch were widespread among the intelligentsia and the bureaucracy, attracting Germans from other states to Prussian service.

In one important respect Prussia remained akin to the rest of Eastern Europe in this period, in that it did not achieve a breakthrough in economic modernisation. This was in part due to the continuing scarcity of resources, despite the annexation of Silesia and the Polish lands, and in part due to the limitations of protectionism and mercantilism as economic stimulants. But in terms of altering the landlord–peasant relationship, Prussian governments also failed to grasp the nettle. A consequence of Frederick II's legal reforms was that peasants for the first time had a legal status, but although Frederick personally considered serfdom an evil he was also conscious that the whole of Prussia's great-power status was built upon serfdom, in that the *Junker* landowners provided the backbone of the officer corps. Recent research suggests that peasants in late eighteenth-century Prussia were increasingly aware of their legal rights and invoked them regularly, but it was not until the Napoleonic period that agrarian reform was forced on Prussia.

For the inhabitants of the new territories Prussian rule did not necessarily mean a change for the better. Silesia at the time of its conquest was the richest single province of the Habsburg Monarchy, its lands supporting a population of 1 million and with significant mining, a weaving and dying industry, and a major commercial centre at Breslau. Prussian annexation came near to killing this golden goose. Cut off from its traditional economic hinterland, Silesia's trade and industry suffered and its woes were increased not only by the devastation of two wars but by a harsh Prussian taxation regime which drained the province's economy. Attempts by Frederick's government to foster new industry failed to halt a general decline which left the province with less manufacturing by 1800 than in 1700.

In the former Polish lands it is clear that a Prussian animus against the Poles was at work from the start, although it should be noted that many of the Commonwealth's Germans deplored the Partitions, which the German mayor of Toruń in 1772 denounced as 'insufferable servitude'; Danzig even took up arms against Prussian occupation in 1793.[16] From Frederick the Great down, Prussians seemed united in their contempt for the Poles as vain, frivolous and incompetent, 'caught in an eternal anarchy', as Frederick himself put it in 1746.[17]

In West Prussia, Prussian taxes and administration were imposed, crown estates confiscated and county diets abolished. Frederick was of the opinion that the Poles needed to acquire 'a Prussian character', but by 1777 his policy had shifted to one of using state funds for buying out Polish land-owners and replacing them with German ones, in order 'to get rid of the bad Polish stuff'.[18] There was a gradual shift in the balance between Polish and German landowners in the province: some of the *szlachta* sold out and migrated to the still independent Polish Commonwealth; others went bankrupt; some carried on as Prussian subjects. In addition, the Prussian government initiated a policy of colonisation: some 3200 German peasant families were settled in West Prussia with free land by 1786.

With regard to the 25,000-strong Jewish community in West Prussia, Frederick succumbed to what might be called the prejudice of the enlight-ened. He despised the Jews for their attachment to what he regarded as an obscurantist religion and made a distinction between supposedly 'useful', wealthy Jews and the 'Jewish ragtag' of poor artisans, traders and the like. By the end of Frederick's reign 7000 Jews had been expelled from West Prussia into rump Poland – as Hagen comments, 'the first systematic expul-sion of any group from Prussia since the sixteenth century' and a blatant departure from Frederick's professed toleration.[19]

The Partitions of 1793–5 represented the culmination of Prussia's aggran-dising *Kabinettspolitik*, but it is only fair to admit that the government of Frederick William II (1786–97) was animated by a genuine alarm at the potential threat posed to the absolutist state by Poland's constitutional reform, given the simultaneous upheaval in France. Again, Prussian law was extended over the huge new acquisitions, and Polish crown lands as well as lands belonging to the Catholic Church were appropriated. A government report of 1793 breathed enlightened condescension towards the 'lackadaisi-cal' Poles who, it was trusted, would soon be brought up to Prussian standards of efficiency and prosperity.[20] The authorities were conscious that they could not now simply 'get rid' of either Poles or Jews, and the policies of estate buy-outs and wholesale colonisation were abandoned. Instead, Prussian bureaucrats displayed a patronising, almost colonial attitude towards the Polish population, while many regarded a posting to these often surly provinces as, in the words of one, 'the Botany Bay of Prussian official-dom'.[21]

The uprising of 1794–5, and the essential reasonableness and moderation of the 1791 constitution, even won the sympathy of some Germans for the Polish Commonwealth's fate. Eminent German figures like Herder and Immanuel Kant went so far as to denounce the Partitions and there was a certain vogue for Kościuszko as Romantic hero. Conscious of the need to win the allegiance, or at least the compliance, of the Polish elite, the Prussian government even tried to cultivate the *szlachta* socially in the 1790s. The Polish nobles, however, together with the hierarchy of the Catholic Church, held aloof for the most part. The truth was that Poles were themselves divided as to how they should respond to the extinction of their state. Some nobles opted for a demonstrative loyalty to the new order, as the best guarantor of their economic and social position. The majority remained disdainful of and hostile to Prussian rule. In 1794–5 several thousand Poles, nobles and commoners fought against the Prussian army in a bitter guerrilla conflict and when the fighting was over some estates were confiscated. The Kościuszko rising, however, had rubbed home not only the Poles' helplessness but also the difficulties of reconciling gentry nationalism, and gentry dominance, with the aspirations of non-nobles.

In the final decade before the Prussian absolutist state met its disastrous defeat at the hands of Napoleon in 1806, the Prussian government took to promoting the mutual study of languages as a means of winning the loyalty of its Polish population. Prussian officials, it was claimed, should be willing to learn Polish, but in return it was time Polish subjects accepted the utility of German as the state language. The aim, clearly, was Prussianisation and not Germanisation, a far cry from the nationalist view of later generations. Poles, it was reasoned, had to accept that they were Prussian subjects. The take-up rate, however, was minimal, not least because the institutional support for such bilingualism never materialised. Poles and Germans would continue to develop within Prussia along separate lines.

PART TWO

NATIONALISM, REVOLUTION AND STATE FORMATION 1804-67

4   Eastern Europe as of 1815. Source: (pp. 414–15) Eastern Europe 1815; *A History of the Modern World*, 3rd edn, by R. R. Palmer and Joel Colton (Alfred A. Knopf, 1965)

7

FORCES OF THE AGE: THE INTERNATIONAL SCENE 1804-67

At the end of the eighteenth century the seeds of fresh conflict and change were already widely sown in Eastern Europe. In addition to the perennial clash of states' interests, both the political ferment attendant on the French Revolution and the Napoleonic Wars, and more gradual social and economic changes, were preparing trouble. In the Ottoman Empire a series of revolts after 1804 led to the formation of new states and began a long process of break-up. The other states, though seemingly more stable, were also shaken by revolts or demands for political change; and although these upheavals were for the most part contained, the combined effect was to alter the regional balance of power by the mid-1860s.

Napoleon Bonaparte's impact on Eastern Europe was considerable. By 1801 he had defeated Austria and Russia yet again, and the Treaty of Lunéville began the final dissolution of the Holy Roman Empire with France's annexation of the west bank of the Rhine. In 1803 the secular princes of the Holy Roman Empire, led by the Emperor Francis, agreed to compensate themselves by annexing the ecclesiastical states; Francis compensated himself even further in assuming the title of Emperor of Austria in 1804. In 1805 Austria, Russia and Britain launched a Third Coalition against France, but Austria's defeat at Austerlitz in December gave Napoleon all the excuse he needed to institutionalise French hegemony in Germany. Thirty German princes formed the Confederation of the Rhine in 1806, in alliance with France; Francis had little option but to abdicate as Holy Roman Emperor. The Treaty of Pressburg in December 1805 had already handed over the former Venetian territories, including Dalmatia, to France, and the Tyrol and Vorarlberg to Bavaria. Continuing hostilities between France and Russia, on the Adriatic coast, led to a French occupation of Ragusa in 1806 and its annexation in 1808.

The Confederation of the Rhine provoked Prussia's suicidal war against France in the autumn of 1806, leading to a crushing defeat. Prussia's prostration was confirmed by the defeat of its ally Russia the following year and the subsequent Treaty of Tilsit. By this Napoleon and tsar Alexander I divided Europe into spheres of influence, but with France's hegemony underscored by Russian adherence to the Continental Blockade against Britain and by the creation of the Grand Duchy of Warsaw out of Prussia's share of the Polish Partitions. This resuscitation of Poland, while it lasted, and despite the duchy's obvious function as Napoleonic puppet state and provider of cannon fodder, ensured Napoleon the loyalty of many Poles, such as Prince Józef Poniatowski, nephew of Stanisław August, who became a Marshal of France and died at Leipzig in 1813.

The uneasy Franco-Russian condominium further destabilised the Ottoman Balkans, where yet another Russo-Turkish war had broken out in 1806 over Russian influence in the Romanian principalities. At Tilsit, grandiose plans were drawn up between Napoleon and Alexander for a partition of the Balkans, but nothing came of these apart from the resumption of French control of the Ionian Islands in 1807. These had fallen under joint Russo-Turkish protectorate as the 'Septinsular Republic', formally 'the first autonomous Greek state of modern times'.[1] British sea power, however, captured most of the islands from France by 1814. In the Eastern Balkans, the Russo-Turkish War lasted until 1812, when the French invasion of Russia forced Alexander to settle for the largely Romanian-inhabited territory of Bessarabia.

Napoleon's reordering of Eastern Europe continued apace when the Habsburg Monarchy once again attacked in 1809. This time Austria's defeat was punished with the cession of its remaining western crownlands to Bavaria, the amalgamation of Dalmatia, western Croatia and the Slovene-inhabited parts of the Austrian crownlands into the 'Illyrian Provinces', annexed to France, and the transfer of West Galicia, the Habsburgs' share of the Third Partition, to the Grand Duchy of Warsaw.

In the end Napoleon's hegemony in Europe collapsed through that most habit-forming of imperial defects, overstretch. The issues that led Napoleon to commit the fatal mistake of invading Russia in 1812 were continental in scope, but Alexander's break with Napoleon also owed much to a legitimate fear that the Grand Duchy of Warsaw would be used as a pretext for reopening the Polish question, and the enthusiastic participation of Polish troops in the 1812 campaign only validated this suspicion. Napoleon's willingness to play the Polish card confirmed the tsar's view of him as a true heir to the Revolution. The disastrous retreat from Moscow heralded the end of the Napoleonic imperium: first Prussia and then Austria deserted Napoleon, and by the spring of 1814 Russian Cossacks were bivouacking on the boulevards of Paris. Eastern Europe had been delivered from France; in its place stood Russia, seemingly more powerful than ever.

The 'restored' Eastern Europe (see Map 4), like everything else agreed by the victors at the Congress of Vienna in 1815, was in fact anything but restored; all aspects of the settlement affecting the region reflected the uneasy balance of power between Austria, Prussia and Russia.[2] The Habsburg Monarchy resumed possession of most of its lost territories in the west: the Austrian crownlands, Croatia and Dalmatia with the addition of Ragusa and, as a buffer against future French aggression, the north Italian provinces of Lombardy and Venetia. The Holy Roman Empire, however, was truly history. Instead, Napoleon's Confederation of the Rhine was continued, but under Austrian leadership and rechristened the German Confederation. Despite the Monarchy's continuing role in German affairs the focus of Habsburg foreign policy was insensibly shifted towards Italy and the Balkans.

In the East, Poland was repartitioned, but here Russia insisted on the lion's share. Prussia regained the province of Posen, Austria the area around Tarnopol, and in a compromise designed to avert conflict between the great powers themselves, the city of Kraków was permitted to govern itself as a free city under great-power guarantee. Otherwise the central bloc of the Polish lands went to Russia. Alexander I, however, was conscious also of the need to placate the Poles, who had fought enthusiastically for Napoleon. Russian Poland was accordingly reconstituted as a kingdom, under Alexander, with a constitution and a modest degree of self-rule. This was enough to win over many Poles, although it remained a sore point that the 'Congress Kingdom' excluded the vast western *gubernii* (governorships); these were henceforth ruled as integral parts of Russia proper.

Europe after 1815 thus gave the appearance of being firmly under control, nowhere more so than in the East, where the most conservative, not to say reactionary, governments dominated the region. Despite attempts by Austria, Prussia and Russia to cooperate with each other in maintaining order, however, through such mechanisms as the 'Congress system' or the 'Holy Alliance', instability was never far from the surface. The identity of interest between the three 'Northern Courts' was real enough, as the Polish question demonstrated, and produced other practical examples of conservative, monarchical solidarity. However, once the instability reached the surface, relations between the powers themselves were apt to deteriorate. A prime example was the so-called 'Eastern Question', revolving around the viability of the Ottoman Empire. The latter was already wrestling with rebellion among the Serbs, which ultimately resulted in Serbian autonomy in 1815. The Greek revolts of 1821 sparked enormous public attention in the rest of Europe, the armed intercession of Russia, Britain and France in 1827, and eventually another Russo-Turkish war in 1828–9. The result was not only the creation of an independent Kingdom of Greece by 1832 but a serious rift between Austria and the other powers.

Likewise the Treaty of Adrianople of September 1829, ending the Russo-Turkish War, established a virtual Russian protectorate over Moldavia and Wallachia, although both, like Serbia, remained formal vassal-states of the sultan. Russia's augmented hold over the Ottoman Empire was a source of grave concern not just to the Habsburg Monarchy but also to France and Britain, which feared a Russian takeover of Constantinople and the Straits, with consequences for the stability of the entire eastern Mediterranean. This fear was exaggerated, in that the Russian government by the mid-1820s had decided that it was more in Russia's interest to preserve a weak Ottoman Empire, over which Russia could exert a preponderant influence, than it was to dismember it.

The Ottoman Empire's northern neighbours had their own internal problems. Russia's honeymoon with the Poles ended abruptly in November 1830 when the Congress Kingdom rose in revolt. It took Nicholas I (1825–55) until September 1831 to re-establish control, and the international ramifications were considerable. The revolt was partly inspired by the July Revolution in France, and one of its unintended consequences was to make any sort of intervention in France by the powers of the 'Holy Alliance' impossible, even had the latter seriously wished to do so. The brutal suppression of the revolt drove another 10,000 Poles into western exile, where for the next generation they were a constant worry to the partition powers. Moderates clustered around Prince Adam Czartoryski at his headquarters in Paris, with its network of agents throughout the continent, fertile in schemes for enlisting the support of foreign governments and allying with discontented nationalities in Eastern Europe. More radical Polish nationalists established links with revolutionary republicans such as Giuseppe Mazzini, the apostle of Italian nationalism. Polish soldiers fought on the side of Hungary against the Habsburgs in 1848–9 and took part in the unification of Italy between 1849 and 1860.

Polish grievances in Habsburg Galicia led to a minor revision of international boundaries in 1846 when Polish nobles staged an uprising designed to spread to the other Partitions. This rebellion too was successfully contained by the Habsburg Monarchy, but the fact that its origins lay in the free city of Kraków gave Austria a justification for annexing Kraków in November 1846.

Such disturbances pale in comparison with the revolutionary year of 1848–9. In the Habsburg Monarchy there were revolutions in Vienna, the north Italian provinces, Bohemia and the Kingdom of Hungary. The fact that revolution broke out in Vienna itself, the imperial capital, resulting in a power vacuum, encouraged the north Italian cities to revolt, which in turn emboldened King Charles Albert of Sardinia–Piedmont to invade Habsburg territory. Despite a rapid Piedmontese defeat, this threat to the Monarchy was not completely contained until March 1849.

Even more cataclysmic was the escalation of events in Hungary, where a liberal revolution in March brought constitutional government and a form of home rule, but where the seeming irreconcilability of Hungarian claims to autonomy with Habsburg rule led in September to confrontation and war.

The Hungarian War of Independence lasted until August 1849 and was resolved only by the assistance of Nicholas I of Russia, who in the name of monarchical solidarity despatched an army across the Carpathians to extirpate the demon of revolution. The twin effect of the Monarchy's loss of control in both Italy and Hungary and the fact that it appeared to owe its recovery largely to Russian power completed the picture of a state whose status as a great power was in question.

The concurrent rash of revolutions in the German states and in Italy also had an inevitable impact on the Habsburg Monarchy. In both regions the Monarchy aspired to play a dominant role; in each it found itself struggling desperately to maintain that position. The fact that a German National Assembly was called at Frankfurt, where it began debating the question of German unity, aroused a strong counter-response in some of the Monarchy's many nationalities. The Czechs in particular rejected the claim that Bohemia was a 'German' land. At the same time the turmoil within the Monarchy, but especially in Hungary, made it painfully obvious that this was far more than just a 'German' state; this undermined its title to lead Germany, let alone unite it, to the corresponding advantage of Prussia. The 'neo-absolutist' government which finally crushed the revolutions in the Habsburg Monarchy was determined to re-establish its standing as a great power. Both the young Emperor Francis Joseph (1848–1916) and his first minister, Prince Felix zu Schwarzenberg, adopted a far more confrontational stance against Prussia's pretensions to leadership in the German Confederation.

Prussia had experienced its own revolution in 1848, but had weathered this storm with far less strain than the Habsburg Monarchy. King Frederick William IV (1840–61) conceded a liberal government and also, to public acclaim, announced that 'henceforth Prussia is merged in Germany', an enigmatic phrase which nevertheless suggested an interest in playing a greater role in German unification.[3] In the province of Posen the new government faced immediate demands from the Poles for some form of autonomy. Despite limited support for this at the Frankfurt National Assembly, opinion in Prussia but also the German Confederation as a whole turned vehemently against any such idea. By November Frederick William, mindful that he still enjoyed the obedience of the army, felt confident enough to dismiss the liberal government. Prussia's role for the rest of the revolutionary year was as a reactionary policeman, stamping out the last vestiges of revolution in the lesser states.

Despite their shared reactionary characteristics, Prussia and Austria were clearly on a collision course over the leadership of Germany after 1849, a rivalry with fateful implications for Eastern Europe. Prussia's attempt to fashion a *kleindeutsch* or 'Little German' union of states at Erfurt in 1850 was vetoed by the Habsburg government, a humiliation the Prussians had to accept, but which reinforced their determination to build Prussian economic and military strength to the point where a repeat of the experience would be impossible. Austro-Prussian rivalry in Germany meant that on international issues affecting the territorial integrity of the Habsburg Monarchy, Prussia was likely to remain neutral, if not actively hostile.

A further blow was dealt the Habsburg Monarchy's international security by the outcome of the Crimean War of 1853–6. This conflict, initially between Russia and the Ottoman Empire, but which by 1855 had dragged in Britain and France and even Piedmont on the Ottoman side, was ultimately about Russia's ability to dominate the Ottomans. It also owed a good deal to the determination of Louis Napoleon Bonaparte, from 1848 president and from 1852 emperor Napoleon III of France, to play a greater role internationally and, if possible, undo elements of the settlement imposed on France in 1815. This involved limiting the threat posed by that settlement's guarantors, in particular Russia and the Habsburg Monarchy. In 1854 Russia was Napoleon III's chief obstacle, in trying to overcome which he could rely on Habsburg support. What made the Crimean War of particular relevance to the Habsburgs was Russia's immediate occupation, on the outbreak of the war in 1853, of the Romanian principalities.

Austro-Russian understanding over the Eastern Question had never been impossible: in 1833 the two powers had agreed to prop up the Ottoman Empire as long as possible and to consult with one another should that prove impracticable. Habsburg toleration of Russia's involvement in the principalities, however, was always conditional upon the preservation of the status quo. The return of Russian troops to the region in 1853 represented a serious alteration of the balance of power, a permanent extension of Russian influence. The Monarchy's response was to demand Russian withdrawal from the principalities in June 1854. Given that Russia was by now under attack by France and Britain, the tsar was obliged to do this; but the result was an indelible sense of betrayal on the part of the Russians, compounded by the fact that Russian withdrawal was followed by an immediate joint Austro-Turkish occupation of the provinces. From this position of security Austria sat out the rest of the Crimean War in armed neutrality, but its future was anything but secure.

For the long-term effect of the war was a fatal undermining of the Monarchy's international position. Its rivalry with Prussia over Germany increasingly in the open, and its hold on Italy ever more likely to be challenged by Piedmont, with the backing of Napoleon III's France, the Monarchy was henceforth bereft of the support of its conservative soulmate Russia. Instead, Russia's humiliation at the Treaty of Paris, which concluded the Crimean War in March 1856, ensured that it was more intent on revising or otherwise evading the treaty's terms than in policing the affairs of Europe. The Habsburg Monarchy, isolated, was obliged to fight its corner unaided in 1859, and again in 1866, and lost both times, with profound results not only for the future shape of Germany and Italy but for the Monarchy's internal construction.

As for Russia, it was stripped of its right to intervene in the affairs of the Ottoman Empire, whose vassal principalities were instead guaranteed their autonomy by all the great powers signatory to the treaty. Russia was forced to cede the southern part of Bessarabia to Moldavia, thus losing access to the mouth of the Danube. Most devastating of all for Russia, the Black Sea was neutralised, meaning that both Russia and the Ottomans were forbidden to maintain a fleet there or military installations on its shores.

In overall strategic terms the following decade and a half of European history is best understood as a power vacuum, in which the ambitions of individual states, combined with the rising force of nationalism, allowed them to redraw the map in the Italian Peninsula and Germany, while the truly global powers, Britain and Russia, remained relatively uninvolved, either from choice or necessity. These upheavals affected Eastern Europe directly, given that the Habsburg Monarchy was their principal victim, but the succession of crises by which this transformation was imposed had an impact in the rest of the region as well. Everywhere in Eastern Europe nationalists, however few in number, felt the force of the example set by the creation of so-called nation-states in Italy and Germany.

The war of 1859, in which the Habsburg Monarchy attacked Piedmont and France and lost Lombardy, was an unmitigated disaster because it demonstrated the Monarchy's essential weakness so plainly. Napoleon III and the Piedmontese openly encouraged the Hungarian nationalist emigration to foment an uprising in Hungary and a Hungarian Legion of 4000 men was formed in Piedmont. At the height of the fighting in Italy the Habsburg government felt obliged to station an entire army corps in Hungary for fear of rebellion. Losing the war completed the Habsburg Monarchy's financial bankruptcy and the impossibility of securing further credit pushed Francis Joseph into a gradual abandonment of neo-absolutism and, by 1867, compromise with the Hungarians.

An essential element of Napoleon III's foreign policy in the post-Crimean decade was his support for the unification of Moldavia and Wallachia. This owed something to a genuine, if vague and selective, sympathy for national liberation movements; it owed even more to Napoleon's desire to exploit the Monarchy's vulnerability. As a result an international conference in 1858 sanctioned the 'United principalities of Moldavia and Wallachia', a curious hybrid, with separate *hospodars* or princes, governments and assemblies, but joined by a Central Commission. The principalities promptly defied the great powers by electing the same man, Alexander Cuza, as *hospodar* in 1859. Any chance that this Romanian *fait accompli* might be overturned then vanished when Austria suffered defeat in the Italian War.

For some years after the Crimean War the former enemies Russia and France found common ground in their hostility to the Habsburg Monarchy. This entente suffered a decisive rupture following the second great uprising in Russian Poland in January 1863. While Austria and Prussia made no secret of their desire to see Russia crush the uprising, the reaction in the West was one of sympathy for the insurgents. Russia's relations with Britain had never ceased to be frosty; because of the Polish revolt Russia's alienation from France was prompt and bitter, a key factor in 1870.

The final revolution in East European affairs was effected by the Austro-Prussian War of 1866. Once again, conflict in a completely different arena, Germany, facilitated change in the Habsburg Monarchy as well as the Balkans. Prussia's steely minister-president from 1862, Otto von Bismarck, pursued confrontation with Austria precisely because he perceived the necessity of excluding the Habsburgs totally from German affairs if Prussia's territorial expansion into the Confederation was to be achieved. Bismarck also knew that the acquiescence in this project of France, Russia and Britain was essential. Napoleon III was willing to sit on the sidelines in the belief that the two German states would fight one another to a standstill. Russia, ill disposed towards Austria in any case, saw a strong Prussia as a useful, conservative counterweight to French power. Britain also favoured a strong central European state capable of restraining both France and Russia. Finally, Bismarck secured a useful distraction against the Austrians in Italy, which signed an alliance with Prussia in return for the promise of Habsburg Venetia.

The Austro-Prussian War was bloody but brief, climaxing in the Austrians' defeat at Sadowa on 3 July 1866. By the Treaty of Prague, in August, the Habsburg Monarchy accepted its expulsion from the German Confederation. Venetia was ceded to Italy, despite the Italians' comprehensive defeat by the Austrians on land and sea. Most importantly, the Habsburg defeat meant that Francis Joseph was all the more inclined to accept home rule within the Monarchy for Hungary and a parallel constitutional government for the 'Austrian' half of the Habsburg realm. The Monarchy, bereft of its Italian and German role, was henceforth to take an even more intense interest in south-eastern Europe and the threat of Russian influence there.

As a coda to this period, it is worth noting that the Franco-Prussian War of 1870–1, and France's defeat at the hands of Prussia and the other German states, confirmed the Habsburg Monarchy's inability to regain its former primacy in German affairs. Instead, the Monarchy's reorientation towards the Balkans was strengthened, as was its fundamental opposition to Russia, while at the same time giving it common cause with the new German Empire. The underlying antagonism of interests which was to help produce the First World War was thus in evidence by the early 1870s.

8

FORCES OF THE AGE: LIBERALISM, NATIONALISM AND ECONOMIC CHANGE 1804-67

Despite the apparent 'restoration' of order in 1815, beneath the surface there were ideological stirrings deriving in large part from the revolutionary turmoil, but drawing some of their force from developments going back into the eighteenth century. One of these ideologies might loosely be termed liberalism: the dawning consciousness among a growing number of Europeans after 1789, even in Eastern Europe, that individual political rights, however narrowly defined, ought to count for something, and that this basic principle should in some way be translated into a constitution, or other institutional framework defining these rights, as well as the obligations of governments. The other main force of the age was nationalism, or as contemporaries referred to it, the 'principle of nationality'. Of the two, nationalism might now seem to us the more significant, but it is important to remember that in the minds of people at the time the concept of liberty was the starting point. Political upheavals in this period were arguably more about basic issues of political rights than they were about nationalism, although in some cases they rapidly took on a nationalistic character. In addition, there were serious economic and social tensions building up, which possessed their own dynamic.

IDEOLOGICAL FERMENT

The revolution in people's minds was perhaps the most potent force unleashed in this period, even if we must always stress the relatively small numbers involved. The French Revolution confronted all the East European empires with the spectres of republicanism, popular sovereignty, the overthrow of the existing order and the nation in arms. This in turn provoked a reaction, in that these conservative monarchies abandoned what modest plans they had hitherto envisaged for both political reform and economic modernisation. Concepts such as popular sovereignty and political rights were now associated with red revolution.

The problem for the rulers of Eastern Europe was that reaction was not enough. Not only were their armies not proof against the revolutionary *élan* of the French Republic, but the ideas that drove the Revolution had been abroad for too long. The revolutionary wars threatened the eastern empires in an obvious territorial sense, but also morally, in that the entire edifice of monarchical absolutism, noble privilege and serfdom was potentially at risk. The impact of this was felt in Eastern Europe for generations.

An essential role in consolidating and deepening the effects of the revolutionary period was played by Napoleon. His redrawing of the international map, however ephemeral, created aspirations towards a later unity. Thus, the creation of the Confederation of the Rhine and the Kingdom of Italy is commonly held to have generated later nationalist demands for 'unification'; this example had force elsewhere. The Grand Duchy of Warsaw, while patently a Napoleonic satellite, was nevertheless a partial reconstitution of the Polish state. The Illyrian provinces, briefly carved out of the South Slav territories of the Habsburg Monarchy, were the first experience these peoples had of a unitary government and furnished the kernel for later concepts of 'Yugoslavism'. In the Balkans the fact that such territorial units were created at all served as a powerful incentive to self-help.

Even more unsettling was Napoleon's demonstration of the efficiency of the modern nation-state, with its centrally controlled administration, regular tax collection, emphasis on legal equality and security of property, and above all its ability to project its power by virtue of a citizen army. The contrast with even the most advanced of the enlightened absolutist monarchies of the *ancien régime* was painful. Throughout the nineteenth century, therefore, the Napoleonic state was very much the template for East European rulers and elites. All saw the centralised, bureaucratic state as the key to modernisation.

Napoleon's opponents were particularly fearful of the appeal of liberal ideas. True, by 'liberal' Napoleon meant 'enlightened' and 'rational', as opposed to our modern usage of the word; in this sense he was heir to the absolutist, not the democratic, strand of the Enlightenment. This may account for the enthusiasm with which in the early years of his reign Alexander I of Russia experimented with projects for enlightened, even constitutional, reform: such limited projects were not, after all, incompatible with autocracy. Yet the rulers of the old Europe rightly mistrusted even the facade of liberalism. Even in Napoleon's time the conviction spread that the rights of man and a constitution and a representative assembly should really mean something, or could be made to do so; in the post-Napoleonic period, liberalism as a political ideology assumed increasing coherence.

The architects of the so-called 'Restoration' following the fall of Napoleon were consequently alert to the stirrings of liberalism as a revolutionary, subversive force, however feeble the threat was in reality. As Prince Clemens von Metternich, Austrian chancellor and the self-appointed architect-in-chief of this conservative order, put it, liberal ideas were a sort of 'moral gangrene', issuing from the excessive and 'presumptuous' application of reason and corrupting the body politic.[1] Fortunately, in Metternich's view, this malady affected only the middling or 'agitating' classes, since the masses were innately conservative. For Metternich this meant in domestic terms the maintenance of monarchical control and a rigid control of the press and public opinion. In international affairs it implied a balance of power agreed among the great powers and the suppression of any sign of revolution.

This immobile attitude was futile in the long run. First of all the interests of these conservative powers conflicted. Secondly, governments found it impossible to resist availing themselves of the more useful elements of the revolutionary and Napoleonic legacy: centralised administrative control, the codification of laws and an educated populace were all as tempting as ever. Francis I, on visiting the newly regained Dalmatia in 1815 and being told that the excellent roads were French built, famously quipped, 'Four years, I wish they had been here for four centuries.'[2] It was an apt, if sublimely unreflective, comment on the irreversible impact of the preceding period.

In the decades following the Congress of Vienna, therefore, it became increasingly apparent that the tide of revolutionary ideas could not be turned back; this was especially true of the range of political values commonly termed *liberalism*. In the Ottoman Balkans, for instance, by some calculations the most backward region on the continent, the ideas and literature of the Enlightenment had long circulated among the Greek population. Rigas Velestinlis was the most striking exponent of liberal as well as nationalist ideas, publishing in 1797 a bill of rights and a draft constitution for liberated Greece, consciously modelled on the French constitutions of 1793 and 1795. Secret societies dedicated to revolt and independence flourished across the Levant. And when, in 1821, the Greek revolt against the Ottomans began, there was no shortage of learned Greeks who justified the uprising with reference to Rousseau's theory of the general will. The Greek war of independence became a *cause célèbre* in Western Europe and attracted the support of famous 'Philhellenes' like Lord Byron, who died at Mesolongi in 1824, precisely because it was seen as a struggle for basic freedoms and human dignity.

What was true of the Greeks held true for most of the rest of Eastern Europe. Thus, the Grand Duchy of Warsaw was endowed by Napoleon with a constitution and legal code, which proclaimed legal equality and personal liberty and abolished serfdom. Although the Napoleonic system was replaced by Russia, the memory of it survived. Some, if not all, Polish patriots began to argue that, until the concept of Polishness was extended to include burghers and peasants as well as nobles, in short became truly popular, there could be no hope of reconstituting a Polish state.

The Polish diaspora, after 1831, was another important factor in spreading subversive ideas. Polish exiles kept turning up in odd corners of Eastern Europe for decades and joined the Hungarian struggle for independence in significant numbers. Most gravitated to Paris, where Czartoryski spent the next 30 years encouraging plans for a confederation of East European peoples which would somehow supplant the Romanov and Habsburg empires. Czartoryski also funded, from his considerable private fortune, a chair in Slavonic literature at the Collège de France, where in the early 1840s Poland's most acclaimed poet, Adam Mickiewicz, preached a Romantic message of 'a universal war for the freedom of peoples', influencing not only his fellow Poles but a whole generation of Romanian students.[3]

One could multiply examples of the spread of ideas in Eastern Europe; the basic point here is the permeability of the divide between Western and Eastern Europe when it comes to ideology. Quite apart from the legacy of 1789 and Napoleon, the power of the example set by France in particular is hard to exaggerate. This was especially strong among Romanians, whose language, like French, is Latin-based. Romanians studied in Paris; some fought on the barricades during the July Revolution of 1830; and one, Ion Brătianu, attempted to assassinate Napoleon III, in 1853, because the latter was not supporting the union of Moldavia and Wallachia more actively. Serbs, Greeks, Poles and others also flocked to Paris and when, in February 1848, the July Monarchy succumbed to revolution, the news triggered revolution in Hungary, which in turn sparked events in Vienna and elsewhere.

The essential lure was that of westernisation, and from the 1820s an increasing number of East Europeans sought a university education in the West. The first generation of Serbian students to study abroad, for instance, left for Austria and Saxony in 1839; most completed their studies in Paris.[4] Once back in their native lands, such men (there were no women) as often as not became exponents of political as well as economic modernisation. They founded newspapers, campaigned for constitutions and started to form embryonic parties. Underlying much of their discourse was the perception that Eastern Europe was backward in comparison with Western Europe and, given the onset of industrialisation in the West, was likely to become more so. These first East European liberals might have differed over which should come first, economic development or national liberation, but they agreed that representative institutions, and government by progressive, moderate figures like themselves, were preconditions for either. They were far from being democrats; on the contrary, most liberals in this period were opposed to universal suffrage.

Liberals in Eastern Europe, for all their essential moderation, were seen by their rulers as dangerous subversives. Conservative regimes down to 1848 kept a tight lid on freedom of expression, with the partial exception of Hungary, where the need to reconvene the Diet in 1825 provided a forum for moderate reforms proposals. More radical critics of the system, however, paid for their temerity with prison sentences. The revolutions of 1848 were thus a flashpoint, which prompted a whole range of demands for constitutional government, for autonomy, for political rights generally; and once this genie had been released from its bottle, often attracting mass support in the process, it proved extremely difficult to put it back in again. The very fact that, in the 'Austrian' half of the Habsburg Monarchy, or in Prussia, constituent assemblies were convened, represented a momentous development in itself. Despite the suppression of the revolutions, the whole issue of representative government had been raised in such a way that it could never subsequently be ignored.

The most explosive ideological development of this period was undoubtedly the emergence of *nationalism* among most of the peoples of Eastern Europe. This was a complex process, but in a regional context a number of general observations are in order. The spread of nationalism was limited by three factors. Firstly, in the cases of the Hungarians and Poles, the rhetoric of nationalism was to begin with the preserve of the nobility. Secondly, the extent to which nationalism spread was, with two significant exceptions, dependent on a people's level of socio-economic development; without an educated elite, some peoples' nationalism was slower to emerge than others'. Thirdly, not just literacy but the extent to which a literary language existed was also crucial, given that many East European languages at the start of the nineteenth century still had no agreed alphabet, formal grammar or common dialect for literary usage.

The two exceptions were the Serbs and the Greeks, or rather the non-urban Greeks of the Greek mainland. Among these largely illiterate peasant or pastoral peoples, who were among the first to revolt against the Ottoman Empire, it is clear that much of the impetus for revolt lay in their inferior socio-economic status and in the religious differences between them, as Orthodox Christians, and their Ottoman Muslim overlords. (The same was not true of urban and mercantile Greeks, who were more typical of an emerging nationalist elite.) Both Serbs and non-urban Greeks nevertheless demonstrated a consciousness of themselves as distinct groups, derived in part from the survival of their respective Orthodox churches throughout the Ottoman period. As a result these two groups have been singled out as the exceptions that prove the rule, peoples who developed nationalism without possessing an educated native elite.

The French Revolutionary and Napoleonic period provided a powerful long-term stimulus to nationalism across Europe. The spectacle of the French nation in arms, sweeping the old Europe before it, was an object lesson in the mass-mobilising appeal of nationalism, not least because it was conflated in most people's minds, in this early period, with the concepts of liberty, equality and political rights. Just as individuals were liberated by these principles, it was argued, so too were other nations – and the French Republic made it its business to ensure this. This force of example was felt even in Eastern Europe.

The Poles' response to the French Revolution has already been alluded to. Elsewhere the results were less obvious. Napoleon, invading the Habsburg Monarchy in 1809, issued a 'Manifesto to the Hungarian Nation', drafted by a lifelong admirer of the French Revolution and former Hungarian 'Jacobin'. It fell sadly flat. The Hungarian nobility, having seen off Joseph II's central-ising reforms in 1790 and regarding the French influence as dangerously subversive of the social order, rallied around the Habsburgs instead. In the Illyrian provinces, the evidence suggests a negative rather than positive reaction to the French. Among German speakers in the Habsburg Monarchy, as in Prussia, there was certainly something of a reactive nationalism produced by hostility to the French, and which the Habsburg government in 1809 tried to whip up, with indifferent success. But in societies where the overwhelm-ing majority of the population were peasants and illiterate, it was unlikely that the immediate response to the French example would be widespread.

The real effect could be discerned only after some decades, and here the work of the 'awakeners' in each society was crucial. Herder's thinking in this respect was the starting point for many, in that it stressed the central-ity of language as the 'soul' of the nation and the importance of recording and studying popular culture as an artefact of the nation's history. Herder particularly singled out the Slavonic peoples as peaceful and industrious and, as a result of these virtues, likely to dominate the region. Equally notorious was Herder's warning to the Hungarians that they risked extinc-tion as a people if they allowed themselves to be Germanised or failed to preserve their uniqueness in a sea of other nationalities.

The national 'awakenings' can best be seen as taking place in two main phases. In the first phase were those peoples whose intellectuals had begun this process in the eighteenth century and continued it into the nineteenth; this includes the Hungarians, Czechs, Poles and Greeks. The second phase includes peoples such as the Slovaks, Serbs, Croats and Romanians, for whom this process got under way mainly in the early nineteenth century. The problem facing most of the peoples of the second wave of awakenings was that the main vehicle for national consciousness, their language, was spoken largely by illiterate peasants and was hence uncodified.[5]

A preoccupation with the history, real or imagined, of the nation and its language was characteristic of national revivals across Eastern Europe. Much of the literary and scholarly output among the Serbs, Slovaks, Czechs and others was focused on the collection of folk tales, epic poetry, historical records and any other evidence that reinforced the message that one's nation had a long and venerable pedigree. Often this involved claims, some of them spurious, that one's own nation had settled in its 'homeland' before another or, better still, had always been there. This sort of dispute was to bedevil relations between Czechs and Germans, for instance, or between Serbs and Croats, or Serbs and Albanians, for generations. History became a weapon on the nationality front, with German and Hungarian nationalists claiming precedence and superiority, on the basis that they at least had a history and a culture, whereas largely peasant nationalities were supposedly 'unhistorical', without culture and hence identity.

With linguistic and literary legitimisation, and with historicisation, came politicisation and conflict. In the case of the new Balkan states, nationalism made only a limited contribution to their formation, but was very much a consequence of this process. The very existence of an autonomous Serbia after 1815, of the Kingdom of Greece after 1832 and of a united Romania from the 1850s, called for a whole panoply of institutions, all of which helped create the sense of belonging to a nation: a 'national' ruler (even if in most cases this was a foreign prince), a national government, an army, an educational system. With these new states there was the additional incentive of national liberation, of releasing from what was seen as bondage co-nationals still under Ottoman or Habsburg or Romanov rule. The foreign policy of the new Balkan states, therefore, and to a large extent their domestic priorities, were heavily influenced by a nationalist agenda of expansion.

In the multinational empires a rising national consciousness inevitably implied political friction. The Polish revolts against Russia have already been mentioned. The Balkan nationalities remaining under direct Ottoman rule became the object of solicitude and propaganda by their national brethren in Serbia and Greece, and by the 1850s a Bulgarian nationalism was appearing too.

The consequences of nationalism were most striking in the Habsburg Monarchy. Hungarian liberal reformers who, as nationalists, also assumed that the language of state should be Hungarian, ran full tilt into the protests of Croats, Serbs, Romanians and Slovaks. Galician Poles discovered that the hitherto unregarded Ruthenes disputed their right to speak on behalf of the province they both inhabited. Bohemia by the 1840s could only with difficulty be defined as a German land. The conflict revolved everywhere around basic issues of education, administration and justice, and in the two decades prior to 1848 a plethora of cultural organisations sprang up, dedicated to promoting each nation's language and sense of identity and defending it against the pretensions of other nations.

Another politicising factor was the inspiration East European nationalists derived from their forerunners in Central or Western Europe. The influence here of the Italian Giuseppe Mazzini was incalculable. Mazzini was arguably the first modern nationalist, an ideologue who believed in the nation as in a religion and who spent his entire life not only fighting and scheming for Italian unification but proselytising the cause of the nation to others. His importance lay in the realisation he spread that the nation required sacrifice and direct action, as typified by the programme of his conspiratorial organisation Young Italy, founded in 1831. Episodes such as the siege of the Roman Republic in 1849, or Giuseppe Garibaldi's thrilling expedition to Sicily in 1860, enthused a generation of nationalists. Some, like the Romanians driven into exile in Paris in 1848, associated themselves directly with Mazzinian revolutionary organisations. Others rejected Mazzini's republicanism, but admired his vision and felt that 'all national movements in this period are expressions of one general aspiration'.[6]

The revolutions of 1848–9 demonstrated that East European nationalism had come of age. The demands of the Hungarian Diet for autonomy, and the war of independence, were about Hungary's vision of itself as a sovereign nation. By the same token the reaction of the national minorities within Hungary to this prospect was no less nationalistic. The final proof of the maturation of nationalism was the fact that blood was shed and events degenerated into an interethnic conflict, with Hungarians pitted against the rest.

In the immediate aftermath nationalism appeared to have been contained. The mass of the population remained peasants and hence on the whole indifferent to the new ideology. Yet hundreds of thousands, if not millions, of ordinary people had been politicised, if only by virtue of being dragged into conflicts which were, in some respects at least, about issues of nationality.

ECONOMIC AND SOCIAL DEVELOPMENTS

The societies of Eastern Europe remained largely agrarian in this period, yet not only was economic and social development happening of its own, but the perceived gap between Eastern and Western Europe was beginning to attract serious attention. This was not least because the gap was getting wider all the time. The crucial problem was posed by the system of land tenure and whether and how it might be altered.

The *Habsburg Monarchy* saw perhaps the most complicated change. This was an empire which enjoyed the reputation of a great power, but whose outstanding economic characteristic was backwardness and financial weakness. The Monarchy had a problem for decades with securing international credit, a vulnerability heightened by the post-1815 slump in grain prices, yet in Italy and Germany it had a position to maintain. Competing with Prussia, which had the edge as an industrialising power, the Monarchy soon found itself shouldered out of the German market by the Prussian-led *Zollverein* or customs union of 1834, which specifically excluded Austria.

In the 'Austrian' lands, excluding Hungary, there was gradual economic recovery, even growth, by the beginning of the 1830s. This was despite the personal opposition to modernisation of the emperor Francis, who initially refused to sanction the importation of steam engines and railway technology, on the ground that it 'would only bring revolution into the country'.[7] The advent of steam in fact transformed the Monarchy's prospects and it is significant that the first major application of the new technology was to river traffic, with the founding of the Danube Steam Navigation Company in 1831. The first railway was opened in 1832 and by 1848 there were 1025 kilometres of track. The improvements in infrastructure meant that exports of agricultural produce, especially from Hungary, could expand; this in turn

stimulated the arrival or the expansion of certain industries: food processing, brewing, textiles and some metal working. Urban centres grew: Vienna
in 1800 had 247,000 inhabitants; by 1850 the figure was 444,000.[8]

In Hungary, despite the market for agricultural produce, economic growth
was less marked and industry non-existent. Here the redundant class was
the numerous gentry, most of whom did not have enough land or income;
this noble proletariat gravitated to genteel occupations like the law, literature, journalism and politics, and Hungarian politics from the 1820s was
dominated by the pressure to accommodate this class, increasing demands
for autonomy in order to gain control of the jobs in the state bureaucracy.

Another peculiarity of Hungarian society, however, was the acute consciousness of the country's backwardness shown by some nobles. Count István
Széchenyi was a pivotal figure, not only in articulating this predicament but
in trying to do something about it. His travels in Western Europe, especially
industrialising Britain, convinced him that 'the century is on the march but,
unfortunately, I live in a country that is dragging one leg behind'.[9] Immensely
wealthy, Széchenyi personally sponsored steamship navigation, the improvement of livestock, the building of infrastructure like Budapest's famous Chain
Bridge, and much else. He also had the insight to perceive the immense drag
on modernisation imposed by serfdom, the free labour from which would be
unnecessary if greater credit, and the liberalisation of property laws, could be
allowed to create a genuine market, attracting investment.

The greatest single economic change in the Monarchy in this period was
the Act of Peasant Emancipation, passed by the Austrian Constituent
Assembly in September 1848 and subsequently extended to Hungary after
its reconquest; both governments had in any case decreed emancipation early
in 1848. Austrian peasants had to pay for their freedom from manorial dues,
as well as for the land they tilled, because the landowners were to be
partially compensated for the loss of free peasant labour. For those peasants
who could manage it, the life of a smallholder beckoned, but for the millions
who could not, a whole class of landless agricultural labourers was created.
Among the landowners, smaller landowners tended to go bankrupt and sell
out, while the big estates expanded. Research has shown that the ending of
serfdom did not, in itself, produce economic development; certainly the lot
of most peasants was not appreciably improved and for many it was
worsened. Rather, the economic growth that did characterise the period after
1850 was the result of several factors, including railway construction and
the foundation of credit banks.[10] The true impact of emancipation was that,
by giving the peasant masses their legal and physical freedom, it put in place
one of the essential preconditions for the deepening of industrialisation in
the Austrian lands and, later, in Hungary.

Prussia, by virtue of its possession of Silesia and, after 1815, the mineral-
rich Rhineland, was in a different league in the modernisation stakes. From
about 1830 industrialisation was well under way in the western provinces,

while leadership of the *Zollverein* conferred on Prussia real economic advantage over Austria, in securing it a large domestic market. The eastern provinces were profoundly agrarian, yet even here a series of reforms after 1806 changed the entire nature of the lord–peasant relationship. The reforming ministry of Baron Karl vom und zum Stein formally proclaimed all peasants free men in October 1807, and from then until 1821 a series of acts worked out the details. Landowning peasants could commute their labour dues in return for cash or the surrender of the land they farmed, and as a result of their relatively favourable circumstances most paid it in cash. Things were not so easy for the landless tenant farmers, since the compensation required was steep and beyond the means of most in this category. The result was a gradual flight from the land in their case, even though the effect of the reforms was on the whole 'quite favourable for the majority of peasants'.[11]

The Prussian Junkers did well out of the abolition of serfdom, since the majority received compensation for the loss of labour dues. In addition, noble estate owners were able to buy up the plots of emancipated peasants who found they could not make ends meet. The result was that the big estates got bigger and because of this could start making the transition to industrial agriculture. Prussia's agricultural revolution, which began to take effect from about 1850 because of technological improvements, was another ingredient in its economic supremacy, but in the process it also consolidated the social, economic and political power of the Prussian landowning class.

Economic development in the *Ottoman Balkans* fell into two distinct compartments. In the newly autonomous or independent Balkan states, political self-rule did not make for economic advance; on the contrary, these societies can be said to have regressed in this period. In parts of those Balkan provinces which remained under direct Ottoman rule, by contrast, something like an economic rebirth took place. The Balkans as a sub-region undoubtedly remained an economic backwater throughout the nineteenth century. Population density overall remained low. Between 1790 and 1910 the population grew by only 0.97 per cent per year and much of the peninsula was desolate or under-cultivated, with a transport system ranging 'from the bad to the non-existent'. As a consequence of the poor infrastructure, agriculture was largely on a subsistence level, supplemented by extensive livestock raising.[12]

Balkan nation-states thus inherited a dismal economic legacy and found themselves unable to achieve much in the way of development, even where they were minded to do so. In addition, both Serbia and Greece started life at the end of savage and destructive insurrections against the Ottomans, and in all the Balkan states the expulsion or gradual expropriation of the Muslim landowners and urban community caused further economic dislocation. In the Romanian principalities most formerly Muslim-owned land was snapped up by the native *boyar* landowners; elsewhere it was at the disposal of the rulers of peasant societies with no native nobility.

Serbia's government thus created a class of peasant smallholders which remained a feature of Serbian society into the twentieth century. This was not, however, a recipe for modernisation: Serbian peasants remained inefficient, subsistence farmers, which meant the government's tax revenue remained low. Serbia became in some respects more backward in the course of the century, and by the end of the 1860s a period of not just political but economic dependency on the neighbouring Habsburg Monarchy was all too predictable.

Greece's experience was similar. Widespread devastation and disorder followed the Ottoman withdrawal at the end of the 1820s and the new government struggled for decades to impose control on a fractious and lawless population. The question of land tenure was especially chaotic. The result, as in Serbia, was a nation of miserably poor smallholders. As with Serbia, this made Greece the plaything of the great powers.

The Romanian principalities were entitled, under the terms of the 1829 Treaty of Adrianople, to expel all Ottoman subjects. *Boyars* received legal title to their land, but the peasants who farmed these estates had no such rights and in fact saw their labour service increased. The era as a whole was a profitable one for the landowner class, while the condition of the peasantry clearly worsened.

The bane of Ottoman rule in the Balkans, and ultimately the reason for Christian revolt, was the breakdown of central control in the late eighteenth century. In the Bulgarian provinces this chaos came to an end with the crushing of janissary power by Mahmud II in 1826. The Ottoman government repossessed lands held by janissaries, which increased revenue, but in addition the restoration of order led to a revival of trade and economic activity.

Much of this economic activity was led by the Christian population, yet the latter traditionally occupied an inferior status in courts of law in any dispute involving Muslims. The need to safeguard this Christian wealth generation therefore put pressure on the government to regularise the position of Christians. The imperial rescript of Gülhane, of November 1839, promised legal equality between Christians and Muslims. Well before this it was apparent that what Michael Palairet describes as 'proto-industry' was taking root in the Bulgarian-inhabited uplands.[13] Here the rural population had turned their hands to cottage industry, and after 1826 the restoration of order meant that these Bulgarian manufactures could reach the Ottoman domestic market again. The result was a considerable manufacturing industry, which compared favourably with the progressive immiseration of the independent nation-states of the Balkans.

In terms of economic and social development *Russia* brought up the rear, even in comparison with the Ottoman Balkans. Russia in the early nineteenth century was by no means economically stagnant, yet it was evidently backward and getting more so. The Empire's trade with Western Europe went up significantly in this period and some of this was due to improvements in infrastructure, notably canals in the Baltic region, the arrival of steam naviga-tion on the river system in the 1830s and the first railways from 1837.[14] Yet in this all-important indicator of economic modernisation Russia was woefully slow: by 1855 there were still only 1060 kilometres of track in the entire Empire.[15] The imperial finance minister from 1823 to 1844 was opposed to railways as leading to 'unnecessary travelling'.[16] During the Crimean War, it took Russian troops longer to reach the theatre of conflict than it did the French and the British because there was no rail link between northern Russia and the Black Sea.

Manufacturing, largely in textiles, continued to grow and the urban population doubled between 1811 and 1863, although at 10 per cent of the total population its proportion was tiny. The population, like the manufac-turing, was concentrated in the big cities; Warsaw and Lódź, in Russian Poland, were significant centres for textiles and metal working by the 1860s. None of this economic growth, however, owed much to government policy; rather, it derived mainly from the expansion of Russian agriculture, which in turn was finding a growing market, for grain especially, in industrialis-ing Western Europe.[17]

The most obvious factor perpetuating Russian backwardness was its overwhelmingly agrarian, serf-based agriculture. Long before the Crimean conflict showed up Russia's disastrous lack of modernity, it was generally agreed that, in the words of the Westerniser B.N. Chicherin, 'serfdom is a shackle which we drag around with us, and which holds us back just when other peoples are racing ahead unimpeded'.[18]

Alexander II (1855–81) finally acted to remedy this situation with the issue of the Edict of Emancipation of 1861. As in the rest of Eastern Europe, emancipation was a legal measure, not an act of social welfare. The peasants were legally freed from bondage and in theory guaranteed land. Few peasants could afford to buy, or keep, the land they had previously tilled; instead the government favoured corralling them into village communes or *mirs*, where they were obliged to remain as long as they still owed their former landlords compensation and in conditions which Geoffrey Hosking has called 'a form of social (though not racial) apartheid'.[19] The rural popula-tion continued to rise and increasing sub-division of the *mirs* put yet more pressure on the land and lowered productivity. Nor was there any dramatic increase in the labour available for industry, which in any case was hardly sizeable enough to soak up this surplus population. All that can be said is that more peasants were, potentially, free to leave the land if they could find the wherewithal to escape, but in the succeeding period this all too often took the form of emigration.[20] As a consequence Russian society remained one of extraordinary tensions and economic backwardness, conditions bound to exacerbate the discontent of not just Russians but also the large number of non-Russians in the population.

9

THE HABSBURG MONARCHY FROM ENLIGHTENED ABSOLUTISM TO THE *AUSGLEICH*

The Habsburg Monarchy, as personified by the Emperor Francis after 1792, might be said to have opted for unenlightened absolutism as a system of government.[1] The Monarchy's victory over Napoleon confirmed this preference for immobility, yet in the next half-century, the Habsburgs found that economic and social change, no less than liberalism and nationalism, forced movement upon them. Since the Monarchy attached great importance to maintaining its position as a great power, its failure to modernise mattered, as did its inability to accommodate the strains of being a multinational state.

The unimaginative conservatism of Metternich proved self-defeating, as the revolutions of 1848 showed. Equally futile was the Monarchy's experiment in neo-absolutism in the decade after 1848. Driven by domestic unrest and external defeat, the Emperor Francis Joseph cut his losses in 1867 and concluded a deal with his most obstreperous nationality, the Hungarians. This might have bought time, but by ignoring the claims of the Monarchy's other peoples it stored up trouble for the future.

UNENLIGHTENED ABSOLUTISM 1804-48

Francis I was an upright but unenquiring and stubborn personality. Committed to combating the principles of the French Revolution, his resistance to innovation of any sort was intransigent and lifelong. 'I want no change,' he told one of his ministers in 1831, the year of a disquieting peasant uprising in Hungary. 'This is no time for reform.'[2]

This ostrich-like conservatism was impracticable. Francis reigned over a population of which an increasing proportion was literate. The rational approach to government and economic management stimulated by the Enlightenment could not be banished, and indeed survived in the minds of many of Francis's own officials. Nationalism was a contagion which, once propagated in one people, had a habit of spreading to others. And although Francis would have been glad to govern without reference to the Monarchy's historic institutions, particularly the Hungarian Diet, he repeatedly found that the Monarchy's weakness, as a state, made this untenable.

Some of the confusions inherent in abandoning the modernisation project became obvious in the course of the French Revolutionary and Napoleonic wars. The Monarchy's six wars against France required, willy-nilly, the cooperation in voting taxes and recruits of the Hungarian Diet which, according to the settlement of 1791, had to be convened every three years. Combating the appeal of French revolutionary ideas involved, logically, a supply of rival concepts, but apart from loyalty to himself as dynast Francis's sole weapon was an ever more draconian and absurd censorship: of the press and literature, of productions of Shakespeare's *Hamlet* for depicting regicide, of the images on fans and snuff boxes, and so on. By the war of 1809, some of the emperor's advisers were convinced that fire had to be fought with fire and an attempt was made to whip up patriotic sentiment against the French invaders. There was, however, an inevitable conundrum in this, for these appeals were couched largely by Austrian Germans in terms of joining a 'national' movement of other Germans, and their allure for the Monarchy's non-Germans was conjectural at best.

Francis's right-hand man after 1809, Metternich, owed his office solely to the emperor's confidence and thus was never the all-powerful minister of legend. Rather, Metternich was trusted by Francis precisely because he too abhorred the prospect of change and believed in constant vigilance against liberal and nationalist ideas. As foreign minister Metternich enjoyed a free hand; in domestic affairs he played a more ambiguous role. He was state chancellor after 1824, but this was a largely honorific post which gave him no authority over the amorphous government structure favoured by Francis, who preferred to keep his ministers independent of each other. There was nothing like a collective government; instead all decisions were referred directly to Francis, who was notoriously averse to making decisions. Metternich had a rival for the emperor's ear in Count Franz Anton von Kolowrat-Liebsteinsky, responsible for internal affairs from 1826 and finance from 1827. Kolowrat and Metternich were so jealous of each other's influence that they effectively cancelled each other out.

When Francis died in 1835 and his amiable but mentally subnormal son Ferdinand became emperor, a sort of regency, the State Conference (*Staatskonferenz*), was established, chaired theoretically by Ferdinand but in practice by his uncle, Archduke Ludwig, and consisting otherwise of Archduke Franz Karl, Metternich and Kolowrat. This arrangement was virtually a guarantee that government would take no steps that were not positively forced on it. 'Drift' seems too mobile a term with which to characterise the policy of such a regime.

The one area where Metternich exercised a real, even fateful influence in domestic policy was in his control of the police system and censorship. It was Metternich's determined attempts to stifle debate and new ideas that made the Monarchy such a byword for costive repression. The censorship was irritating but on the whole ineffective in preventing the influx of new publications and ideas. Recent studies demonstrate conclusively that Metternichian Austria hardly deserves the epithet 'police state'. The gravest charge against the regime was that it sought to inhibit change but was too weak to do so competently.[3]

This resistance to modernity might not have mattered, had the Monarchy not been so clearly paying the penalty for postponing a controlled adaptation. The Monarchy's pretensions as a great power were constantly undermined by its financial weakness. Budgetary constraints were such that the effective strength of the army was never more than 230,000 men. This led to a 'catastrophic decline' in Austrian influence in the 1820s.[4] Metternich's inability to oppose much of the international upheaval of the period was ultimately due to the government's failure to harness the Monarchy's real economic potential.

Despite clear signs of economic growth, the social stresses attendant upon a rising population, changing methods of industrial production and an inherently inefficient agricultural base were becoming greater by the year. This was despite the fact that a growing section of noble opinion, as typified by Széchenyi in Hungary, perceived the need for some resolution of the agrarian question that did not involve social upheaval. At the same time, the marginalised artisan class was beginning to experience the worst effects of unbridled capitalism: undercut by the cheapness and ubiquity of the new industrialism, this group found itself driven into the ranks of the unskilled labourers. The simmering restlessness of peasants whose folk memory dwelt fondly on the promises of liberation held out, briefly, by Joseph II, and the hatred of the artisans for a system which could not protect them against boom-and-bust, were potent sources of revolution by the time the harvests failed in 1846 and 1847. Peasant unrest in Hungary in 1831, but even more the murderous rage of peasants against their lords in Galicia in 1846, convinced many of the possessing classes that they were sitting atop a social volcano.

Politically the Monarchy seemed on the surface quiescent, largely because Francis, and after him the State Conference, governed almost entirely without reference to the Diets of the Austrian and Bohemian crownlands and Galicia, ruled the Italian provinces directly from Vienna and consulted the Hungarian Diet only when they had to. In the non-Hungarian lands there was little enough evidence of a demand for constitutional government as such, merely a weariness of the censorship and a growing sense that economic and legal reform was long overdue. In Hungary, although Francis avoided convening the Diet from 1813 to 1825, the discontent this bred at such flouting of the Hungarian constitution proved too costly to ignore. Hungarian nobles and county assemblies had an awkward habit of refusing to vote taxes and recruits if the Diet were sidelined, and from 1825 a succession of Diets gave voice to an increasing debate about how to redress the kingdom's problems.

THE RISE OF NATIONALITY

Within this framework of near-absolutism in the 'Austrian' lands, and an undoubted political space in Hungary, the most prominent feature of the political landscape in this period was the spread of national consciousness and an increasing conflict of national interests. The implications for specific parts of the Monarchy are worth examining.

In the *Bohemian crownlands* of Bohemia, Moravia and Silesia, but especially in Bohemia itself, the relationship between Germans and Czechs was becoming tense by the 1840s. This was despite a lingering sense on the part of some aristocrats, public figures and intellectuals that there was something to be said for a Bohemian identity which accepted the coexistence of both ethnic groups but still saw value in a shared *Landespatriotismus* or provincial patriotism. As one noble of German descent put it as late as 1845, 'I am neither a Czech nor a German, but only a Bohemian.'[5] While most Germans assumed that Bohemia was essentially a German land because of the supposed superiority of German culture, which was bound to assimilate the culturally 'weaker' Czechs, a minority dissented. Some, like the Catholic professor of religious philosophy Bernard Bolzano, argued that Germans and Czechs would ultimately merge into a new, common identity, but in the meantime urged each people to learn the other's language.[6]

Given the prevailing German disdain for the mere idea of the Czechs as a people of culture, however, it was hardly surprising that by the early nineteenth century a new generation of Czechs had emerged, committed to a more aggressive assertion of nationality. Typical of this new hard line was Josef Jungmann, who argued that, because of the language division, it was unrealistic to hope for a merger of the two peoples. Jungmann practised what he preached: as a secondary school teacher he was the first to offer instruction in the Czech language at this level, teaching several generations to appreciate their language more and to see the language of the peasant as the truly national language. In addition to writing the first *History of Czech Literature* (1825) and compiling a Czech–German dictionary, Jungmann translated many foreign authors into Czech, thereby demonstrating its flexibility of expression. For this new generation of Czech 'awakeners' the old *Landespatriotismus* was clearly inadequate, especially since it failed to address the question of which nation, Czech or German, should predominate.

The historian František Palacký was, after Jungmann, the most influential of the Czech nationalists. Appointed the official historian of the Bohemian Diet in 1829, Palacký edited the first Czech-language version of the journal of the National Museum. With the enthusiastic assistance of fellow awakeners, Palacký turned the scholarly activity of the National Museum into a vehicle for promoting the Czech language, publishing an increasing number of works in Czech and waging a sort of genteel culture war against what he saw as the undue hegemony of German. The cultural organisation *Matice česká*, founded in 1831, existed expressly to publish works by Czechs, in Czech.[7] Palacký's *History of the Czech Nation in Bohemia and Moravia* may have been originally published in German, in 1836–42, as a simple *History of Bohemia*, but there was no denying the combative nature of its message that the Czech people were every bit as historical, if not more so, than the German.

In *Galicia*, the greatest national awareness before 1848 was demonstrated by Polish nobles, but towards the end of this period a rival Ruthene, or Ukrainian, nationalism appeared. Polish nationalism was still largely gentry-based, nor could it contemplate the admission that Galicia was anything other than a 'Polish' land. In fact, of a population estimated in 1817 at 3.5 million, 47.5 per cent were Poles, 45.5 per cent Ruthenes, with 6 per cent Jews and 1 per cent Germans; Poles predominated in the western part of the province, Ruthenes in the eastern part.[8]

The relationship between Polish nobles and their serfs, whether Poles or Ruthenes, was complicated by annexation to the Monarchy. Josephinian taxation fell most heavily on the peasants and arguably worsened their condition. Yet implementation of new legislation in the countryside, especially taxation, had necessarily to be entrusted to the noble landowners, so the result of Joseph's reforms was to sharpen the hatred felt by peasants for the nobles rather than for the imperial government.

The Habsburg authorities regarded the Polish gentry, with some justice, as inherently subversive. The real centre of Polish nationalist ferment in this period, however, was the formally independent Republic of Kraków, a postage-stamp territory of 1164 square kilometres with a population, by 1827, of 127,000. Although Kraków was under the 'protection' of the partitioning powers and thus subject to occasional intervention, it nevertheless became a beacon for Polish nationalists, not least because the modest prosperity it enjoyed, and even more the existence of its ancient university, which drew students from all three Partitions, maintained a sizeable urban middle class of merchants, professionals and intellectuals.

Galicia and Kraków were thoroughly unsettled by the revolt of 1830–1 in Russian Poland. With the revolt crushed, large numbers of refugees settled in Galicia and the Republic of Kraków. The latter, together with the even greater Polish diaspora in Paris, became one of the centres of conspiratorial activity aimed at winning Polish independence. All Polish nationalist factions, however, still drew most of their support from the same narrow, noble social base, a factor which was to have terrible consequences in 1846.

In the meantime another complication had arisen with the development of a Ruthene national consciousness. The Ruthenes of Galicia were an excellent example of the revolutionary impact achieved by the reforms of Maria Theresa and Joseph II, and of how difficult it was to undo such changes. For the first time, Ruthenian children were being educated in their own language, albeit to begin with the liturgical book language derived from Old Church Slavonic and known as 'Slaveno-Rusyn'. The result was that by the 1820s the first generation of Ruthenian intellectuals was becoming active, even if, as is characteristic of this sort of development, much of their work initially was in recognised literary languages like Latin, German or Polish.

An increasing number of educated Ruthenes, however, was sufficiently moved by their contacts with fellow Slavs to interest themselves in their own language. The so-called 'Ruthenian Triad' of young seminarists led by the poet Markiian Shashkevych deliberately rejected the Latin alphabet as a written medium for Ukrainian, preferring a Cyrillic alphabet; more importantly, they also used the vernacular, rather than 'Slaveno-Rusyn', for their works. Shashkevych and his friends published in 1837 *Rusalka Dnistrovaia* (The Nymph of the Dniester), an almanac of folk songs and original poems; this was the first work ever published in modern Ukrainian. The reaction of the imperial authorities in Galicia to the book was revealing: 'We already have enough trouble with one nationality [the Poles], and these madmen want to resurrect the dead-and-buried Ruthenian nationality!'[9] The reaction of Polish Galician patriots was no less dismissive. Clearly there was a growing sense, on both sides, of opposing interests.

Polish noble nationalism received its death blow with the failure of the Galician revolt of 1846, which exposed the abyss between nobles and peasants. The decision was taken in Paris to stage yet another uprising in all three Partitions; it was hoped to avoid the disaster of 1830–1 by calling on the peasants for support, promising them emancipation. The peasantry of West Galicia, however, saw their landlords only as oppressors; they were certainly not susceptible to the blandishments of nationalism. Scheduled to start in February 1846, the conspiracy was betrayed to the Prussian authorities and the ringleaders in the Prussian and Russian Partitions promptly rounded up. Only in Kraków and Galicia was an insurrection proclaimed and an appeal issued to the countryside for support. The response horrified everyone. Encouraged by the Habsburg authorities to defend the existing order, the Polish peasants of West Galicia turned on their noble landowners, massacring some 2000. The memory of peasant carts heaped with noble corpses being dragged into the nearest town was the main reason the Poles remained relatively quiet during the revolutions of 1848.

Finally, nationality problems were becoming undeniable in the Kingdom of *Hungary*. Here the focus was initially on the demands of the Hungarian nobility for a regularisation of the kingdom's relationship with the crown. From 1825 a succession of Diets provided a forum for Hungary's fledgling liberal reform movement. The Diets also saw the articulation of a growing sense of Hungarian nationalist purpose, which in turn elicited a response from the non-Magyar minorities of the kingdom. In so far as there can be said to be a 'first generation' of Hungarian reformers after 1825, Széchenyi was its undoubted leader. Yet Széchenyi's audience was almost invariably his fellow magnates. Though typical of his peers in his essential conservatism and loyalty to the Habsburg dynasty, Széchenyi was however thoroughly atypical in the breadth and genius of his vision for levering Hungary out of its humiliating backwardness. The essence of this vision was that Hungary must achieve economic modernisation fast by opening the country to foreign capital and investment; only after this might political liberalisation be conceivable. Széchenyi insisted that this influx of capital would be possible only if the nobility accepted taxation. He was not an overt nationalist and because of his conservatism this high-minded thinker was thus increasingly outflanked and sidelined by a younger generation of reformers, for whom political liberalisation but also the nation were all-important.

This new generation was becoming more vocal by the early 1830s and one of the keys to understanding them is to grasp that most of the younger opposition came from the ranks of the gentry rather than the magnates. The gentry saw themselves as the defenders of Hungary's ancient constitution and laws. They were opponents of arbitrary government, were influenced by the new liberal ideas of the age and were more obviously nationalist than the titled aristocracy. Precisely because some of them regarded the Hungarian nation as threatened with extinction in a sea of hostile national-ities, a few could even envisage the extension, with time, of political rights to the whole nation in an ethnic sense. Unlike western liberals, however, Hungarian gentry liberals were less interested in *laissez-faire* economics and freedom from an interfering state. On the contrary, they 'wanted to strengthen rather than weaken the state', provided it was under their control, because only through state action, they reasoned, could economic development be generated and the interests of the Hungarian nation – by which they understood primarily themselves – be safeguarded.[10] Hungarian liberals, like their emerging leader, Lajos Kossuth, saw the Habsburg Mon-archy as both politically oppressive and economically exploitative.

The 'Long Diet' of 1832–6 saw an increased number of the new breed of reformers. Among the new deputies was Kossuth, who hit upon a novel way of communicating his own ideas to a larger public, by publishing handwrit-ten accounts of the parliamentary debates, the first in the country's history. These journals became an eloquent vehicle for the liberal agenda. The issue that was uppermost in liberal reformers' minds, and which contributed power-fully to the poisoning of relations with Hungary's national minorities, was the language question. The leaders of the reform generation of 1832 were obsessed with the idea that the Hungarian nation could be swamped by a sea of Slavs and Romanians. They saw language as the integrator of the state and objected to the use of Latin in the Diet and the administration as incompatible with a modern society. The Diet of 1830 had succeeded in passing a law which required applicants for positions in public service or the legal profession to speak Magyar and which confirmed the counties' right to communicate with the Hungarian Chancellery and the courts in Magyar and to be answered in that language. The 'Long Diet' saw calls for this principle to be extended and before it rose in 1836 Magyar had been made the legally binding text of all laws and the language of parish registers where it was also the language of the sermon.

Kossuth, given the priceless platform of editor of the newspaper *Pesti hírlap* (Pest Newssheet), from 1841 to 1844, continued to exert a tremendous influence, constantly inveighing against the tyranny of Vienna, the timidity of the magnates and the dangers threatening the Hungarian nation from its increasingly dissident national minorities. His liberalism, his protectionism and his nationalism found a ready echo among his fellow Magyars, some of it distinctly illiberal. The central nationalist obsessions were the reunification of Transylvania with Hungary and the language question. As Kossuth put it in an editorial of 1842, 'Magyar must become the language of public administration, whether civil or ecclesiastic, of the legislative and the executive, of the government, of justice, of public security, of the police, of direct and indirect taxation and of the economy.'[11] Only a single admonitory voice was raised. Széchenyi, to his credit, warned of the danger the new agenda posed for relations not only with the Monarchy but with Hungary's own minorities. While he supported making Magyar the official language, Széchenyi insisted that the real priority must still be modernisation and that any attempt at forcible Magyarisation would alienate non-Magyars at precisely the moment their support was most needed.

Széchenyi's intervention made him popular with non-Magyars but lost him support among his fellow Hungarians. In the end the nationalists achieved their desire in the Diet of 1843–4, when a law was passed in 1844 making Magyar the official language of government and of the Diet in Inner Hungary, excluding Croatia and Transylvania. Croatia, because of its special status within Hungary, was free to use Latin for its own internal administration, and Croatian deputies to the Hungarian Diet could continue to address it in Latin for another six years, but all communication between the Croatian and Hungarian authorities was henceforth to be in Magyar.

For the non-Magyars in Hungary the rise of Hungarian nationalism was increasingly worrying, and nowhere more so than in *Croatia*. Formally a subordinate kingdom within Hungary, Croatia had its own Diet, the *Sabor*, which also sent representatives to the Hungarian Diet. This was precisely why the language issue was of such concern and had been since the 1790s: Latin (or German) was the only effective means of communication between Hungarians and Croats, given that Croatian nobles were reluctant to learn Magyar and Hungarian nobles disdained learning Croatian. The Croatian nobility, however, had not done much to oppose Hungarian language legislation. Active protest came from only a few nobles, such as Count Janko Drašković, who in 1832 proposed that the South Slavs should be joined in a single unit within the Monarchy.

A more coordinated opposition came from Croatia's fledgling middle-class intellectuals, notably the journalist Ljudevit Gaj, who had done much to establish a Croatian literary language and was influenced by other Slav thinkers' belief that all Slavs were in reality a single nationality. Gaj was an advocate of a common 'Illyrian' identity shared by the Croats with Slovenes, Serbs and Bulgarians. The 'Illyrian movement' thus founded was arguably the beginning of modern Croatian nationalism. It was virulently anti-Hungarian and rapidly assumed political dimensions as the Illyrian Party, founded by Count Drašković in 1841. Renamed the National Party, it continued to denounce Hungarian language legislation and, especially after passage of the law of 1844, relations worsened. Some sort of clash was therefore likely even before revolution overtook both countries.

The *Serbs* of Hungary were divided between the Military Border, which stretched across the southern frontiers of Croatia–Slavonia and Hungary proper, and the region Serbs referred to as the Vojvodina. Serb demands for some form of autonomy within Hungary went back to the reign of Joseph II, but fell foul of both Hungarian intransigence and the exaggerated nature of the claim, since Serbs were not a majority in any of these regions except perhaps the area around Sremski Karlovci. The Serbs' minority status, however, was no hindrance to a lively sense of identity.

Political leadership traditionally came from the Serbian Orthodox clergy. The Church's leadership, however, was increasingly challenged by a younger, more secular generation, the product of the Josephinian educational system. By the 1840s, however, even the Church was becoming more adventurous. The synod of 1842 also called for a Serb 'National Assembly' and the Serb Patriarch himself was an advocate of making common cause with the Croats against the Hungarians.

The *Romanians* of Hungary were divided physically between the Grand Principality of Transylvania, the counties of Inner Hungary bordering the principality and the Military Border. The Romanians were also divided confessionally between the Uniate majority, predominant in Transylvania, and the Romanian Orthodox, more numerous in Inner Hungary. The vast majority of Romanians were peasants; in the towns Romanians were still outnumbered by Hungarians and Saxons.

Transylvania was administered separately from Vienna and had its own Diet. Romanians of either confession were politically unrepresented in Transylvania, since they did not constitute one of the three 'historic' nations: the Hungarians, the Szeklers and the Saxons. Their sole voice in the Diet was the Uniate bishop of Transylvania, who as a landowner held a seat. The Uniate Church was nevertheless tolerated because of its allegiance to

Rome; it qualified for state support. The Orthodox Church, by contrast, received no support at all.

As with the Serbs, political and cultural leadership until the early nineteenth century was almost entirely in the hands of the Uniate Church. By the 1830s, however, a lay, middle-class intelligentsia was beginning to take the lead, articulating a new sense of Romanian nationality which consciously sought to bridge the Uniate–Orthodox divide. The publication of histories and literature in the Romanian language gradually increased. Probably the greatest single factor in disseminating the idea of the nation was the *Gazeta de Transilvania*, the principality's first political newspaper in Romanian, which began publication in 1838 under the editorship of Gheorghe Barițiu. This not only gave a platform to Romanian intellectuals but also, despite the censorship, introduced its readership to western ideas and literature, created links between Transylvania and the Danubian principalities and raised consciousness generally.

Finally, a national consciousness had clearly emerged among the *Slovaks* by 1848 and very much in reaction to Hungarian nationalism. It was only towards the end of the eighteenth century that individual scholars like Bernolák identified Slovak as a distinct language, and for some decades both Czechs and Slovaks were capable of arguing that Slovaks were merely a subordinate element in a single, 'Czechoslovak' nationality. By the 1830s, however, there was a small elite of nationalist intellectuals, even if the peasant mass of the population remained indifferent.

The succeeding generation, galled by the language law of 1840 and the active discrimination against Slovak cultural activities, was even more vocal. L'udovít Štúr, a teacher at the Slovak secondary school at Pressburg, led a circle of nationalist zealots who celebrated the Slovaks' ties to other Slavs but also increasingly stressed the individuality of Slovak language and identity. In 1842 Štúr and 200 other Slovak pastors addressed a petition to the Emperor Ferdinand, complaining about the new law and requesting a chair for the study of Slovak at Pressburg. The mere fact that the Slovaks had taken their case to Vienna, however, enraged the Hungarian nationalists. Kossuth denounced the petitioners, deriding the very idea of a Slovak nation: 'Wherever we look in Hungary, nowhere do we see the substance of any Slovak [*tót*] nationality.'[12] Štúr was forced out of his teaching post in 1844 as a dangerous 'Pan-Slavist', but discovered an alternative vocation as the editor of one of the first Slovak-language newspapers. He also produced a grammar in 1846 which did much to popularise the central Slovakian dialect and hence bridge the gap between Protestant and Catholic Slovaks.

The elections to the Diet of 1847 took place in an atmosphere of tremendous excitement. The Hungarian liberal opposition, Kossuth to the fore, was convinced that the time had come for radical reform: constitutional government, a bill of rights, the reunion of Transylvania with Hungary, and much else. Looming over everyone was the grim lesson of the Galician revolt:

something must be done to defuse the social timebomb ticking in the countryside. Yet there was one gap in the agenda: 'Only the nationality question was left unmentioned and this for the simple reason that, in the eyes of the liberals, the nationality question did not exist.'[13] They were soon to be undeceived.

REVOLUTIONS AND REACTION 1848-9

The year of revolutions that overtook the Habsburg Monarchy in 1848–9 can appear bewildering, given the multiplicity and complexity of events in all corners of the realm. Although some sort of storm was expected, the revolutions caught many contemporaries off guard, including the imperial government, and the rapidity with which events unfolded had much to do with the regime's loss of nerve and momentary collapse. Yet the success of the revolutions was illusory. Not only were the forces for change weaker than they seemed, but once the individuals in charge of the Monarchy recovered their nerve, or were replaced by more determined personalities, the reimposition of order, however arduous, was relatively straightforward. The fact that the Monarchy weathered this crisis enabled it to survive another 69 years.

The events themselves are easiest to comprehend if seen, geographically, in four main compartments. There was a revolution in the imperial capital, Vienna, which toppled the Metternich regime and went through several phases before being extinguished in October 1848, while the constitutional 'spin-off' from this continued into the next year. There was a revolution in Hungary, in that a genuinely autonomous Hungarian government, within the Empire, was created; this Hungarian revolution however subsumed a variety of revolts against the new Hungarian government and led to a war between Hungary on the one side and the imperial government and the non-Magyar nationalities on the other. There was a revolution of sorts in Bohemia, or to be more precise in Prague, which saw a brief but ultimately self-defeating tug-of-war between Czechs and Germans over what sort of country Bohemia was, and who should run it, before this interesting episode was brought to an end by the imposition of martial law. And there were revolutions, or rather revolts, against Habsburg rule in the north Italian provinces of Lombardy and Venetia, which tempted the neighbouring Kingdom of Piedmont to invade the Monarchy not just once but twice.

There were different types of revolution. Some disturbances had socio-economic causes such as the agrarian problem and the strains occasioned by the beginnings of industrialisation. All four main areas of revolution had obvious political origins or soon developed political foci such as demands for constitutional government or even independence. And all revolutions except the Viennese were to a greater or lesser extent nationalist in nature, in that the demands for change were inextricably bound up with the national aspirations of one people, which in many cases provoked the nationalism of other peoples.

The Monarchy was inescapably affected by revolutionary events in the rest of Europe, but especially the German Confederation and the rest of the Italian Peninsula. Not only did the convening of a German National Assembly at Frankfurt and the debate on the possible unification of all Germans in one state have implications for the Austrian Germans and the very existence of the multinational Monarchy, but retrieving the Monarchy's position in both Germany and Italy was crucial to its survival as a great power.

A succession of poor harvests, in 1846 and 1847, drove food prices upward; inflation in turn forced government to raise consumer taxes, which fell with especial harshness on the poor in both countryside and town. The economic recession afflicting most of Europe in the late 1840s meant that urban factories were laying off workers instead of hiring more. The government's financial problems forced the decision to call a meeting of the Estates or Diet of Lower Austria for 13 March 1848. It was in this situation that the news arrived in Vienna, on 29 February, of a revolution in Paris the week before.

The initial gains of the revolutions were spectacular, in part because of the domino effect produced by news of revolutions elsewhere. In Vienna there was a run on the banks and a general heightening of economic uncertainty because it was suspected, quite rightly, that Metternich intended going to war, if he could find the allies, to nullify the French Revolution. In Pressburg, where the Hungarian Diet was in session, Kossuth in a speech on 3 March demanded the creation of an autonomous Hungarian government, responsible to the Diet, as well as the emancipation of the peasantry, the taxation of nobles and the limited extension of the suffrage among the urban middle class and the better-off peasantry. Crucially, Kossuth also demanded a proper constitution for the non-Hungarian lands of the Monarchy, as a safeguard against further interference by Vienna in Hungary's traditional liberties. Kossuth's speech was being distributed on the streets of Vienna within days and caused intense excitement. By the time the Estates of Lower Austria convened, its deputies found themselves besieged by thousands of students from the University of Vienna, who invaded the proceedings and forced a delegation to carry a petition to the imperial palace, echoing the Hungarian demands and calling for Metternich's dismissal. When the troops guarding the imperial palace fired on the crowd, killing 45 people, mayhem ensued. Artisans from the suburbs joined the students and started burning the factories, which they saw as the cause of their destitution. The imperial family, intimidated by the violence, rejected Metternich's advice to use brute force to suppress the disturbances and instead sacked him. On 15 March, in response to continuing unrest, the emperor issued a rescript promising to convene an imperial Diet or *Reichstag* for the purpose of drafting a constitution for the non-Hungarian 'half' of the Monarchy. At the same time the citizens of Vienna were granted permission to form a National Guard and

Only in Croatia, whose separate status within Hungary was acknowledged even by Hungarian nationalists, did the Hungarian government from the start promise to respect Croatian rights. Yet it was precisely in Croatia that nationalist opposition to Hungary was most obdurate and where a common interest with elements of the court and the imperial government first emerged. Croatia's own revolution occurred in March, when a 'National Congress' dominated by the Illyrian Party assembled in Zagreb. This National Congress announced the abolition of serfdom and demanded the reincorporation of the Military Border into Croatia–Slavonia, formal autonomy comparable to Hungary's and even the right of Croatia to conduct its own 'foreign affairs'. In the meantime, in an attempt to retain some form of conservative control over Croatia, the Vienna government appointed Colonel Josip Jelačić as *Ban* (governor) of Croatia. This was a fateful appointment, since Jelačić, although no Illyrian, was a fierce Croatian nationalist, not only loyal to the Habsburgs but also animated by an abiding hatred of Hungary. His popularity enabled Jelačić to assume command of the Border Guard regiments and whip up hostility to Hungary, and it is clear that some imperial officials at least encouraged him.

In these circumstances the Batthyány government, which was in any case dominated by the ultra-nationalist Kossuth, could probably do nothing right. Certainly its reaction to Jelačić's open defiance of Hungarian authority was unequivocal. The Hungarians banned any elections for a new *Sabor*; Jelačić held the elections on 5 June, and the *Sabor* when it met promptly handed over supreme power to him. Despite Batthyány's attempts throughout the summer to resolve the situation, Jelačić continued to defy the Hungarians and to gather troops with an obviously belligerent intent.

By 5 July it was clear that in addition to the spread of conflict with the nationalists, relations with the imperial government were breaking down. At the heart of the rift was the unresolved paradox of the April Laws and what Hungarian autonomy meant in practice. Already Hungary had spurned a plea from Vienna that it shoulder a quarter of the interest on the state debt and, even more alarmingly, started creating a national militia or *honvéd*, as well as appealing to soldiers of imperial regiments to join this new Hungarian army. On the issue that mattered most to the imperial government, Italy, the Diet in effect refused to send troops there. The court, in response, accused the Hungarians on 31 August of violating the Pragmatic Sanction of 1723, in other words of destroying the unity of the Monarchy itself.

Matters were tipped over the edge by Jelačić, who invaded Hungary on 11 September with an army of 40,000 men. With the Batthyány cabinet breaking up under the strain, the Hungarian Diet voted to create a National Defence Committee, comprising Kossuth and five others. Jelačić was met by forces loyal to the Hungarian government and defeated and driven back towards Vienna. In the interval a loyalist Hungarian general, sent by the court to reimpose control over Hungary, was attacked and murdered by an angry mob. In despair, Batthyány and other moderates resigned on 1 October, leaving Kossuth in charge as president of the National Defence Committee and symbol of national resistance.

The news of the war with Hungary, and more particularly of Jelačić's defeat, sparked the final flare-up of revolution in Vienna. When the capital's garrison was ordered to march to Jelačić's assistance, the students and artisans rose in revolt, physically attempting to prevent the troops' departure. The imperial war minister was murdered and the government fled to Olmütz in Moravia, while the *Reichstag* relocated to the nearby town of Kremsier. Windisch-Graetz, with the enthusiastic assistance of Jelačić, stormed Vienna on 31 October with considerable brutality. The Viennese revolution was over.

Windisch-Graetz, *de facto* ruler of Austria but the ultimate loyalist, proposed his brother-in-law Prince Felix Schwarzenberg to the imperial family as minister-president and the best man to regain control of the Monarchy. Schwarzenberg was a conservative anxious to resume the modernisation of the Empire and not averse to using the ideals and talents of the new breed of constitutional liberals to this end. He was also determined to restore the centralised structure attempted by Joseph II, as the precondition of maintaining the Monarchy's position as a great power.

In a final signal of the Monarchy's renewed sense of purpose, the monarch himself was changed. The weak-minded Ferdinand was persuaded by his family, Windisch-Graetz and Schwarzenberg to abdicate on 2 December in favour of his 18-year-old nephew Francis Joseph. The latter was the ideal instrument for this project: uncompromised by his uncle's pledges to the forces of revolution, Francis Joseph was himself a conscientious, stubborn and ultimately unimaginative conservative who believed in his mission to rule and accepted wholeheartedly Schwarzenberg's precepts on the need to so with as little reference as possible to popular institutions.

The first priority of this new team was to subdue Hungary, a task easier said than done. Throughout the autumn a vicious guerrilla war raged in southern Hungary and especially Transylvania, where the Romanians, both Orthodox and Uniate, the Saxons and imperial forces made common cause against the Hungarian authorities. The Hungarian government was forced to relocate to Debrecen and Buda-Pest fell to Windisch-Graetz in January 1849. The Hungarians made a final rebound, driving the imperial forces out of the country and retaking Buda-Pest in May. By this point, however, the political tide had turned against the Hungarians.

Schwarzenberg on taking office had left the Kremsier *Reichstag* in session, hopefully working on a draft constitution, in part to convince public opinion that the Monarchy was an acceptable leader of the German Confederation. The draft completed by Kremsier in March 1849 was arguably one of the Monarchy's great missed opportunities. Although it scrupulously avoided making provision for either Hungary or Lombardy–Venetia, its proposals for the rest of the Monarchy constitute one of the first attempts in history specifically to address the problems of running a multinational state. Ministers were to be responsible to parliament as well as to the monarch. Only in foreign affairs would the crown retain virtually unfettered control. With regard to nationality, the constitution announced, 'All peoples of the Empire are equal in rights. Each people has an inviolable right to preserve its nationality in general and its language in particular.'[18] This included equal rights to the use of one's language in local matters such as education, public administration and the courts. The bicameral legislature provided for a directly elected lower house on a fairly wide franchise and, most innovatively, for an upper house representing each province, and the 'circles' or districts within those provinces, on what was in effect an ethnic basis.

The Kremsier constitution was never adopted, largely it seems because its first draft, later withdrawn, also insisted on the principle of popular sovereignty, which neither Francis Joseph nor Schwarzenberg would accept. Instead, the *Reichstag* was dissolved on 4 March, at which point interior minister Count Franz Stadion issued an alternative constitution which made clear the new regime's centralising drive. The Stadion constitution guaranteed civil liberties and self-government at municipal level and reiterated the principle of the equality of nationalities. In other respects it concentrated power far more obviously in the hands of the monarch. Ministers were responsible to the crown alone and not to the *Reichstag*. Hungary was reduced to a relatively small province, in a position of parity with all other territories of the Monarchy.

Stadion's constitution was never formally implemented, ostensibly on the ground that control over Hungary was not yet re-established. In Hungary, however, the damage was done and in response to this proposed centralisation Kossuth's government on 14 April deposed Francis Joseph and five days later defiantly proclaimed Hungary's independence. Hungarian independence was nevertheless an illusion. Not only was no great power willing to intervene on Hungary's behalf, but on the contrary Russia's Nicholas I was increasingly anxious to help the Habsburgs suppress this hearth of revolution on his doorstep. The additional pressure put on the Hungarian war effort by Russia's 200,000-man invasion helped tip the balance. Despite desperate appeals by Kossuth's agents abroad for intervention, numbers prevailed. The Hungarian army capitulated to the Russians at Világos on 13 August, while Kossuth and a host of others fled into exile.

FROM NEO-ABSOLUTISM TO DUALISM 1849–67

For the next ten years Francis Joseph and a succession of ministers attempted to govern the Monarchy along 'neo-absolutist' lines. The Stadion constitution was theoretically the legal basis of government, but as the months passed it became obvious that the young emperor himself was disinclined to abide by any constitution. The whole point of neo-absolutism was to preserve the Monarchy's position as a great power and for this purpose, it was reasoned, the monarch had to have at his disposal a completely centralised, unconditionally subordinate, modern state machinery. Every corner of the Monarchy must be brought under the direct supervision of an expanded bureaucracy controlled from Vienna, and preferably with German as its administrative language.

The neo-absolutist regime is sometimes referred to as the 'Bach system', after Alexander Bach, who took over from Stadion as interior minister in 1849. Bach was an 1848 liberal, but he was also an Austrian German patriot committed to the preservation of the Monarchy and hence to the maintenance of order and efficient administration. It was Bach who implemented the centralising goals of neo-absolutism with an army of bureaucrats, many of them Germans, but an increasing number bilingual Czechs. The government also, inevitably, reimposed a strict and pettifogging censorship and disposed of an equally large number of police informants.

From 1849 until the end of 1851 Francis Joseph appears to have been content to rule the Monarchy by administrative decree. Finally, at the end of 1851, Francis Joseph abolished the Stadion constitution outright. This made explicit the intention of governing absolutely in future: all representative institutions, whether *Reichstag* or Diet or local assembly, were abolished; the principle of equality of nationalities and languages was set aside; and Austrian law would henceforth apply throughout the Monarchy, including Hungary. The latter was divided into five administrative units, the county system sidelined and German made the language of state. No one nationality, however, was favoured, despite the support non-Magyar nationalities had given the Monarchy in 1848–9; as one Hungarian put it, non-Magyars received as reward what Hungarians got as punishment. After 1852, when Schwarzenberg died unexpectedly, Francis Joseph dispensed even with a minister-president; henceforth he alone coordinated the work of his ministers.

This was centralisation with a vengeance; the question was, would it work? One of the ironies of the neo-absolutist period is that, although it was ultimately a self-defeating failure, the regime, freed for the moment from the tiresome necessity of consulting local sensibilities, did much economically to haul the Monarchy into the nineteenth century. The foundations of this economic development were laid earlier; nor was peasant emancipation as decisive a factor as previously thought. There was certainly no great jump in agricultural productivity after 1853, when the commutation of labour services began in earnest. In most of the 'Austrian' half of the Monarchy emancipation may even have retarded economic efficiency by creating a larger class of struggling peasant proprietors; in Galicia and Hungary the effect was to drive many peasants off the land entirely or into an expanding class of immiserated landless agricultural labourers.

Nevertheless the period of neo-absolutism undoubtedly saw the continuation and intensification of economic growth. Such reforms as the abolition of the customs barrier between 'Austria' and Hungary in 1851, a uniform currency, credit institutions and above all the creation of a modern infrastructure of railways, roads and canals all contributed to the establishment of a native manufacturing base, with the predictable knock-on effect of generating further growth.

Politically, however, neo-absolutism was a resounding failure. The reason, paradoxically, was precisely the preoccupation of the regime with maintaining its great-power position, which in the eyes of the monarch and his advisers justified neo-absolutism in the first place. From a still fundamentally weak economic base, the Monarchy was trying to project its power too far and exceeding its resources. Revenue simply failed to keep pace with the costs of being a great power, such as keeping the army mobilised during the Crimean War as a means of putting pressure on Russia, or fighting the Italian War of 1859. By 1859, 40 per cent of the government's income was devoted to servicing the interest on the state debt.[19] Just as crippling was the cost of maintaining thousands of troops in Hungary, in peacetime as well as wartime, for fear of an uprising. So it was neo-absolutism itself which, by making it impossible to muster the necessary resources, vitiated the Monarchy's ability to prosecute an aggressive foreign policy or even to hold on to its existing territory.

The war of 1859 was the breaking point for neo-absolutism. After this defeat and the loss of Lombardy, the Monarchy's richest province, the refusal of the Viennese and foreign banks to continue lending to such a shambolic regime made some form of domestic reorganisation imperative. Francis Joseph reluctantly embarked on a period of constitutional experiment. By November 1859 the emperor had announced the convening of a 'reinforced' *Reichsrat*, in other words an enlarged council to represent the Monarchy's constituent parts.

Once on the slippery slope of concessions, the emperor found it hard to go back. The mere act of convening a 'reinforced' *Reichsrat* raised the conundrum of how to add to it without reviving the provincial diets, including Hungary's. The 'reinforced' *Reichsrat* which met in May 1860 was hardly representative: most of its members had to be appointed precisely because there were no diets. Yet even this apology for a popular assembly managed to extract a promise from the emperor not to raise taxes without its consent. It also produced two distinct factions, each with its own proposal for a way forward. A group of Hungarian, Bohemian and Galician magnates proposed a sort of federated Monarchy, with each province represented by its diet and crowned with a number of overarching central institutions. The other faction was made up largely of Austrian Germans and favoured a unitary system, but with greater popular representation.

Francis Joseph was temperamentally more inclined to listen to the conservative, aristocratic faction. The result was the October Diploma of 1860, which restored the diets and provided for a *Reichsrat* of 100 members, drawn from the diets' members. The key to the Diploma's conservatism, however, was in the electoral system proposed for the provincial diets: this was weighted so heavily in favour of the landed nobility everywhere that the whole scheme was vehemently attacked by all other sections of society. It was no sooner announced than it became clear that it satisfied no group except its conservative authors. Even though the latter were chiefly Hungarians, they found themselves repudiated by mainstream political opinion in Hungary, which reflected largely the gentry class. Ferenc Deák, one of the moderates who had retired from active politics in September 1848, had become the *de facto* leader of the gentry and insisted that the restoration of Hungary's historic constitutional status, as defined in the April Laws, was the irreducible minimum for a political settlement. The various nationalities in both halves of the Monarchy also denounced the Diploma bitterly. Just as angry were the representatives of the growing Austrian German middle classes, who identified most with the Habsburg state and felt that they should be more obviously the dominant element in it.

Francis Joseph yielded to this argument in December 1860, when he appointed Anton von Schmerling, another 1848 liberal, as 'minister of state'; the emperor also clearly hoped to strengthen his hand in the competition with Prussia for primacy in Germany by thus ostentatiously giving the German element of the Monarchy a dominant role. Schmerling proceeded to issue the February Patent of 1861, which opted for the solution now probably closest to Francis Joseph's preference: the centralised, unitary state, but in constitutional form. The Patent provided for a much-expanded *Reichsrat* of 343 members, in effect a parliament for the entire Monarchy. As with the October Diploma, the deputies were to be drawn from the provincial diets, but this *Reichsrat* was to have the power to initiate legislation, as well as to approve the budget. Matters not concerning Hungary would be debated by a 'narrower' *Reichsrat* consisting only of the non-Hungarian deputies. What made the Patent a veneer, however, was that the indirect electoral system set in place for all provinces, instead of favouring just the nobility, was this time weighted in favour of the German-speaking element throughout the Monarchy.

The Schmerling system lasted all of four years but proved itself effectively unworkable from the start because of the refusal of the Monarchy's non-Germans to participate. The Hungarian Diet, though elected for the first time since 1848, was dissolved almost as soon as it met, for daring to demand the restoration of the April Laws; under Deák's leadership it also refused to send any of its deputies to the *Reichsrat*. The Croats, Poles and Czechs followed a similar policy after 1868, as did the Italians of Venetia. The blatantly German-oriented nature of the system alienated all the other nationalities.

The deadlock was finally broken, once again, by a crisis in foreign policy. By the mid-1860s, the looming confrontation with Prussia was beginning to concentrate Francis Joseph's mind. Faced with a continuing budgetary deficit, the emperor gradually recognised the need to do a deal with the Hungarians. Crucially, the Hungarian leadership had also subtly altered its position by this point, in that it accepted the fatal ambiguity of the April Laws in relation to foreign affairs and control of the Monarchy's armed forces and the need to resolve this.

Deák in particular recognised that these two issues were sticking points for Francis Joseph. Deák succeeded in convincing the monarch that the Hungarians were willing to modify the April Laws in so far as these were incompatible with the Monarchy's ability to function as a great power. The essence of the deal eventually struck was that the emperor was to be left with more or less undisputed control over foreign policy and the armed forces. In return, Hungary would receive constitutional autonomy within its historic borders, including Croatia. An essential part of the settlement, for the Hungarians, was that there must also be a constitutional government in the 'Austrian' half of the Monarchy; this would be a safeguard against a return to neo-absolutist rule.

By July 1865 Francis Joseph was convinced that the Hungarians could be trusted. He sacked Schmerling and authorised new elections for the provincial diets. In December the Hungarian Diet convened to debate the terms of the settlement. The Austro-Prussian War of 1866 and the decisive defeat of Austria, coming in the middle of these deliberations, only served to demonstrate afresh the interdependence of both the Monarchy and the Hungarian political elite. Forced to cede Venetia to Italy and to renounce leadership of and membership in the German Confederation, Francis Joseph was finally brought to see the necessity of Hungarian support if he were ever to recoup these losses. Deák and his principal partner in the negotiations, Count Gyula Andrássy, for their part, appreciated all the more that Hungary was too weak to stand on her own and needed to be part of a great power in order to have any influence over her fate at all. In October 1866 the emperor appointed as foreign minister Count Friedrich Ferdinand von Beust. It was Beust and Andrássy who hammered out the basic points of the agreement.

The Austro-Hungarian *Ausgleich* or Compromise was essentially one reached between the monarch, not 'Austria', and the appointed representatives of the Hungarian Diet, which in turn largely represented the Hungarian nobility. As such, the *Ausgleich* was a deal that excluded all the other nationalities of the Monarchy, including the Germans. It was accepted by the Diet and promulgated in March 1867; only after that, in June, could Francis Joseph be finally crowned King of Hungary. A parallel constitutional law was enacted for 'Austria' in December 1867.

The result was something quite unique: a constitutional monarchy in two halves, united by the person of the monarch as Emperor of Austria and King of Hungary. Responsible to the monarch were three 'common' or joint ministers, for foreign affairs, war and common financial matters such as tariffs and trade treaties. All other matters were reserved to the governments and parliaments of the two halves, 'Austria' and Hungary. Each half had autonomy, with its own parliament, ministry and minister-president. 'Delegations', consisting of deputies from the two parliaments, sitting apart, were designed to monitor the workings of the three common ministries, but in practice the delegations were powerless and the emperor and his common ministers were free to run foreign and military policy as they saw fit. The contribution of each half of the Monarchy to common expenses was fixed, at 70 per cent for 'Austria' and 30 per cent for Hungary, but this and the other common financial matters were subject to renewal every ten years.

The most serious defect of this 'dualist' constitution was that, in satisfying the minimum requirements of the dynasty and the Hungarians, it recognised only imperfectly, if at all, the rights or aspirations of the other peoples of the Monarchy. Even the Germans, who thought of themselves as the natural leaders of 'Austria' and who to begin with did indeed control its government, were estranged when they found, some years later, that the emperor was quite capable of ruling without them. The other nationalities, in both halves of the Monarchy, felt even more aggrieved and this has been the main criticism of the *Ausgleich* ever since: it did not solve, and indeed exacerbated, the 'nationality problem'. As a consequence, it has been argued, the Habsburg Monarchy was doomed to self-destruct because it was incapable of further change, and the 'uncompromising compromise', in George Barany's words, was the reason.[20]

There is an alternative view, put most cogently by C.A. Macartney, which seeks to place the *Ausgleich* in context. According to this, the deal done in 1867 was probably the best, or even the only one possible; 'unjust but realistic', as Istvan Deak puts it.[21] But this second view, though a sounder historical argument, can also be criticised. As Alan Sked points out, not every solution had been tried as of 1867; on the contrary, the general principles of the abortive Kremsier constitution of 1849, if probably too radical for the time in some of their detail, nevertheless constituted a genuine attempt to wrestle with issues of nationality.[22] What is indisputable is that the settlement of 1867 left more inhabitants of the Monarchy dissatisfied than satisfied. The Monarchy was to pay the ultimate price for this half a century later.

Legend:

- Gains by Russia
- Gains by Rumania
- Gains by Serbia
- Gains by Montegero
- Gains by Greece (1881)
- ·········· Bulgarian frontier according to the Treaty of San Stefano

Iaşi

BOSNIA

Belgrade

ROMANIA

Bucharest

SERBIA

Sarajevo

HERCE-GOVINA

SANJAK OF NOVI PAZAR

Niš

BULGARIA

MONTENEGRO

Sofia

EASTERN RUMELIA

Plovdiv

OTTOMAN

Constantinople

San Stefano

Salonika

EMPIRE

GREECE

Athens

5 The Ottoman Empire 1856–78. Redrawn from The Berlin Settlement in the Balkans (p. 213), *The Eastern Question* by M. S. Anderson, Macmillan (1966)

10

THE OTTOMAN EMPIRE AND THE BALKAN NATION-STATES

The Ottoman imperium in the Balkans rested on a fundamental distinction between Ottoman Muslims and a variety of Christian underclasses. Yet until the eighteenth century the latter were not conspicuously oppressed, save perhaps in time of war with Christian powers. In a pre-nationalist age, the Empire's multitudinous peoples coexisted without undue friction, as long as the state was administered with reasonable efficiency. It was the institutional degeneration of the Ottoman state, in particular its loss of control over Muslim elites in outlying provinces, which loosened the allegiance of the sultan's Christian subjects.

The outstanding feature of the Ottoman Empire between 1804 and 1867 is the emergence of autonomous or independent nation-states at its expense. The Serbian revolt of 1804 signalled the beginning of a long process of self-liberation by Balkan Christian peoples, albeit one always heavily dependent on great-power intervention. By the end of the 1860s an independent Greece had emerged and *de facto* if not formal independence had been achieved by Serbs, Romanians and Montenegrins. The very creation of these states fostered an ever greater nationalist fervour. Not only did the new rulers find themselves driven to promote national sentiment through the apparatus of the state itself; all the new states were 'incomplete', in that there were still fellow nationals living under direct Ottoman rule, who must be liberated. This twin agenda of nation-building and national liberation dominated the agenda of the new states.

At the same time the Ottoman Empire had no intention of submitting passively to such a carve-up. Successive sultans wrestled with increasing determination to reverse the Empire's fortunes. Ottoman reformers, however, continued to be hampered by the conservatism or outright opposition of influential elites; worse, they had to cope with physical revolt against imperial authority, not just by Balkan Christians but by Muslims. The record of

Ottoman modernisation in this period, therefore, is one of well-meaning initiatives frustrated by internal resistance as much as inertia.

As if this were not enough, the Empire continued to be the focus of international conflict and great-power intervention. This was only partly because so many of its Balkan subjects were Christians, for whom the governments of European powers, if not their citizens, professed sympathy. Just as important was the Empire's strategic location astride the Straits and its increasingly titular possession of the Middle East and North Africa. France was a traditional supporter of the Ottomans as a counterweight to the Habsburg Monarchy and, increasingly, Russia. Britain, because of its Indian empire, had an abiding fear of Russian influence in the Ottoman realms, especially if this threatened the status quo in the eastern Mediterranean. The Habsburg Monarchy by the late eighteenth century had ceased regarding the Ottomans as a threat, in view of the more worrying possibility of Russian expansion into the Balkans. Russia itself saw the Ottoman Empire as a legitimate sphere of influence, not least for its importance as a trade route via the Straits, but by the early nineteenth century Russian policy was arguably more concerned to preserve the Ottoman imperium, as a suitably weak and hence biddable neighbour, than it was to acquire fresh territory.

THE EMERGENCE OF THE BALKAN NATION-STATES

None of the new states emerged entirely in isolation. Not only were international context and great-power involvement crucial, but there were numerous points of contact, ideological and practical, between the Balkan peoples themselves. The Serbian revolt was assisted not just by South Slavs from the Habsburg Monarchy but by Greeks and Bulgarians. The Greek revolt was a two-headed affair, with greater hopes pinned initially on the rising in the Romanian principalities than on that in present-day Greece. The Balkan statelets, once established, built up links with each other and reached out to their co-nationals in Ottoman territory; they also, however, found that their longer-term plans for expansion often clashed.

The social composition of the Balkan revolutions varied. Although the majority of participants came from the peasantry, it would be misleading to characterise these as peasant uprisings. In the case of the Serbs and Greeks, many of the leaders were local 'notables', men who had amassed some wealth as merchants or outlaws and had already assumed a leadership role in their communities, often one recognised by the Ottoman authorities. Only in the Romanian principalities did the eventual leadership come from the landowning *boyar* class, even if the initial revolt of 1821 was led by a non-noble.

A final aspect of the Balkan revolutions worth mentioning is the calamitous consequences for the Muslim population, whether Ottoman officials, ethnic Turks or Muslim Slavs. Modern scholarship has only recently caught up with the fate of the Balkan Muslims, which was long obscured by Christian indignation over Ottoman atrocities. Yet wherever Christians rose against Ottoman rule, the first to die were usually the local Muslims, and the well-documented barbarities of Ottoman forces in subsequent fighting were often committed in retaliation. Regardless of who killed whom first, the effect was a huge demographic shift throughout the nineteenth century: in the century following 1821 it has been calculated that 5 million Muslims were forced out of former Ottoman provinces in the Balkans and along the Black Sea coastline.[1]

SERBIA

The Serbian revolt was the classic instance of the breakdown of authority in the Ottoman centre creating chaos in the provinces: janissaries, encouraged or forced to seek a living in the *paşalık* of Belgrade, had by 1804 been terrorising Christians and Ottoman officials alike for years. In response the Serbs, led by the illiterate but forceful Karađorđe [Black George] Petrović, a veteran of the Austro-Turkish wars who was also a wealthy merchant, started arming in self-defence. In January 1804 an attempt by the leading janissaries to round up and exterminate Serb *knezes*, or notables, sparked serious fighting. Karađorđe's rebellion was thus avowedly not against the sultan's authority but against the janissaries and it was at first, with some misgivings, encouraged by the local governor. The janissaries were routed and their leaders executed in August 1804.

The Serbs, however, demanded as reward not only that they should in future collect taxes in the province but that Karađorđe's militia should henceforth be responsible for order and that Ottoman troops should withdraw. Even the reform-minded Selim III balked at this. Mindful of conservative opposition in Constantinople to any concessions to Christians, Selim was also alarmed at Karađorđe's appeal for foreign assistance. Ottoman forces were sent to suppress the revolt, but instead were beaten back in August 1805 and fighting became general. Karađorđe captured Belgrade in December 1806, but long before that he had effectively declared Serbia a self-governing province when, in the autumn of 1805, he convened a Serbian Governing Council.

This new Serbia's existence was a precarious one, always heavily dependent on outside factors. The Russo-Turkish War of 1806 inevitably relieved pressure on the Serbs. Russian assistance, however, was limited, and from 1807 Karađorđe's forces were on the defensive. Although the insurgents were joined by Serbs from the Habsburg Monarchy, this was no substitute for the help of a great power. The Serbs were also riven by internal squabbles. Karađorđe was an autocratic personality, not above personally despatching rivals among his fellow notables, but as the tide turned against the Serbs his leadership was called into question. When Russia as a result of Napoleon's invasion concluded a hasty peace with the Ottomans in 1812, the end was at hand. Ottoman forces returned to the *paşalık* in overwhelming strength in October 1813. Karađorđe fled to Russia and the revolt was put down with considerable brutality.

Matters did not end there, however. The *paşalık* remained a hotbed of unrest, bitterness and violence, despite an Ottoman amnesty and the return of thousands of refugees. Many Serbs, especially the wealthier among the *knezes* who had most to lose, accepted the amnesty, but many did not, and as the months passed the Ottoman authorities' suspicions of the Christian populace, heightened by random acts of violence, translated into ever greater harshness, including systematic torture and executions. In the end it was their fear of arbitrary execution which led even the loyal *knezes*, under the leadership of Miloš Obrenović, to stage a second revolt in April 1815. This second insurrection loudly proclaimed that it was rebelling not against the sultan's authority but against the local pasha's injustice. Such moderation undoubtedly swayed Sultan Mahmud II to do a deal; even more influential was the fact that, in the wake of Napoleon's defeat, Russian pressure on the Porte in favour of a settlement was harder to resist. In November 1815 Miloš was made Supreme *Knez* or Prince of the province, although still a vassal obliged to pay tribute to the sultan. An Ottoman governor remained, as did Ottoman garrisons in six fortresses. In addition, the Serbs were granted their own judicial body, were made responsible for the collection of taxes and local affairs and were entitled to bear arms. It was *de facto* if not formal autonomy.

Autonomy was confirmed formally only in 1830 as a result of the Russo-Turkish War of 1828–9, as was Miloš's hitherto self-proclaimed status as hereditary prince, but from 1815 Miloš worked hard to consolidate his position. Like Karađorđe an illiterate livestock merchant, and intolerant of opposition, Miloš was nevertheless crafty enough to secure by outward subservience and corruption what he would not have been able to gain by force. When in 1817 Karađorđe dared to return to Serbia, Miloš had him murdered and sent his head to the sultan as proof of his loyalty. For the same reason Miloš refused utterly to get involved in the Greek revolts of 1821. Yet all the while he was intent on reducing the Ottoman presence by buying up Muslim estates, conniving at the terrorisation of those who would not sell and bribing Ottoman officialdom to turn a blind eye to this commercialised form of 'ethnic cleansing'. This process was accelerated after 1830 when Muslims other than the fortress garrison were required to leave Serbia. Although Miloš retained much of this Muslim property himself, he sold much of it to his followers, creating in the process the nucleus of a Serbian smallholder class, as Serbs flocked into the principality from neighbouring provinces. At the same time Miloš encouraged the founding of schools and welcomed the assistance of Habsburg Serbs or those few natives of Serbia who had profited from a foreign education. Six additional districts claimed by Serbia as part of the original *paşalık* of Belgrade were ceded by the Porte in 1833.

Miloš's despotic nature, however, created opposition, principally among those of his fellow notables who resented Miloš's authority but also among the handful of town dwellers and intellectuals who objected to the prince's 'Ottoman' ways. Miloš was supposed to rule with the assistance of a *Skupština* or assembly, but those who feared his arbitrariness increasingly argued for some formal restraint on the prince. By the late 1830s this 'Constitutionalist' opposition was attracting the attention of the great powers, anxious for strategic reasons to deny one another influence in this autonomous corner of the Ottoman Empire.

Paradoxically, liberal Britain took the side of Miloš and the Ottoman government in disputing the need for a constitution, while autocratic Russia backed the Constitutionalists. The result was a Russian victory: under pressure in December 1838 the Porte issued the so-called 'Turkish constitution', which obliged the prince to govern in cooperation with a council of 17, whose members he could appoint but whom he could not subsequently remove. Miloš, unable to tolerate these restrictions but without sufficient popular support to resist them, abdicated and went into exile in June 1839. His son Michael succeeded in March 1840, but the Constitutionalists' suspicion of the Obrenović family generally led in 1842 to the deposition and exile of Michael and the acclamation as prince of Alexander Karađorđe, son of Karađorđe.

Alexander's elevation owed more to his surname than to any innate strength of personality. The real powers in the land were the Constitutionalists or, as they liked to call themselves, the 'Defenders of the constitution'. The council was dominated by two notables in particular and an extremely able representative of the new class of educated bureaucrats, Ilija Garašanin. These were conservative authoritarians, who basically believed in rule by their own kind; they were hardly democrats. Yet the Constitutionalist period saw the regularisation of the state bureaucracy, the introduction of a legal code in 1844 and the extension of the educational system. Much of this modernisation was the work of Garašanin as minister of the interior from 1843 to 1852.

Garašanin was also the author of one of the most famous, or infamous, documents in Serbian history, the *Našertanije* or Plan of 1844. This memorandum was partially inspired by the Polish *émigré* Czartoryski, who urged Serbia to act as a unifier of all the South Slavs, against the day when the Slav peoples generally would be able to emancipate themselves from the great multinational empires. Garašanin, however, conceived Serbia's national mission as confined to the liberation of 'Serb' lands, but by this he still understood Bosnia–Hercegovina, Albania, Montenegro and the territory known as 'Old Serbia', among the Ottoman provinces, and the Vojvodina in the Habsburg Monarchy. These lands corresponded roughly to the extent of Serbia's lost medieval empire, but they also contained substantial minorities of non-Serbs. Yet Garašanin's vision of a 'Greater Serbia', the Serbian nation-state as it ought to be, informed generations of Serbian politicians, and Garašanin did what he could to set the process in motion by establishing a network of agents throughout the Ottoman provinces as well as the Habsburg Monarchy.

The Constitutionalist regime had to tread cautiously because of Serbia's vassal status. Serbia provided not so covert support for its fellow Serbs in the Vojvodina during the 1848 revolution, but Garašanin was aware that this was a dangerous game. The Crimean War demonstrated Serbia's vulnerability even more starkly. Russia, in 1853, insisted on Garašanin's dismissal as a 'revolutionary', and when Russia was forced to withdraw from the neighbouring Romanian principalities later that year, its place as Serbia's mentor was promptly filled by Austria. The 1856 Treaty of Paris formally annulled Russia's right to pose as the 'protector' of the Ottoman vassal-states; they were instead subjected to the invigilation of all the great-power signatories.

By 1858 the leading Constitutionalists were increasingly at odds with those whose loyalty lay with Prince Alexander and it was resolved to call a *Skupština* to resolve the issue of control. The 'St Andrew's' *Skupština* of December 1858, however, backfired on both parties by deciding to depose Alexander and recall the ageing Miloš Obrenović to the throne. Miloš returned in triumph in February 1859 and although he died in 1860, leaving his son Michael as prince, his reappearance spelled the end of the Constitutionalists' dominance.

The reign of Michael Obrenović (1860–8) saw a renewed concentration on national liberation. Michael, in contrast to Miloš, was educated and cosmopolitan, having spent much of his life abroad. He was determined to free Serbia from Ottoman control and saw the best route to this goal in building up Serbia's military strength while at the same time concluding alliances with other Balkan states and peoples. Conservative by temperament, he found an ideal coadjutor in Garašanin who, restored to favour, acted as prime minister from 1861 to 1867. Both men frowned upon the new generation of Serbia's foreign-educated, liberal youth, some of whom were becoming politically active by the late 1850s, and argued in vain for a greater popular participation in public life. Strongly nationalist, they supported the expansion of the Serbian state, but incurred censorship, prison sentences and exile for their criticisms of Michael's domestic rule. In 1866 Vladimir Jovanović and others founded the *Ujedinjena omladina srpska* (United Serbian Youth) or *Omladina* at Novi Sad in Habsburg Hungary. Though short lived as a coherent organisation, the *Omladina* alarmed not only Prince Michael but also the Habsburg Monarchy because it demonstrated the strength of Serb nationalism on both sides of the border.

Serbia's military build-up under Michael and Garašanin meant that, on paper, the government disposed of a national militia of 90,000 men by the end of the decade. In reality, like the frog that puffs itself up to impress its enemies, Serbia's military potential was well below this, but both friends and enemies were obliged to take its pretensions seriously. A network of agents was built up throughout the Balkans, but especially in Bosnia and

Old Serbia. Alliances envisaging eventual joint military action against the Ottomans were concluded with Montenegro in 1866, Greece in 1867 and the new united Romania in 1868; although in the event these were never activated, the sense of impending crisis was palpable. Relations with the Porte had been especially abysmal since 1862, when the Ottoman governor of Belgrade had bombarded the town. In 1867, following repeated appeals to the powers by Serbia, the Ottoman government finally withdrew its garrisons from the principality. Serbia in 1867 seemed poised to make the decisive breakthrough to independence and national liberation.

GREECE

Any attempt to explain the emergence of an independent Greece in the 1830s is complicated by the fact that the Greeks were scattered across the Balkans, the Black Sea littoral and the Ottoman Levant. Equally confusing, there were two main revolts against Ottoman rule in 1821, one in the Romanian princi-palities, the other in what became the Greek state, primarily the Peloponnesus and the southern area of mainland Greece. The Danubian revolt was quickly snuffed out, not just by the sultan's armies but by the hostility of the surrounding Romanian population. It was in the heartlands of the south that the state was established, a circumstance which made its domination by outside powers for the remainder of this period all the easier.

The significance of the Greek diaspora, and the eighteenth-century roots of Greek nationalism, has already been described. More Greeks lived in the trading capitals of the Empire and Europe than lived in what is now Greece. The Greek merchant class had grown in size and wealth throughout the eighteenth century and the numbers of educated, cosmopolitan Greeks, alive to the ideas of the Enlightenment and the French Revolution, increased accordingly.

Yet it was not the wealthiest merchants who provided the advance guard of Greek nationalism. Still less was it the Phanariots, integrated as they were into the Ottoman governing system. Active nationalists were instead typified by Emmanouil Xanthos, Nikolaos Skouphas and Athanasios Tsakaloff, the impoverished and bankrupt merchants who founded the *Philiki Etairia* (Society of Friends) at Odessa in 1814. These men, influenced by their contacts with Western Europe and inspired by the example of forerunners like Velestinlis, saw in revolt and national independence a meaningful role for themselves. Their vision was not so much of a nation-state as of a revival of the medieval Byzantine Empire, centred on Constantinople, on the basis that this had been the apotheosis of the Greek nation.

The *Etairia* relied on a secret, cellular organisation and a fearsome oath of loyalty and attracted similar idealists and malcontents from among petty merchants, professionals like teachers and physicians, and local notables. Its recruitment was minimal until, in 1818, it moved headquarters to Constantinople and started promoting the rumour that it had Russian support for its plans. This quite misleading impression was reinforced by the fact that the *Etairia* had established contact with Count Ioannis Kapodistrias, a Greek from Corfu who had risen through the Russian diplomatic service to become joint foreign minister, with Count Karl Nesselrode, to Alexander I. As a servant of the tsar, Kapodistrias did not encourage revolt but almost certainly knew that the *Etairia* was preparing one. By 1821 the *Etairia* was well established in the Danubian principalities and southern Greece, with a membership of around 1000. Its preparations were assisted by the Greek nationality of many of Russia's consuls in these regions, and it had secured for the military leadership of the revolt the services of General Alexandros Ypsilantis, the son of a former Phanariot *hospodar* of Wallachia, who also happened to be a personal *aide-de-camp* to the tsar. It was assumed that the revolt would profit from the concurrent conflict between the Porte and Ali Pasha, the warlord of the western Balkans, who from 1820 was besieged in his stronghold Ioannina and was sending out feelers to the *Etairia* for concerted action.

The main focus of the revolt was to be in Greece, with a diversionary uprising in the Romanian principalities, but since there was little coordination of effort the initial outbreaks were in the principalities. In Moldavia the ruling *hospodar* was a member of the *Etairia*; in Wallachia the Society recruited the Romanian notable Tudor Vladimirescu, who was also a commander of the local militia. The *Etairia* assumed, against all the signs, that they would gain support from the other Balkan Christians, especially the Serbs; they also reckoned, disastrously, on Russian intervention. Ypsilantis, when he crossed into Moldavia from Russia on 6 March 1821, ostentatiously wore a Russian uniform and created the impression that a Russian army was on its way, which encouraged others to join him. Muslims in Iaşi and Galaţi, in Moldavia, were deliberately massacred, in the hope that Ottoman reprisals would prompt the tsar to step in.

These calculations were shattered when the tsar disavowed the revolt as an offence against the legitimate order. But in the Romanian principalities the fundamental weakness was that this was a Greek uprising, in a population largely Romanian, and the Greeks were hated there because of their identification with the corruption of the Phanariots. Romanian *boyars* and peasants alike were intent on shaking off Greek rule, not breaking away from the Ottoman Empire. Even Vladimirescu, when he joined forces with the *Etairia*, assumed the Greeks would carry on to Greece itself, leaving the Romanians to make their peace with the Ottomans. In the meantime, however, Vladimirescu's proclamation in February 1821, by calling on the peasants for support, unleashed a social rather than a national uprising, in which the peasants attacked *boyar* estates.

The result was chaos. Ypsilantis and Vladimirescu both marched on Bucharest, where they met in April, but the complete absence of outside support, and the approach of the sultan's armies, soon forced both to retreat.

Vladimirescu, suspected by the Greeks of betrayal, was executed by Ypsilantis' men in June, an act which confirmed Romanians' view of Greek perfidy. Shortly after Ypsilantis was defeated and driven into Austrian territory by the Ottomans. The events in the Danubian principalities were a tragic sideshow compared with the main Greek revolt, but in the principalities themselves the most important outcome was the end of Phanariot rule. At this proof of Greek disloyalty, the Porte acceded to Romanian pressure and handed over the administration of both provinces to native Romanians.

In the Peloponnesus and mainland Greece, by contrast, the revolt soon passed out of *Philiki Etairia*'s control and degenerated into several different conflicts which the Ottomans found much more difficult to extinguish. This was in part a matter of geography: in the mountainous hinterland, or among the inlets and islands of the coast, the insurgents were hard to get at; they were also harder to subject to any central authority. Here most of the leaders were local notables or entirely self-made men. As in Serbia, the spark for revolt came when the Ottomans, anxious to forestall cooperation between the Greeks and Ali Pasha, tried to round up community leaders. Greeks started attacking and slaughtering Muslims, killing 15,000 out of 40,000 in the Peloponnesus alone.[2] The Ottomans responded in kind and the revolt became general by early April.

The main Greek revolt succeeded in attracting outside help. In Western Europe the so-called Philhellenes, Romantics and liberals, whose classical education gave them a sympathy for the Greeks as Europe's cultural forebears, raised money and public consciousness on behalf of the insurgents, and not a few, like Lord Byron, participated personally. Even more decisively, the possibility of Russian intervention was heightened when in April the Ottoman government ordered the lynching, in Constantinople, of the Greek Orthodox Patriarch and several other bishops, on the ground that they had not done enough to deter their co-religionists from rebellion. Accompanied by a general massacre of Constantinople's Greek community, this barbarity led to a rupture of relations with Russia, for although Alexander had not supported revolt, he took seriously his right to protect his fellow Orthodox Christians.

Politically as well as militarily the struggle for Greek independence was confused in the extreme. The revolt was in reality a number of local revolts, under no overall direction that any of the participants would accept. In December 1821 Dimitrios Yspilantis, brother of Alexandros, succeeded in convening at Epidaurus delegates from the various insurgent regions, who drew up a constitution. However, no one paid this would-be government much attention and fighting broke out between different factions. In the meantime the Ottomans' initial preoccupation was with Ali Pasha, but on the latter's betrayal and execution in January 1822 they could devote their full attention to the Greeks. In 1824, moreover, the sultan secured the help of his most powerful vassal, the virtually independent Pasha Mohammed Ali of Egypt. The entry of the western-trained Egyptian army and navy turned the tide.

Beaten back on all fronts, the Greeks in 1826 made a formal appeal to the great powers for assistance. Russia, Britain and France, each acting out of suspicion of the others, agreed in the Treaty of London, in July 1827, to attempt a 'reconciliation' between the Greeks and the Porte. An Anglo-Russian–French fleet was despatched to the Levant with instructions to mediate, an offer which the winning Ottomans were inherently less likely to accept than the losing Greeks. The result was the notorious battle of Navarino, in October, when the allied fleet, having been fired on by the Ottoman–Egyptian fleet, promptly destroyed it. Russia used this incident as an excuse for declaring war on the Ottomans in March 1828, which had the effect of relieving the pressure on the Greeks. Long before the Treaty of Adrianople concluded this Russo-Turkish War, in September 1829, the great powers had already settled that some form of autonomy, for some part of the Greek-inhabited areas of the Ottoman realms, was essential. At the same time the Ottoman forces effectively conceded defeat by the Greek insurgency.

In the meantime the Greeks had been trying to reach agreement among themselves as to what shape a Greek state should take. A National Assembly was convened at Troezene early in 1827 and a second constitution agreed in May. Kapodistrias, who had left Russian service in 1822 to devote himself to independence, was elected provisional head of state, but soon found that, as a perceived 'Russian' figure, his authority was disputed by the 'French' and 'British' factions in the assembly. Authoritarian by temperament, Kapodistrias was assassinated in October 1831. This domestic chaos only confirmed the great powers in their determination to impose their own settlement on the Greeks, but it was Britain's fear that a merely autonomous Greece would be too easily manipulated by Russia which led it to push for complete independence. By the second Treaty of London in July 1832 a sovereign Kingdom of Greece was accepted by the Porte and the 17-year-old Otto of Bavaria selected as king. Otto arrived with a retinue of Bavarian troops and advisers in February 1833, to rule over a state which comprised the Peloponnesus, southern Rumeli and the islands of the western Aegean, and 800,000 people, between a quarter and a third of all Greeks.[3] The new government was provided with a massive capital loan sponsored by the great powers to enable it to function. It is no exaggeration to say that the new state would not have been created without great-power intervention, and its continued existence depended on the protection of the powers, which came at the cost of constant outside interference. Because the kingdom contained only a fraction of all Greeks, the overriding preoccupation of successive governments was with the liberation of those fellow nationals still under Ottoman rule.

Throughout the first decade of King Otto's reign, what structure and order there was depended on the king's Bavarian ministers and 3500 German mercenaries, who remained until the late 1830s. The government attempted to impose a Napoleonic-style, centralised administration on the country, but rapidly found that authority in the provinces still relied on the cooperation of local notables and former insurgent leaders. The country was plagued by banditry and insecurity. Economically Greece remained backward, with 60 per cent of the population peasants.

Normal political parties were slow to emerge. Instead factions continued to be identified as 'Russian', 'French' and 'British', depending on which great power's patronage they enjoyed. In September 1843 there was a sort of *coup*, the result of growing discontent at the lack of constitutional government, the continuing influence of the king's Bavarian advisers, the level of taxation forced on the government by its need to service the foreign loan, and above all the failure to liberate the Ottoman Greeks or even to support an uprising in Crete in 1841. Otto was obliged to grant a constitution which, when finalised in March 1844, established a bill of rights and a lower chamber of the National Assembly elected by universal manhood suffrage. Liberal though this constitution was, Otto was able largely to ignore it because whichever clique the king favoured with office could then manipulate the electoral system through a mixture of bribery and intimidation. Party politics continued to reflect the priorities of the great powers, with the dominant figure down to his death in 1847 being the leader of the 'French' party, Ioannis Kolettis. Kolettis in particular became an exponent of what Greeks referred to as the *Megali Idea* (Great Idea), the expansionist dream of nineteenth-century Greek nationalism. This posited that the Greek state ultimately should take over all those lands formerly belonging to Byzantium and that its capital should be Constantinople.

Such a megalomaniacal vision completely ignored the fact that the former Byzantine lands were now inhabited by millions of non-Greeks. It also ignored the brutal realities of Greece's position, which made it the shuttlecock of international politics. The British government was especially inimical to the implications of the *Megali Idea*, which threatened the territorial integrity of the Ottoman Empire. When, in 1850, the property of a Portuguese but Gibraltar-born Jew, Don Pacifico, was damaged by an anti-Semitic Athenian mob, Britain seized the opportunity to humiliate Greece with a naval blockade until compensation was paid. The Crimean War exposed Greece to further dangers. Ottoman Greeks staged an uprising and volunteers from the kingdom flocked to join them. This led Britain and France to occupy Piraeus, the port of Athens, from 1854 to 1857, and a government of the 'British' party under Alexandros Mavrokordatos was forced on Otto. In the post-Crimea period Otto's continuing inability to achieve territorial expansion, coupled with his lack of an heir and the kingdom's economic problems, finally led to another army-led coup. With the approval of the great powers, Otto was forced to abdicate in October 1862.

It was the great powers once again who determined Otto's successor, a Danish princeling who, on being accepted by the National Assembly, acceded as George I (1863–1913). The Assembly also voted in a new constitution, ratified in October 1864. This explicitly limited the king's power by making his ministry responsible to the legislature rather than the crown. The legislature was made unicameral and elected by secret ballot. As a sort of international 'dowry', Britain ceded to Greece the Ionian Islands, which it had administered since 1815. This first territorial increase since the foundation of the state served only to remind Greek nationalists that realisation of the *Megali Idea* was still unfinished business.

The obsession with nation-building, as well as the Greek government's crippling indebtedness to the great powers, meant that modernisation was next to impossible. There was no likelihood of a native industry emerging while the country was forced to remain open to foreign imports. What revenue the state received from taxation went on servicing the foreign debt, with little left over for the building of roads or other infrastructure, the improvement of local government or education; of a population of 1 million by 1860, only 45,000 pupils were in elementary school. Greece remained a society of small towns and villages, where political influence depended on clientism and corruption and the average Greek was 'hardly aware of the state'.[4]

ROMANIA

The unification of Moldavia and Wallachia as the autonomous Principality of Romania was an obvious product of great-power rivalry, but it also corresponded to the wishes of an increasing number of the Romanian *boyar* elite, if not the downtrodden peasantry.

Given the anarchy reigning in the Ottoman Balkans, the dominant influence in the principalities for the first half of the nineteenth century was in fact Russia. During the Russo-Turkish War of 1806–12, Russian troops were in occupation, the presence of the French-speaking noble officers among them paradoxically reinforcing the spread of French cultural influences, and hence nationalism, already under way among the Romanian elite. Although Russia was forced temporarily to withdraw in 1812, it negotiated before doing so the cession of the Romanian-inhabited territory to the east of Moldavia known as Bessarabia. This not only secured Russia access to the mouth of the Danube, it permanently poisoned Romanian patriots' view of their huge neighbour. After Napoleon's fall Russia's influence was as unchallengeable as ever and although the tsar refused to support the revolutionaries of 1821, he backed the replacement of Phanariot rule with Romanian autonomy as an even greater surety of Russian influence.

The opposition of Greek and Romanian interests revealed in 1821 was an important point in the emergence of Romanian national identity, but the appointment in 1822 as *hospodars* of two Romanian *boyars* was even more of a milestone. For the first time in centuries Romanian rulers, assisted by *divans* or councils of their fellow *boyars*, were entrusted with government. Autonomy was deepened by the Convention of Akkerman between Russia and the Porte in 1826: the *divans* would now elect each *hospodar* for seven years, subject to the approval not only of Constantinople but of St Petersburg too. The Treaty of Adrianople in 1829 not only brought the Russian troops back but rendered Ottoman suzerainty almost completely nominal. The *hospodars* were to be elected for life, Ottoman garrisons were withdrawn and all Muslim subjects of the sultan were to sell their property and leave the principalities. In return the principalities would continue paying tribute.

From the Romanian viewpoint the only problem with autonomy was that it too was nominal as long as Russia's grip on the principalities remained. Nevertheless the period after Adrianople was also one in which the institutions of the modern constitutional state were set in place in each. As with Serbia, absolutist Russia presided over the drafting of the Organic Statutes, issued formally by the Ottoman government for Wallachia in 1831 and Moldavia in 1832. These provided for oligarchical rule by the landowning class. *Hospodars* would continue to be elected from special assemblies of their *boyar* peers. Neither *hospodars* nor assemblies had decisive control of the legislative process, or the power to dismiss the other; instead disputes were to be settled by appeal to both the Porte and the Russian government. The Statutes, however, regulated the affairs of each principality in minute detail and always in favour of the *boyars*, who did not pay taxes and for the first time were assigned clear ownership of land, formal title to which had been denied them by the Ottoman system. Peasants, by contrast, were allotted a heavier labour service. Political but also economic power was thus firmly concentrated in the hands of the *boyars*, but the effect was to make Romanian society a social time bomb.

This was a period of Russian dominance but also economic development. In Moldavia Michael Sturdza proved an able if authoritarian ruler, who managed to fund considerable building of infrastructure and schools. Wallachia, too, gradually improved basic infrastructure and education and in both principalities the *boyars* profited from the growing European market for Romanian foodstuffs. In 1847 the principalities received permission to effect a customs union, and the removal of economic barriers between the two accelerated economic growth.

Romanian nationalism in the principalities assumed coherence. Before 1821 this owed much to the influence of the 'Transylvanian School', with their stress on the Latinity and hence antiquity of the Romanian language and identity. But in the principalities, although French culture was rapidly becoming dominant among the native *boyars*, the language of administration, commerce and all schooling was entirely Greek until 1817, when the *hospodar* of Wallachia gave permission for some teaching in Romanian. Gheorghe Lazăr, the Transylvanian who took up this task, had an immense influence on the succeeding generation. His pupil and successor, Ion Eliade

Rădulescu, published the first Romanian grammar in 1828, in 1829 launched the first Romanian-language newspaper in Wallachia and in 1830 set up his own printing press. An important collaborator of Rădulescu was the *boyar* Constantin Golescu, who not only bankrolled Rădulescu's publishing but, with him, founded a Literary Society which attracted attention to the essential modernising prerequisite of spreading Romanian-language education. In Moldavia a similar role was filled by the western-educated Gheorghe Asachi, the first to teach in Romanian at the Greek Academy of Iaşi and who in 1829 began the first Romanian-language journal in Moldavia.

After 1821 Romanian nationalism was focused on Russian influence, but even more on whether the principalities should be allowed to unite as one state. Patriotic societies sprang up dedicated to achieving this goal. An important role was played by the generation of young Romanians who acquired an education in the West, especially in Paris. On returning to their native country, these Romanian liberals pressed for a properly constitutional government and civil liberties although, as the sons of landowners, they were less keen on universal manhood suffrage and peasant emancipation. But above all they believed that the Romanian nation should be brought together in one political unit. Nationalists also established an increasing number of links with their fellow Romanians in the Habsburg Monarchy, but the Habsburg Romanians tended to regard the idea of any political union with the principalities as impractical.

The principalities had radically different experiences in the revolutionary year of 1848–9, although the result was similar in that Russian influence was simply strengthened. Prince Sturdza in Moldavia suppressed all signs of unrest immediately and determinedly. In Wallachia, by contrast, Prince Bibescu was toppled in June 1848 by a revolutionary movement, many of whose leaders had rushed home from Paris to take part. This revolution was radical by Romanian standards, calling for representation of all social classes as well as peasant emancipation, provided landowners were compensated, but its main thrust was against the Russian protectorate. Because of this its extinction was predictable: in May 1849 Russia and the Porte agreed that *hospodars* would be appointed, not elected, and would rule with *divans* hand-picked by each *hospodar* with joint Ottoman–Russian 'advice'. As the ultimate safeguard, Russian troops remained in occupation yet again until 1851. The revolutionaries fled abroad, many now convinced that, for unification to have any chance, the backing of some great power was essential.

Formation of a Romanian nation-state was finally facilitated by the Crimean War. Although Moldavia and Wallachia were occupied by Russia in 1853–4, this was reversed by Austria's ultimatum and the Anglo-French attack on the Crimea, and the Habsburg Monarchy then installed its own forces in the principalities for the duration of the war. The 1856 Treaty of Paris spelt the end of Russia's hegemony in the Danube basin: both principalities remained autonomous within the Ottoman Empire, but this was now jointly guaranteed by all the signatory powers; in addition, Russia was forced to cede southern Bessarabia to Moldavia. Just as crucially, Napoleon III of France made it clear at the peace negotiations that he supported Romanian unification, in part because of a vague sympathy with national movements, but mainly to discomfit the Habsburg Monarchy.

The French government accordingly pressed for elections of *divans* in each principality, which would then vote on the question of union. Conducting elections became a tussle of wills between the powers: the first elections in July 1857 were blatantly rigged by the Ottoman authorities in favour of continued separation and only after lengthy negotiations was it agreed to hold reruns in September, which produced *divans* clearly minded for union. An international conference hosted by Napoleon in 1858 resulted in the oddity of the 'United Principalities of Moldavia and Wallachia': parallel but separate *hospodars* and governments, 'united' by a Central Commission of 16 representatives of each principality and charged with any legislation affecting both, such as tariffs and communications.

That this compromise was soon set at nought was due to the undoubted strength of Romanian national feeling, even as measured by a highly restrictive franchise which ensured that the *divans* of both principalities were exclusively *boyar* in composition. First the Moldavian assembly in January 1859, and then the Wallachian, in February, voted by clear majorities for the same man, Alexander Cuza, a liberal of the 1848 generation, as *hospodar*. This purely personal union, though technically forbidden, was nevertheless able to stand because the power most likely to have insisted on its annulment, Austria, was overwhelmed by its own crisis in Italy later that year. Cuza remained *hospodar* of both principalities, and by early 1861 the essential impracticality of the arrangement had persuaded the great powers and even the Porte to sanction the abolition of the Central Commission and the formation of a single, unitary government. The first united cabinet took office in February 1862.

Cuza's brief reign saw significant advances towards the consolidation of a Romanian nation-state. Party politics in both principalities had already become a competition between the Conservatives, who represented the biggest landowners, and the Liberals, whose constituency included lesser nobles, officialdom and the small but growing middle class. The Conservatives dominated the National Assembly by virtue of the narrow franchise, but this did not deter Cuza from appointing the Liberal historian Mihai Kogălniceanu as minister-president in October 1864, and whichever party was favoured with office soon found that an increasingly centralised state bureaucracy was the key to staying in power through the manipulation of elections. Kogălniceanu's ministry changed the face of Romanian society in a number of ways. The educational system was deepened with the founding of universities at Bucharest and Iaşi. A legal code was introduced along French lines. From December 1863 the government started secularising the lands of

Orthodox monasteries, a step which proved popular because it involved dispossessing Phanariot Greeks, but which also released a quarter of the country's arable land on to the market. A less happy result was achieved by the Agrarian Law of August 1864: this aimed to create a class of peasant small-holders by abolishing labour services, allotting the peasants land and compensating the landowners from state funds. In reality much of the best land was taken by the *boyars* anyway and the peasants tended to run rapidly into debt and sell out, becoming landless agricultural labourers, as in so many other parts of Eastern Europe.

Despite these achievements Cuza was not personally popular and his lack of an heir made his position precarious. His dismissal of Kogălniceanu left him isolated, and a conspiracy of both parties, with the assistance of disaf-fected army officers, forced him to abdicate in February 1866. All the great powers by this point accepted the practical irreversibility of unification. Their compromise choice for ruler fell on Prince Charles of Hohenzollern-Sigmaringen, who was duly approved by a national plebiscite. The provi-sional government in the meantime had drafted a liberal constitution which, while guaranteeing basic liberties and legal equality, nevertheless confined real political power to the propertied elite through indirect elections and to the prince by giving him the right to appoint and dismiss ministers as well as veto legislation. United Romania was in for a long spell of constitutional but essentially oligarchical rule.

MONTENEGRO

Tiny Montenegro, although technically not even autonomous in this period, enjoyed a *de facto* independence by virtue of its inaccessibility and the renowned orneriness of its people. The *Vladika* or prince-bishop from 1782, Peter I, pursued an active policy of expansion during the French Revolutionary and Napoleonic wars, especially in the direction of the Adriatic and despite the near-constant threat, not so much from the Ottomans, as from neighbouring warlords like Ali Pasha. Peter sought the protection of Russia, but the latter clearly saw the Montenegrins as pawns in its larger struggle with France. In 1806 a Russo-Montenegrin force unsuc-cessfully besieged French-held Ragusa and later captured Cattaro (Kotor), which Montenegro then held, but in 1807 Russia handed Cattaro over to France and in 1815 it was reassigned to Austria, to assuage Habsburg fears of Russian influence on the Adriatic.

The great powers' disregard of Montenegro was understandable, since from their perspective it hardly qualified as a state. The *Vladika* 'ruled' from the mountain stronghold of Cetinje over a population of 120,000 scattered across an inhospitable terrain with no roads, and who lived according to tribal customs, including a refusal to pay taxes or tribute, constant warfare with the Ottomans, mutual raids against one another and blood feuds. There was virtually no administration, because the *Vladika* had no income beyond what he got from warfare and intermittent Russian subsidies, so what armed force he disposed of always depended on the willingness of local chieftains to follow him. An assembly of headmen, convened in 1798, had agreed on a code of laws and a central court, but the applicability of these institutions remained conjectural. The *Vladika*, who traditionally came from the Petrović clan, in theory shared power with the 'governor', a post which, equally traditionally, was filled by a member of the Radonjić clan.

A more recognisable state structure began to emerge only in the reign of Peter II (1830–51), also known as Peter Njegoš. Njegoš's accession bloodily resolved the tensions between his clan and the Radonjić family, whose attempt to claim complete temporal power led to their virtual extinction. Able to rely on Russian subsidy, as well as the hands-on encouragement of Russian-appointed advisers, Njegoš convened another assembly of notables in 1831 and won approval for an Administrative Senate of 16, chosen from among the tribal leaders but who, innovatively, would be paid a salary out of the Russian funds. A regional police force, the Guard, was also put together, whose salaried commanders were also local strongmen. Going beyond this proved harder: the unruly Montenegrins resisted even a notional tax and state revenue continued to consist mainly of Russian gold. Njegoš spent much of his reign in desultory warfare with the Ottomans as well as his own subjects. He was also a leading poet of the Serbian language: his sanguinary epics, such as *The Mountain Wreath* (1847), are among the classics of Serbian literature, whatever one might think of the values they represent.

Njegoš's nephew Danilo I (1851–60), who wished to marry, finally secularised the office of prince in 1851 by refusing to take holy orders. In 1853 open war broke out with the Ottomans; only an Austrian ultimatum to the Porte saved Danilo from all-out invasion. During the Crimean War, Danilo was unable to exploit Ottoman vulnerability due to pressure from Austria, but when, in 1858, the freelance incursions of Montenegrin tribesmen into Hercegovina provoked another war with the Ottomans, the principality was not only saved by the intervention of France and Russia but was ceded the town of Grahovo, the one territorial acquisition of the reign. In domestic terms Danilo tried to build up a central armed force and in 1855 issued another legal code, but Montenegrins continued to elude the tentacles of the state.

By the time Danilo fell victim to an assassin in 1860 and was succeeded by Nikita I (1860–1918), Montenegro's position within the Ottoman Empire was as ill defined as in the eighteenth century. Formally its prince was the sultan's vassal; informally Montenegro exercised the freedom of a sovereign state. Yet not only did Montenegro not possess most of the attributes of a state, but its indeterminate position and poverty meant it remained constantly manipulated by the great powers. In the 1860s Montenegro enjoyed relatively close relations with the kindred Serbia, partly because of the dynastic link between Petrović and Obrenović, partly as an aspect of Prince Michael Obrenović's schemes for a Balkan alliance. Yet the two principalities were also potential rivals for the position of 'Piedmont' of the Serbs, and exploitation of this difference remained an option open to the chancelleries of Europe.

THE OTTOMAN EMPIRE'S ATTEMPTS AT REFORM

Any account of the Ottoman Empire in this period which starts with its breakaway provinces risks putting the cart before the horse. While much of what the Ottoman government attempted in the way of reform was clearly reactive, not least to the prospect of partition by the great powers, it would be misleading in the extreme to suggest that the sultans had not been interested in reform in the first place. The problem was how to get there.

By the turn of the century, Selim III had pioneered change by driving many if not all of the janissaries into the provinces and building up in their stead a 'New Model' army of professional troops. Yet there was arguably an even greater obstacle to reform than the obstreperousness of janissaries and Balkan Christians. This was the innate conservatism of the Ottoman elite and its suspicion that modernisation might come at the cost of Westernisation.

The New Model was understandably opposed by the janissaries, who correctly saw it as a threat to their own primacy. But the fact that it relied on European-style training and command structures was also seen by conservatives as an unsettling break with tradition. Much of the opposition to Selim came from the *ulema*, the clerical interpreters of Islamic law, who feared that reform would lead to European forms of education and European legal practices and hence the corruption of Ottoman Muslim values. Selim simply had not built up enough of a support base to overcome these forces. In addition he was faced, by 1806, with simultaneous Serbian revolt and war with Russia, to say nothing of the continuing unruliness of warlords such as Ali Pasha and Pasvanoğlu.

Matters came to a head in May 1807, when an alliance of janissaries, conservative notables and *ulema* staged a revolt in Constantinople and deposed Selim, who preferred to accept defeat rather than risk civil war by calling on the New Model for support. Selim's cousin was made Sultan Mustafa IV and a conservative government promptly disbanded the New Model. Enough of Selim's adherents, however, had fled to the provinces to make possible a counter-coup, led by Mustafa Pasha Bayraktar. When Mustafa Pasha's army entered Constantinople in July 1808, the conservatives managed to kill Selim before being toppled themselves and executed, and the last surviving member of the imperial house was installed as Mahmud II (1808–39). Mahmud's position was nevertheless precarious: the bulk of Mustafa Pasha's forces had no sooner been sent back to the Russian front than the conservatives struck again, killing Mustafa Pasha and retaining Mahmud on the throne, on condition that reform was abandoned.

Mahmud II, as one historian justly notes, was 'a man of incredible patience'.[5] Isolated and mistrusted, he spent years winning over religious conservatives by donations to schools and mosques and the ostentatious support of tradition. He gradually inserted men he could trust into positions of power and in particular built up an alternative military force in the non-janissary units of the army like the artillery, but without obviously Europeanising them. The janissaries, in the meantime, did themselves no favours by their continuing corruption and violence and their palpable inefficiency in various wars and revolts; on one occasion they set fire to houses in the capital to demonstrate their indignation at being asked to fight. By June 1826 Mahmud felt strong enough to strike: the janissaries were provoked to revolt by rumours of renewed attempts to reform them, but this time the sultan had enough military and popular backing to crush them. Janissaries in Constantinople and the provinces were literally slaughtered and their reign of terror ended.

Free at last, Mahmud concentrated on administrative changes, which laid the groundwork for more far-reaching reforms later. Officials were paid salaries instead of being expected to do their jobs for a fee. Something like a 'cabinet' of ministers was formed, with specific administrative remits. A post office was created in 1834 and in the same year permanent embassies in foreign capitals were established. This last, together with the founding in 1833 of a Translation Office for teaching officials foreign languages, had an incalculable effect by introducing an increasing number of Ottoman public servants to outside customs and outside ways of thinking. The first Ottoman newspaper, the weekly *Takvim-i Vekayi* (Calendar of Events), was started by the government in 1831 to provide officials and foreigners with the texts of laws and basic news, but proved the prototype for other journals. Mahmud even dared to resume the European-style organisation of the army and in 1835 entrusted this to a young Prussian, Helmut von Moltke, more famous as the later military genius of German 'unification'.

These reforms, however, came too late and were not enough. The Empire as we have seen was not strong enough to suppress the Serbian and Greek revolts, far less avert defeat by Russia in 1829. Even before Russia's intervention in the Greek revolt Mahmud had been forced to turn for back-up to the most powerful Ottoman warlord of all, Mohammed Ali of Egypt, and to promise him Crete and the Peloponnesus as a reward. The rise of the Albanian-born Mohammed Ali was itself symptomatic of the Empire's weakness. Most humiliatingly of all, when Mohammed Ali decided to invade Syria in 1832, as compensation for being denied the Peloponnesus, Mahmud's forces were soundly defeated at Konya in the heart of Anatolia in December. Constantinople itself was saved only by the paradox of Russian support. In return for signing the Treaty of Hünkâr Iskelesi in July 1833, which guaranteed Russia closure of the Straits to foreign warships in time of war, Mahmud bought protection from Mohammed Ali, albeit at the cost of leaving him in control of Syria. In 1839 Mahmud attempted to regain Syria, but the result was catastrophic. The Ottoman army was again defeated at Nezib in June, after Moltke had recommended an attack and the Ottoman commander had refused, revealingly, on advice from the *ulema* attached to the army. Mahmud died before learning of this, but in the meantime the Ottoman fleet had deserted to the Egyptians. The 'Mohammed Ali crisis' was eventually resolved when the great powers ejected the Egyptians from Syria, but induced the Porte to recognise Mohammed Ali as hereditary Pasha of Egypt. A 'Convention of the Straits', in 1841, effectively internationalised this vital strategic waterway, closing it to all foreign warships in peacetime. The sultan could not even control his own doorstep.

Despite these disastrous events, the accession of the 16-year-old Abdülmecit I (1839–61) was nevertheless the start of the most concerted attempt yet at reform, the period of the *Tanzimat* (Reordering). This was due to the emergence by this stage of a certain class of Ottoman official, committed to the preservation of the Empire and yet more alive to the need for modernisation and the value of western examples than had hitherto been the norm. Abdülmecit's first grand vezir, Mustafa Reşit Paşa, was the archetype, having travelled widely and served as a diplomat in Paris and London. Reşit Paşa's two principal protégés and co-adjutors, Ali Paşa and Fuat Paşa, followed him up a similar career ladder and alternated in the highest offices with him and after his death.

The defining document of the *Tanzimat* was the *Hatt-ı Şerif* (Imperial Rescript) of Gülhane, the courtyard of the sultan's palace where the decree was read out on 3 November 1839. This announced three main resolutions with potentially revolutionary implications. All subjects of the sultan, regardless of religion, were entitled to 'security for life, honours and fortune'; there would henceforth be 'a regular system of assessing and levying taxes'; and the levying of troops would be equally regular.[6] In effect the Empire was saying that all subjects were equal before the law, with equal rights as well as responsibilities. Christians were entitled to fair treatment in courts, even *vis-à-vis* Muslims; all subjects would be taxed fairly and proportionately; and all subjects would be liable to conscription.

The Gülhane rescript was obviously intended to convince the great powers that the Empire was still a going concern, intent on rejuvenation. It was equally, however, an attempt to win over the Empire's millions of subjects, so many of whom were disaffected, especially in the Balkan provinces. Whether the new-found rights of non-Muslims could be reconciled with the traditional dominance of Muslims was another matter; certainly the decree's authors hedged their bets when they also represented it as a 'return' to traditional Ottoman values. Whatever the rhetoric, the basic aim was undoubtedly a greater centralisation and control from the centre.

In 1840 a new legal code was issued, formally based on strict equality before the law. Taxes, formerly collected by governors or tax 'farmers', who extorted extra for their own profit, were now entrusted to salaried officials responsible to the sultan's treasury. In administrative terms provincial governors were now to be assisted by councils of notables, thirteen in number, of which seven would be officials and the rest local notables, and include non-Muslims. Below this were local councils of five, one of whose members had to be a non-Muslim notable. The armed forces, especially the army, were subjected to a thoroughgoing reorganisation along regimental lines and a reserve force was established in which ex-conscripts were enrolled for seven years. Commissariat supply depôts were created and a rudimentary educational network for recruits was set up.

Admirable though these reforms were, their practical implementation was more problematical. To begin with there were simply not enough educated and trained bureaucrats to go round, and in many corners of the Empire the sultan's ordinances remained paper only or met with deliberate obstruction. Then, too, the collection of taxes was necessarily an imperfect exercise, with the result that the government frequently could not pay for its own reforms. The poll tax on non-Muslims was not even abolished until 1855, at which point the government also ruled that non-Muslims were entitled to bear arms and were thus, in theory, liable to be conscripted. In practice Christians preferred to buy their way out of military service and the Ottoman army was happier not recruiting them. And although the reformers were granted a relatively long period of calm in international affairs, the outbreak of the Crimean conflict set things back generally. The government was obliged to cease construction of all public works and even to suspend council officials' salaries. Apart from the expenses of the war itself, an influx of hundreds of thousands of Muslim refugees, expelled from Russia at the war's end, imposed an additional burden on the state.

At the peace negotiations in Paris the great powers, assuming a collective responsibility for the Empire's vassal-states in the Balkans, also insisted on a reiteration of Ottoman intentions of reform. The result was the *Hatt-ı Hümayun* of 18 February 1856, which again proclaimed the complete equality before the law of all the sultan's subjects. As the Empire's subsequent history shows, this good intention proved easier to announce than to fulfil. Instead, most of the modernisation that took place in the post-Crimean period was in physical infrastructure and technical education rather than in political and social institutions. Slowly the Empire began to construct a railway system, to bind its domains together by telegraph, and to acquire a small cadre of native engineers, physicians and technocrats.

Yet with modernisation came also, in the end, foreign debt. In 1854, after consciously resisting the temptation hitherto, the Ottoman government bowed to the exigencies of the Crimean War and took out its first overseas loan. Thereafter the Ottoman state debt ballooned from year to year, and as the interest on the debt increased so too did the Empire's vulnerability to outside pressure and its potential inability to continue modernisation and hence ensure its own internal stability. By the time Ali Pasha, the last of the original *Tanzimat* generation, died in 1871, the Ottoman imperium was about to be rocked to its foundations by a combination of bankruptcy, nationalist revolt and foreign intervention.

11

RUSSIA AND PRUSSIA 1804-67

There were certain parallels between Russia and Prussia in the first half of the nineteenth century. Both were still largely agrarian societies, ruled by monarchies with far fewer restraints on their pretensions to absolute rule than the Habsburg Monarchy. Both were conscious of the need to modernise and had already devoted some energy to this agenda. Both demonstrated that absolutism itself, because of its inherent inefficiency, could pose practical difficulties to modernisation. Both were committed to the continuing suppression of Polish independence.

There were also, however, increasing differences. Prussia in the nineteenth century had far better prospects for genuine modernisation, whereas Russia dropped further and further behind its European competitors. In terms of political modernisation, Prussia after 1848, while hardly a democratic state, at least became a constitutional one. As for nationality problems, Prussia's only concern, at least until the 1860s, was with its Polish minority, whereas Russia was a truly multinational empire, with all the headaches that promised in an age of nationalism.

THE RUSSIAN EMPIRE: THE LIMITS OF AUTOCRACY

The fundamental problem of the Russian Empire was that its position as a great power was increasingly undermined by its political and economic backwardness and by its multinational composition. The Empire continued to expand territorially, acquiring in Eastern Europe alone Finland in 1809, Bessarabia in 1812 and the lion's share of repartitioned Poland in 1815, not to mention its conquests in the Caucasus and Central Asia. By the standards of the Napoleonic Wars, sheer size and population were decisive. By the standards of the Crimean War, however, size was no longer enough: Russia's industrialised western opponents were able to bring a decisive concentration of force to bear against it.

The tsars recognised there was a problem; the conundrum was how to address it. Alexander I (1801–25) made a sincere but ultimately half-hearted attempt to modernise and made constitutional concessions to newly acquired peoples. His successor Nicholas I (1825–55) abandoned any thought of wide-ranging reform as too dangerous, a policy then reversed by Alexander II (1855–81) under the impact of the Crimea. In the meantime nationality was becoming an issue, not just among non-Russians but among ethnic Russians themselves, a development frowned upon by the autocracy wherever it emerged.

Alexander I, influenced by enlightened thinking, came to the throne an avowed lover of constitutions, even if he owed his accession to the palace coup which strangled his unstable father Paul I. The genuinely idealistic Alexander dismantled the regime of police surveillance by which the paranoid Paul had monitored his subjects, permitted nobles to travel abroad again and encouraged the importation of foreign publications. He believed that the evil of serfdom would somehow have to be abolished and, with his friend Prince Adam Czartoryski, deplored the eighteenth-century Polish Partitions. Yet constitutional rule, for Alexander, meant essentially that he should govern in accordance with law rather than in tandem with representative institutions. Excellent reasons could always be found for postponing emancipation of the peasantry, such as the opposition of landowners. The undoubted constitutional status of not only Finland and Poland but also the Ionian Islands, during their brief experience of Russian rule, did not give their peoples the right to criticise the imperial will.

For all Alexander's good intentions he effected little constructive change. Government was made notionally more coherent by the creation in 1802 of ministries responsible for specific departments, but since this was set up alongside, rather than as a replacement for, the 'colleges' or committees of officials which had hitherto run things, the result was simply more bureaucracy; and the creation of a State Council in 1810, separate from the ministries, made things even more complicated. From 1807 to 1812 Alexander's principal minister was the remarkable Mikhail Speransky, a non-noble with wide-ranging plans for introducing the rule of law, the separation of powers and even a representative assembly or *Duma*. Apart from the State Council, however, and the requirement, in 1809, that senior bureaucrats undergo examinations of their fitness for their jobs, not much else of Speransky's programme was implemented. Alexander's reign saw more progress in education: six universities were founded, including those of Dorpat in Livonia and Vilna in Lithuania, as well as several hundred schools, and although state funding for these latter was inadequate, it was supplemented by private donations.

Speransky fell from favour in 1812, a victim in part of Alexander's growing preoccupation with the French threat, but also of criticism from conservative opponents. The most articulate of these was the historian Nikolai Karamzin, whose 'Memorandum on Ancient and Modern Russia' (1810) forcibly argued that for the tsar to subordinate himself to the rule of law was positively dangerous because the sheer size and complexity of the

Empire required an untrammelled and undisputed authority. The tsar, Karamzin claimed, exercised this authority most effectively through the nobility, which was why it was essential that serfdom be retained as the guarantee of noble prosperity. Such arguments struck a chord with many patriotic Russians, who saw Speransky as an impractical dreamer out of touch with Russian realities, trying to impose institutional forms derived from French models.

The titanic struggle with Napoleon was quite enough to distract Alexander from internal affairs, but his decision to carry the war into Europe, shape the peace settlement at Vienna and act as one of its guarantors thereafter meant that Russia was taking on a far greater international role than hitherto. This, together with Alexander's increasingly conservative reaction against the revolutionary manifestations of liberalism and nationalism, is generally assumed to be the reason for his lack of commitment to further modernisation. Yet it remains the case that, in territories regained or newly acquired, Alexander either confirmed existing institutions and privileges, as with the Grand Duchy of Finland, or granted some form of autonomy or constitutional rule, as in Bessarabia and the 'Congress' Kingdom of Poland. The tantalising question is how far Alexander might have been prepared to extend constitutionalism to the rest of the Empire. As late as 1818–20 a draft constitution, produced for the emperor by his friend Nikolai Novosiltsev, actually proposed a federal structure, with the Empire divided into 'vice-regencies', guaranteed civil liberties, and regional and national assemblies. This appears to have been too radical for Alexander, but the circulation of such ideas, even in the narrow circles of the nobility, created expectations of change which were to be bitterly disappointed.

Alexander died suddenly in November 1825 and the confusion over his successor – he had designated Nicholas, the younger of his two brothers, as heir rather than the elder, Constantine, but without publicising this decision – prompted an attempted coup on Constantine's behalf by a group known ever since as the 'Decembrists'. This label obscures the decade-long build-up of frustration among some of the nobility, most of them army officers, with the slow pace of reform. The Decembrists, whose numbers never exceeded more than a few hundred, had been conspiring in a succession of secret societies since 1816, and their common goal, despite the divisions among them, was the transformation of the Russian state and society.

The Decembrists believed that serfdom should be abolished, although the moderates among them did not think this obliged the state to give the peasants any land. They differed as to whether there should be a constitutional monarchy or a republic and whether a centralised or federal state was best. What is most interesting about the Decembrists in an East European context is, firstly, that their views were shaped largely by contact with Western Europe and, secondly, that the impetus for their initial formation was hostility to non-ethnic Russians. Thousands of Russian nobles experienced the West for themselves during the Napoleonic Wars and after, and they brought back a vivid sense of Russia's backwardness. The war itself created for probably the first time a sense of national solidarity with the peasant masses, who fought and suffered and yet whose only reward was the continuation of serfdom. And the Decembrists bridled at the number of ethnic Germans in the state bureaucracy and the fact that non-Russians like the Poles received constitutional rights while the Russians received none. The most radical Decembrist of all, Pavel Pestel, argued for giving the Poles formal if not *de facto* independence, but otherwise aiming at the assimilation of all other peoples of the Empire into '*one* single nation', the Russian; Pestel excepted the Jews, whom he thought should be forcibly deported to the Ottoman Empire.[1]

Nicholas I used the Decembrist revolt as a cue, not for wide-ranging reform but for more piecemeal tinkering. For 30 years this strong-minded tsar conducted a personal war against the subversive forces of liberalism and nationalism at home and abroad. Nicholas was open to suggestions for reform and indeed anxious to effect change, but was determined that the initiative had to come from the centre. Russia became a byword for censorship, police surveillance and an ultimately self-defeating attempt at bureaucratic control. Nationalist revolt in Poland was brutally suppressed, and in the name of monarchical solidarity Nicholas acted as the policeman of Europe, with the exception of Greece where intervention happened to coincide with Russia's strategic interests.

At the heart of Nicholas's autocracy was the vain conviction that the forces of revolution could be kept at bay through sheer bureaucratic vigilance. To this end the 'Third Section' of the imperial chancellery, which was responsible for internal security, became an all-pervasive organ of surveillance. The tsar personally censored the work of Russia's greatest poet, Alexander Pushkin, whose closeness to the Decembrists earned him a captive existence at court under the imperial eye.

Nicholas, however, was intelligent enough to perceive that his subjects had to be taught loyalty. The Polish uprising of 1830–1, coming so soon after the Decembrist revolt, was decisive in pushing Nicholas towards an early attempt at creating what was subsequently termed 'official nationality': all subjects, regardless of their ethnic identity, had to accept that they were servants of the tsarist state.[2] The architect of this ideological counter-offensive was Count Sergei Uvarov, whose seminal report of December 1832 recommended that education be firmly linked to 'the quintessentially Russian protective principles of Orthodoxy, Autocracy and Nationality'.[3] Only thus, reasoned Uvarov, who served as the aptly named minister for public instruction from 1833 to 1849, could the Empire be safeguarded: religious belief, obedience to the tsar and an emphasis on the Russianness of the state would counteract the vitiating influence of western liberalism and the subversion of subject peoples.

The cautiousness of Nicholas I's government ensured that Russia remained backward. The insistence on controlling everything from the centre increased the overall numbers of the state bureaucracy, but without any obvious gain in efficiency or reduction in venality. Speransky was brought back into government service and entrusted with the codification of existing laws which, when completed in 1833, at least laid the groundwork for future legal reform. Nicholas could see the value of the universities in producing trained minds for state service, but in his view this was their main purpose, and after 1848 the study of law and politics was banned and higher education restricted to those intending a career in state service. At the same time the stifling of open debate was not enough to discourage covert dissent, some of it increasingly radical, among Russia's superfluous intelligentsia. Above all, serfdom was tackled only marginally.

There is a large literature on whether Russia's continuing backwardness was due to serfdom, with the consensus now suggesting that serfdom was still sufficiently profitable for most landowners to prefer its retention and that, as in the Ottoman Empire, peasants in some areas were able to participate in enough economic activity on the side to justify the term 'proto-industrialisation'.[4] The real arguments against serfdom were the moral case against treating human beings as chattels, the possibly exaggerated fear of peasant rebellion and the purely practical insight that, without emancipation, Russia was never going to achieve genuine modernisation. Serfdom may not have been the economic drag its critics said it was, but as long as it was retained the economic growth the Russian Empire was capable of could simply not be attained. Russia paid the penalty in the Crimean War.

Alexander II, succeeding his father in the middle of the war, grasped the nettle of peasant emancipation in 1861. He also learned the essential lesson of the Crimea, which was that Russia would have to modernise or perish. Even conservatives were convinced of this. A country whose troops had to march all the way to the Black Sea for want of railroads, and were armed with flintlock muskets as opposed to their enemies' rifles, was clearly in urgent need of reform.

Alexander had no intention of submitting his autocratic authority to any form of popular assembly, but he recognised that a more open debate on how to reform the Empire was essential. The censorship and police surveillance were accordingly relaxed in 1856, and throughout the 1860s and 1870s considerable, though never absolute, freedom of expression prevailed. In the process, and in conjunction with the growth in a university-educated class, something like 'public opinion' in Russian society finally took shape. The sense of a civic identity was also encouraged by legal reforms, such as the introduction of public court proceedings, trial by jury and a right to legal representation.

Emancipation apart, the most striking innovation of the reign was the creation in 1864 of a system of local self-government, in the shape of provincial and district assemblies or *zemstvos*. These were elected indirectly from among the three main classes of landowners, townspeople and peasants, on a franchise heavily weighted in favour of property and tax; they had no executive powers as such, but were expected to advise local administrations on such issues as roads, prisons, hospitals, education and the like. Nevertheless the *zemstvos* were revolutionary in that they were the first genuinely representative institutions in Russia since the seventeenth century: peasants made up 42 per cent of the members of a typical *zemstvo* at district level, with landowners at 38 per cent and townsmen at 17.[5] This contributed to a growing national consciousness. Significantly, however, *zemstvos* were not introduced in provinces where the majority of the population was non-Russian.

THE PARADOX OF RUSSIAN NATIONALISM

Despite Alexander's reputation as the 'Tsar Liberator' of the serfs, it was clear by the 1860s that, for a significant section of the intelligentsia, especially the younger generation, his reforms were not enough. A minority of alienated intellectuals was beginning to gravitate towards radical solutions such as nihilism, populism and revolutionary socialism, and the regime's sole response to such radicalism was repression. In addition to the rise of what might be called the left-liberal opposition, however, dissatisfaction with tsarist rule was also increasingly taking the shape of what can only be termed an ethnic or Great Russian nationalism.

It is conventional to date the emergence of Russian nationalism from the period of the Crimean War, a humiliation which forced Russians to identify themselves *vis-à-vis* the outside world and which was qualitatively different from the largely religious and dynastic loyalties which had fired most Russians to resist Napoleon in 1812. Yet historians are also increasingly aware of the paradox of Russian nationalism in the nineteenth century. What did being Russian mean, in a multinational empire? And given that Russia was an autocracy, which rejected the participation even of Russians in the governance of the state, how could nationalism, an ideology whose founding premise was the sovereignty of the people, be tolerated by the tsars?

Some of the preoccupations of the Decembrists were early focal points for Russian nationalism: a sense of inferiority or hostility towards the West, but also a pride in Russia's separateness and resilience, coupled with an animus against the Empire's non-Russians. In the reign of Nicholas I the first coherent expression of Russian nationalism was the movement known as Slavophilism. The Slavophiles by definition exalted everything Slav, but especially Russia's pre-eminence in the Slav world. They held not only that Russia was unique and different from the West but that it was culturally and morally superior because of its Orthodox faith, which had ensured that Russians preserved a spiritual apartness. Like nationalists everywhere, Slavophiles such as the historian Mikhail Pogodin and the publicist Konstantin Aksakov stressed the deep historical roots of the Russian language and enthusiastically collected folklore. They also considered the

Russian autocracy obtaining before Peter the Great to be a natural, indeed necessary part of national character because the Russian people were unpolitical and did not want to rule themselves, trusting instead to the tsars to hold Russia together.

As an early variant of nationalism, it has to be admitted that Slavophilism was hardly a roaring success. Progressive-minded Russians, who hoped for political reform, denounced the Slavophiles as obscurantist apologists for reaction, while Nicholas I regarded them with suspicion, in part because their name implied a revolutionary desire to see all Slavs in the same state. Arrested in 1849, several Slavophiles talked themselves out of prison only by protesting the unpolitical nature of their goals. In reality the Slavophiles were not a threat to the autocracy; they shared many of the values of Uvarov's 'official nationality', including its hostility to the non-Russian nationalities of the Empire.

Something like a modern ethnic Russian nationalism appeared only with Pan-Slavism, a movement first articulated under the shock of the Crimean War. Pan-Slavism posited that all Slav peoples had a common cultural identity, despite the obvious differences of language and, in the case of West Slavs and some South Slavs, religion. More importantly, Pan-Slavists like the scientist Nikolai Danilevsky and the journalist Mikhail Katkov assigned leadership of this Slav community to Russia. The basis for this hegemony, as with the Slavophiles, was the innate superiority of Russian culture and the greatness of the Russian state.

As a means of buttressing Russia's international position, as well as rational-ising its continuing domination of recalcitrant Slav peoples like the Poles, Pan-Slavism was essentially an apologia for Russian imperialism. It was often assumed by foreign observers that Pan-Slavism was the guiding force behind Russia's foreign policy, which it never was, although in the 1870s it did exert consider-able influence on Alexander II's reaction to the Balkan crisis. Yet at the heart of Pan-Slavism was something which set it on a collision course with the tsarist regime, which was precisely its appeal to the ideal of the nation. Unlike the Slavophiles, Pan-Slavists were highly critical of the autocracy, whose inefficiency and unaccountability, in their view, had produced the catastrophe of the Crimea. A truly national policy, for Pan-Slavists, must harness the energy of the people by involving their representatives in government, modernising the economy and the state, repressing the subject nationalities and wielding Russian power more forcefully abroad. Some of these aims coincided with those of the tsars, but the crucial ingredient of nationalism, the recruitment and involvement of the Russian people, was out of the question. The Russian autocracy saw national-ism as a threat and that included the nationalism of ethnic Russians.

THE CHALLENGE OF NON-RUSSIAN NATIONALISM

Russian nationalism was in part a response to the nationalism of the Empire's non-Russian minorities. This was especially true of Polish nationalism, which had a pedigree going back into the eighteenth century. Dealing with the Polish question was thus an existential task for Russian patriots. Yet the early nineteenth century also saw the emergence of additional national movements, the repression of which was increasingly the preoccupation of tsarist governments.

The *Poles* were the most high-profile of the minorities and their two revolts in this period tested the Empire to the limits. Both revolts failed, however, because the gentry base of Polish nationalism was still too narrow to attract mass support. As a consequence we can discern two strands in the Polish relationship with Russia. The first hankered after the old Polish–Lithuanian Commonwealth, in a political rather than ethnic sense, and whether at home or in the sizeable Polish emigration plotted to regain independence by force or diplomacy. The second was accommodationist: Poles who accepted the unlikelihood of reviving the old Poland but hoped, by working with the tsarist regime, to mitigate the treatment of their people.

One of the ironies of the situation after repartition in 1815 was that, while more Poles than ever before lived under Russian rule, Alexander I seemed genuinely to intend ruling them constitutionally. It was largely on Alexander's insistence that the Treaty of Vienna recognised the existence of a Polish nationality and promised the Poles 'a Representation and National Institutions' in each of the three Partitions.[6] The problem was that 'constitution' for Alexander meant 'an orderly system of government based on the rule of law' rather than one where the ruler was bound to respect certain fundamental rights of his subjects or to consult some form of representative assembly.[7] Thus, Congress Poland had a genuine autonomy: although Alexander was king, it had its own administration and army; the language of state and of education was Polish, with a new University of Warsaw founded in 1816; a *Sejm* (parliament) was elected every two years on a franchise wider than that of France; and civil liberties such as freedom of expression were guaranteed, while the abolition of serfdom under Napoleon was confirmed. Nevertheless Alexander was quick to appoint his own men to positions of influence, including his younger brother Constantine as viceroy, and when the *Sejm* of 1820 criticised him he ignored it. The Poles were particularly disappointed that Alexander had not reunited Congress Poland with the western provinces or *gubernii* of the Empire, formerly part of the old Commonwealth. At the same time conservative, nationalist opinion in Russia itself pointed out the incongruity of a constitutional Poland within autocratic Russia.

Nicholas I progressively restricted the Poles' constitutional freedoms. In November 1830 a group of young army officers proclaimed an insurrection against Russian rule. Moderates like Czartoryski condemned the uprising, but were drafted in to negotiate a revision of the constitution with the tsar and soon found themselves sharing the revolutionary government with radicals like the historian Joachim Lelewel, who urged appealing to the masses for support. The *Sejm* then in January 1831 radicalised the situation irrevocably by deposing Nicholas as king. The result was disaster. Despite having a disciplined army of 80,000 men, which initially held the Russians off, the National Government under Czartoryski suffered from a succession of inept military commanders; just as decisive, the revolt 'lacked wide social support'.[8] When Russian troops re-established control, Nicholas abolished the constitution, the *Sejm* and the army, forbade the teaching of Polish in schools and closed down the universities of Warsaw and Vilna. Some 10,000 Poles, headed by Czartoryski, fled abroad and Russian Poland entered a new dark age.

The Polish emigration was divided between Czartoryski's aristocratic moderates and democratic radicals like Lelewel. Lelewel's 'Young Poland' was eventually superseded, in the 1830s, by the Polish Democratic Society, also based in Paris. All factions of the diaspora agreed, after 1831, on the need to involve the peasant masses by holding out some form of emancipation; significantly the Poles envisaged extending this programme to the Lithuanian, Belorussian and Ukrainian peasants of the nine western *gubernii*, in the hope that they would thereby be won over for inclusion in a restored Polish Commonwealth. Not all Polish landowners, however, were happy with this and getting the message across even to Polish peasants that the hated *szlachta* were on their side was fraught with difficulties, as the events of 1846 in Habsburg Galicia demonstrated.

The other problem Polish nationalists faced was that the autocracy was also feeling its way towards emancipation, especially after Alexander II's accession. It was precisely the issue of emancipation, however, which led to renewed revolt. Poles generally, whether moderate or radical, were anxious that the tsar should not be able to claim credit for emancipation either in the Congress Kingdom or the western *gubernii*, yet plans for a two-stage emancipation were accompanied by demonstrations which met with a crackdown and several killed. Further attempts to establish order simply resulted in more demonstrations, more deaths and the imposition of martial law in the autumn. The radicals, increasingly known as 'Reds' as opposed to the moderate 'Whites', were encouraged by this to start planning revolt and a Central National Committee was formed in mid-1862, which recruited an underground army of some 6000. In January 1863 the authorities provoked a premature uprising by ordering the conscription of 12,000 young Poles known for their radicalism. The Reds proclaimed themselves the Provisional National Government of Poland and 'declared war' on the Russians on 22 January.

The revolt of 1863–4 lasted as long as it did not because of the absolute numbers of insurgents, who at any given point cannot have been higher than 20–30,000, and totalled perhaps 200,000 out of a population of 4 million, but because it was more deeply rooted in the hopes of the people generally, compared with 1830. It was also more diffuse, conducted as a series of guerrilla campaigns which the Russian army found difficult to stamp out. The revolt was soon joined by the Whites, desperate to associate themselves with the national cause and, in the process, give it a more moderate direction, but the insurgents were riven by factionalism and received no help from outside, apart from volunteers from Austria and Prussia. What kept the revolt spreading, and provided it with additional recruits, was the proclamation at the outset that the peasants would be granted ownership of the land they tilled; there was even a promise of land for landless labourers. This won over 30,000 peasants, not just in the kingdom but in the Lithuanian and Belorussian *gubernii*. Peasant support faded only when, in March 1864, the tsar was persuaded to offer the same terms himself, which were considerably more generous than the settlement in Russia.

The last serious resistance was overcome by August 1864. Apart from those executed, thousands of rebels were marched to exile in Siberia and 3400 noble estates in both the kingdom and the western *gubernii* were confiscated. A heavy police regime was imposed and Russian made the language of administration and justice. The Catholic Church, seen as a hearth of dissidence, was penalised by the abolition of a fifth of its parishes, the non-appointment of bishops to vacant sees and the closure of monasteries. As we have seen, the *zemstvo* system was not extended to Russian Poland, nor was trial by jury introduced. Poles after 1864 tended to accept that they were confined to Russian rule for good. What was different, however, was that the old, gentry-based nationalism was broken and a new, more socially inclusive concept of the nation began to gain ground.

The *Ukrainians* still laboured under something of an identity problem in this period. Not only had the area now known as the Ukraine, historically, been divided between Russia and the Polish–Lithuanian Commonwealth, but after the Partitions a substantial number of Ukrainian speakers remained in Austrian Galicia. In Russia the social elite of the former Hetmanate, on the left bank of the Dnieper, consisted largely of Cossacks, who by the turn of the century were completely Russianised and remote from their Ukrainian-speaking serfs. In 'right-bank Ukraine', which had remained longest in Poland–Lithuania, the nobility was overwhelmingly Polish or Polish speaking; in both areas the predominant cultural medium was undoubtedly still Polish. The peasant masses and the elite on the left bank were Orthodox, while on the right bank the Polish elite was Catholic, but the few Ukrainian-speaking landowners and the peasantry were Orthodox, since the Uniate Church was barely tolerated in Russia. Russians were in the habit of assuming that Ukrainian was simply a 'South Russian' dialect of Russian, and in the absence of a Ukrainian-speaking elite few Ukrainians took issue with this until the early nineteenth century.

What changed this situation was in part the Russian Empire's perceived need to dismantle the Polish cultural hegemony in the area. After the 1830–1 revolt the noble status of 64,000 lesser Polish gentry on the right bank was revoked and these gradually assimilated into the Ukrainian-speaking mass of the population; the largest Polish estates, however, remained intact. The Uniate Church, seen as a tool of Polish Catholicism, was formally absorbed into the Orthodox Church in 1839.

Ukrainians were affected by the general quickening of interest across Europe in the origins of languages and peoples. Left-bank Ukraine was the focus of what national consciousness arose, ironically as a result of the founding by the tsars of universities at Kharkiv, in 1805, and Kiev in 1834. Uvarov's policy of 'official nationality' initially encouraged research into the Slavic peoples, as a counter to Polish predominance but also in the assumption that Ukrainians were essentially Russians. Although teaching at both universities was in Russian, each created a generation of Ukrainian intellectuals. Much of the early activity collecting folklore, writing histories and the like was not only the work of Russians but was also written in Russian, and for decades the attitude prevailed, even among Ukrainians, that Ukrainian as a mere 'dialect' was unsuitable for literary expression. One of the greatest Ukrainian writers, for instance, the novelist Nikolai Gogol, wrote exclusively in Russian.

It was not until the 1840s that a generation emerged arguing, firstly, that Ukrainian was in fact a literary language and secondly, that this implied the existence of a separate Ukrainian nationality. The historian Mykola Kostomarov promoted the idea of a Ukrainian literature and history. The novelist and ethnographer Panteleimon Kulish wrote historical fiction, originally in Russian, then increasingly in Ukrainian, as well as in-depth studies of the history of the Ukraine. Above all, the peasant poet and painter Taras Shevchenko demonstrated the flexibility of the language, as well as denouncing the oppression of the Ukrainian masses not just by Russia but by their own Cossack elite. Such activities, as well as the formation of an ill-focused secret society called the Cyril and Methodius Brotherhood, eventually drew down the wrath of the authorities. Some ten of them were arrested in 1847 and sentenced to various terms of imprisonment and exile; with characteristic harshness, Nicholas I insisted that Shevchenko be drafted into the army and 'forbidden to write or to sketch'.[9]

The Ukrainian nationalists were able to regroup after 1855 under the more relaxed regime of Alexander II. Kostomarov and Kulish were both allowed to publish and Shevchenko was released from the army. Ukrainian cultural societies, known as *hromadas*, sprang up in imitation of the original, founded in the early 1860s, and which promoted creative literature, scholarly journals and the compilation of grammar books and other school texts. Following the second Polish revolt, however, the government cracked down yet again on nationalist movements other than Russian ones, and by this point it was reacting in part to denunciations of all non-Russian minorities by Pan-Slav activists like Mikhail Katkov. In July 1863 the interior minister, Count Peter Valuev, issued a decree which flatly asserted that 'a Little Russian [Ukrainian] language has not, does not, and cannot exist, and that its dialects as spoken by the masses are the same as the Russian language'.[10] The Valuev Decree accordingly banned the publication as well as the importation of instructional books in Ukrainian, Lithuanian and Belorussian, restrictions later reinforced by the Ems Decree of 1876. Given that the teaching of these languages was effectively banned as well, it was plain that even the 'liberal' Tsar Alexander was reluctant to admit the very existence of national minorities.

Among the *Baltic* peoples, as among the East Slav *Belorussians*, there was still very little identifiable cultural or political activity because these were peasant peoples as yet untouched by social differentiation, let alone nationalism. This was despite the fact that the one area of the Empire where the abolition of serfdom came early, apart from the lands formerly in Napoleon's Grand Duchy of Warsaw, comprised the Baltic provinces of Estonia, Livonia and Courland. Between 1802 and 1804, with the encouragement of Alexander I, the Livonian and Estonian diets passed legislation regulating personal obligations and giving peasant leaseholders hereditary title to the land they farmed. Full emancipation followed in all three Baltic provinces between 1816 and 1819, but there was a catch. Serfs were made legally free but given no land; instead, those who wished to remain on the land were forced to negotiate with their former masters for the right to remain as tenant farmers, or go elsewhere; in addition they were still liable for labour services. This was initially at least a solution which left most peasants worse off. Subsequent peasant ordinances passed by the Baltic provinces in the 1850s and 1860s partially rectified this situation by setting aside some land for purchase or hire by peasants. Combined with the greater provision of primary schools for the children of Latvian and Estonian peasants, this put the Baltic provinces economically a generation ahead of the rest of the Empire.

In terms of national consciousness it is instructive to compare the experiences of ethnic Lithuanians with Belorussians. The former Grand Duchy of Lithuania, when part of the Polish Commonwealth, had been a vast state comprising not just present-day Lithuania but all of modern Belarus and most of the Ukraine. 'Lithuania' for the duchy's Polonised gentry meant this medieval entity, but for the very few educated Lithuanian speakers, such as the historian Simonas Daukantas, it represented an historic identity which could be claimed, however bogusly, for Lithuanians. For the masses of Lithuanian, Belorussian and Ukrainian peasants, however, it meant nothing. Yet in the decades following emancipation, a tiny number of Lithuanian peasants gradually prospered, while the Russian government's drive to break the cultural hegemony of Polish, after 1863, meant that some state schools changed from Polish to Russian instruction, but also for the first time taught Lithuanian as part of the curriculum. The first generation of Lithuanian nationalists was being produced.

For Belorussian peasants there was no national myth to draw on, nor did anyone emerge even after emancipation willing to champion the unique character of the Belorussian language. Instead, like Ukrainian, Belorussian was accepted by most scholars in the nineteenth century as a dialect of Russian. Translations of works in other languages into Belorussian were being made as early as the 1840s by the Lithuanian–Polish poet Vincent Dunin-Martsinkevich, but in the absence of any agreed grammar or alphabet this sort of exercise was seen as a form of linguistic curiosity and there was no literate, Belorussian-speaking market for it. Those few Belorussians who gained an education, after 1861, did so in Russian, whose similarities to their native tongue made it easy enough to master, and possession of which was their ticket to upward mobility.

The Baltic German nobility, and *Germans* generally, continued in this period to function as a sort of factotum class for the autocracy, supplying so large a proportion of the Empire's bureaucrats and diplomats that, as we have seen, they became the object of ethnic Russians' hostility. Baltic German nobles were prominent among the assassins of Paul I, and in the reign of Nicholas 19 out of 134 members of the State Council were Germans. One German, Benckendorff, headed the Third Section; another, Nesselrode, though not of Baltic extraction, functioned as foreign minister for more than 40 years without ever mastering Russian. A Russian general, told by Alexander I to name his reward for distinction on the battlefield, allegedly asked to be 'promoted to the rank of German'.[11] Both German and Russian nobles were part of a cosmopolitan elite, but the perceived ubiquity of Germans undoubtedly contributed to the growing nationalism of ethnic Russians by the 1860s.

Finally, thanks to the Polish Partitions the Russian Empire contained the largest population of *Jews* in Europe, some 400,000.[12] In theory Jews had been granted full civil equality by Alexander I's Jewish Statute of 1804, but in practice they remained outcast and discriminated against. The Statute did not apply in Congress Poland after 1815, for instance, where equality was made conditional on assimilation into Polish society, and restrictions were placed on Jews' economic activity. In Russia proper, Jews were still confined to the Pale of Settlement. Despite the enlightened intentions of 1804, discrimination was rife and the enforcement of restrictions was taken far more seriously than the upholding of rights. Matters got worse under Nicholas I, who favoured forcible rather than voluntary assimilation. In his reign Jewish self-regulation was abolished, Jews were forcibly deported from border areas and in 1827 their exemption from military service was brutally reversed, with some conscripts for 25 years' service being taken as young as 12. Alexander II rescinded this particular cruelty in 1856, but otherwise did little to protect his Jewish subjects.

THE KINGDOM OF PRUSSIA 1804-67

The larger story of Prussia's role in the creation of the German Empire is tangential to a history of Eastern Europe, whereas that of Prussia is quite central to it. Our main concern here is with Prussia's increasingly poisonous relationship with its Polish subjects.

For Prussians the Grand Duchy of Warsaw, formed largely from Prussian territory in 1807, was part of the trauma of defeat, a proof that Prussia was not modern enough and a spur to reform. For Poles it was the partial realisation of their dream of national rebirth, a dream which Napoleon consciously appealed to when he called on them to rise up against the Prussians: 'I will see if the Poles are worthy of being a nation.'[13] The Poles duly rose up and were rewarded with a puppet state, whose fortunes rose and fell with the emperor's.

The Poles' behaviour in 1806 shaped Prussian attitudes thereafter in two ways. Some were already urging King Frederick William III (1797–1840) to accept that the Poles were thoroughly unreliable, which meant Prussia should begin the 'Germanisation' of its Polish lands by compulsorily purchasing the estates of the Polish *szlachta*. Reformers like Baron vom Stein, by contrast, argued in response to this that the government should win the Polish nobles' loyalty by involving them in local government. Stein's 'Nassau memorandum' of June 1807 acknowledged the Poles' loyalty to their own nation and suggested that Frederick William play to this patriotism by adopting the title of King of Poland.

Conciliation remained the key note when, in 1815, Prussia regained control of the Grand Duchy of Posen; as Frederick William proclaimed to the Poles, 'You too have a fatherland . . . You will be incorporated in my monarchy without having to relinquish your nationality.'[14] A Polish magnate was appointed governor of Posen and a diet was convened in 1827, in which the Polish gentry were well represented. The *szlachta* remained the dominant social class, constituting the judiciary and retaining their seigniorial status in towns. Economically, Polish nobles were affected by the gradual implementation of peasant emancipation after 1807, the terms of which were extended to Posen after 1815. There was a slump in grain prices after the Napoleonic Wars and a mortgage and credit society for landowners, the *Landschaft*, set up by the Prussian government in 1821, supported them down to 1848. As for the peasants, between 1823 and 1858 40 per cent managed to survive as independent smallholders; the majority, however, found it impossible to survive on their own and became landless labourers.

Polish gentry nationalism refused to die away. On the contrary, secret student societies and disgruntled Napoleonic veterans kept resentments alive and the *Diet*, when it met in 1827, promptly complained about the number of German officials in the duchy, the lack of a separate Polish division in the Prussian army and the use of German in senior secondary schools. There were demands for a Polish-language university and even for sovereign status. The Prussian government's response was to tighten rather than loosen control, since the practical view of many ministers and officials was that the Poles were not to be trusted. This attitude was only hardened by the revolt of 1830 in Russian Poland, when some 3000 volunteers from Prussia crossed the border, and the appointment in 1831 of a new provincial president, or chief administrator, Eduard Heinrich Flottwell, signified an end to the policy of conciliation. Flottwell, as a Lutheran, based his administration on the assumption that the Catholic Poles were not only disloyal but fundamentally 'illogical' and priest-ridden.[15] He disqualified Polish nobles from nominating provincial councillors, replaced Polish officials with Germans, abolished noble jurisdiction in towns, insisted on the use of German in the bureaucracy and, most significantly, inaugurated a policy of settling German peasants in the Duchy. In post until 1841, Flottwell sent a clear message to the Poles that the Prussian state regarded them as enemies; the weapon of internal colonisation was to remain a favourite one of Prussian governments down to 1918.

One Polish response was to disengage from state service. Another, more effective in the end, was to form self-help societies for sharing improvements in agricultural technique, but also as a network for defending Polish interests. In 1841 a middle-class doctor, Karol Marcinkowski, founded the Society for Academic Aid, designed to raise funds for the education of the sons of townspeople and peasants; this was a key development in broadening the social base of Polish nationalism in Prussia.

There was a brief respite when Frederick William IV (1840–61) succeeded his father. Frederick William appears to have conceived a Romantic-minded enthusiasm for the Polish *szlachta*, but he was at odds with his own ministers in this. In the 1840s, there was a certain common ground between the increasingly visible, and economically powerful, class of Prussian German liberals and some Poles, who could unite in the desire for representative, constitutional government. Conversely, Prussian Junkers and the Polish *szlachta* had a common interest in confining political power, if it were ever to be extended, to the landowning class.

The revolutionary year of 1848 led to a rupture between the Prussian state and its Poles. German liberal opinion, in Prussia as in other German states, assumed that a war with Russia was inevitable because of the tsar's opposition to German unification and in this scenario German and Prussian liberals initially supported the restoration of Poland as an ally against tsarist reaction. In Berlin, Frederick William caved in to popular pressure, appointed a liberal government and made noises vaguely in favour of 'merging' into Germany. In Posen, a Polish National Committee was formed on 23 March and Ludwik Mierosławski, the military leader of the failed 1846 revolt in Galicia, was released from prison and started recruiting an army of 10,000 landless peasants. These Polish actions, however, were immediately mirrored by German ones. A German National Committee sprang into being, opposed to any Polish autonomy or secession, and units of the Prussian army stationed in the province unilaterally attacked Mierosławski's forces and dispersed them in April and May. The Polish National Committee dissolved and the Prussian government resumed control.

Equally revealing was the overwhelming opposition, in the German National Assembly which convened at Frankfurt in May, to a liberal motion calling for the restoration of Polish independence. In a debate in July the Assembly rejected the motion and some of the speeches showed a steely new German nationalist hostility to the Poles. Back in Prussia, reaction was triumphant before the end of the year. The Prussian National Assembly voted in October to leave Posen as it was and the conservative constitution approved by the king in December made no mention of the Poles' place in the state and gave no guarantees of minority rights.

The paradox, however, was that Prussia after 1848 was a constitutional state, albeit one where the franchise was heavily weighted in favour of the landowning elite, and in this restricted arena the Poles could at least attempt to defend their interests against an increasingly Polonophobe government. There was some awareness, too, that Polish gentry nationalism no longer offered a broad enough base for this project. In 1848–50 a Polish League was created to reach out to non-nobles by promoting a popular press and economic cooperatives. The government dissolved this in 1850, but since the wealthier among the Polish were still entitled to vote they set up a strong network of local committees, dominated by the gentry, the Church and the professional middle class. In 1859 a liberal newspaper, *Dziennik Poznański*, started to appear and in 1861 the Central Economic Society was formed, initially simply to promote good agricultural practice, but increasingly a political network.

In response Prussian state policy hardened yet further in the 1850s and 1860s. Eugen von Puttkammer, provincial president in 1851, described the Polish population as 'an element hostile to the Prussian government . . . To conciliate it is impossible. To extirpate it is inhumane . . . nothing remains but to confine it energetically to the subordinate position it deserves.'[16] Prussian policy returned to the idea of colonisation, implemented by the state-assisted purchase of Polish nobles' estates by Germans. This was a policy also favoured by Otto von Bismarck, Prussian minister-president from 1862 and from his youth one who regarded the Poles as the 'sworn enemies' of Prussia.[17] Such intransigence was only strengthened by the revolt of 1863–4 in Russian Poland, suppression of which was actively encouraged by Prussia. Nor, when the process of German 'unification' began in 1867 with the formation of the North German Confederation, was any attempt made to address Polish concerns about their inclusion in the new German 'nation-state'. In 1867 the Poles argued in vain against the inclusion of Posen in the North German Confederation, a federal state which foreshadowed the eventual Empire of 1871, but in which Prussia was clearly going to be the dominant element. As the Polish deputy Kazimierz Kantak put it in February 1867, 'It lies in the principle of nationality and the right of self-determination, that a nation which claims this principle for itself and its own development as a state must admit the same right to other nationalities.'[18] It was an appeal that fell on deaf ears.

PART THREE

NATIONALISM, INDEPENDENCE AND MODERNISATION 1867–1918

12

NATION-STATES AND MODERNISATION

The period between the 1860s and the First World War saw the most rapid and profound change to date in the lands of Eastern Europe, even if the foundations of that change had been laid in preceding generations. The emancipation of millions of peasants in the mid-century made possible a quicker and more diverse economic development and the beginnings at least of the capital investment needed in both agriculture and industry for modernisation. Economic development brought social change: migration within as well as between states, urbanisation, and an increasingly varie-gated social structure. Social change begat political pressures, facilitated by the greater incidence of constitutional government almost everywhere except Russia, and even in Russia after 1905. The political spectrum, in addition to reflecting the concerns of particular classes or interests, was shaped above all by the dynamic of nationalism. In this period the new nation-states, as well as nationalities within states, seemed increasingly on the offensive, with the multinational empires fighting a rearguard action, often with apparent success but in the end with disastrous consequences for international harmony.

ECONOMIC AND SOCIAL CHANGE

Economically the paradox of this period was that, although labour mobility had been achieved by peasant emancipation, the gap between Western and Eastern Europe was arguably as great in 1914 as in the 1860s. Significant parts of Eastern Europe, notably the German-speaking lands of the Habsburg Monarchy, parts of Hungary and Russian Poland, were closer to the West than ever before in terms of economic diversification and appearance, but even these were still primarily agrarian societies. As of 1900, 50 per cent of the population of the 'Austrian' half of the Habsburg Monarchy still lived off the land and two-thirds of Hungary and Russian Poland. The percent-ages were far higher elsewhere in the region.[1]

The terms under which emancipation was agreed in most of the Habsburg Monarchy, Prussia and Russia enabled only a minority of peasants to establish themselves as independent smallholders. Those who could not make this transition had to accept a precarious existence as tenant farmers or landless labourers. Among the noble landowners, many small to middling gentry also found it hard to survive once bereft of their peasants' free labour. The biggest landowners tended to buy out the lesser ones, as well as the even more vulnerable smallholders. In some parts of Eastern Europe, therefore, most strikingly in Prussia, this finally facilitated the modernisation of agriculture because the big estates were wealthy enough to invest in new techniques and machinery. In some Balkan states, by contrast, in the absence of a native aristocracy, the predominant peasant proprietors were sheltered from economic reality by government, which forbade the confiscation of farms for debt. This preserved the smallholder class, but at the cost of perpetuating the inefficiency of agriculture, whose practitioners were not wealthy enough to modernise their production methods. In the Ottoman Balkans the chief burden on the peasantry was the high level of taxation.

All the while rural population was steadily rising, doubling between 1860 and the turn of the century.[2] This, coupled with the general inefficiency of agriculture, had certain consequences. Firstly, elemental peasant revolts were still a possibility in some parts of the region into the twentieth century. The uprisings in Ottoman Bosnia and Bulgaria in the 1870s, the widespread peasant unrest in Russia in 1905–6 and the terrifying revolt of 1907 in Romania were all testimony to the grinding poverty of the rural masses. Secondly, the natural reaction of most East European peasants to their rising numbers was to subdivide their plots still further to provide for the new arrivals; while understandable in human terms, this only made the inefficiencies of scale more obvious. Thirdly, peasants could now migrate: from region to region and at times from state to state in search of work; from countryside to town, swelling the urban population; and increasingly after 1890 from Eastern Europe entirely, emigrating in their millions to the Americas or Australasia or, in the case of Russia, to Siberia.

Labour mobility and population increase both facilitated the spread of industrialisation. In most areas this was a cumulative process going back generations, given extra impetus by emancipation, the founding of banks and credit institutions and, in the case of the Habsburg Monarchy, the abolition of internal customs barriers. Prussia's industrialisation, which was based partly on Silesia but really took off in the Rhineland, was stimulated by the customs union formed with other German states in the 1830s, but then massively reinforced by the creation of the Empire in 1871. In Russia, by contrast, large-scale industrialisation came late, largely after 1890, and was state-led, a consequence of the tsarist regime's recognition that Russia's effectiveness as a great power was being seriously imperilled by its backwardness. So capital-poor was the Russian economy, however, that much of the capital for industrialisation had to come from foreign, mainly French, banks, as well as from a huge effort by the state to maximise grain exports. A similarly government-led attempt at modernisation was made by some of the Balkan states, but with indifferent success due to the impoverished revenue base from which these states were starting.

Where industrialisation did take hold, it was characterised by the greater exploitation of mineral resources, the building of railways and other infrastructure and the emergence of factory-based production, although much of the latter evolved around the processing of the region's agricultural products: milling, brewing, sugar-beet refining, farm machinery and the like. The rudiments of a regional infrastructure were achieved by the completion of such projects as the Semmering rail link between Vienna and Trieste in 1853, the Vienna–Constantinople route in 1888, the clearing of the Danube for navigation, Russia's opening up of the grain-growing Ukraine in the 1860s and 1870s and its building of the Trans-Siberian Railway after 1891.

Industrialisation, and the quickening of trade that went with it, led to a rapid growth of some cities, even if these were still islands in a sea of agrarian society, and the average size of towns remained small. Between 1850 and 1910, for instance, the population of Vienna exploded from 444,000 to 2.03 million; Budapest from 178,000 to 880,000; Warsaw from 100,000 to 856,000; Moscow and St Petersburg from 365,000 to 1.4 million and 485,000 to 1.9 million respectively.[3] The rapidity of this urbanisation meant that overcrowding, sub-standard accommodation, poor hygiene and disease were endemic problems, resulting in social unrest and the formation of labour organisations and political movements focused on the amelioration of conditions, if not the overturning of the entire economic order. Urbanisation also meant a steady increase in the number of literate East Europeans as more and more people had access to education, the beginnings of a mass media and an introduction to politics. In terms of nationality issues, the growth of towns also spelled change. Whereas at the start of the century the urban population in large parts of the Habsburg Monarchy, and in the Baltic provinces of Russia, had been German, by the end of the century the balance had shifted the other way: both Budapest and Prague, largely German speaking in 1848, were mainly Hungarian and Czech centres by 1900. Overall the economic and social change in this period had the effect of heightening political awareness, including nationalism.

POLITICAL DYNAMICS

In the broadest sense, the political development of East European societies after the mid-nineteenth century was conditioned by two factors. Firstly, the increasing social variegation just described was reflected in the type of political aspirations and organisations that emerged. Secondly, the adoption of constitutional government by so many states in the region, however limited this was in some instances, meant that for the first time there was a forum within which political conflict could be worked out, albeit on the whole unsatisfactorily.

'Constitution' was a word capable of differing interpretations. In the sense of a decree or other legislative instrument specifically binding a ruler to certain norms of behaviour, however, constitutions were gaining ground. Prussia after 1848, and subsequently the German Empire from 1871, the two halves of the Habsburg Monarchy after 1867, and the Balkan states as they achieved autonomy or independence, were all constitutional monarchies. The Ottoman sultan in 1876 felt obliged to grant a constitution, but then promptly annulled it; its restoration became one of the principal aims of the succeeding generation of reformers who finally seized power in 1908. Even the Russian autocracy experimented with local self-government in the 1860s and 1870s, and in 1905 Nicholas II was forced to concede the October Manifesto, which bound him at least in theory to govern with the assistance of representative institutions.

'Representative', however, was another term with elastic connotations. Initially most assemblies were elected on an extremely narrow franchise determined by property qualifications, like the notorious three-class suffrage in Prussia, which gave most representation to the wealthiest elite, the Junkers. Similar restrictions applied in the Habsburg Monarchy. In the Balkan states the system was ostensibly liberal, with the vote exercised by all male taxpayers or, in the case of the Bulgarian constitution of 1879, universal manhood suffrage. Yet electorates were all too easy to manipulate through corruption, outright intimidation or the manipulation of citizenship rights, as with Romania's Jews and Muslims, disenfranchised because they were not Christians. Some Balkan states, like Serbia, had several constitutions, depending on how often the ruler felt obliged to change the goalposts or how many revolutions there were. Nevertheless, within this inadequate and unsatisfactory framework, politics after a fashion was still possible, as was progressive change. In the 'Austrian' half of the Habsburg Monarchy, the franchise was widened in the 1880s and then, to general astonishment, extended to universal manhood suffrage in 1907. Serbia returned to democratic politics in 1903, admittedly as a result of a bloody palace coup.

The constitutional spaces in so many polities, and the political spectrum which filled them, reflected the balance of power in each society. Outside the Balkans the landowning aristocracy and gentry remained the dominant social class, and in Prussia and Hungary the most powerful political one as well. The landowners' interest in high protective tariffs against grain imports, for instance, exerted a baleful influence in Prussia and Hungary, and by extension on relations with other powers. The emerging middle class, by contrast, was less sure of its ground, and politically the heyday of liberal parties in both 'Austria' and the German Empire was confined to the period 1867–79. Socially conservative, liberals feared the eruption of the lower classes and did what they could to impede their enfranchisement; they also tended to defer to the prevailing aristocratic ethos of their societies and were susceptible to the lure of ennoblement.

Further down the social ladder, the evils of rapid urbanisation and the uncertainties of the new industrialism made the lower middle class and artisans susceptible to calls for social welfare legislation, as well as a new, more negative type of politics which blamed liberal capitalism itself but also Jews and national minorities for society's problems. For the small but concentrated factory proletariat, meanwhile, the nostrum was initially self-help organisations such as trades unions and cooperatives, but increasingly, from the 1880s, Marxist socialist parties committed, in theory, to a revolutionary overthrowing of the social and political order. In the countryside, the peasant masses' politics were, to begin with, vaguely socialist as well. Marxism, however, was a political philosophy inimical to peasants, considering them to be inherently capitalist because of their desire to farm their own land. The alternative, for peasants, was 'populism', a world view with an emphasis on cooperativism in the formation of credit associations and land banks, but conservative in social values, strongly religious, hostile to the urban or gentry elite and convinced that the peasant was the true embodiment of the nation. The appearance of populist parties by the end of the century was a sign that nationalism had indeed become a mass political phenomenon, extending even to the peasantry.

Almost everywhere, in this period, nationalism became the common currency of politics, gradually spreading to something like a mass audience. In the Habsburg Monarchy the very act of creating representative institutions meant that, from the start, and even with a limited franchise, the Austrian *Reichsrat* and provincial diets contained parties representing national minorities; with the growth of these minorities' middle classes their representation also grew. Political discourse focused on such issues as educational provision and the right to administrative and judicial decisions in one's own language, as well as access to employment in the state bureaucracy. In Hungary it was rather the almost complete absence of minority representation in parliament, thanks to the Hungarian elite's control of the electoral machine, which was the overriding grievance. In Germany, although Polish representation in the Prussian Diet was artificially limited, at federal level the Polish faction in the *Reichstag* complained bitterly about this situation for decades. In the Balkan states governments were concerned from the first with creating a mass loyalty to the idea of the nation which had hitherto been impossible, through such instruments as the educational system, a conscript army and the constant iteration of the goal of liberating fellow nationals still under Ottoman rule. Even those 'stateless' nations still subsumed within the Ottoman and Russian empires developed a sense of themselves as nations in this period, sometimes in isolation, sometimes under the influence of contact with fellow nationals across the border.

INTERNATIONAL REPERCUSSIONS

Some of the implications for international affairs of the political trends outlined above, and in particular the emergence of multiple nationalisms, will be readily apparent. It should not be forgotten, however, that traditional great-power rivalries, some of them rooted in clashes of economic interests, also played a role.

All the great powers, for instance, but especially Russia, Austria–Hungary and Britain, took an interest in the 'Eastern Question', that is, how to manage the perceived decline of the Ottoman Empire. In particular this revolved around the powers' strategic interests in the Straits and with them access to both the Mediterranean and the Black Sea. The Crimean War had already been fought over this issue, and until 1870, when the Black Sea clauses of the Treaty of Paris were finally revoked by international agreement, Russian diplomacy was dominated by the desire to shake off restrictions on its right to maintain naval bases on the Black Sea. Both Russia and Austria–Hungary continued to fear one another's presence in the Balkans. The Habsburg Monarchy in particular was apt to see a 'Pan-Slavist' tendency in Russian policy, erroneously assuming that every Slavic people and government in the region was a puppet in Russia's hands. This did not prevent periodic *ententes* between the two powers over Balkan issues, but the fundamental antagonism remained. Britain also feared Russian influence in the Balkans and the Ottoman Empire generally, at least until the late 1890s, when the British government concluded that an Ottoman Empire which either could not or would not reform itself was no longer defensible.

In addition to strategic concerns there were economic conflicts of interest. The drive to modernise led the Ottoman government further and further into debt to West European banks and by the mid-1870s more than half of state revenue went towards paying the interest alone. When in 1876 the Ottomans suspended payment, the great powers intervened and by 1881 an international financial commission, the Ottoman Public Debt Administration, was empowered to earmark certain revenues for debt servicing. Western capital, with the tacit and occasionally overt support of western governments, continued to seek concessions for trade and investment in the Ottoman realms. The same was true in the Balkan states, where competition to lend money to these countries' impoverished governments, to build their railway lines, to arm their troops, was increasingly fierce.

One final aspect of great-power rivalry which deserves mention is the looming antagonism between Russia and Germany. Until the late nineteenth century the conservative community of interest between the three northern empires had sufficed to keep Russia and Germany on relatively cordial terms. The industrialisation of Russia from the 1890s, however, reinforced Russia's strategic interest in the Straits because of the overriding necessity of exporting grain along this route; any threat to this economic windpipe was increasingly seen as a life-or-death issue for Russia. At the same time the rapidity of Russia's industrialisation, and the seeming certainty that this would enhance its military effectiveness despite Russia's defeat by Japan in 1905, helped to radicalise German policy in the two decades preceding 1914.

German nervousness was also increased by the conclusion of a Franco-Russian defensive alliance in 1894. German fear of a two-front war against the French and Russians was an obsession by 1914; Germany's own growing economic interest in the Balkans and the Ottoman Empire as fields for investment gave this an added edge. But this area where Germany's drive to establish economic and political hegemony, short of outright colonial empire, was strongest and most successful was also of vital interest to Russia.

The complications that nationalism introduced took several forms. Firstly, the very existence of the Balkan nation-states, and their increasing number, was potentially destabilising. Greece, Serbia, Montenegro and, after its creation in 1878, the autonomous Principality of Bulgaria all sought to expand at the expense of the Ottoman Empire or other neighbours, and in the process liberate fellow nationals. Only Romania did not seek such expansion, although this did not prevent its nationalists from eyeing Habsburg Transylvania, nor did it stop Romania in 1913 exploiting the Balkan Wars to seize Dobrudja from Bulgaria. In the meantime, those peoples still under Ottoman rule were encouraged to seek independence or unification with their 'home' state, aspirations which could lead to international crisis and great-power involvement.

The multinational empires, thus threatened, had their own strategies for containing nationalism. Continuing to sit on the Polish question was one of the few causes Russia, Germany and Austria–Hungary had in common by the end of the century. The Habsburg Monarchy and Russia, traditional rivals in the Balkans, could nevertheless live and let live for substantial periods, through active commitments to consult one another over contentious issues such as Macedonia. Austro-Hungarian diplomacy, in addition, coped with the potential danger of nationalism in three main ways. Firstly, it secured the occupation of Bosnia–Hercegovina in 1878, a move designed above all to forestall the expansion of Serbia, whose attractive power over the Monarchy's own South Slav population it feared. Secondly, the momentous decision was taken in 1879 to conclude a defensive alliance with Germany, which gave the Monarchy the ultimate insurance against Russia. Thirdly, the Monarchy coped with the threat of 'irredentism' by prophylactic alliances with each of the three nation-states on its borders which shared nationality with minorities within the Monarchy. By concluding alliances with Serbia in 1881, Italy in 1882 and Romania in 1883, the Monarchy hoped to neutralise the nationalism that undoubtedly existed in each.

The great powers generally exercised a form of clientism among the Balkan states, but these attempts at control could backfire. Russia, through its war against the Ottomans in 1877–8, created Bulgaria in the belief that the new state would act as an outpost of Russian influence in the Balkans; no one, however, was more surprised than Russia when it turned out in the 1880s that the Bulgarians had minds of their own and repudiated Russian tutelage. Most fatefully, the Habsburg Monarchy's long political as well as economic domination of Serbia blew up in its face when, in 1903, a revolution in Belgrade ushered in a new, democratic regime which was also strongly nationalist, anxious to throw off the restraints imposed on Serbia in the 1880s. Trade relations between the Monarchy and Serbia broke down in 1906 and the so-called 'Pig War' resulted in Serbia finding alternative markets for its produce and escaping from its dependent position.

The crises which shook the European state system between 1871 and 1914 almost all had their origins in the Balkans. Revolts in Bosnia and the Bulgarian *vilayets* in 1875–6 provoked Ottoman reprisals, international outrage, an unsuccessful Serbo-Montenegrin war against the Ottomans in 1876 and finally, by prior agreement between Russia and Austria–Hungary, Russian intervention. The resulting crisis over Russia's attempt to create a 'big Bulgaria' in 1878 led to the Congress of Berlin and a paring down of Bulgaria to the area between the Balkan Mountains and the Danube, with a strip to the south-east accorded a limbo-like existence under great-power supervision as Eastern Rumelia. The Berlin Congress was also a milestone because it sanctioned the Habsburg takeover of Bosnia–Hercegovina and the formal independence of Serbia, Montenegro and Romania.

Bulgarian nationalism produced another crisis in 1885–6 when there was a revolution in Eastern Rumelia and the principality responded to calls for a union of the two halves. This was subsequently ratified by the great powers, but not before Serbia had gone to war with Bulgaria in 1885 in a vain effort to win territorial compensation. In 1897 Greece provoked its own crisis when it responded to an uprising in Ottoman Crete by attacking the Empire on its own; despite a speedy defeat, Greece was saved from re-conquest by great-power intervention and effectively rewarded for its aggression when the powers pressured Constantinople into granting Crete autonomy, with a son of the Greek king as high commissioner.

The 1890s also saw the eruption of the Macedonian question: the attempts by armed bands, armed and financed by the governments of Greece, Serbia and Bulgaria, to carve out territory in advance of any partition of this remaining corner of the Ottoman domains, by 'ethnically cleansing' entire areas of their national rivals. For years this murderous state of affairs bedev-illed international politics, with the powers reluctant to sanction a predictably ferocious suppression of the bands by the Ottoman authorities, yet unable to agree on an effective international police force to maintain order in Macedonia.

In the end it was the Macedonian question, and the sultan's powerless-ness to resist either Balkan nationalism or the ceaseless interference of the powers, which prompted the 'Young Turk' revolution of 1908. This final effort to reform from within, while at the same time holding the Empire together, led to a crisis over Bosnia, which the Habsburg Monarchy decided formally to annex in October 1908, to forestall Bosnian delegates being summoned to a parliament planned by the revolutionary government.

judicial independence were enacted, with a special constitutional court to invigilate their infringement; this court became one of the levers available to national minorities for gaining fairer treatment. All religions were declared equal in status by an act of 1868, which gave Jews among others civil rights, civil marriage was relegalised and the Church's role in the school system limited. There was a burst of economic growth, including much new railway construction, which was halted only by the stock-market crash of 1873.

The only interlude in this pattern of German dominance was in 1871, when Francis Joseph, disturbed at the enthusiasm of many Austrian Germans for the German cause in the Franco-Prussian War, briefly contemplated restructuring the Monarchy to give greater voice to Slavs, especially the Czechs. Negotiations began for a 'Czech Compromise', whereby the Bohemian crownlands would enjoy the same autonomy as Hungary. These proposals, however, raised such a storm of protest not just among Austrian Germans but on the part of the Hungarian government that Francis Joseph backed down. This one effort between 1867 and 1918 to reconfigure the Monarchy failed, and non-German and non-Hungarian opinion was further alienated.

German liberal dominance was restored until 1879, yet the drawbacks of this dominance were increasingly apparent. Not only did most non-Germans continue to feel excluded from the system, but the decade-long fall-out from the 1873 crash, which bankrupted many firms and caused widespread unemployment, did much to discredit liberalism itself and to split the Austrian Germans politically. The disenfranchised working class turned increasingly towards socialism, a trend culminating in the founding of a Social Democratic Party in 1888. The lower middle class also deplored the evils of capitalism, but turned instead to Christian Socialism, a movement which stressed the need for social justice based on Catholicism, but which also specifically associated liberalism with Jewish influence. There was a marked rise in anti-Semitic prejudice in the 1870s, fuelled by an influx of Jews from the eastern provinces following emancipation and by the increased prominence of Jews in the professions and economic life, including the financial market. Finally, a small but violently vocal minority of Austrian Germans embraced Pan-Germanism: these German nationalists (and anti-Semites) argued for the dissolution of the Monarchy and the incorporation of its German population in the new German Empire.

Francis Joseph broke decisively with the German liberals in 1879 when they objected to the occupation of Bosnia–Hercegovina, on the ground that it upset the ethnic balance of the Monarchy still further. Incensed at this interference in his exclusive domain of foreign affairs, the emperor found an acceptable replacement in Count Eduard Taaffe. Taaffe's government, nicknamed the 'Iron Ring' because of its supposed durability, lasted in fact for 14 years. It rested on an assortment of conservative, clericalist Germans, landowners and non-German minority parties. The Poles were happy to support Taaffe in return for a continued free rein in Galicia. Most eye-catchingly, however, the Czechs were brought into the magic circle of government, much to the disgust of many Austrian Germans, and Czech deputies resumed attendance at the *Reichsrat*.

The Iron Ring was founded on a calculated strategy of securing the loyalty of the Monarchy's Slavs by judicious concessions in matters relating to education, language rights and, crucially, the suffrage. The paradox of this was that, necessary as such concessions were, they nevertheless made nationality problems worse. Austrian Germans found it hard to accept a situation where they were no longer the dominant element in the state, while among Czechs in particular the concessions heightened nationalism as well as a sense of grievance at the immutability of Dualism. And all the while the demographic balance was shifting steadily in favour of the non-German nationalities, in that economic development was increasing the number of educated and propertied non-Germans, who were likely to qualify for the vote even without suffrage reform.

The trend was accelerated in 1880 with language ordinances for Bohemia and Moravia, whereby all administrative and judicial decisions were required to be in the language of the petitioner, while criminal trials had to be in the language of the accused. The practical effect of this was to give an advantage in gaining civil service employment to Czechs, who were more likely to be bilingual. The numbers of non-Germans in the provincial and imperial bureaucracy started climbing. There was also an increase in the number of schools founded for national minorities generally. Most revolutionary was the suffrage reform of 1882, which halved the property qualification for town dwellers and thus enfranchised large numbers of non-Germans, with a consequent jump in the number of non-German deputies in the *Reichsrat*. The effect was felt soonest in provincial diets: in the Bohemian Diet elections of 1883 the majority swung decisively from Germans to Czechs.

Bohemian Germans in protest boycotted the Diet from 1886 to 1890, at which point a conference of moderate Czechs and Germans agreed to Czech-language schooling in any community with 40 or more Czech children and the division of Bohemia along language lines into separate administrative and judicial areas. Neither side, however, really spoke for its respective community. Most Czech nationalists refused to countenance the division of historic Bohemia and obstructed the bill physically in the Diet, leading to its suspension. In the *Reichsrat* elections of 1891 the Young Czechs supplanted the older moderate Czechs, threatening the stability of the Iron Ring itself. Taaffe tried to neuter the effects of nationalism in 1893 by persuading Francis Joseph to introduce a bill for universal manhood suffrage. This proved too much for Taaffe's conservative supporters and the Iron Ring disintegrated.

The following decade and a half was a period of mounting nationalist cacophony and parliamentary paralysis, in which government both provincially and centrally was often forced to suspend diet or *Reichsrat* and rule by emergency decree. In 1896 the Polish Count Kazimir Badeni succeeded in passing a complicated system of indirect suffrage and the elections held on this basis in March 1897 returned a kaleidoscope of 25 parties to the *Reichsrat*, which made government more than ever dependent on the votes of the Czechs. To keep the latter sweet, Badeni introduced new language ordinances for Bohemia and Moravia, but designed to be applicable elsewhere. By these all civil servants were to be fully bilingual by 1901 and plaintiffs in the courts were to be entitled to proceedings in their own language at all levels.

The Badeni language ordinances unleashed a tempest of nationality conflict. Germans everywhere demonstrated violently against the legislation and were met with equally violent Czech counter-demonstrations. German obstruction led to the prorogation of the *Reichsrat* and mass protests on the street. Francis Joseph at this point dismissed Badeni in favour of Baron Paul von Gautsch. A compromise proposed by Gautsch, whereby Bohemia and Moravia would be divided into three administrative zones depending on which language, or neither, was dominant, was attacked by the Czechs as an unacceptable weakening of the 'historic' Czech crownlands. A succession of ministries governed by decree into the new century, scrapping the Badeni ordinances on the way but suffering constant Czech obstruction as a result. This was the period in which even foreign observers began to wonder how long the Monarchy could survive such stress.

In January 1900 Francis Joseph appointed as minister-president Ernest von Koerber, a bureaucrat specialising in commercial and transport matters. Koerber's novel approach to nationality problems was to attempt to nullify them by economic development. Modernisation itself, it was hoped, would give all the nationalities a common, uniting interest. The government initiated a major programme of railway building, drafted plans for an extension of the canal network and, above all, invested heavily in railway connections from the interior of the Monarchy to Trieste, its principal sea port. Despite this stimulus, and the maintenance of industrial production artificially through high tariff barriers, the economy remained depressed. Worse, economic development showed no sign of allaying acrimony between the nationalities. The general election of 1901 returned an even greater number of nationalist Czechs and Pan-Germans. Relations in Galicia between the Polish elite and the Ruthenes remained poisonous. Conflict in Trieste between Italians and Germans over Italian-language education facilities led to riots, causing Koerber to resign late in 1904.

Throughout 1905 Francis Joseph, the former neo-absolutist, pondered the strategy of defusing nationality problems by extending the suffrage. The emperor's willingness to contemplate such a radical step was increased by the constitutional crisis in Hungary (see below) and by the revolutionary events of that year in Russia, where even the tsar was forced to concede a popularly elected *Duma*. In 1906 the government of Baron Max von Beck introduced a suffrage bill enfranchising virtually all adult males. The bill was signed into law by the emperor in January 1907.

The *Reichsrat* elected under the new dispensation in May 1907 was radically different in composition. Out of the 516 seats, each nationality was allotted a fixed number: Gemans 233, Czechs 107, Poles 82, Ruthenes 33, Slovenes 24, Italians 19, Serbs and Croats 13 and Romanians 5. What was novel was the type of parties represented: explicitly nationalist parties were in fact severely reduced in strength, with a corresponding increase in the size of socially based parties. Thus the Czech nationalists and Pan-Germans shrank dramatically, while the biggest groups were the Christian Socialists, the German Clericals, the Social Democrats and the Czech Agrarians. Shared nationality was certainly no guarantee against party division: the Polish deputies were distributed among five different factions, while Ruthenes were split between so-called Ukrainophiles and Russophiles.

More democratic representation nevertheless did not make Austria any easier to govern. Beck was forced to resign in 1908 when his criticism of the annexation of Bosnia incurred the wrath of Francis Joseph, but there was no let-up of nationality disputes: Czechs versus Germans, Germans against Italians, Italians against Slovenes. Elections in 1911 produced a pandemonium of factions and the last peace-time government, under Count Karl Stürgkh, managed largely by ignoring parliament or doing without it entirely. As a result the Austrian representative assembly was not even sitting when, in July 1914, the Monarchy undertook the fateful step of going to war.

Numerous observers in the last decades before the war speculated as to whether the Habsburg Monarchy was doomed. Parliamentary government in the Austrian half was certainly not a success and most of the nationalities were in some way disaffected. Yet, with the exception of the Italians, whose ambitions of joining Italy were increasingly open by 1914, no nationalities in the Austrian part of the Monarchy actively sought independence, since the only circumstance that could make such an option even conceivable, the Monarchy's dissolution, was itself almost unthinkable. It took the solvent of a world war for the unimaginable to become practicable.

HUNGARY

The situation in the Kingdom of Hungary, including its subordinate Kingdom of Croatia–Slavonia, was by contrast considerably less fluid. Here the political elite, the Hungarian gentry, remained firmly in charge throughout the Dualist period and worked towards a Hungarian nation-state with some success, even though ethnic Hungarians or Magyars were a minority of the population. Romanians, Serbs, Slovaks and Ruthenes had genuine cause for complaint, yet to the end of his reign Francis Joseph remained loath to alter the basic terms of the *Ausgleich*.

The initial premises of the new constitutional era in Hungary, however, as represented by the 'Deákist' government of Count Gyula Andrássy (1867–71), were impeccably liberal. Deákists like Andrássy were ardent nationalists who insisted on the integrity of historic Hungary, but they also believed in constitutionalism, the rule of law and civic equality. Accordingly there was no problem in recognising the historic rights of Croatia by a sub-Compromise, the *Nagodba*, in 1868. By this Croatia retained its own government and *Sabor* (assembly) in Zagreb and the right to send delegates to the Hungarian Diet, although the Hungarian government exerted a crucial control in that it appointed the *Ban* or governor of the kingdom. The brightest achievement of the Andrássy government was the Nationalities Law of 1868, which for the time was an enlightened attempt to ensure the rights of Hungary's minorities. While declaring that 'all citizens of Hungary constitute a single nation', whose official language could only be Hungarian, the Law nevertheless gave local authorities the right to decide their language of business and individual citizens the right to justice in their own tongue at communal and district level, as well as education in their mother tongue up to secondary level.[1] What the Nationalities Law did not recognise was any corporate identity of non-Magyar nationalities. The Deákists feared applying federalism to a multinational state like Hungary, and the stress on the political unity of the state meant that nationality rights were conditional on this and hence liable to capricious interpretation by later Hungarian governments.

For this is what soon happened. Implementation of the Nationalities Law was already impeded by the fact that, because of the narrow suffrage, the county assemblies responsible for ensuring this remained gentry dominated; a restriction of the suffrage pushed through in 1874 ensured that this remained the case. In the meantime the Deákists were losing ground to the new Liberal Party under Kálmán Tisza, who came to power in 1875 and represented an increasingly nationalist variant of Hungarian politician, more nationalist indeed than liberal.

Tisza ruled through a combination of blatant electoral corruption and policies designed to reinforce the Magyar character of the state. The mainstay of his ministry (1875–90) was the policy of 'Magyarisation', the forcible conversion of the nationalities to the Magyar language and culture by means of systematic legislation and discrimination, and which was continued by subsequent governments. Magyarisation involved the closure of non-Magyar cultural institutions and especially schools, making Magyar the language of instruction in state-run primary schools, and close regulation of secondary schools. The aim, according to a contemporary Hungarian observer, was to make the education system 'like a big engine, which takes in at one end hundreds of Slovak youths who come out at the other end as Magyars'.[2] Non-Magyar newspapers were harassed by fines and censorship, and the language of public transport and communications, of public notices and even inscriptions on tombstones was made Hungarian. Electoral intimidation and gerrymandering ensured that representation of minorities remained tiny: after the last pre-war elections, ethnic Hungarians held 405 out of 413 seats in the Diet.

Magyarisation had some limited success, especially among ethnic Germans and Jews, many of whom in the Dualist period did their best to assimilate. Certainly the remarkable economic and cultural flowering of the late nineteenth century owed much to the genuine tolerance extended to this Magyarised Jewish community. On the other nationalities, however, Magyarisation undoubtedly had a profoundly alienating effect, yet its proponents equally clearly saw it as essentially progressive, designed to enhance 'national' cohesion through cultural assimilation.

Economic modernisation intensified in Hungary under Dualism, with great development in the period 1867–72 and an additional influx of Austrian capital after the Vienna stock-market crash of 1873. After 1890 there was a renewed spurt of growth when a combination of the internal market offered to Hungarian agriculture by its inclusion in the Monarchy, the accumulation of capital and the initial springboard provided by the country's extractive and food-processing industries led to yet further industrialisation and a sizeable factory proletariat, at least in the Budapest area.[3]

Despite this growth, the period after 1890 saw the rise of a new generation of Hungarian nationalists convinced of Hungary's oppressed status and determined to win greater autonomy or even independence. The main focus of nationalist grievance was the common imperial and royal army and the German language of command used even in Hungarian units. Control of the armed forces, however, was one of the areas considered by Francis Joseph as his exclusive prerogative. The result was the bruising constitutional crisis of 1903–6, when the emperor-king's rejection of nationalist demands for a more explicitly Hungarian army led to the fall of the last Liberal government under István Tisza (Kálmán's son) and the shock election in 1905 of a coalition led by the Independence Party. Francis Joseph defused this crisis by threatening to introduce universal manhood suffrage, as in Austria. The coalition government managed to avoid implementing this, which would have destroyed Magyar supremacy, but at the price of abandoning its demands regarding the army.

A pro-Vienna but still fiercely hegemonist National Party of Work, founded by Tisza, gained power in 1910 and showed no more inclination towards real democratisation than any of its predecessors. The nationalities' position remained completely subordinate, with the attendant danger, in the case of the Romanians and Serbs, of the spread of irredentist leanings towards neighbouring Romania and Serbia.

In Croatia, Hungarian governments maintained close control for most of this period through their appointment of the *Ban*, the narrowness of the electorate and the exercise of wholesale electoral corruption. A Croatian

National Party, formed in the 1860s, strove unavailingly for greater genuine autonomy, while a more extreme nationalist faction, the Party of Right, voiced increasing intolerance, not just of Hungarian domination but of Croatia's Serb minority. The governorship of Count Károly Khuen-Héderváry (1883–1903) was distinguished by its deliberate policy of divide-and-rule, by making concessions to the Serbs which inflamed Croatian nationalist opinion. For a brief period in the new century, a Croatian–Serb Coalition was formed, reflecting a new-found enthusiasm for a common 'Yugoslav' or South Slav identity, and in 1906–7 this alliance actually managed to form a government. This coincided, however, with rising tension between the Monarchy and Serbia, and in an atmosphere of heightened suspicion of South Slavs in both Budapest and Vienna over Bosnia, the Croatian–Serb government was forced from office and a number of prominent South Slavs were tried for treason in 1908–9. As a consequence Croatia was seething with disaffection by 1914.

FOREIGN POLICY

The interaction between domestic affairs and the Monarchy's foreign policy was potentially fateful. The *Ausgleich* enabled the Monarchy to function as a great power, but it also fundamentally weakened it. Financially the fixed nature of contributions to common expenditure, and the requirement every ten years to renegotiate this, limited the size of the armed forces and raised doubts as to their efficacy. The multinational composition of the Monarchy made it peculiarly vulnerable to certain pressures, both internal and external, and apprehensive about these; the chronic conflict between nationalities advertised this weakness. Finally, the direction of foreign policy was subtly affected by the fact of the *Ausgleich* itself. Francis Joseph's control of foreign affairs was effectively absolute but, by the terms of the *Ausgleich*, the Austrian and Hungarian ministers-president had a right to be consulted on foreign policy. The Hungarians, if not the Austrians, availed themselves of this right, especially in the early period, with the consequence that policy towards Russia and the Balkans assumed a more readily Russophobe hue than it might otherwise have done. Hungarians were well represented in the diplomatic service and one, Andrássy, was foreign minister for most of the crucial 1870s.

Certain abiding features of Austro-Hungarian foreign policy emerged at an early stage. Given the prevailing suspicion of Russia's intentions, and despite recurrent attempts at conservative solidarity with the tsars as well as Germany, Francis Joseph at Andrássy's urging eventually gravitated towards a formal alliance with the German Empire in 1879. The German alliance remained a constant down to 1918, since in the eyes of the emperor and successive ministers Germany was the essential safeguard against Russia, and even though Germany's own diplomacy, after 1890, became increasingly adventurous and alarming to other powers.

The Monarchy also sought to avert the threat of irredentist nationalism by cultivating the monarchical, conservative elements in all three of its potential enemies to the south, concluding alliances with Serbia, Italy and Romania in the 1880s. This was only a limited success. Italy and Romania stayed allies until the outbreak of the First World War, but were never seen as trustworthy by Vienna and indeed ended by joining the opposite side. In the case of Serbia a series of treaties was forced on the country in 1880–1, designed to keep it in a state of political and economic subjection. Serbia's rulers undertook not to conclude alliances with other states without Vienna's consent and its principal export, livestock, was made entirely dependent on the Austro-Hungarian market. This policy backfired disastrously after 1903, however, when a palace revolution in Belgrade brought to power a new dynasty and a more stridently nationalist government, determined to emancipate Serbia from its subordinate position.

In 1878–9, before any of these ties of doubtful value had been forged, the Monarchy took the ultimately self-defeating step of occupying the Ottoman province of Bosnia–Hercegovina. Andrássy agreed with Francis Joseph, who needed no persuading, that this first acquisition (rather than loss) of territory of the reign was vital for strategic reasons, but above all to prevent the aggrandisement of Serbia, whose attractive power over the Monarchy's own Serbs would otherwise be strengthened. The Monarchy thus assumed control over a mixed population of Orthodox Serbs, Catholic Croats and Muslim Slavs, possession of which earned it the implacable hatred of Serb nationalists on both sides of the frontier. Bosnia was a constitutional anomaly, administered by the common finance minister because neither the Austrian nor the Hungarian government wished to see it in the hands of the other, and for the next 40 years a succession of able bureaucrats strove to make it a showcase for Habsburg rule, establishing a secure and efficient government and considerable economic modernisation. Yet the basic contradiction remained: although Croats accepted Habsburg rule readily, and Muslim landowners did likewise in return for security of tenure, the Serbs persisted in dreaming of union with Serbia and were increasingly seen as internal enemies by the Habsburg authorities.

The Bosnian question was at the root of the downward spiral in the Monarchy's international security after 1903. Resentment at the occupation of the province had contributed to the nationalist backlash in Serbia which produced the revolution of that year, and once the new regime in Belgrade had dared to break off economic relations with the Monarchy in the so-called 'Pig War' of 1906–11, when the Monarchy closed its borders to Serbian livestock and Serbia was forced to find alternative markets elsewhere, the inherent antagonism between Austria–Hungary and Serbia could only escalate. Formal annexation of Bosnia in 1908, and the unsuccessful prosecution of South Slav politicians within the Monarchy for treasonable dealings with Serbia during the crisis, only made matters worse. The Balkan Wars of

1912–13 completed the deterioration in the Monarchy's perceived strategic position: a strengthened Serbia, perhaps this time with Russian backing, appeared to enjoy increased prestige as the potential 'Piedmont' or unifier of the South Slavs. What has sometimes been described as the militarisation of Habsburg decision making, with both civilian and military leaders resolved somehow 'to eliminate Serbia as a political power-factor in the Balkans', was already a reality by June 1914.[4] It was at this point that the assassination at Sarajevo of Francis Joseph's heir, Archduke Francis Ferdinand, by a Bosnian Serb mistakenly assumed to be acting at Belgrade's behest, offered what seemed the ideal pretext for war against Serbia.

Legend:
- Serbian gains in 1912–13
- Romanian gains in 1912–13
- Bulgarian gains in 1912–13
- Greek gains in 1912–13
- Montenegrin gains in 1912–13

BOSNIA

HERCE-GOVINA

MONTE-NEGRO

ALBANIA

Shkodër

Durrës

SERBIA

Belgrade

Skoplje

Salonika

GREECE

Athens

ROMANIA

Bucharest

Iaşi

BULGARIA

Sofia

Adrianople
Constantinople

OTTOMAN EMPIRE

CRETE

7 The Ottoman Empire and the Balkans 1878–1913, showing territory gained by other nationalities in 1912–13. Redrawn from The Balkans in 1913 (p. 300), *The Eastern Question*, by M. S. Anderson, Macmillan (1966)

14

OTTOMAN RETREAT AND THE BALKAN NATION-STATES TO 1914

The half-century before the First World War saw the final crumbling of the Ottoman Empire's European domains. Despite its rulers' attempts at modernisation, the Empire fell victim to a combination of great-power interference and the expansionist ambitions of Balkan nation-states, and by 1913 was reduced to the south-east corner of the Balkans.

It was customary at the time, and in much written since, to portray the Ottoman Empire as the 'sick man of Europe', whose decline was as much the result of his own misrule and 'oriental' inefficiency as it was of external assault. Yet a counter-argument has been mounted to the effect that the Empire was not so much sick as mugged. If it was economically ailing, a primary producer importing more than it exported, it was the imposition of unfair trading terms by the more advanced great powers which made it so. If it was weak militarily, this was because of the necessity of defending itself with inadequate revenue and insufficient manpower against a host of internal and external foes.[1] Ottoman rule has for too long been seen through the prism of Christian prejudice against a Muslim-dominated state.

There is some truth in this. The Balkan states were themselves backward, inefficient and militarily weak, and their advances against the Ottomans owed much to great-power backing or the interventions of the great powers on their own behalf. In disputes between the Empire and the Balkan Christians, the great powers almost invariably sided with the Christians. We should also not overestimate the strength of Balkan nationalism. The majority of Balkan Christians, to say nothing of Balkan Muslims, probably were indifferent to the ideal of the nation even in the late nineteenth century. And the great powers undoubtedly had compelling reasons for intervening in Ottoman affairs, either for fear of ceding strategic advantage to one another or because they saw opportunities for economic profit.

Yet the fundamental weaknesses of Ottoman rule in the Balkans were cultural ones, which no amount of latter-day lauding of its 'tolerance of diversity' can obfuscate.[2] Firstly, the Empire was a Muslim state ruling over a multiplicity of Christian peoples, whose disaffection and readiness to be subverted were, in the end, decisive factors. The Ottomans' enemies continued to exploit this weakness to the end. Secondly, the emergence of nationalism, however few its adherents initially, accentuated this vulnerability. Nationalism, moreover, was possible not just among Christians but among non-Turkish Muslims too, like the Albanians or, in the Empire's non-European provinces, Kurds and Arabs. Nationalism even emerged, towards the end of this period, among the Turks themselves, a development which made it impossible to retain the allegiance of the sultan's non-Turkish subjects.

OTTOMAN REFORM AND ATTEMPTS AT CONSOLIDATION TO 1912

Under Sultan Abdül Aziz (1861–76) the reforms initiated in the *Tanzimat* period continued, albeit at a slackened pace. The premise of the *Tanzimat* was that the Empire could be preserved only through modernisation and that this was possible only by establishing full legal equality for all subjects, Muslim and non-Muslim, and ensuring a fair taxation system. A law of 1864 extended the principle of representative government by creating provincial assemblies, elected from local notables of all faiths. Public education made painful progress, with the products of the teacher training colleges, set up under Mahmud II, going on to found a widening network of primary and middle schools. Christians and Jews were able to attend the new schools and were eligible for positions in the state bureaucracy.

The real sticking point, though, was taxation. A programme of land registration, started in 1858, was still not completed by 1914 and in its absence the inefficient and abusable system of tax-farming had to continue. Revenue from foreign imports was kept low by the Capitulations or trade agreements forced on the Porte by the great powers. Worst of all was the soaring state indebtedness to western banks: by 1860 the government was paying a fifth of its meagre revenue on the interest alone, a figure which by 1875 had climbed to 50 per cent.[3] To top it all, the Empire was host to a steady stream of Muslim refugees. Russia between 1854 and 1876 expelled 1.4 million Crimean Tartars and in the mid-1860s another 600,000 Circassians from the Caucasus. Their arrival produced further economic dislocation and expense.[4]

If the *Tanzimat* constituted the first practical attempt at modernisation, the group of thinkers known as the Young Ottomans, emerging in the 1860s, represented the first generation of western-educated elite to formulate something like an 'Ottoman nationalism', a state-reinforcing ideology that would give the sultan's subjects a common identity. Young Ottomans like Namık Kemal and Ali Suavi were proponents of western-style liberalism, in that they believed representative institutions and a constitution were essential preconditions for modernisation. As opposed to the secularisers of the *Tanzimat*, however, the Young Ottomans also held that Islam was the crucial binding element for an Ottoman identity. Adept at exploiting the new Turkish-language newspapers, they initially appealed to all Muslims, but increasingly their emphasis was on ethnic Turks. Kemal, for instance, was responsible for popularising the term 'fatherland' (*vatan*), but it was always unclear whether this could ever include non-Turks. Suavi specifically advocated an educational system which would be Turkish-language only, which begged the question whether the Turkish used would be the elite's Ottoman Turkish, heavily influenced by Arabic and Persian and virtually unintelligible to the masses, or the demotic language of Anatolian peasants. The Young Ottomans' liberalism put them on the wrong side of Abdül Aziz's regime and their influence was necessarily confined to the literate elite, but they won some adherents to constitutionalism and sowed the seeds of a modern Turkish nationalism.

The Young Ottomans' case for constitutional accountability was reinforced when the Empire was overtaken by catastrophe in 1875–8, with revolts in Bosnia–Hercegovina and then Bulgaria triggering war and partition. The rising in Bosnia in 1875 was due to resentment of oppressive tax collection rather than nationalism, but as it progressed the insurgents were joined by genuine nationalists, both Serb and Croat, from neighbouring Serbia, Montenegro and the Habsburg lands. It was these outsiders, often, who were responsible for the worst atrocities against the province's Muslims; Ottoman army reprisals were equally fierce and prompted a flood of refugees into Habsburg territory.

In the Bulgarian provinces, in April 1876, the revolt led by the Bulgarian Revolutionary Committee was calculated to provoke outside intervention. Bulgarians had profited from the proto-industrialisation begun earlier in the century; they were also largely responsible for running their own affairs. Yet tax collection was problematical here too and some among the younger generation were determined to take advantage of Ottoman preoccupation with Bosnia. Nationalism had been slow to appear among the largely peasant Bulgarians and the nationalists were split between moderates who would have settled for autonomy and revolutionaries who had been trying for years to foment an uprising from bases in Serbia and Romania. The rising never progressed beyond the Balkan Mountains and it is clear that the vast majority of Bulgarians wanted nothing to do with it. But the massacre of Muslims at the start led to murderous reprisal by Ottoman irregular troops, and it was these 'Bulgarian horrors' which caught the attention of the western and Russian press and ultimately led to intervention.

It was great-power pressure on the Ottoman government, in the shape of proposals for reform of its European provinces, which drove the Empire to transform itself into a constitutional monarchy. In May 1876 a coalition of conservatives and reformers, headed by Midhat Pasha, deposed Abdül Aziz;

after the brief reign of the mentally unstable Murad V, the latter's brother became sultan as Abdül Hamid II (1876–1909). Midhat's government, determined to justify Ottoman rule in the Balkans and thus avert further foreign dictation, induced Abdül Hamid to promulgate the first constitution of an Islamic state on 23 December 1876.

This remarkable document represented a fundamental political change, in that its mere existence implied that the sultan was no longer the absolute ruler and sole lawgiver. Instead, the constitution's provision for a bicameral legislature, with a nominated senate of 25, and a lower chamber of 120 deputies elected on a restricted franchise, constituted an admission of the principle of popular sovereignty. Modelled on Belgium's 1831 constitution, the Ottoman constitution retained the sultan as central: he still appointed ministers, who were responsible to him, not parliament, and he had the power to approve or reject all laws, as well as to dissolve the assembly. To the astonishment of observers domestic and foreign, the first elections were held early in 1877 and the parliament duly met in March. A second election was held towards the end of the same year and a second parliament met in December.

The only problem with the 1876 constitution was that its lynch-pin, Abdül Hamid, had no intention of governing constitutionally if he could help it. Abdül Hamid was as anxious as anyone to modernise and shake off foreign influence, but he was autocratic and mistrustful by disposition. He dismissed Midhat Pasha in February 1877 and, when the second elected assembly dared criticise the disastrous loss of the war with Russia, he dismissed it as well in February 1878. Censorship and police surveillance took the place of debate and the dreams of the Young Ottomans seemed doomed to disappointment.

Instead their worst fears were realised when, in June 1878, the sultan's diplomats signed the Treaty of Berlin. This product of international mediation between the Ottomans and Russia, while modifying the peace terms originally imposed by Russia at San Stefano, nevertheless forced major losses on the Porte. An autonomous Principality of Bulgaria, whose prince would be a vassal of the sultan, was created; its territory amounted to roughly a third of that considered at the time to be inhabited by Bulgarian speakers. A slice of territory between the Balkan and Rhodope Mountains, christened Eastern Rumelia, was to be administered by an Ottoman Christian governor under great-power supervision. Serbia, Montenegro and Romania all became formally independent; there were minor territorial gains for the first two and for Romania a forced exchange of Southern Bessarabia, ceded to Russia, for the territory south of the Danube estuary known as Dobrudja. Greece was also empowered to negotiate territorial demands and by 1881 great-power intervention had secured it parts of Thessaly and Epirus. Most humiliating of all from the Ottoman point of view was the handing over of Bosnia–Hercegovina and Cyprus to Austro-Hungarian and British administration respectively; although both provinces remained formally Ottoman possessions, there was little disguising the intended permanence of these transfers. As before, the Muslim population of the territories in question paid the heaviest price of all. Thousands were massacred or forced to flee by Russian troops during the war of 1877–8. It has been estimated that of the 1.5 million Muslims in Bulgaria, 800,000 were either killed or died of disease or starvation, or emigrated to Ottoman-ruled territory. The Muslim population of Bosnia was reduced by about a third between 1875 and the completion of Austro-Hungarian occupation in 1879.[5]

Abdül Hamid's strategy for holding together what was left of the Ottoman imperium has been described as 'Pan-Islamism'. This stressed the essentially Islamic nature of the state and the sultan's role as leader of the Muslim faithful. To inculcate in his subjects a sense of loyalty to himself, Abdülhamit encouraged the spread of education. He also recognised the importance of rapid communications as a means of physically holding things together and his reign saw a big increase in railway and road construction, as well as telegraph facilities. Overriding everything was an insistence on maximum centralisation and control.

Pan-Islamism proved an inadequate substitute for constitutionalism. Apart from its obvious lack of appeal to Christians, it was increasingly clear that non-Turkish Muslims were hardly wooed by it either. Among Albanians, for instance, 1878 saw the first stirrings of nationalism when the League of Prizren was formed to agitate for the use of Albanian in schools; by 1896 this had evolved into an appeal to the great powers for administrative autonomy. The expansion of education, too, was a double-edged weapon. Not only did the spread of literacy increase the number of subjects inclined to question authority, a decree of 1894, that henceforth Turkish must be used in all schools, alienated Christians and non-Turkish Muslims alike. Finally, expenditure, especially on railways, could be maintained only by borrowing from the West and by 1881, after the Ottoman government had defaulted on its debts, a consortium of European powers forced it to accept the Ottoman Public Debt Administration. This international body earmarked the revenue from certain government monopolies and taxes for the Empire's foreign creditors. The arrangement enabled the government to continue borrowing, but at the price of sacrificing 29 per cent of real income; it was also a highly visible symbol of the Empire's helplessness *vis-à-vis* the European powers.

The combination of autocracy, nationalist unrest and above all humiliation by the great powers prompted the beginnings of a specifically Turkish nationalism. In 1889, a number of young Muslim scholars in Constantinople, of predominantly middle-class background, formed a secret revolutionary society, the Committee of Union and Progress (CUP), later known as the Young Turk movement. The Young Turks' principal aims were the overthrow of Abdül Hamid and the restoration of the 1876 constitution, but they also initially envisaged a federalised Empire which would be able to retain the loyalty of its peoples. As the movement expanded and acquired more ethnic Turks, however, it was also influenced by Namık Kemal's concept of *vatan* and a tendency to equate 'Ottoman' with 'Turkish'. A major influence in this direction was the Russian Tartar *émigré* Yusuf Akçura, who disputed the point of trying to win over non-Turks and wrote in 1903, 'The Young Turks' attempts to found an Ottoman nation is [a] cul-de-sac. Nationalism is the only road to take.'[6] This appealed especially to the increasing number of army officers who joined the movement. For these there were additional spurs to action in the shameful outcome of the Greco-Turkish War of 1897 (see below), but especially the situation in Macedonia. This Ottoman-ruled area of the Balkans was claimed by Bulgaria, Serbia and Greece, all of which supported armed bands there. The great powers repeatedly interfered with Ottoman efforts to control Macedonia and in 1903, following an unsuccessful Bulgarian-led uprising, imposed an international police force to maintain order. For the Young Turks this was the ultimate indignity.

In July 1908 a CUP-inspired revolt, demanding the restoration of the constitution, was mounted by officers of the Third Army Corps, stationed in Macedonia. Supported to begin with by Muslims and Christians, Turks and non-Turks across the Empire, it spread rapidly to other army units and by 24 July Abdül Hamid had conceded defeat and reinstated the constitution. A government was installed dominated by the CUP, although the latter stayed in the background at this stage, insisting that it was not a political party.

The Young Turk revolution was no sooner accomplished than events demonstrated the 'unworkability of a multi-national Ottoman state'.[7] At the prospect of a parliament being elected which would once more represent all provinces of the Ottoman Empire, the Habsburg Monarchy hastened formally to annex Bosnia–Hercegovina in October; at the same time Bulgaria proclaimed itself independent and Crete, effectively under Greek administration since 1897, announced its union with Greece. The tendency of the Young Turk government, moreover, was decidedly centralist. The CUP itself soon split between a Liberal wing which still hoped to placate the nationalities by concessions such as local autonomy, and the 'Unionists', whose reaction to the loss of the Balkan provinces was an ever greater emphasis on 'Turkification'. Turkish was made the official language of state in 1908 and a compulsory element at all levels of the educational system. As a result of a conservative Muslim attempt at a counter-coup, in the spring of 1909, which was accompanied by revolts by Armenians and, in Kosovo *vilayet*, Albanians, the CUP formed its own political party, deposed Abdül Hamid in favour of Sultan Mehmet V (1909–18) and announced measures to crack down on nationalist unrest, especially in the Balkans. The three years before the outbreak of the Balkan Wars in 1912 saw a hardening of attitudes on both sides, with non-Turks increasingly alienated and an increasingly authoritarian government pursuing policies that amounted to 'Turkification with lip-service to Ottomanism'.[8]

THE BALKAN NATION-STATES TO 1912

That the Kingdom of *Greece* in this period remained independent at all, and indeed expanded territorially, owed less to its own exertions than to the favour of the great powers. At the same time the country's economic dependency on those same powers continued, while politically much of Greek society remained in thrall to the goal of national unification.

Under George I (1864–1913) political parties continued to function through clientage rather than coherent ideologies, with the state itself running the biggest client system of all through its control of employment in the swollen bureaucracy. Patronage, corruption and electoral violence were an open book for leaders such as Theodoros Deliyannis and Kharilaos Trikoupis, who alternated as minister-president throughout the 1880s and 1890s, while in foreign policy the predominant influence was exercised by the king. Deliyannis' faction was broadly conservative and hotheadedly nationalist, clamouring for the realisation of the *Megali Idea* and the liberation of fellow Greeks from Ottoman rule. It was this party which kept public opinion fired up over Crete, where Greek governments inspired no fewer than four revolts between 1866 and 1896, and which finally led Greece into the calamitous one-month war of 1897, from which, thanks to the great powers, Greece was lucky to escape with an indemnity of 4 million Turkish pounds and, to the fury of the Ottomans, an autonomous regime for Crete itself. Nationalist opinion was also behind increased support for Greeks in Macedonia from the 1890s.

Trikoupis' New Party stood for a less adventurous foreign policy and sought to encourage modernisation; the three Trikoupis ministries increased roads by a factor of three in ten years and railways from 12 to 1000 kilometres between 1882 and 1896, and oversaw completion of the Corinth Canal by 1893.[9] Modernisation, however, was constantly overshadowed by Greece's economic vulnerability. Trikoupis was forced to declare a state bankruptcy in 1893 when the country's main export trade in currants collapsed and the foreign loans necessitated by the 1897 war indemnity resulted, as with the Ottomans, in the imposition of an International Financial Commission, with the right to collect revenue from Greece's state monopolies and customs for foreign creditors. Much of the economy was sustained only by remittances from the 350,000 Greeks who emigrated to America between 1890 and 1914.

The Young Turk revolution, with its potential to regenerate the Ottoman Empire, provoked something like a revolution in Greece itself. Army officers concerned at the country's poor state of preparedness formed a Military League and in August 1909 demanded improvements in the armed forces. Their favoured candidate for office was the popular Cretan Eleftherios Venizelos, whose Liberal Party won a convincing majority in the elections of 1910. Venizelos pushed through a variety of measures to increase political efficiency and modernise Greek society. Parliamentary filibustering was restricted and public employment made conditional on examinations; land was expropriated for redistribution, trade unions legalised and a minimum wage for women and children and a progressive income tax were introduced. The resulting surplus permitted increased spending on the armed forces. The result was that, when the Balkan League was formed in 1912, Greece was in a much better position to realise its long-standing ambitions against the Ottomans.

Much of *Serbia*'s development, or lack of it, from the 1860s was conditioned by its relationship with the Habsburg Monarchy. The assassination of Prince Michael Obrenović, in 1868, not only put his ambitious plans for a Balkan alliance against the Ottomans on hold but was followed by a Regency on behalf of his nephew Milan (1868–89) which was anxious not to upset Vienna, although not above flirting with Russia. Milan, on attaining his majority in 1872, was equally unadventurous, not least because of the emergence of party politics. A constitution agreed by the Regency in 1869 had legitimised greater political activity, even if the dominant Liberal Party of Jovan Ristić showed little inclination to share power. Serbia in this period has been cited as an example of 'politics as development': despite remaining an essentially peasant society due to its lack of economic development, it nevertheless was well on the way to becoming a functioning democracy, with effectively universal manhood suffrage, a critical press and a new political force emerging by the 1870s, the Radical Party, which represented the views of its smallholder supporters.[10] All parties were strongly nationalist, but differed as to how liberation of fellow Serbs under Ottoman rule should be achieved. For economic investment Serbia remained totally dependent on foreign, which meant Austro-Hungarian, capital.

The Near Eastern crisis of 1875–8 starkly illustrated Serbia's weakness. The war against the Ottomans for Bosnia, entered into so vaingloriously in 1876, ended in humiliating defeat, from which Serbia was rescued only by Russia; the latter then forced Serbia back into the wider Russo-Turkish conflict, only to abandon it in favour of the Bulgarians at the peace negotiations. Recognition of Serbia's independence, and minor territorial gains to the south-west, were secured only with the help of Austria–Hungary, but in return Serbia was obliged to look on while the Habsburgs occupied Bosnia and to accept the treaties of 1880–1 which kept it in political and economic subjection to Vienna for the next generation. Elevation to the status of a kingdom, in 1882, was poor consolation and an unprovoked attack on the new Bulgaria, in 1885, seeking compensation for the latter's union with Eastern Rumelia, resulted in another mortifying defeat.

King Milan, an Austrophile playboy with little affection for his subjects, abdicated in 1889, leaving his under-age son Alexander (1889–1903) a Regency and a new, even more democratic constitution. Alexander, however, proved precociously authoritarian, staging his own coup in 1893 at the age of 16, reinstating the 1869 constitution and ruling through an unpopular clique, while persecuting Radical opponents of the regime and maintaining close relations with Austria–Hungary. The king's marriage to his mistress, in 1900, lost him the support of the officer corps of the army and in June 1903 a conspiracy of the military and the Radical Party brutally murdered the royal couple, installed Peter Karađorđević, descendant of Karađorđe, on the throne, and restored the 1889 constitution.

The 1903 revolution marked a decisive shift in Serbian policy. Henceforth governments were dominated by the Radical Party under Nikola Pašić, which in 1906 dared to make the economic break with Austria–Hungary, without which a more aggressive pursuit of nationalist goals would have been impossible. Given the danger of confronting the Habsburgs too openly over Bosnia, as shown by the crisis of 1908–9, Serbia focused increasingly on a military build-up and the formation of an alliance against the Ottomans. By 1912 these twin preoccupations were about to bear fruit.

Romania in this period was a country of paradoxes. Politically stable, it remained governed by an oligarchical elite. Economically it became increasingly diverse and achieved greater modernisation than other Balkan states, yet the gulf between its richest and poorest grew ever wider. The constitution agreed in 1866 on the accession of Prince Charles I (1866–1914) established an indirect voting system, whereby four electoral colleges were elected by voters according to property qualifications. The wealthiest three classes of electors in turn elected 118 deputies to the National Assembly, while the college representing the peasantry, 60 per cent of the population, returned 30 deputies. Politics was dominated by two parties, with the prince occupying a pivotal role as arbiter between them: the Conservatives represented the landowning *boyars*, while the Liberals spoke for the urban, and more overtly nationalist, middle classes. The Liberals, once in power, modestly amended the system in 1884 to three electoral colleges, with the peasant college returning 38 out of 183 deputies, but this hardly altered the disenfranchisement of peasants, since a literacy requirement for voting excluded the 60 per cent of them who could not read.

Internationally Romania had a foot in both camps. Forced to participate in the Russo-Turkish War of 1877–8, mainly as a transit camp for Russian troops, its reward was independence and the Dobrudja, followed in 1881 by recognition as a kingdom. Its penalty was the retrocession of Southern Bessarabia to Russia and the revision of its constitution, demanded by the great powers in 1878 but intensely resented, to make discrimination against non-Christians, but especially Jews, illegal. Partly from Russophobia, the Liberal government of Ion Brătianu concluded a defensive (and secret) alliance with Austria–Hungary in 1883. This, however, was never more than a marriage of convenience, given the general strength of feeling against the Habsburgs over the position of fellow Romanians in Transylvania.

Romania's economic development was impressive. It was the first Balkan state to attract serious investment in railways and as a result the big estates profited immensely from a boom in the international grain trade – by 1914 Romania was the third greatest exporter of corn and the fourth greatest of wheat in the world.[11] An increasing proportion of the economy was devoted to agricultural processing industries such as sugar refining and tobacco, a development encouraged by the government's decision, in 1885, to emancipate itself commercially from Austria–Hungary and seek other markets for its produce. Extractive industrial activity also took off, based initially on forestry and then, following the discovery of major deposits in the 1860s, oil, of which Romania produced 1.8 million tonnes by 1913.[12] Much of the oil industry was controlled by foreign corporations, given the lack of indigenous capital accumulation. Yet on the eve of the First World War Romania presented an increasingly modern face to the world.

Under the surface, however, there were serious socio-economic tensions. Apart from the fact that the corruption and closed nature of Romanian politics made even the urban classes feel excluded from decision-making, the condition of the peasant majority worsened appreciably. The agrarian legislation of the 1860s had failed to create a peasant smallholder class; instead 200,000 peasants had no land at all at the start of this period and 300,000 at the end of it, while a growing number of the rest either leased more land and fell increasingly into debt as a result or laboured on bigger estates while trying to maintain their own plots.[13] Peasant indebtedness, and the use of force to ensure debt collection, led to chronic unrest and violence in the latter decades of the century, ameliorated only marginally by the creation of an Agricultural Credit Bank in 1881 and the legalisation of cooperatives in 1904. In 1907 a spontaneous and generally directionless peasant uprising, put down with exemplary brutality, cost 10,000 lives, but although both main parties agreed that something must be done to avert a repetition, legislation to redistribute land and introduce a universal suffrage system was only being considered in 1914.

Autonomous *Bulgaria*, after 1878, was intended by its creator Russia to be an outpost of influence in the Balkans, but proved more independent-minded than expected. The new state was indeed dominated in its early years by Russians, who drafted the constitution finalised by an Assembly of Notables at Tŭrnovo in February 1879; ironically, given its tsarist provenance, this was yet another model democratic document, providing for direct, universal manhood suffrage, with power shared between a prince and his appointed ministers and the National Assembly or *Sŭbranie*. The Russians also hand-picked Alexander of Battenberg (1878–86) and provided officers for the fledgling army, but soon found that neither the prince nor his government took kindly to constant interference. Party politics divided initially between the Conservatives, paternalist and elitist, and the more nationalist and democratic Liberals; not until the formation in 1899 of the Bulgarian Agrarian National Union (BANU) did the peasant masses find a powerful political voice of their own.

The breaking point with the Russians came over Eastern Rumelia, whose separation from the principality was deplored by Bulgarian nationalists and whose regional assembly was in any case dominated by Bulgarians. In 1885 a revolutionary committee in Plovdiv, Eastern Rumelia's capital, proclaimed union; the Bulgarian government, fearful of its own public opinion, hastened to accept. Russia, furious at this wilfulness, withdrew its military personnel, while Serbia, hoping for easy gains, attacked Bulgaria but, to everyone's surprise, was decisively routed. Russia insisted that it would sanction the union only if Alexander abdicated, and the unwilling prince was actually kidnapped in 1886 by officers acting for the tsar and, after a prolonged international crisis, replaced by Ferdinand of Saxe-Coburg-Gotha (1887–1918).

The government of Ferdinand's first minister-president, Stefan Stambolov, was authoritarian in the extreme and resorted to unprecedented electoral violence to maintain its majority. This was partly to shore up a shaky new regime and partly a reaction to the malign effects of the 'Macedonian Question'. Some 200,000 Macedonian Slav refugees lived in Bulgaria after 1878 and their efforts to foment rebellion in Ottoman territory were a standing embarrassment to Stambolov, who repressed them. He could do nothing, however, to hinder the formation in 1893, in Ottoman-ruled Salonica, of a Macedonian Revolutionary Organisation. The ministry which succeeded Stambolov, on his dismissal in 1894 (he was murdered by embittered Macedonians a year later), felt less able to withstand Macedonian demands for support and a Supreme Macedonian Committee was formed in Sofia that year in an attempt to control the movement and work for the incorporation of Macedonia into Bulgaria. The Salonica-based group, however, was less amenable to such direction and ambivalent about annexation; to distinguish itself from the 'Supremacists' in Bulgaria it eventually renamed itself the Internal Macedonian Revolutionary Organisation (IMRO). IMRO complicated matters dangerously for the Bulgarian government, which was held by most outside observers to be complicit in IMRO's extremist tactics.

In its domestic development Bulgaria was hag-ridden by debt, obliged from the start of its existence to borrow in order to function at all. Much of Bulgarian politics revolved around land tenure. Some of the land belonging to the 150,000 Muslims who fled the principality in 1878 was confiscated, but some Muslims returned and by the turn of the century 15 per cent of arable land was still in Muslim hands. A majority of Bulgarian peasants, however, as in Serbia, were smallholders, most of them self-sufficient but not producing much surplus. The country remained an overwhelmingly agrarian society, with what industry there was being extractive or food processing. In 1899 the government, desperate to increase revenue, introduced a tithe payment in kind on arable land, which was vastly unpopular and led directly to the formation of the Agrarian Union. Alexandŭr Stamboliiski, leader of BANU, epitomised the gulf between town and countryside, a genuine populist who extolled the peasant as the backbone of the nation and distrusted everything urban. Governments after 1900 struggled to contain the rising electoral presence of the Agrarians, as well as increasing labour and socialist unrest, by electoral fraud and violence; the particularly harsh policies of one minister-president, Nikola Petkov, led to his assassination in 1907. Independence in 1908 did little to alleviate these internal tensions, even if it meant Bulgaria now controlled its own trade and the income from its own customs.

THE COLLAPSE OF OTTOMAN POWER IN THE BALKANS 1912-14

The sudden roll-back of the Ottoman imperium in 1912–13 surprised most observers, yet should perhaps have been expected. With hindsight it was clear that the Young Turk revolution, though an attempt to preserve the Empire, had temporarily weakened it, while the Balkan states, uncharacteristically and briefly united, had modernised, militarily at least, just enough to prevail. In doing so they unintentionally contributed to the establishment of a final nation-state, Albania.

The Balkan League, forged between Serbia, Bulgaria, Greece and Montenegro between March and May 1912, was promoted by the Russian government in an effort to limit Habsburg influence in the peninsula, but the Balkan states, demonstrating once again that they had minds of their own, promptly turned the alliance against the Ottomans. They were encouraged by Italy's successful war of 1911–12 in pursuit of Ottoman Libya and were fearful lest the Young Turks regenerate the Empire, as well as alarmed by growing Albanian calls for an autonomous unit to be carved out of the four *vilayets* in which Albanians were concentrated. A revolt against Young Turk centralisation had in fact been simmering among the Albanians of Kosovo since 1909, spreading to neighbouring *vilayets* by 1911. Serbia, Bulgaria and Greece were all therefore anxious to wrest the remaining Balkan provinces from Ottoman control, so much so that they concluded only the vaguest of agreements as to how these territories should be divided in the event of victory.

Hostilities, initiated on the flimsiest of pretexts in October 1912, were brief but savage, with Ottoman forces actually outnumbered two to one because of the Italian War, and the Balkan armies assisted by guerrilla activity behind Ottoman lines. Serbia, Montenegro and Greece mopped up the western Balkans, while Bulgaria and Greece attacked in the east, Bulgaria advancing almost to Constantinople and Greece taking Salonica. Most of Macedonia, to Bulgaria's annoyance, fell to Serbia and Greece. The fighting was accompanied by considerable brutality on all sides, with well-documented atrocities recorded by a famous international enquiry, published to much western tut-tutting on the eve of the First World War.[14]

An armistice was agreed in early December, at great-power insistence. This was in part in response to appeals by Albanians, who had set up a provisional government under Ismail Qemal at Vlorë in November and protested against the takeover of territory by the Balkan states, but it owed even more to Austria–Hungary's determination to deny Serbia access to the Adriatic. At the peace negotiations in London the creation of an Albanian state was settled in principle, but proceedings were interrupted by the Ottomans' resumption of hostilities in February 1913 and their loss of yet more territory to their enemies. Peace negotiations resumed in April, at which point it became clear that the planned Albania was being used by Serbia and Greece as justification for hanging on to their Macedonian conquests. The Treaty of London, in May, fixed the limits of Ottoman territory in the southeast and sketched in Albania, but left adjustment of borders in Macedonia to the later agreement of the three states concerned. Bulgaria's sense of injustice was only heightened by intimations from Romania, hitherto not involved in the fighting, that it wished compensation, which could come only from Bulgaria. The latter rashly attacked Serbia and Greece in June, but was soundly defeated not only by these states but by Romania and the Ottoman Empire, which seized the opportunity to claw back the area around Adrianople.

The final territorial redistribution, at the Treaty of Bucharest in August 1913, can be seen from Map 7. The Ottoman reconquest of Adrianople was allowed to stand, but elsewhere the Empire's Balkan dominions were no more. In their place the Balkan nation-states had become in their turn multi-national, with Serbia incorporating Albanians, Macedonian Slavs and Turks, Montenegro Albanians and Turks, Greece Albanians, Macedonian Slavs and Turks, and Romania Bulgarians.

In the new Albania, the provisional government of Qemal, whose writ hardly extended beyond Vlorë, was ignored by the great powers, who set up instead an International Control Commission, empowered to draft a constitution, assemble an international police force and draw boundaries. The title of Prince was offered to a minor German princeling, Wilhelm of Wied, who arrived in March 1914 but whose 'reign' lasted barely half a year. Albania's tribal factions, split additionally between Muslims, Orthodox and Catholics, proved intractable and when the First World War broke out, the International Control Commission promptly disbanded.

The end of Ottoman rule was a seeming triumph for Balkan nationalism, but in reality had been brought about by state-led war and territorial aggrandisement. In the process, however, the antagonisms of the different Balkan nationalities to each other were undoubtedly exacerbated, while the emergence of a specifically Turkish nationalism was expedited by defeat and the loss of non-Turkish population. Finally, the elimination of 'Turkey-in-Europe', and the expansion of Serbia in particular, strengthened the conviction in Vienna that the Habsburg Monarchy was next in line.

15

THE RUSSIAN AND GERMAN EMPIRES TO 1914

The divergence between the Russian Empire and Prussia could only widen in the second half of the nineteenth century, when Prussia assumed the leading role in the new German Empire of 1871. German 'unification', which in reality excluded large numbers of ethnic Germans from the new state, nevertheless created the most formidable economic and military power on the continent. Russia, by contrast, appeared more backward and hence more vulnerable than ever before, yet it was this vulnerability which finally spurred tsarism to embark on a crash course in industrialisation after 1890. Thereafter Russia's phenomenal growth began to close the gap once more. The German government's consciousness of this growth was a contributory factor in its decision to risk war in 1914.

The two empires in this period were very different politically. Germany was a constitutional monarchy and a genuinely federal empire, even if its head of state retained significant powers and its greatest component, Prussia, remained a bastion of conservatism. Russian autocracy survived even the 1905 Revolution, when a constitution of sorts and a representative assembly were forced on the tsar. Yet both empires shared one characteristic: each in reality was multinational, despite efforts to identify the state with a single nationality. Germany, or rather Prussia, coped with its principal minority, the Poles, by waging a campaign of legal discrimination and internal colonisation. Russia, with multiple nationalities, attempted with notable lack of success to create a supranational sense of 'Russian' identity, even though the nationalism of ethnic Russians increasingly complicated the picture, in reaction to the nationalism of non-Russians.

RUSSIA – EMPIRE WOES

Russia's experiences in this period illustrate starkly not only the perils of backwardness but also one of the central dilemmas of modernisation:

economic development unaccompanied by political reform could produce deadly tensions within a society. Add to this the complications of nationality, and the impression of a state straining at the seams is unavoidable.

Since Russia was an autocracy, it is legitimate to consider the great-power preoccupations of its rulers first. Alexander II (1855–81) began his reign all too aware that Russia's vulnerability could affect its ability to maintain itself as a great power. The Empire's fundamental weakness *vis-à-vis* its European rivals was obvious by the 1860s, as was the reason for it, a lack of economic modernity. Emancipation of the serfs in 1861 was only the first step in this direction and one which certainly failed in its aim of creating a stable class of peasant smallholders. The most visible symbol of Russia's weakness, however, was its lack of railways. A government commission on railway construction concluded in 1865, 'The longer we delay, the further we shall fall behind Western Europe and the less we shall be able to develop our agriculture or even prevent its decline.'[1] Alexander's finance minister, Michael von Reutern, put it even more bluntly in 1866: 'Our whole future depends on the railways.'[2] The problem was that although there was a growing iron and cotton industry in Russia by the 1860s, the Empire was not capital-rich and the finance for railways had to come from foreign banks. To attract such capital the Russian government had to guarantee foreign investors a profit, as well as ensuring political stability and avoiding foreign adventures and wars.

Yet precisely because it was a great power, Russia found it impossible to avoid expansion, war and crippling expenditure on armaments. Its conquest of much of Central Asia, in what has been described as psychological compensation for its Crimean defeat but which also had strategic and economic motives, continued for several decades after 1856. It entered into the war against the Ottoman Empire in the 1870s partly for reasons of prestige, partly because of the novel pressure on the tsar of Pan-Slavist-generated public opinion, and partly for strategic advantage, but in defiance of the financial consequences. Reutern, who had painfully stabilised Russia's currency and funded railway construction, largely through borrowing, resigned in 1878 in despair over the costs of the war. The Ottoman war left Russian finances 'almost where they had been after the Crimean War'.[3]

The penny finally dropped in the late 1880s when the crisis over Bulgaria's union with Eastern Rumelia raised the possibility of war with Austria–Hungary and Germany. A major reason for Russia's climb-down was the poor state of the Russian armed forces as a result of successive cuts in expenditure and the impossibility of funding their improvement. Alexander III (1881–94) was simply forced to recognise the limitations of Russian power and it was in these circumstances that the decision was taken to embark on a state-led industrialisation programme.

The tsar's resolve owed much to the persuasiveness of Sergei Witte, who as finance minister from 1892 to 1903 masterminded Russia's breakneck modernisation. Witte was in many respects building on the efforts of his predecessors to fuel economic take-off through a combination of high tariffs against foreign manufactures and raw materials, continued borrowing and a drive to push up grain exports, and thus foreign currency earnings, by raising indirect taxes. The latter policy hit the peasantry hardest, by forcing many to sell their own supplies of grain, resulting in widespread famine in 1891–2, but it undoubtedly boosted government revenues. Witte continued these policies. He also commissioned huge infrastructure projects such as the Trans-Siberian Railway, to open up the natural resources of Russia's vast Asiatic hinterland, while offering low freight charges to make the railways profitable. The result was a massive spurt in economic growth: 20,000 kilometres of track laid between 1896 and 1901, a doubling of iron production between 1892 and 1899, with comparable figures for coal and steel, and rapid urbanisation.[4] Russia's industrial revolution was well under way.

DEVELOPMENT WITHOUT POLITICS

The second striking aspect of Russia's history in this period is the political dilemma inevitably accompanying modernisation, given that the Empire remained an autocracy. All the tsars took their role as autocrat seriously. Even the reforming Alexander II had no intention of relaxing control and saw the *zemstvos* or local assemblies essentially as talking shops, charged with implementing decisions made in St Petersburg. Alexander III and Nicholas II (1894–1917) were reactionaries as well as unimaginative mediocrities, whose natural preferences were even tighter control. They regarded the landowning nobility as unreliable and relied instead on an ever-expanding bureaucracy and police apparatus. The result was a regime inherently inefficient and unresponsive to the pressures building within Russian society.

The lack of any meaningful political space, and the sidelining of even the educated and public-spirited, had already radicalised Russia's intelligentsia, and this trend intensified in the late nineteenth century. In their attempts to effect change, young Russians turned first to well-meaning but impractical proselytising among the common people and finally to revolutionary socialism and political violence. Government in response resorted to ever greater repression, especially in the wake of Alexander II's assassination in 1881. For the remainder of the imperial period revolutionary movements committed to the destruction of tsarism formed a constant backdrop of tension, and however tiny the numbers involved, their appeal could only increase once industrialisation took off. The displacement of population from countryside to town, the miserable living conditions of the new proletariat and the continuing pressure on those still farming the land constituted the ideal matrix for revolution.

Nicholas II's government compounded these problems by its imperialist ambitions in the Far East, which were in turn driven by Witte's vision of opening up Siberia, while muscling in on territories and markets, such as

China and Korea, which Russia could plausibly hope to dominate. The resulting clash with imperial Japan lies outside this story, but the catastrophic consequences of the Russo-Japanese War of 1904–5 are highly relevant. Defeat at the hands of an Asiatic power which had modernised more effectively seemed the ultimate indictment of Russian backwardness, its military unpreparedness and above all its incompetent leadership. The economic privations of the war, and the outrage at impending defeat, sparked strikes and revolutionary unrest throughout 1905, which in October finally forced the tsar to issue a manifesto, in effect Russia's first constitution, which legitimised political parties and promised a representative assembly or *Duma*.

This creation of a political arena, however, unleashed fresh tensions. Not only were the limitations placed by the October Manifesto and the *Duma* on the tsar's power – in particular his ability to appoint ministers and decide policy – minimal, but the very emergence of political parties, even ones elected through a restricted and indirect suffrage, ensured that economic and social grievances were voiced with even greater vehemence. It also meant that the Pandora's box of Russia's nationality problems was now opened.

RUSSIAN AND OTHER NATIONALISMS

The complications of nationality arose from the fact that, as of 1897, ethnic or Great Russians constituted only 44.3 per cent of the population. As far as Russians were concerned there were arguably two nationalisms, one 'official' and the other popular. Official nationalism was the sense of loyalty to tsar and state, regardless of a subject's ethnicity, which had been promoted since the 1830s. Popular Russian nationalism was being vocally expressed in the new print media by the 1860s, by such figures as Katkov. Thereafter the slow production of an educated class by the schools, the improvements in physical communications and above all the emergence of a mass newspaper culture finally created that 'imagined community' we call nationalism.[5]

Yet popular nationalism, by definition, was viewed with trepidation by the tsars, even when they shared some of its objectives. Pan-Slavists like Katkov or A.S. Suvorin, publisher of the mass-circulation *Novoe vremia* (New Times), were bitterly hostile to national minorities, like the Poles in 1863–4 who did not accept their subordinate status within the Empire. They bayed for intervention in the Balkans in the 1870s, the one occasion when Pan-Slavism could be said to have shaped tsarist foreign policy directly, and howled with outrage at the compromise Treaty of Berlin, which the journalist Ivan Aksakov denounced as 'an open conspiracy against the Russian people . . . with the connivance of Russia's own representatives'.[6] They were increasingly critical of the regime for not being nationalist enough and, by implication, not basing its policies on the national will. As a consequence tsarism continued to look nervously over its shoulder at these populist tribunes, whose views were undoubtedly shared by a growing number of government officials, diplomats and even ministers.

Thus pressured from below, Russian governments in the 1880s started to articulate a more aggressive, if not more coherent, official nationalism than hitherto. One of the chief architects of what was called 'Russification' was Alexander III's former tutor, Konstantin Pobedonostsev, who was procurator or lay administrator of the Orthodox Church's Holy Synod from 1880 to 1905, but whose frankly reactionary influence extended across the reigns of the last two tsars. Pobedonostsev as early as 1876 recognised the challenge posed to the monarchy by popular nationalism: 'The government must either take this popular movement in hand and lead it, or it will inundate the authorities and spread, wild and uncontrolled, animated by a sense of mistrust and hostility to the government.'[7] Yet riding the nationalist tiger could not, for Pobedonostsev, involve any concessions to western-style representative government. Instead the government must inculcate a sense of belonging to the Empire by an ever greater centralisation and by giving cultural primacy to the Russian language and the Orthodox religion. This did not mean that non-Russians were expected somehow to become ethnic Russians; it did mean that their own languages and cultures would be severely restricted. How this was to be achieved was less clear, and Russification varied considerably from nationality to nationality in how it was implemented. The overall effect, however, was disastrous. Where a nationality was already disaffected, it made things worse; among hitherto loyal peoples it stirred up resentment and nationalist sentiments where they had not existed.

In the case of the *Poles* Alexander II's government abandoned all attempts to rule through the local elite after the 1863–4 revolt. Henceforth Russian Poland was administered as an integral part of the Empire, with a Russian-language administration and judicial system, staffed by Russians, a much restricted role for the Catholic Church and the substitution of Russian for Polish in middle and secondary schools. From 1879 speaking Polish in schools became a criminal offence, although in practice the ban proved hard to enforce, and Russian was made the language of instruction even in elementary schools in 1885. The Main School in Warsaw was made a Russian-language institution in 1869, with the result that the number of Poles in higher education dropped dramatically. A large Orthodox cathedral was constructed in the centre of Warsaw.

Poles reacted with a pragmatic, surface acceptance of what they could not alter, beneath which, however, Polish nationalism not only survived but intensified, despite increasing social divisions as industrialisation set in. The Polish provinces were one of the hearths of industrialisation, responsible for a quarter of the Empire's manufacturing by 1914, and this was accompanied by rapid urbanisation, with a third of the population town-dwellers by 1909.[8] There was a growing industrial working class as well as middle class.

Among the former, underground Marxist socialism was making inroads by the 1870s, but it was not until 1892 that the Polish Socialist Party was founded by exiles in Paris. Under the leadership of Józef Piłsudski this peculiarly Polish socialism was also strongly nationalist: only a reunified and independent Poland, Piłsudski argued, could achieve modernisation and hence progress to socialism. The Socialists found themselves after 1893 with a rival in the shape of the Social Democrats, led first by Róża Luxemburg and later Feliks Dzierżyński; these more orthodox Marxists rejected Piłsudski's nationalism as incompatible with socialism. Middle-class political activity, also perforce clandestine, was in this period gradually shouldering aside the impoverished nobility as representative of a truly modern Polish nationalism. The National League, started in 1893 by Roman Dmowski and later renamed the National Democratic Party, abbreviated in Polish to *Endecja*, appealed to Poles of all classes because it saw the nation as socially inclusive, as well as Catholic. On the negative side, *Endecja's* nationalism was also indebted to Social Darwinism and racism. It assumed that non-Polish nationalities within 'Polish' territory would have to assimilate; it was also explicitly anti-Semitic.

Ukrainians were victims of something 'unique in nineteenth-century Russia', in that the government over several decades did its best to suppress Ukrainian, not as a literary language but as the language of the common people.[9] The publications banned under the Valuev Decree of 1863 and the Ems Decree of 1876 were textbooks, grammars and other educational aids, rather than literary works. This particular aspect of Russification has been dubbed the 'demographic approach': since Ukrainians were, at 17.81 per cent of the population by 1897, the second-largest ethnic group in the Empire, after the Russians, it would, as one official remarked in 1876, be 'the utmost political carelessness' to allow a separate national consciousness to develop among the peasant millions, as opposed to the tiny Ukrainian intelligentsia.[10] Russians on their own were a minority within Russia, but if, as Russian nationalists tended to assume, Ukrainian and Belorussian were classed as mere dialects of Russian, the three peoples together constituted a clear majority. Uneasily aware of the potential attraction of the Ukrainian national movement in Habsburg Galicia, the governments of Alexander III and Nicholas II maintained this policy of linguistic repression and persecuted any Ukrainian intellectuals who objected. It was encouraged by the fact that industrialisation was steadily altering the demographic balance of the Ukraine by attracting significant numbers of ethnic Russians as workers, entrepreneurs and officials.

In the *Baltic provinces* Russification scored a remarkable 'own goal' by risking the alienation of the German nobility, arguably the most loyal of the Empire's minorities. Russian nationalists had long resented the German nobles as privileged aliens, but the autocracy traditionally prized these efficient landowners and servants of the crown. The foundation of the

German Empire, however, inclined even the tsars to question German loyalties, and on his accession in 1881 Alexander III refused to confirm the Baltic nobility's privileges. Although he left the self-governing *Ritterschaften* in place, he deprived them of judicial authority in the 1880s and introduced Russian-language schools for administrators, whose graduates, many of whom were Estonian and Latvian, were envisaged as 'agents of future Russian domination'.[11] Russian was gradually made compulsory throughout the Baltic provinces' educational system above primary level and in 1893 Dorpat University was turned into the Russian-language Yuriev University. As in Poland, Riga and Reval were blessed with ostentatiously large Orthodox cathedrals.

The Baltic German nobles, ironically, were just as nervous as the autocracy about nationalism, even among their fellow, but non-noble, Germans in the towns, but especially among their Estonian and Latvian peasants. This period finally saw the emergence of a modest class of Estonian and Latvian smallholders, delayed beneficiaries of the earlier agrarian reform in these provinces. The children of these farmers constituted the first generation of urban factory workers, shopkeepers, artisans, teachers and the like, who then acted as the real 'carriers' of nationalism, campaigning for native-language secondary schools and producing textbooks, newspapers and literature. Industrialisation, which affected the Baltic provinces as it did the Polish lands, accelerated this process. Politically, therefore, the Baltic peoples were split. The sizeable factory proletariat gravitated to socialism, with a Latvian Social Democratic Party being formed secretly in 1904. But key elements of all Estonians' and Latvians' desiderata were the abolition or democratisation of the *Ritterschaften* and the break-up and redistribution of the German nobles' estates. These social tensions broke out during the 1905 Revolution, when there were bloody strikes and demonstrations in the towns and angry Estonian and Latvian peasants burned down large numbers of manor houses. Alarmed at these events, the government rediscovered the virtues of the German nobility, but the latter's confidence in the tsar's ability to protect them was shaken. The decade before the First World War saw the rise of German economic and political associations embracing both nobles and middle class, and the beginning of the very thing Russifiers had most reason to fear: a Baltic German nationalism.

Lithuanians' experiences in this period were similar to those of the other Baltic peoples. A tiny educated elite was in place by the 1860s, and as Catholics the Lithuanian reaction to Russification was partly religious. The first Lithuanian-language review, *Aušra* (The Dawn), was started in 1883 by Jonas Basanavičius, whose studies in Moscow and abroad inspired him to engineer his people's 'awakening'. *Aušra* had to be printed in Prague, in Cyrillic, and then smuggled into Russian territory, but it was the first of several such periodicals. The first political organisation was a Social Democratic Party, in 1895, followed by a liberal Democratic Party in 1902.

Finally, Russia's *Jews* were the unenviable exception to the rule, in that tsarist governments in the end abandoned attempts to assimilate or at best tolerate them, in favour of a policy of renewed discrimination and exclusion. Alexander II partially emancipated the Jews: although the majority were still confined to the Pale of Settlement, it became possible for certain classes of merchant, craftsman or degree-holder to move to the Russian heartland. Enough Jews were able to gain an adequate education and enter business or the professions to create a Jewish middle class.

Alexander III, by contrast, reacted harshly to the fact that one of his father's assassins was of Jewish origin, but the widespread violence that broke out against Jews in 1881 owed much also to a growing conviction among Russians generally that Jews were unfairly exploitative and alien to Russian culture. Ivan Aksakov was one of the first to promote the view that Jews were undermining the Empire from within and were in league with Russia's enemies, a view adopted by Alexander III's first minister of the interior, Count N.P. Ignatiev. From 1882 Jews were once again restricted in what property they could own, barred from the law and other professions and subjected to an upper limit in higher education. In 1891 two-thirds of Moscow's Jewish population, some 20,000 people, were expelled as illegal residents. The police department of the interior ministry, in the late 1890s, had a hand in embellishing and disseminating the notorious French forgery, *The Protocols of the Elders of Zion*, purporting to prove the existence of a Jewish conspiracy to dominate the world. It is now generally accepted that the tsarist government did not directly incite *pogroms*, or organised violence, against Jewish communities, as happened in 1903 in Bessarabia and again in 1905–6 across the Empire, but by its generally anti-Semitic stance it undoubtedly gave the perpetrators the impression that they had official approval. Unsurprisingly, 2 million Jews emigrated from Russia between 1890 and 1914. Among those who remained, the first mass political movements appeared. Zionism, tolerated by the government because its programme was resettlement in Palestine, won recruits in the middle class. Socialism, however, had more appeal if the 25,000-strong membership of the Jewish wing of the Social Democratic movement, the *Bund*, was any indication. The *Bund* opposed Zionism and insisted that the Jews, as yet another distinct nation within the Empire, deserved cultural autonomy and Yiddish-language schooling.

1905 AND BEYOND

This is not the place to consider the 1905 Revolution and its aftermath as part of the larger history of Russia, let alone as an aspect of what Lenin (unhistorically) considered the 'dress rehearsal' for the 1917 Revolutions. Rather, the main interest in a history of Eastern Europe is how the Revolution affected the Empire's non-Russian subjects and their relationship with Russia and the Russians.

The revolutionary events themselves demonstrated just how fissile this multinational realm had become. Most of the unrest that destabilised the Empire immediately after 'Bloody Sunday' in St Petersburg, in January 1905, was not in the Russian heartland but in the non-Russian periphery. The most prolonged violence was in Poland, with a terrorist campaign by Piłsudski's Socialists and more deaths than the 1863 revolt; at one point 300,000 troops were stationed there, while the Japanese War was still in progress.[12] There was widespread agrarian unrest in the Ukraine as well as the Baltic provinces, and a general 'mobilizing effect' upon nationalities across the board.[13] The Jewish *Bund* was active in organising its members, not least in self-defence against the threat of *pogroms*.

Even in advance of the October Manifesto nationalist parties were being formed among the Baltic peoples and existing underground organisations like the *Endecja* prepared to come out in the open. The Manifesto's promise of civil rights and freedom of expression spawned a rash of non-Russian newspapers and cultural bodies: Ukrainians were quick to take advantage of the new press freedoms, and even the Belorussians published their first periodicals and demanded autonomy. The first *Duma*, which assembled in April 1906, was a striking reflection of the Empire's multinational nature. There were 220 non-Russian deputies, as opposed to 270 Russians, and although most of the non-Russians gravitated to parties according to political persuasion rather than national allegiance, most of the Poles followed *Endecja*, and there was a Ukrainian parliamentary 'circle' in both the first *Duma* and that of 1907.[14]

Diffused among Russia's new party system, yet highly visible, the presence of national minorities in the *Duma* prompted a backlash from both the government and Russian nationalists. While the historian Pavel Miliukov, leader of the main middle-class party, the Constitutional Democrats (*Kadets*), sincerely advocated granting all nationalities the broadest cultural autonomy, other parties were returned to the *Duma* bearing a radically different message. The Union of the Russian People, in particular, flatly asserted its belief in autocracy and the 'indivisibility of the Russian Empire'; it was also openly anti-Semitic and was known to have the support of Nicholas II himself, as did the ultra-nationalist vigilante groups, the Black Hundreds, which attacked socialists, liberals and national minorities and were especially active in the *pogroms* of 1905–6.[15] From the viewpoint of the tsar and P.A. Stolypin, his prime minister from 1906 to 1911, the high representation of nationalities in the *Duma* was undesirable; it was to restrict this that Stolypin, in 1907, introduced an electoral reform bill specifically designed to reduce the number of non-Russian deputies. As the imperial edict announcing this change put it, 'The State Duma, created to strengthen the Russian state, should be Russian in spirit.' Accordingly, non-Russians 'should have sufficient representation in the State Duma for their needs, but should not have so many that they have a deciding voice . . .'[16]

The result was that, in the third *Duma* of 1907–12, and the fourth (1912–17), the number of non-Russian deputies was substantially reduced, as was the strength of parties representing specific nationalities. By contrast the representation of Russian nationalist parties went up significantly. Stolypin, rightly described as a 'modern nationalist', proceeded also to crack down on minority cultural associations and freedoms of all sorts.[17] As he admonished the Polish deputies in 1907, 'Admit that the highest good is to be a Russian [*russkii*] citizen, bear this title as proudly as Roman citizens once did . . . and you will receive all rights.'[18] V.N. Kokovtsov, the assassinated Stolypin's successor, reiterated in 1912 'the hallowed unity and indivisibility of the empire, the predominance of the Russian nationality within it, and of the Orthodox faith'.[19] It was a message the Empire's non-Russians found increasingly unpalatable.

THE GERMAN EMPIRE

When the North German Confederation was joined by the South German states to form a 'united' Germany in 1871, it transferred to the new Empire its federal constitution as well as the leading role of the largest state, Prussia. At the federal level Germany had striking democratic features: the *Reichstag* or imperial diet was elected by universal manhood suffrage, and although appointment of the chancellor and his government rested solely with the emperor, German governments in this period increasingly found it convenient to dispose of a working parliamentary majority, since the *Reichstag*'s consent was required for legislation. The individual states retained their own princes, governments, assemblies and real administrative control over their own affairs; the imperial government was responsible for defence and foreign relations.

The problem with regard to national minorities came from this strong position assured the states: some states, including Prussia, retained highly undemocratic constitutions, in Prussia's case a 'three-class suffrage' which ensured the dominance of the Junker landowners. And with Prussia came a substantial minority of Poles: 2.4 million in 1871, or 5 per cent of the total population, their numbers had risen to 3.5 million by 1910. One out of ten subjects of the King of Prussia was a Catholic Pole.[20] The Poles therefore had continuous representation in the federal *Reichstag*, but were entirely unrepresented in the Prussian *Landtag* or diet.

Bismarck, until 1890 Prussian minister-president as well as imperial chancellor, shared the jaundiced views of most Protestant Germans against Catholics as potential 'enemies of the *Reich*', whose allegiances to the new Germany were bound to be divided; Polish Catholics were doubly suspect. The German government's self-defeating *Kulturkampf* or 'war of civilisations' against Catholicism lasted throughout the 1870s, but was eventually abandoned when it became obvious that persecution had merely strengthened the *Zentrum*, the party representing the 36 per cent of Germans who were Catholic. The Poles, by contrast, came in for more concentrated fire in the 1880s. Bismarck's personal views on them were virulent: they were primitive, obscurantist, fundamentally untrustworthy and ready to revolt 'on twenty-four hours' notice'.[21] On security grounds alone, Bismarck felt, it was imperative to control and if possible reduce the Polish presence in Prussia's eastern provinces, and especially 'to rid the country of the trichinosis of the Polish nobility'.[22]

The Prussian government had already, in the 1870s, sought to strengthen the German character of the state by language ordinances which made German the official language, to be used in the school system, public administration and the courts, and in commercial transactions. It followed this up in 1883–5 with the forcible expulsion of 32,000 illegal Polish migrant workers from Russia and Austria, a third of whom were Polish Jews. In 1886 a Settlement Act was passed and a Royal Prussian Colonisation Commission set up, with the aim of buying out Polish landowners and resettling their estates with German colonists. This 'inner colonisation' campaign was a near-complete failure. Although 150,000 Germans were settled, most of the land had to be purchased from Germans, not Poles. The Poles, moreover, fought back, establishing their own Land Bank in 1889, buying extra land and organising cooperatives. Between 1896 and 1914 more land passed from German hands into Polish than the other way; this was despite the passing in 1908 of an Expropriation Act which provided for compulsory purchase. A higher Polish birth rate helped negate the Prussian government's attempts to reverse the balance, more than compensating for the 400,000 Poles who had migrated to the industrial Rhineland by 1914.[23]

Polish national consciousness in this period, as in Russia, was undoubtedly strengthened by Prussia's anti-Polish measures, not least because, again as in Russia, it became in the process socially more inclusive. A larger educated and middle class, the formation of peasant cooperatives, the cohesion of the Polish National Democratic Society in the *Reichstag*, and not least the constant need to mobilise Poles of all classes in self-defence, meant that Polish nationalism was a truly mass phenomenon by 1914.

Conversely, what many Germans, from Bismarck down, clearly saw as an equally defensive struggle against a creeping tide of Slavdom, was clearly a factor in the formation of a genuinely German, as opposed to Prussian, nationalism. 'United' Germany was an artificial amalgam of disparate elements, divided by loyalties to individual states, by religion, by class and by political beliefs. In addition to better-known bonding agents such as imperialism, and the imperial navy launched in 1898, an animus against Poles in the Prussian east was by the 1890s an important focus for German chauvinists and a variety of nationalist pressure groups. The Pan-German League, founded officially in 1891, represented a new type of radical or 'integral' nationalism. It stood by definition for dissatisfaction with the German Empire as incomplete and for its expansion to include all Germans, broadly defined as anyone of 'Germanic' stock and wherever they lived. Pan-Germans also enthusiastically supported 'inner colonisation' at the expense of what they saw as racially inferior Slavs. Even more focused on the Prussian east was the German Eastern Marches Society, founded in 1894 and known as the *Hakatisten* from the initials (HKT) of its three co-founders. The *Hakatisten* existed to maintain the pressure on what it saw as a backsliding government, insufficiently active in Germanising Prussian Poland; it was they who floated the idea of not simply buying out but positively expelling the Poles. Organisations like these did much to alienate Germany's Poles still further in the generation before 1914.

A final point should be made about the peculiar contribution that the German Empire made to the breakdown of international order, by the very fact of its existence. Germany's *Weltpolitik* or 'world policy', aiming at the acquisition of a colonial empire backed up by a world-class navy, as well as an economic and political influence in Europe and the wider world commensurate with its industrial and military power, was pursued vigorously from the late 1890s. It was both a function of the new German nationalism and helped powerfully to reinforce it. At the same time it expressed an understandable interest on the part of German governments and industry in achieving that 'world power status' enjoyed by powers such as Britain and France. But by the early twentieth century *Weltpolitik* was beginning to boomerang. It helped consolidate the Triple Entente of France, Russia and Britain around Germany and its ally Austria–Hungary, while encouraging expectations in German nationalists which could ill be met. More importantly, because more dangerous than mere diplomatic encirclement, was the increasing focus of German imperialism closer to home, in the Balkans and the Ottoman Empire. German investment in these regions, often even at the expense of its Habsburg ally, and Germany's involvement in training the Ottoman army, sounded alarm bells in London, Paris and especially in St Petersburg. Each of the Entente powers, in 1914, was reacting to a perceived threat to its vital strategic interests, posed not by the ostensible instigator of the July crisis, Austria–Hungary, but by imperial Germany.

16

THE FIRST WORLD WAR 1914-18

The importance of the First World War as a catalyst for change in Eastern
Europe can scarcely be overstated. Simply in terms of political geography the
war saw the near total break-up of the great multinational empires and their
succession by 'Eastern Europe' itself, a region of putative nation-states. Yet
although the war can be seen as a war of nationalities, it was first and foremost
a war of states. Nationalism on its own could never have accomplished such
a cataclysm, even if it exacerbated the effects. Only in its latter stages did the
conflict take on ideological overtones, not all of them nationalist.

ORIGINS

In its origins this defining conflict of the twentieth century had an obvious
East European locus, in the Austro-Serbian antagonism and the assassination
of the Habsburg heir, Francis Ferdinand, at Sarajevo on 28 June 1914. The
assassin was a Bosnian Serb and he and his six fellow conspirators, all
Habsburg subjects, were motivated by an animus against Habsburg rule and
a desire to see Bosnia united with Serbia. They had been recruited, trained
and armed by Colonel Dragutin Dimitrijević, the *de facto* head of 'Unification
or Death', otherwise known as the Black Hand, a nationalist secret society
founded in Belgrade in 1911, with Serbian government approval, to organise subversion and guerrilla activity in Ottoman territory during the Balkan
Wars. After the wars the Black Hand played a destabilising role in Serbia
itself, disputing government authority in the newly occupied south and
raising fears of a military coup, since Dimitrijević was not only head of
Serbian army intelligence but had been a participant in the bloody 1903
revolution. The Serbian government was not behind the Sarajevo plot,
although minister-president Nikola Pašić had received intimations of it and
had attempted to warn the Habsburg authorities, albeit obliquely and
ineffectively.

None of this mattered very much, since the Habsburg government was
already determined to do something forceful about Serbia before Sarajevo. It

made the assumption, for which it uncovered no proof, that the Serbian government was responsible and it used this as the ideal justification for action. Sarajevo was a pretext for war, rather than the cause of conflict between the Monarchy and Serbia, whose government for reasons of nationalist pride was admittedly unlikely to back down from such a confrontation. To act against Serbia, however, Vienna knew perfectly well that the backing of its ally Germany was essential, against the high likelihood of Russian intervention. And for reasons which had very little to do with Habsburg interests, this support was forthcoming: on being consulted early in July, the German government urged Vienna to go ahead.

Controversy has raged over this ever since, but the documentary evidence is compelling for the conclusion that, despite its Balkan occasion, the outbreak of war in 1914 had more to do with the conflicts generated by Germany's *Weltpolitik* and, in particular, Germany's increasing interests in the Near East and the Ottoman Empire. Germany's economic and political involvement in these areas rode across the economic and strategic interests of all three Entente powers. German investment in the Balkan states competed directly with French capital, and its long-term interests in infrastructure projects like the Berlin to Baghdad railway aroused British apprehensions about German ambitions in the oil-rich Persian Gulf. It was German pressure on Russian interests, however, which provided the greatest flash-point, and since Russia for all its weakness in the past was the real counterweight to Germany, this was of natural concern to Britain and France. In this sense the war was in essence a conflict between the two continental giants, Russia and Germany.

Russian governments were traditionally jealous of Habsburg influence in the Balkans, but by 1914 their fear of German hegemony in the region was even greater. Russia itself, despite its dependence on French capital, illustrated the power of German economic penetration, in that its imports from Germany went up by 150 per cent between 1905 and 1913.[1] More alarming by far were German trade with the Ottomans, German talk of a 'land bridge' to the Middle East, German missionary activity in Eastern Anatolia and, above all, Germany's military presence. The despatch to Constantinople, in the winter of 1913–14, of a Prussian general, Liman von Sanders, charged with training the Ottoman army, provoked near hysteria in St Petersburg, because it suggested a real possibility that Germany might physically control the Straits. For Russia this was simply a life-or-death issue and not just because of its strategic implications. Economically, since the 1890s the Straits had become Russia's windpipe to the outside world, the only practicable conduit through which it shipped 37 per cent of its exports, including three-quarters of the grain with which it paid for industrialisation. Russia's slow strangulation during the war, when the Straits were indeed closed to it, showed how justified such sensitivity was.[2]

Behind Austria–Hungary's aggression against Serbia, therefore, the Russian government saw the hand of Berlin, and it was not long before the French and British governments suspected it too. Concern in the Entente capitals was not allayed by the secrecy with which Vienna concocted its ultimatum to Serbia, which with Berlin's knowledge it drafted in such terms as to guarantee rejection, nor by the uncertainty as to what Austria–Hungary intended, once it had declared war on Serbia on 28 July. The German chancellor, Theobald von Bethmann Hollweg, was in any case intent on letting the crisis intensify, in the hope that the Entente would fall apart under the strain, thus giving Germany full freedom of movement in pursuing its *Weltpolitik*. When it turned out, however, that Russia would not back down, that its ally France saw its own vital interests in backing Russia, and that Britain's interest lay in preventing a French defeat by the premier military and naval power on the continent, the German government accepted war against all three, confident that it could win. It was a far cry from Sarajevo.

THE WAR OF STATES

By mid-August 1914 the original Austro-Serbian war had been engulfed by the larger conflict between the Entente powers and the 'Central Powers', Germany and Austria–Hungary. Italy, a member of the Triple Alliance, and Romania, an ally of the Habsburg Monarchy, stayed neutral on the legitimate ground that these defensive alliances did not justify entry; each in any case harboured designs on Habsburg territory. For the Entente the conclusion, on 2 August, of an alliance between Germany and the Ottoman Empire, and the latter's entry into the war in October, were a major blow, isolating Russia from its allies by closing the Straits. Yet the Ottoman government was motivated by a fear of Russia fully equal to Russia's fear of Germany.

The fighting in 1914 set the pattern for much of the next three years both in its savagery and its inconclusiveness. Compared with the massive clashes of the great powers with each other, the Balkans was a sideshow. Landlocked Serbia was cut off from any external help, unless Greece could be involved in the war. Nevertheless, the Serbian army managed to repel not just one but two Austro-Hungarian attacks before Christmas and even conducted a raid into Habsburg territory. The incompetence of the Habsburg supreme commander, General Franz Conrad von Hötzendorf, in allowing troops to be soaked up on the Serbian front meant that his forces paid a terrible price in Galicia. Russia, which to everyone's surprise put its forces in the field faster than was assumed possible, not only overran much of Galicia, inflicting about 1 million casualties on the Habsburg armies between September and December, but launched an invasion of East Prussia, where German strategy relied on simply holding the line while the main offensive was under way against France. The division of Russian forces, however, and mediocre Russian generalship, enabled the Germans to surround and annihilate them at Tannenberg in late August, with an overall Russian loss of 242,000 men.[3]

Notoriously, deadlock and trench warfare became the norm on the western front, but on the eastern front matters remained more fluid, though no less sanguinary. Germany and Austria–Hungary squandered further lives in a series of winter offensives against Russia, as a result of which the Austro-Hungarian army suffered catastrophically high losses, especially of officers. German forces, and German strategy, increasingly took the lead. It was largely to avert a total Habsburg collapse that the German commander, Erich von Falkenhayn, resolved on a major new offensive centred on Gorlice in May 1915, which against all expectations rolled the Russians back hundreds of miles, across the whole of Russian Poland and well into Belorussia and the Baltic provinces by September. This was in part offset by Italy's declaration of war against the Monarchy in May, although the subsequent Italian offensive was so inept that even the debilitated Austro-Hungarian army was able to contain it. Finally, the British and French attack on the Dardanelles in the spring, undertaken to gain access to their Russian ally, highlighted the Central Powers' inability to assist the Ottomans and spurred their invasion of Serbia. Facing overwhelming odds, including a vengeful Bulgaria, Serbia succumbed in the autumn of 1915, although the Serbian government and a remnant of its army survived a nightmare retreat across Albania to the coast and found refuge on Corfu. They were able to do so because Britain and France, in an attempt to bring the Serbs aid, had already violated Greek neutrality by landing troops at Salonica; this split Greece between the nationalist and interventionist prime minister Eleftherios Venizelos and the pro-German King Constantine, a division bridged only in July 1917 when the Allies expelled Constantine. In the meantime, however, the Gallipoli campaign failed and Russia remained cut off from the West, a circumstance which contributed to its breakdown.

Massive casualties were not the only factor weakening all combatants, but especially Austria–Hungary and Russia, by the end of 1915. Although the multiple nationalities of the two sides' armies showed remarkable loyalty and courage for years, there were also numerous signs of disaffection and lack of enthusiasm for the war, as well as a steady trickle of desertions from Habsburg forces. Equally damaging were the economic dislocation and privation caused by the war. Harvests had already been affected by the call-up in 1914. Large areas of Galicia, East Prussia and the Polish–Lithuanian–Ukrainian borderlands were physically devastated. Serbia was a wasteland, its population decimated by typhoid as well as war. Economic life generally was disrupted by the interruption of normal commerce and the gradual harnessing of industry to the 'war economy'. The Entente's blockade started causing serious food shortages for the Central Powers by 1916–17, but Russia, too, a former grain exporter, was facing comparable hardship due to the closure of the Straits. Food shortages brought malnutrition and increased vulnerability to disease. It was this slow death by blockade which drove the German government, in January 1917, to return to a policy of unrestricted submarine warfare, whereby even neutral ships trading with the Entente would be targeted. The momentous consequence was that in April the United

States entered the war against Germany, a development which in the long term sealed the Central Powers' fate.

In these circumstances, continuing the war was suicidal for the multi-national empires. Russia's General Brusilov undertook another successful offensive in the summer of 1916, which pushed the front westward again some 50 miles in places and completed the demoralisation of its main target, the Austro-Hungarian army. The latter by this stage had lost over half its men, either killed, wounded or taken prisoner, and henceforth Austro-Hungarian units were increasingly of use only when mingled with German ones, and in many cases under German command. Matters were only alleviated for the Central Powers, paradoxically, by the declaration of war on them, in August, by Romania, emboldened by Brusilov's successes to attempt its own conquest of Transylvania. A German-led offensive swiftly defeated the phenomenally ill-commanded Romanian army and occupied Bucharest by December.

If Austria–Hungary was struggling by the end of 1916, Russia too had shot its bolt. This was not a military failure so much as a collapse of the home front. The sheer incompetence of Nicholas II's government and its conduct of the war, coupled with the huge casualties and food shortages, prompted increasingly bitter denunciations in the *Duma*, and when Nicholas attempted to dissolve it in March 1917 its refusal to accept this was supported by mass strikes, the formation of revolutionary councils or soviets and, crucially, disaffected military and naval units in the capital, Petrograd.[4] This first Russian Revolution forced the tsar's abdication and installed a provisional government headed by a liberal aristocrat, Prince Georgii Lvov, and initially composed mainly of representatives of the liberal middle-class parties.

The provisional government, however, suffered from a fundamental contradiction: its liberal but patriotic leadership was determined to carry on the war by prosecuting it more efficiently, yet this very aim rapidly eroded what popular support it had. Russia's army disintegrated under the strain of a final summer offensive, which failed miserably, while the revolutionary socialist parties strengthened their grip on the soviets. In particular, the Bolsheviks under Vladimir Lenin were able to exploit the masses' desire for 'land, peace and bread'. The second, Bolshevik Revolution in November had the completely revolutionary aim of establishing a socialist system, but Lenin, on seizing power, while denouncing both sides in the war as 'imperialist' and issuing a call for world revolution, also immediately sought an armistice with the Central Powers.

Russia's collapse and withdrawal from the conflict raised in acute form the issue of war aims. The longer the war lasted, and the higher the 'butcher's bill', the greater the war aims governments came up with to justify these sacrifices. The Habsburg Monarchy never resolved what to do with occupied Serbia, but this was the least of its problems. Its leaders would have been glad of peace, had their German allies permitted it, but they still could neither contemplate the territorial cessions which might have bought peace nor accept any internal restructuring of the Monarchy to allay nationality discontents. The German government and political classes, by contrast, not to mention the military, had wide-ranging plans for territorial and economic conquests in both Western and Eastern Europe as well as overseas. In addition to establishing a *Mitteleuropa* or Central European customs union, dominated both politically and economically by Germany, the most extreme annexationist war aims, adopted by the government at the insistence of the high command in April 1917, envisaged carving a sort of economic hinterland out of western Russia. This would include the puppet 'Kingdom of Poland', which the Central Powers, finding themselves in possession of all the Polish lands, had already proclaimed in November 1916, but it also involved detaching a whole swathe of territories, from Finland to the Caucasus, for annexation or otherwise subordinate status.

In March 1918, at the Treaty of Brest–Litovsk with Bolshevik Russia, Germany succeeded in imposing its maximalist aims in the East. Its task was facilitated by the Bolsheviks, who briefly withdrew from negotiations in protest at the extent of Germany's claims and thus encouraged the Germans to advance even further into an already disintegrating Russia before discussion was resumed. By the Treaty, Finland and the Ukraine were recognised as 'independent' states, although German forces were firmly in occupation of both. Poland, Lithuania and Courland were detached from Russia, earmarked for eventual incorporation in the *Reich*; by a separate agreement in August, Livonia and Estland were also detached, clearly intended to be maintained as protectorates controlled through the ethnic German element. The grain- and mineral-rich Ukraine was the centrepiece in this constellation of satellite states, but German influence in Eastern Europe generally was massively strengthened by Brest–Litovsk.

Germany and its allies never reaped the expected harvest of Brest–Litovsk. Before the year was out the Central Powers were brought down by their increasing debility and the overwhelming manpower and resources now available to the western powers through American participation in the war. The revolutionary chaos and disintegration which overtook Eastern Europe in the autumn of 1918 had its origins partly in war-weariness, hunger and a political radicalism quickened by the Bolshevik Revolution. It was also, however, a function of the region's multinational composition.

THE WAR OF NATIONALITIES

As the war dragged on, nationalism became an ever greater factor. Although the majority of people had no choice but to obey the call-up, fight and die in the trenches, and endure the privations of the home front, a minority did urge exploitation of the conflict for nationalist purposes, in some cases from exile abroad. These lone voices struggled initially to make themselves heard, but they were pushing at an open door. There was an inherent risk for the multinational empires in going to war at all: given the strain involved, the likelihood of a territorial shake-up and the interest of nationalists in promoting change, fault-lines were bound to emerge.

With *Poles* fighting on both sides, nationalist leaders were confronted with a choice between working for the Central Powers' victory or Russia's, in the certainty that neither side would necessarily offer them anything more than domination by a single power rather than three. Piłsudski, though a Russian subject, had already opted for the Central Powers in 1908 when he migrated to Austrian Galicia, where he was allowed to organise a paramilitary force, the Riflemen's Union, for possible deployment in a war with Russia. The National Democrats under Dmowski put their faith in Russia, but their hopes of an autonomous Poland under tsarist rule were undermined by Russification. On the outbreak of war Piłsudski led his riflemen on a brief but hopeless foray into Russian territory, after which the Habsburg authorities firmly subordinated his force to regular army command. Meanwhile, the *Endecja* continued to argue that an autonomous Poland under Russia was the only realistic prospect, even though by August 1915 the whole of Poland was under Central Power control. Dmowski transferred his activities to the West in November, setting up a Polish National Committee to lobby the French, British and American governments for support.

One of the lonest voices, on behalf of the *Czechs*, was the academic and politician Tomáš Masaryk who, in 1914, finally convinced by the attack on Serbia that the Habsburg Monarchy was unreformable, fled to the West and started campaigning for an independent, Czecho-Slovak state, on the ground that Czechs and Slovaks were so closely related that they should combine. Masaryk was joined by a fellow Czech, Edvard Beneš, and the *émigré* Slovak astronomer Milan Štefánik, and was vocally assisted by eminent sympathisers in the West such as the Scottish historian R.W. Seton-Watson, H. Wickham Steed of *The Times* and others, as well as the sizeable Czech *émigré* community in the United States. The Entente powers, however, were not yet ready to commit themselves to a break-up of the Monarchy; in Austria–Hungary itself the political parties representing Czech and Slovak interests were hardly in a position to respond. On the eastern front Czech and Slovak troops were perpetually suspected of disaffection and tendencies to desert which, combined with the persecution of Czech and Slovak political leaders at home, soon became a self-fulfilling prophecy: sporadic disobedience and desertions began, especially after the Monarchy's catastrophic losses in 1915.

For the *South Slavs*, also, the war made the hitherto almost inconceivable conceivable. The first formal expression of Serbia's war aims was the Declaration of Niš in December 1914, which informed the Entente powers that Serbia's ultimate aim was 'the liberation of all our captive brethren Serbs, Croats and Slovenes'.[5] Whether this amounted to a genuine 'Yugoslavia' or

South Slav state, however, as opposed to a Serb-dominated Greater Serbia created by the annexation of Bosnia, Montenegro and part of the Adriatic coastline, remained to be seen. In the meantime, two Croat politicians, Frano Supilo and Ante Trumbić, decamped from the Habsburg Monarchy to the West in 1914 and formed a Yugoslav Committee, dedicated to the establishment of a Yugoslav state on federal lines, an appeal backed by western friends such as Seton-Watson, although not by western governments. Between the Serbian government and the Yugoslav Committee there seemed little common ground other than the dismemberment of the Habsburg Monarchy. Serbia's premier Pašić hoped to use the Committee to undermine the Monarchy, but intended a centralist, Serb-dominated state; the Yugoslav Committee saw federalism as the only feasible option. Both sides were driven together by circumstance. The Yugoslav Committee needed Serbia's support against Italy's claims, endorsed by the Entente in May 1915, to Habsburg territory inhabited by Croats and Slovenes. The Serbian government, once driven physically out of Serbia, needed whatever help it could get. The two parties came together at Corfu in July 1917 to affirm their common commitment to the formation of a Yugoslav state, but little else was agreed.

The reaction of warring governments to nationalist pressure varied. In the Habsburg Monarchy to begin with there was little sign of overt disloyalty among national minorities at home or at the front, but grievances were created by the government's internment of political leaders and the trial of some for treason. In the Austrian half of the Monarchy, at least, the military were given virtually dictatorial powers for the first two years of hostilities and made it plain they regarded the Slav and Romanian population as unreliable; in Bosnia, southern Hungary and Galicia the army behaved 'as an occupying power in enemy territory'.[6] Habsburg troops began to be targeted by propaganda leaflets on the Russian and especially the Italian front, promising the Monarchy's peoples 'the fulfilment of national desires', and although the immediate effect was minimal, the cumulative impact by 1918 cannot be ignored.[7] As the Monarchy's casualties mounted, cracks did begin to appear in front-line troops' morale, with units surrendering wholesale and in some instances deserting. When Francis Joseph died in November 1916, his successor Charles relaxed the censorship and reconvened the Austrian *Reichsrat*; the result was a swelling chorus of nationalist discontent, which really did begin to have an incremental effect on military morale. However, Charles could do nothing about the situation in Hungary, where the government refused even to consider concessions to the nationalities.

In the larger strategic context the Monarchy was fatally tied to its dominant German partner and here the Central Powers found themselves in competition with their enemies for the allegiance of certain nationalities. In November 1916 they announced the creation of a Polish constitutional monarchy, the precise extent of which remained unspecified. This was always intended to be a puppet state; indeed, the German high command's

8   Territorial changes 1918–23. Source: (p. 137) The Peace Settlement, *Independent Eastern Europe: A History* by C. A. Macartney and A. W. Palmer (Macmillan, 1962)

CONCLUSION

The end of the First World War is in many respects an inappropriate closing point for a history of Eastern Europe. Fighting continued or flared up anew in some parts of the region for several years after 1918, borders were still being disputed, and it was not until 1923 that the last of the peace treaties was signed. When the dust had settled, the multinational empires were no more, replaced by that belt of smaller states which now came to be known as Eastern Europe. Even then there was enough unfinished business to ensure that Eastern Europe remained a source of international instability throughout the interwar years.

In the Baltic states there were vicious civil conflicts raging for over a year between forces loyal to the new national governments, ethnic Germans, and Communists, both local and Russian. German troops remained in the area at the request of the victorious Allies, to prevent the new states falling to Bolshevik revolution, until late 1919. In the Ukraine the Hetmanate was replaced in November 1918 by a Ukrainian National Republic. This independent Ukraine, however, was not only a base for the 'White' reactionary forces ranged against Lenin's regime in the Russian civil war, it was also the scene of confused fighting between the Red Army and the Republic, which the latter finally lost in 1920. The Ukraine was reincorporated in what became the Soviet Union as the 'Ukrainian Soviet Republic'. Poland's western borders, including the 'Polish Corridor' to the Baltic, were decided by the Treaty of Versailles imposed by the Allies on Germany in June 1919, but its eastern frontiers were in a state of flux until 1921, following a war with Bolshevik Russia, which ended with Poland conquering most of the former territories of the old Polish Commonwealth, together with large numbers of Belorussians and Ukrainians. In 1920 Poland also seized the region around Wilno, a predominantly Polish and Jewish city, despite Lithuania's 'historic' claim to it. Hungary lost substantial territories to Czechoslovakia, Romania and Yugoslavia, but in the process succumbed to a brief Bolshevik dictatorship in 1919, which was then extinguished by a Romanian invasion and a 'White' reaction; a peace treaty with Hungary was possible only in 1920.

The Kingdom of Serbs, Croats and Slovenes (only formally named Yugoslavia in 1929) was eventually compelled to accept borders with Italy in 1920, which left substantial numbers of Slovenes and Croats under Italian rule, although Yugoslavia itself was a decidedly multinational state, not all of whose subjects were Slavs and even more of whom were unhappy with their lot. Albania was lucky to escape partition between Yugoslavia, Italy and Greece by 1920; as it was, large numbers of Albanians still lived in Yugoslavia and Greece. Bulgaria lost territory to Yugoslavia and Greece, including its access to the Aegean. Finally, the partition of the Ottoman Empire produced a Turkish nationalist backlash and resistance to the peace terms imposed in 1920 coalesced around a Young Turk army officer, Mustafa Kemal. Greece, awarded the right by the Allies in 1919 to occupy the Anatolian, but largely Greek, port of Smyrna and a large portion of its hinterland, overreached itself in 1921 by launching an even more ambitious invasion of the Turkish heartland. This attempt to realise the *Megali Idea* backfired when the Turks literally drove the Greeks into the sea in 1922. The result was not only a revised peace treaty in 1923 but the first negotiated population transfer in modern history, whereby 1.1 million Greeks and 380,000 Muslims were expelled from their ancestral homelands and deported to a 'nation' they had never seen.[1]

Over this chaos the great powers of the war's winning side presided, at the Paris peace conference of 1919–20 and through innumerable interventions and attempted deals both before and after.[2] It is important to dispel the notion that the great powers simply ordained the peace settlement in Eastern Europe. Although they had considerable leverage and could in some cases force a solution, their reach was limited by their resources, the war-weariness of their own electorates and not least the actions of East European governments and peoples. The great powers' exhortations were in any case diluted by their self-interest. Awards of territory were made to serve broader strategic desiderata, principally the limitation of German power and the insulation of Europe against the plague bacillus of Communism. To these ends the principle of national self-determination was implemented only partially, and in some case not at all, in Eastern Europe. Territory containing substantial minorities was either seized by states or awarded to them for strategic reasons. The result was a region of supposed nation-states which were in fact anything but that. Economically and militarily weak, politically faction ridden and liable to slide into authoritarianism, the states of Eastern Europe were scarcely in a position to serve as a *cordon sanitaire*, hemming in Germany from the East while also guarding the continent against Communism. In reality the region was a vast power vacuum, which the true regional superpowers, Germany and Russia, would strive to fill as soon as they recovered from defeat and revolution.

How, then, to summarise the developments that had made Eastern Europe such a distinct region in this formative period from the early eighteenth century to the end of the First World War? In particular, what can be said about the underlying themes of modernisation, nationalism and supra-nationalism? Despite considerable advances in several parts of Eastern Europe, it is clear that economically the region had not caught up with Western Europe; indeed, the gap might even be said to have been widened by the outcome of the war. Apart from the physical damage inflicted on some areas, the division of the region into yet more sovereign states, each with its own customs barriers, currency, legal and institutional systems, and each desperate to protect what industry it had, constituted a serious retardation of economic development. The inefficiency of agriculture was not lessened by the rise, under constitutions which to begin with almost everywhere relied on universal suffrage, of mass-based peasant parties; these were able to put land redistribution on the political agenda in several states, which created a larger class of smallholders, not noted for high productivity. Only in the Soviet Union did forced collectivisation in the 1930s produce an agricultural revolution, but at hideous human cost and with as yet unsuspected inefficiencies of its own; the export of this self-defeating model to Communist Eastern Europe after 1945 is arguably one of the reasons it has remained economically backward down to the present.

Politically, too, Eastern Europe might be said to have remained backward after 1918. Democratic constitutions and universal suffrage were introduced to most of the region, but did not seem to take easy root. Before the 1920s were out several states had succumbed to dictatorship or authoritarianism and political instability and violence were endemic. We should, however, beware of seeing this as a peculiarly East European problem, since Western Europe in the interwar period had its fair share of violence and political extremism. Nevertheless it may be that there was something in the political culture of the pre-1918 period, or in some cases, as in tsarist Russia, the absence of political culture, which helps explain this political immaturity.

The end of our period saw the seeming triumph of nationalism, with the formation of so many 'national' states. Yet this triumph was only partial and indeed deeply flawed. Fresh injustices were perpetrated in creating these states, but the mere fact of state creation was enough to ensure the continued strength of nationalism's appeal. Now there were new grievances on which nationalism could feed. Macedonians were stranded in Yugoslavia, Hungarians in the three successor states around Hungary; above all, Austrian Germans were permanently excluded from union with Germany and Germans were a vocal minority in the Baltic states, in Poland, in Czechoslovakia and elsewhere.

Finally, the concept of supranational states seemed discredited and discarded. The old empires were gone, and although the Soviet Union was still a multinational state it was not only appealing to a different, and supposedly higher ideology, socialism, for its *raison d'être*; the 'Union of Soviet Socialist Republics', to give it its full name, was deliberately given a federal appearance, if not reality, in order to defuse the nationalism of its constituent peoples. Curiously, however, the new Eastern Europe contained two states, Czechoslovakia and Yugoslavia, purporting to represent a composite, 'state' nationalism. Each officially promoted the fiction, unsupported by ethnography or philology, that there was such a thing as a 'Czechoslovak' or a 'Yugoslav' national identity. Neither was a convincing advertisement for such a thesis. In Eastern Europe as a whole, in the interwar period, there was little sign of any sustained ability to cooperate internationally, let alone return to some larger political unit.

At the end of the Second World War Eastern Europe had the Soviet supranational model, Communism, imposed on it. This had the effect, obvious as early as the 1950s but even clearer after the fall of Communism in 1989, of making nationalism stronger. Not only did nationalism, especially among the peoples of the Soviet Union itself, appear to be the one disintegrative factor the Soviet leadership had not reckoned with, it has so far demonstrated its continuing importance to East Europeans. Yet the eagerness of the post-Communist states to join the European Union, whatever their disappointment since doing so, may be some indication that a different form of supranationalism is now acceptable.

NOTES

Introduction

1   Palmer, A., 1970, *The Lands Between: A History of East Central Europe since the Congress of Vienna*, London.

2. Wolff, L., 1994, *Inventing Eastern Europe: The Map of Civilization on the Mind of the Enlightenment*, Stanford, 4–6.

3. Arguably the first real attempt at modernisation by an East European ruler was that of Peter the Great of Russia in the early eighteenth century. For the purposes of this study, however, Russia as a whole has been excluded, although many of its subject peoples have not. In any case Petrine Russia had not yet expanded to include the territories of Eastern Europe as defined above, with the exception of the Baltic littoral and parts of present-day Ukraine.

4. For a general introduction see Alter, P., 1994, *Nationalism*, 2nd edn, London.

5. Anderson, B., 1991, *Imagined Communities: Reflections on the Origin and Spread of Nationalism*, revised edn, London, 47 ff. One might also cite, as an even earlier example of an artificially created sense of state loyalty, the United Kingdom (1707) and the idea of being British, as opposed to English, Scottish, etc.

6. Nisbet, H.B., 1999, 'Herder's Conception of Nationhood and its Influence in Eastern Europe', in R. Bartlett and K. Schönwälder (eds), *The German Lands and Eastern Europe: Essays on the History of the Social, Cultural and Political Relations*, Basingstoke, 116–17.

7. Alter, *op. cit.*, 7. The phrase 'conscious cherishing' is from Hayes, C.J.H., 1960, *Nationalism: A Religion*, New York, 15.

8. A seminal study of the 'stages' by which national consciousness emerges is Hroch, M., 2000 [1985], *Social Preconditions of National Revival in Europe: A Comparative Analysis of the Social Composition of Patriotic Groups among the Smaller Nations*, B. Fowkes (trans.), New York; see especially 22–4.

9. Nicholas I of Russia, quoted in Miller, W., 1966 [1927], *The Ottoman Empire and its Successors 1801–1927*, 3rd edn, London, 203–4.

10. Quoted (without attribution) in Taylor, A.J.P., 1964 [1948], *The Habsburg Monarchy 1809–1918: A History of the Austrian Empire and Austria–Hungary*, Harmondsworth, 25.

11. It is worth noting here, however, that 1804 is the starting point for Part Two not because it saw the start of the Napoleonic Empire but because it was the point at which the Empire of Austria was proclaimed and the year in which the Serbian revolt against the Ottoman Empire began.

Chapter 1

1. Coleman, D.C., 1977, *The Economy of England 1450–1750*, Oxford, 97; Cobban, A., 1963, *A History of Modern France*, vol. I: *Old Régime and Revolution 1715–1799*, Harmondsworth, 48.

2. Coleman, *op. cit.*

3. Ingrao, C., 1994, *The Habsburg Monarchy 1618–1815*, Cambridge, 101.

4. Okey, R., 1986, *Eastern Europe 1740–1985: Feudalism to Communism*, 2nd edn, London and New York, 32.

5. McCarthy, J., 1997, *The Ottoman Turks: An Introductory History to 1923*, London and New York, 257.

6. Okey, *op. cit*; Bideleux, R. and Jeffries, I., 1998, *A History of Eastern Europe: Crisis and Change*, London, 153; Király, B.K., 1969, *Hungary in the Late Eighteenth Century: The Decline of Enlightened Despotism*, New York, 49.

7. Chirot, D., 1989, 'Causes and Consequences of Backwardness', in D. Chirot (ed.), *The Origins of Backwardness in Eastern Europe: Economics and Politics from the Middle Ages until the Early Twentieth Century*, Berkeley, 4.

8. *Ibid.*

9. Okey, *op. cit.*, 26; Király, *op. cit.*, 37, giving figures for the 1780s.

10. Evans, R.J.W., 1979, *The Making of the Habsburg Monarchy 1550–1700: An Interpretation*, Oxford, 81.

Chapter 2

1. Jelavich, B., 1991, *History of the Balkans*, vol. I: *Eighteenth and Nineteenth Centuries*, Cambridge, 68–70, and text of Article VII of the Treaty, quoted, 69; see also Anderson, M.S., 1966, *The Eastern Question 1774–1923: A Study in International Relations*, London and Basingstoke, xi–xiv.

2. Scott, H.M., 1990, 'Introduction: The Problem of Enlightened Absolutism', in H.M. Scott (ed.), *Enlightened Absolutism: Reform and Reformers in Later Eighteenth-Century Europe*, Ann Arbor, 19; Ingrao, C., 'The Smaller German States', *ibid.*, 226, 231.

3. From Frederick's own 'Essay on the Forms of Government and the Duties of Sovereigns' (1777), quoted in Blanning, T.C.W., 'Frederick the Great and Enlightened Absolutism', in Scott (ed.), *Enlightened Absolutism*, 278.

4. Extract from *Ideas for a Philosophy of the History of Mankind* (1784–91), in D. Williams (ed.), 1999, *The Enlightenment*, Cambridge, 210.

5. Properly speaking, France was still a monarchy when it declared war on Austria and Prussia in April 1792. The French Republic was declared in September 1792.

Chapter 3

1. Blanning, T.C.W., 1994, *Joseph II*, London and New York, 205: 'The Habsburg Monarchy was not a state, it never became a state and it never could have become a state.'

2. Macartney, C.A., 1969, *The Habsburg Empire 1790–1918*, London, 3–11.

3. Ingrao, C., 1992, *The Habsburg Monarchy 1618–1815*, Cambridge, 165.

4. *Ibid.*, 164, 174.

5. *Ibid.*, 186.

6. Davies, N., 1981, *God's Playground: A History of Poland*, vol. I: *The Origins to 1795*, Oxford, 521.

7. Okey, R., 2001, *The Habsburg Monarchy c. 1765–1918: From Enlightenment to Eclipse*, Basingstoke and London, 18.

8. Padover, S.K., 1967, *The Revolutionary Emperor: Joseph II of Austria*, London.

9. Ingrao, *op. cit.*, 197.

10. Blanning, T.C.W., 1970, *Joseph II and Enlightened Despotism*, London, 73.

11. Quoted, Blanning, 1994, *Joseph II, op. cit.*, 58.

12. *Ibid.*
13. *Ibid.*, 60, 58.
14. Blanning, *Joseph II and Enlightened Despotism, op. cit.*, 70.
15. The initial Patent was issued only for the Bohemian lands, in 1781, and was extended to the Austrian lands and Galicia in 1782; Ingrao, *op. cit.*, 201.
16. Text in Macartney, C.A. (ed.), 1970, *The Habsburg and Hohenzollern Dynasties in the Seventeenth and Eighteenth Centuries*, London, 180–4.
17. Quoted, Blanning, *op. cit.*, 71.
18. Quoted, Macartney, *Habsburg Empire, op. cit.*, 139.
19. Since 1437 these three 'nations' had been considered the constituent peoples of Hungary, a division reaffirmed in Transylvania in 1542; Macartney, C.A., 1962, *Hungary: A Short History*, Edinburgh, 50, 78. The Szeklers (*székelyek*) were a nomadic people possibly related to the Magyars, and granted privileged status after the Magyar conquest of present-day Hungary; *ibid.*, 5, 10.
20. Quoted, Blanning, 1994, *Joseph II, op. cit.*, 203.
21. Ingrao, *op. cit.*, 220.
22. Cushing, G.F., 1960, 'The Birth of National Literature in Hungary', *Slavonic & East European Review*, XXXVIII, no. 91, June, 463.
23. Okey, R., 1986, *Eastern Europe 1740–1985: Feudalism to Communism*, 2nd edn, London and New York, 78.

Chapter 4

1. In Polish, '*Rzeczpospolita Oboga Narodów, Polskiego i Litewskiego*'; see Lukowksi, J., 1991, *Liberty's Folly: The Polish–Lithuanian Commonwealth in the Eighteenth Century 1697–1795*, London and New York, 3. *Rzeczpospolita* is ultimately derived from the Latin *res publica* and has been variously translated into English ever since 1569 as both 'commonwealth' and 'republic'. I have opted for 'commonwealth', on the ground that the Polish *pospolita* suggests 'public' in the sense of community and *rzeczpospolita* 'common weal'. (I am indebted to Prof. Michael Bernhard for advice on this.)
2. *Ibid*; cf. Lukowksi, J., 1999, *The Partitions of Poland, 1772, 1793, 1795*, London and New York, 2.
3. Lukowski, *Liberty's Folly, op. cit.*, 3–4.
4. *Ibid.*, 9; *idem, Partitions*, 2.
5. Rousseau, J.-J., 1771, *Considérations sur le gouvernement de la Pologne*, quoted in R.R. Palmer, 1959 *The Age of the Democratic Revolution: A Political History of Europe and America 1760–1800*, vol. I: *The Challenge*, Princeton, 411–12.
6. Lukowski, *op. cit.*, 8.
7. Zamoyski, A., 1987, *The Polish Way: A Thousand-Year History of the Poles and their Culture*, London, 199.
8. Zamoyski, A., 1992, *The Last King of Poland*, London, 8.
9. Rostworowski, E., 1982, 'War and Society in the Noble Republic of Poland–Lithuania in the Eighteenth Century', in G.E. Rothenberg *et al.* (eds), *East Central European Society and War in the Pre-Revolutionary Eighteenth Century*, New York, 165.
10. Zamoyski, *op. cit.*, 222.
11. Grochulska, B., 1982, 'The Place of the Enlightenment in Polish Social History', in J.K. Fedorowicz *et al.* (eds), *A Republic of Nobles: Studies in Polish History to 1864*, Cambridge, 245, 249–50.
12. Zamoyski, *The Polish Way, op. cit.*, p. 223; *idem, Last King of Poland, op. cit.*, 10.
13. Frederick II to the Prussian ambassador, 28 June 1744; quoted, *ibid.*, 25.

14. Quoted, Lukowski, J. and Zawadzki, H., 2001, *A Concise History of Poland*, Cambridge, 91–2.
15. From Frederick's mocking poem 'La Guerre des Confédérés', quoted in Hagen, W.W., 1980, *Germans, Poles, and Jews: The Nationality Conflict in the Prussian East 1772–1914*, Chicago and London, 36; see also the critique of the 'just deserts' school in Halecki, O., 1963, 'Why was Poland Partitioned?', *Slavic Review*, XXII, no. 3, Sept., 441.
16. Konczacki, J.M., 1986, 'Stanislaw August Poniatowski's "Thursday Dinners" and Cultural Change in Late Eighteenth Century Poland', *Canadian Journal of History*, XXI, Apr., 27, 33.
17. Zamoyski, *op. cit.*, 215.
18. Lukowski, *op. cit.*, 113.
19. Zamoyski, *Polish Way*, *op. cit.*, 247.
20. Lukowksi and Zawadzki, *op. cit.*, 102.
21. Quoted in Hagen, *op. cit.*, 50.
22. As Catherine put it in 1792, 'I shall fight Jacobinism, and beat it in Poland'; quoted in Palmer, *op. cit.*, 434.
23. Quoted in Lukowski, *op. cit.*, 182.

Chapter 5

1. 'Konstantiniyye' (Constantinople or the city of Constantine) was the name used by the Ottomans themselves, in official documents, for today's Istanbul; Quataert, D., 2000, *The Ottoman Empire 1700–1922*, Cambridge, 4.
2. Vucinich, W.S., 1962, 'The Nature of Balkan Society under Ottoman Rule', *Slavic Review*, XXI, no. 4, Dec., 597.
3. Sugar, P.F., 1977, *Southeastern Europe under Ottoman Rule 1354–1804*, Seattle and London, 3–8; Jelavich, B., 1983, *History of the Balkans*, vol. I: *Eighteenth and Nineteenth Centuries*, Cambridge, 39–40; McCarthy, J., 1997, *The Ottoman Turks: An Introductory History to 1923*, London and New York, 103–10.
4. *Ibid.*, 106.
5. Quataert, *op. cit.*, 5.
6. *Ibid.*, 2.
7. Stoianovich, T., 1960, 'The Conquering Balkan Orthodox Merchant', *Journal of Economic History*, XX, June, 234–5, 259–63, 267–9.
8. Clogg, R., 1992, *A Concise History of Greece*, Cambridge, 27.
9. Jelavich, *op. cit.*, 100.
10. Malcolm, N., 1994, *Bosnia: A Short History*, London and Basingstoke, 52–3, 94–6.
11. *Ibid.*, 72. Even more of these Orthodox colonists were *Vlachs*, a pastoral people speaking a Romance language akin to Romanian and who were scattered across large tracts of the Balkan highlands; *ibid.*, 73–6.
12. Sugar, *op. cit.*, 241.
13. Quataert, *op. cit.*, 45, 46; for a more balanced view, Sugar, *op. cit.*, 241–2.
14. Shaw, S.J., 1971, *Between the Old and the New: The Ottoman Empire under Selim III 1789–1807*, Cambridge, MA, 71–210; see also Jelavich, *op. cit.*, 117–18.

Chapter 6

1. Kappeler, A., 2001, *The Russian Empire: A Multiethnic History*, Harlow, 115–16.
2. Hosking, G., 1998, *Russia: People and Empire 1552–1917*, London, 8.
3. Raeff, M., 1966, *Origins of the Russian Intelligentsia: The Eighteenth-Century Nobility*, New York, 17–18.

4. Hosking, *op. cit.*, 115; Raeff, M., 1970, 'Pugachev's Rebellion', in R. Forster and J.P. Greene (eds), *Preconditions of Revolution in Early Modern Europe*, Baltimore and London, 172, 189–90.

5. Tolz, V., 1997, *Russia*, London, 51; Slezkine, Y., 1997, 'Naturalists versus Nations: Eighteenth-Century Russian Scholars Confront Ethnic Diversity', in D.R. Brower and E.J. Lazzerini (eds), *Russia's Orient: Imperial Borderlands and Peoples 1700–1917*, Bloomington and Indianapolis, 48–9.

6. Georgi, J.G., *Description of All the Peoples Inhabiting the Russian State* (1776–80); quoted in Slezkine, *op. cit.*, 39. For the distinction between *russkii* (ethnic Russian) and *rossiiskii* (inhabitant of the Empire), see Hosking, *op. cit.*, xix.

7. *Ibid.*, 161.

8. Thaden, E.C., 1984, *Russia's Western Borderlands 1710–1870*, Princeton, 2.

9. Kappeler, *op. cit.*, 76; Hosking, *op. cit.*, 33.

10. *Ibid.*, 81–2.

11. Kappeler, *op. cit.*, 82–3; Wandycz, P.S., 1974, *The Lands of Partitioned Poland 1795–1918*, Seattle and London, 18.

12. Kappeler, *op. cit.*, 83–4.

13. These were terms used by the Prussian authorities. West Prussia comprised what the Poles had called Royal Prussia and the Noteć district; South Prussia was most of Great Poland (Wielkopolska); and New East Prussia was formed largely of Mazovia, including Warsaw. See the maps in Hagen, W.W., 1980, *Germans, Poles and Jews: The Nationality Conflict in the Prussian East 1772–1914*, Chicago and London, 8, 53; and Friedrich, K., 1997, 'Facing Both Ways: New Works on Prussia and Polish–Prussian Relations', *German History*, XV, no. 2, 258–9, and note 6.

14. Scott, H.M., 2000, '1763–1786: The Second Reign of Frederick the Great', in P.G. Dwyer (ed.), *The Rise of Prussia 1700–1830*, Harlow, 178.

15. Gothelf, R., 'Frederick William I and the Beginnings of Prussian Absolutism 1713–1740', *ibid.*, 56–8, 59–63.

16. Friedrich, K., 'The Development of the Prussian Town 1720–1815', *ibid.*, 147; Hagen, *op. cit.*, 17.

17. Quoted, *ibid.*, 36; Friedrich, *op. cit.*, 145.

18. Quoted, Hagen, *op. cit.*, 40, 41.

19. *Ibid.*, 45–7.

20. *Ibid.*, 52.

21. Quoted, *ibid.*, 55. The official was referring to Britain's recently founded penal colony in Australia.

Chapter 7

1. Miller, W., 1966 [1927], *The Ottoman Empire and its Successors 1801–1927*, 3rd edn, London, 40.

2. For a still authoritative guide to internation events, see Bridge, R. and Bullen, R., 2004, *The Great Powers and the European State System 1815–1914*, 2nd edn, London.

3. Carr, W., 1991, *A History of Germany 1815–1990*, 4th edn, London, 38.

Chapter 8

1. Milne, A., 1975, *Metternich*, London, 28.

2. Quoted in Okey, R., 1986, *Eastern Europe 1740–1985: Feudalism to Communism*, 2nd edn, London, 60.

3. Lukowski, J. and Zawadzki, H., 2001, *A Concise History of Poland*, Cambridge, 130–1, 135–7; Campbell, J.C., 1944, 'The Influence of Western Political Thought in the

Rumanian Principalities 1821–1848', *Journal of Central European Affairs*, IV, no. 3, Oct., 267–8.

4. Petrovich, M.B., 1976, *A History of Modern Serbia 1804–1918*, vol. I, New York and London, 285–6.

5. Hroch, M., 2000 [1985], *Social Preconditions of National Revival in Europe: A Comparative Analysis of the Social Composition of Patriotic Groups among the Smaller Nations*, Ben Fowkes (trans.), New York, 22–4.

6. Stokes, G., 1975, *Legitimacy through Liberalism: Vladimir Jovanović and the Transformation of Serbian Politics*, Seattle and London, 61–3, quoting a pamphlet written by the Serbian liberal Vladimir Jovanović in 1862.

7. Quoted, Macartney, C.A., 1969, *The Habsburg Empire 1790–1918*, London, 258–9.

8. Bideleux, R. and Jeffries, I., 1998, *A History of Eastern Europe: Crisis and Change*, London, 290.

9. Széchenyi Diary, 10 Aug. 1825, quoted in Barany, G., 1968, *Stephen Széchenyi and the Awakening of Hungarian Nationalism 1791–1841*, Princeton, 112.

10. Komlos, J., 1983, *The Habsburg Monarchy as a Customs Union: Economic Development in Austria–Hungary in the Nineteenth Century*, Princeton, 48–51, 90–111; Good, D., 1984, *The Economic Rise of the Habsburg Empire 1750–1914*, Berkeley and Los Angeles, 92–3.

11. Melton, E., 2000, 'The Transformation of the Rural Economy in East Elbian Prussia 1750–1830', in P.G. Dwyer (ed.), *The Rise of Prussia 1700–1830*, Harlow, 124, 113–16, 123–5.

12. Palairet, M., 1997, *The Balkan Economies c. 1800–1914: Evolution without Development*, Cambridge, 22.

13. *Ibid.*, 50.

14. Falkus, M.E., 1972, *The Industrialisation of Russia 1700–1914*, Basingstoke, 32.

15. Seton-Watson, H., 1967, *The Russian Empire 1801–1917*, Oxford, 247.

16. *Ibid.*

17. Falkus, *op. cit.*, 33–6.

18. Quoted, Hosking, G., 1998, *Russia: People and Empire 1552–1917*, London, 317–18. Chicherin was writing in 1856.

19. *Ibid.*, 321.

20. Falkus, *op. cit.*, 43 ff; Hosking, *op. cit.*, 320–2.

Chapter 9

1. As the last Holy Roman Emperor, Francis reigned as Francis II from 1792 to 1806. From 1804 he assumed the title of Francis I, Emperor of Austria.

2. Quoted, Macartney, C.A., 1969, *The Habsburg Empire 1790–1918*, London, 234.

3. Sked, A., 1989, *The Decline and Fall of the Habsburg Empire 1815–1918*, Harlow, 44–52.

4. Bridge, F.R., 1990, *The Habsburg Monarchy among the Great Powers 1815–1918*, Oxford, 27.

5. Count Joseph Thun, quoted in LeCaine Agnew, H., 2003, 'Czechs, Germans, Bohemians? Images of Self and Other in Bohemia to 1848', in N.M. Wingfield (ed.), *Creating the Other: Ethnic Conflict and Nationalism in Habsburg Central Europe*, New York and Oxford, 57.

6. Sayer, D., 1998, *The Coasts of Bohemia: A Czech History*, Princeton, 57–62.

7. Literally 'Czech Queen Bee', a term suggesting maternity as well as collective belonging. There was a proliferation of such organisations among the Slavonic peoples in the early nineteenth century; see Kimball, S.B., 1970, 'The Matica Česká, 1831–1861:

The First Thirty Years of a Literary Foundation', in P. Brock and H. G. Skilling (eds), *The Czech Renascence of the Nineteenth Century: Essays Presented to Otakar Odložilik in Honour of his Seventieth Birthday*, Toronto and Buffalo, 53, note 1, and 58, note 10.

8. Wandycz, P.S., 1974, *The Lands of Partitioned Poland 1795–1918*, Seattle and London, 71.

9. Quoted, Rudnytsky, I.L., 1967, 'The Ukrainians in Galicia under Austrian Rule', *Austrian History Yearbook*, III, Pt 2, 397.

10. Janos, A.C., 1982, *The Politics of Backwardness in Hungary 1825–1945*, Princeton, 60–7.

11. Quoted, Deak, I., 1979, *The Lawful Revolution: Louis Kossuth and the Hungarians 1848–1849*, New York, 45.

12. Quoted, Evans, R., 2003, 'Kossuth and Štúr: Two National Heroes', in L. Péter, M. Rady and P. Sherwood (eds), *Lajos Kossuth Sent Word ... Papers Delivered on the Occasion of the Bicentenary of Kossuth's Birth*, London, 123; original Hungarian cited in note 6. *Tót* is the common, derogatory word in Hungarian for 'Slovak'; the modern *szlovák* is a more recent development.

13. Deak, *op. cit.*, 56.

14. Quoted, *ibid.*, 97.

15. Quoted, Evans, R.J.W., 2000, '1848–49 in the Habsburg Monarchy', in R.J.W. Evans and H. Pogge von Strandmann (eds), *The Revolutions in Europe 1848–1849: From Reform to Reaction*, Oxford, 189.

16. Evans, *op. cit.*

17. Quoted, *ibid.*

18. Quoted, Sked, *op. cit.*, 143.

19. Okey, R., 2000, *The Habsburg Monarchy 1765–1918: From Enlightenment to Eclipse*, London and Basingstoke, 172.

20. Barany, G., 1967, 'Hungary: The Uncompromising Compromise', *Austrian History Yearbook*, III, Pt 1, 234–59.

21. Deak, *op. cit.*, 348; Macartney, *op. cit.*, 567–8.

22. Sked, *op. cit.*, 190.

Chapter 10

1. Mazower, M., 2000, *The Balkans*, London, 11–12, and note 19.

2. Jelavich, B., 1983, *History of the Balkans*, vol. I: *Eighteenth and Nineteenth Centuries*, Cambridge, 217.

3. *Ibid.*, 229; Clogg, R., 1986, *A Short History of Modern Greece*, Cambridge, 43–5.

4. Psomiades, H.P., 1976, 'The Character of the New Greek State', in N.P. Diamandouros et al. (eds), *Hellenism and the First Greek War of Liberation (1821–1830): Continuity and Change*, Thessaloniki, 154.

5. McCarthy, J., 1996, *The Ottoman Turks: An Introductory History to 1923*, Harlow, 291.

6. Quoted, *ibid.*, 296–7.

Chapter 11

1. Quoted, Hosking, G., 1988, *Russia: People and Empire 1552–1917*, London, 178; emphasis in original.

2. The term 'official nationality' was coined in the 1870s by the Russian historian Alexander Pypin; Saunders, D., 1992, *Russia in the Age of Reaction and Reform 1801–1881*, London and New York, 117.

3. Quoted, *ibid.*, 117–18.
4. *Ibid.*, 135–9; more recently, Moon, D., 1992, *Russian Peasants and Tsarist Legislation on the Eve of Reform: Interaction between Peasants and Officialdom 1825–1855*, London and Basingstoke.
5. Hosking, *op. cit.*, 322, 322–6.
6. Article I of the Treaty, in Hurst, M. (ed.), 1972, *Key Treaties for the Great Powers 1814–1914*, vol. I: *1814–1870*, Newton Abbot, 45.
7. Hartley, J.M., 1996, 'The "Constitutions" of Finland and Poland in the Reign of Alexander I: Blueprints for Reform in Russia?', in M. Branch, J.M. Hartley and A. Mączak (eds), *Finland and Poland in the Russian Empire: A Comparative Study*, London, 41–4.
8. Lukowski, J. and Zawadzki, H., 2001, *A Concise History of Poland*, Cambridge, 135.
9. Quoted in Magocsi, P.R., 1996, *A History of Ukraine*, Toronto, 364.
10. Text quoted, *ibid.*, 369–70.
11. Quoted, Hosking, *op. cit.*, 160.
12. *Ibid.*, 33.
13. Quoted, Hagen, W.W., 1980, *Germans, Poles and Jews: The Nationality Conflict in the Prussian East 1772–1914*, Chicago and London, 68.
14. Quoted, *ibid.*, 79.
15. Quoted, *ibid.*, 88.
16. Quoted, *ibid.*, 121.
17. Quoted, *ibid.*, 123–4.
18. Quoted, *ibid.*, 144.

Chapter 12

1. Okey, R., 1986, *Eastern Europe 1740–1985: Feudalism to Communism*, 2nd edn, London and New York, 118–19.
2. Longworth, P., 1997, *The Making of Eastern Europe: From Prehistory to Post-communism*, 2nd edn, Basingstoke, 142.
3. Mitchell, B.R., 1973, 'Statistical Appendix 1700–1914', in C.M. Cipolla (ed.), *The Fontana Economic History of Europe*, vol. IV: *The Emergence of Industrial Societies*, Pt 2, London, table 2, 750.

Chapter 13

1. Text in Macartney, C.A., 1969, *The Habsburg Empire 1790–1918*, London, 560.
2. Quoted, Jászi, O., 1929, *The Dissolution of the Habsburg Monarchy*, Chicago and London, 329.
3. Komlos, J., 1983, *The Habsburg Monarchy as a Customs Union: Economic Development in Austria–Hungary in the Nineteenth Century*, Princeton, 112–14, 126–32, 206–13.
4. Memorandum by Baron Matscheko, undated, but before 24 June 1914; quoted in Bridge, F.R., 1972, *From Sadowa to Sarajevo: The Foreign Policy of Austria–Hungary 1866–1914*, London, 369; full text as document 37, *ibid.*, 443–8.

Chapter 14

1. McCarthy, J., 2001, *The Ottoman Peoples and the End of Empire*, London, 3.
2. *Ibid.*
3. Jelavich, B., 1983, *History of the Balkans*, vol. I: *Eighteenth and Nineteenth Centuries*, Cambridge, 285.
4. *Ibid.*, 286; McCarthy, J., 1996, *The Ottoman Turks: An Introductory History to 1923*, Harlow, 330–7.

5. *Ibid.*, 340–1.
6. Quoted, Poulton, H., 1997, *Top Hat, Grey Wolf and Crescent: Turkish Nationalism and the Turkish Republic*, London, 72.
7. Lewis, B., 1968, *The Emergence of Modern Turkey*, 2nd edn, London, Oxford and New York, 214.
8. Poulton, *op. cit.*, 80.
9. Clogg, R., 1992, *A Concise History of Modern Greece*, Cambridge, 68.
10. Stokes, G., 1990, *Politics as Development: The Emergence of Political Parties in Nineteenth-Century Serbia*, Durham, NC and London, 1–2, 9–13.
11. Hitchins, K., 1994, *Rumania 1866–1947*, Oxford, 171–2.
12. Pavlowitch, S.K., 1999, *A History of the Balkans 1804–1945*, London and New York, 193.
13. *Ibid.*, 133, 194.
14. Carnegie Endowment for International Peace, 1914, *Report of the International Commission to Inquire into the Causes and Conduct of the Balkan Wars* (Washington, DC), republished as Kennan, G. F., 1993, *The Other Balkan Wars: A 1913 Carnegie Endowment Inquiry in Retrospect with a New Introduction and Reflections on the Present Conflict* [i.e. in former Yugoslavia], Washington, DC; Todorova, M., 1997, *Imagining the Balkans*, New York and Oxford, 4–6.

Chapter 15

1. Quoted, Geyer, D., 1987, *Russian Imperialism: The Interaction of Domestic and Foreign Policy 1860–1914*, Leamington Spa, Hamburg and New York, 38.
2. Quoted, *ibid.*, 40.
3. von Laue, T.H., 1963, *Sergei Witte and the Industrialization of Russia*, New York and London, 18.
4. Figures in Geyer, *op. cit.*, 136–41.
5. Anderson, B., 1991, *Imagined Communities: Reflections on the Origin and Spread of Nationalism*, revised edn, London and New York, 33–8.
6. Quoted, Geyer, *op. cit.*, 82.
7. Quoted, *ibid.*, 77.
8. Lukowski, J. and Zawadzki, H., 2001, *A Concise History of Poland*, Cambridge, 167.
9. Hosking, G., 1998, *Russia: People and Empire 1552–1917*, London, 379.
10. Quoted, Saunders, D., 1995, 'Russia's Ukrainian Policy (1847–1905): A Demographic Approach', *European History Quarterly*, XXV, no. 2, Apr., 187.
11. Hosking, *op. cit.*, 383.
12. *Ibid.*, 378.
13. Kappeler, A., 2001, *The Russian Empire: A Multiethnic History*, Harlow, 334.
14. *Ibid.*, 341–2.
15. Programme of the Union of the Russian People, Sept. 1906, in McCauley, M. (ed.), assisted by Waldron, P., 1984, *Octobrists to Bolsheviks: Imperial Russia 1905–1917*, London, doc. 19, 37–9.
16. Text in McCauley, *op. cit.*, doc. 26, 47–9.
17. Weeks, T.R., 2001, 'Official and Popular Nationalisms: Imperial Russia 1863–1914', in U. von Hirschhausen and J. Leonhard (eds), *Nationalismen in Europa: West- und Osteuropa im Vergleich*, Göttingen, 428–9.
18. Speech in *Duma*, 16 Nov. 1907, quoted, Weeks, T.R., 1996, *Nation and State in Late Imperial Russia: Nationalism and Russification on the Western Frontier 1863–1914*, DeKalb, 146.
19. Quoted, Kappeler, *op. cit.*, 344–5.

20. Porter, I. and Armour, I.D., 1991, *Imperial Germany 1890–1918*, London and New York, 29.
21. Quoted, Hagen, W.W., 1980, *Germans, Poles and Jews: The Nationality Conflict in the Prussian East 1772–1914*, Chicago and London, 125.
22. Quoted, Wehler, H.-U., 1985, *The German Empire 1871–1918*, Leamington Spa and Dover, NH, 111.
23. Porter and Armour, *op. cit.*

Chapter 16

1. Geyer, D., 1987, *Russian Imperialism: The Interaction of Domestic and Foreign Policy 1860–1914*, Leamington Spa, Hamburg and New York, 308.
2. Lieven, D.C.B., 1983, *Russia and the Origins of the First World War*, Basingstoke and London, 27–30, 45–6.
3. Figures in Herwig, H.H., 1997, *The First World War: Germany and Austria–Hungary 1914–1918*, London, New York, Sydney and Auckland, 86–7, 88–9, 94, 129.
4. St Petersburg had been renamed on the outbreak of war because it sounded too Germanic.
5. Quoted, Petrovich, M.B., 1976, *A History of Modern Serbia 1804–1918*, vol. II, New York, 630.
6. Zeman, Z.A.B., 1977 [1961], *The Break-up of the Habsburg Empire 1914–1918: A Study in National and Social Revolution*, New York, 44.
7. Quoted, *ibid.*, 53; Cornwall, M., 2000, *The Undermining of Austria–Hungary: The Battle for Hearts and Minds*, Basingstoke and London, 438–44.
8. Lukowski, J. and Zawadzki, H., 2001, *A Concise History of Poland*, Cambridge, 192.
9. Quoted, LaFeber, W., 1994, *The American Age: U.S. Foreign Policy at Home and Abroad 1750 to the Present*, 2nd edn, New York and London, 309–10.

Conclusion

1. Clogg, R., 1992, *A Concise History of Modern Greece*, Cambridge, 93–103.
2. Sharp, A., 1991, *The Versailles Settlement: Peacemaking in Paris, 1919*, Basingstoke and London, 130–58.

BIBLIOGRAPHY

GENERAL

Alter, P., 1994, *Nationalism*, 2nd edn, London.

Anderson, B., 1991, *Imagined Communities: Reflections on the Origin and Spread of Nationalism*, revised edn, London and New York.

Bideleux, R. and Jeffries, I., 1998, *A History of Eastern Europe: Crisis and Change*, London.

Borejsza, J.W., 1994, 'The French Revolution in Relation to Poland and East-Central Europe', in J. Klaits and M.H. Haltzel (eds), *The Global Ramifications of the French Revolution*, Washington, DC and Cambridge, 55–71.

Bridge, R. and Bullen, R., 2004, *The Great Powers and the European States System 1815–1914*, 2nd edn, London.

Chirot, D., 1989, 'Causes and Consequences of Backwardness', in D. Chirot (ed.), *The Origins of Backwardness in Eastern Europe: Economics and Politics from the Middle Ages until the Early Twentieth Century*, Berkeley, Los Angeles, CA and Oxford, 1–14.

Cobban, A., 1963, *A History of Modern France*, 3rd edn, vol. I: *1715–1799*, Harmondsworth.

Coleman, D.C., 1977, *The Economy of England 1450–1750*, Oxford.

Hayes, C.J.H., 1960, *Nationalism: A Religion*, New York.

Herwig, H.H., 1997, *The First World War: Germany and Austria–Hungary 1914–1918*, London, New York, Sydney and Auckland.

Hroch, M., 2000 [1985], *Social Preconditions of National Revival in Europe: A Comparative Analysis of the Social Composition of Patriotic Groups among the Smaller Nations*, translated by Ben Fowkes, New York.

Hurst, M. (ed.), 1972, *Key Treaties for the Great Powers 1814–1914*, vol. I: *1814–1870*, Newton Abbot.

LaFeber, W., 1994, *The American Age: U.S. Foreign Policy at Home and Abroad 1750 to the Present*, 2nd edn, New York and London.

Longworth, P., 1997, *The Making of Eastern Europe: From Prehistory to Postcommunism*, 2nd edn, Basingstoke.

Macartney, C.A. (ed.), 1970, *The Habsburg and Hohenzollern Dynasties in the Seventeenth and Eighteenth Centuries*, London and Melbourne.

Mitchell, B.R., 1973, 'Statistical Appendix 1700–1914', in C.M. Cipolla (ed.), *The Fontana Economic History of Europe*, vol. IV: *The Emergence of Industrial Societies*, Pt 2, London, 738–820.

Nisbet, H.B., 1999, 'Herder's Conception of Nationhood and its Influence in Eastern Europe', in R. Bartlett and K. Schönwälder (eds), *The German Lands and Eastern Europe: Essays on the History of the Social, Cultural and Political Relations*, Basingstoke, 115–35.

Norwich, J.J., 1982, *A History of Venice*, London.

Okey, R., 1986, *Eastern Europe 1740–1985: Feudalism to Communism*, 2nd edn, London and New York.

Palmer, A., 1970, *The Lands Between: A History of East Central Europe Since the Congress of Vienna*, London.

Palmer, R.R., 1959, *The Age of the Democratic Revolution: A Political History of Europe and America 1760–1800*, vol. I: *The Challenge*, Princeton, NJ.

Scott, H.M. (ed.), 1990, *Enlightened Absolutism: Reform and Reformers in Later Eighteenth-Century Europe*, Ann Arbor, MI.

Scott, H.M., 1990, 'Introduction: The Problem of Enlightened Absolutism', in H.M. Scott (ed.), *Enlightened Absolutism: Reform and Reformers in Later Eighteenth-Century Europe*, Ann Arbor, MI, 1–35.

Sharp, A., 1991, *The Versailles Settlement: Peacemaking in Paris, 1919*, Basingstoke and London.

Snyder, T., 2003, *The Reconstruction of Nations: Poland, Ukraine, Lithuania, Belarus 1569–1999*, New Haven, CT and London.

Stone, N., 1998 [1975], *The Eastern Front 1914–1917*, Harmondsworth.

Sugar, P.F., 1994 [1971], 'External and Domestic Roots of Eastern European Nationalism', in P.F. Sugar and I.J. Lederer (eds), *Nationalism in Eastern Europe*, Seattle and London, 3–54.

Vital, D., 1999, *A People Apart: The Jews of Europe 1789–1939*, Oxford.

Wheeler-Bennett, Sir J., 1939, *Forgotten Peace: Brest–Litovsk, March 1918*, New York.

Williams, D. (ed.), 1999, *The Enlightenment*, Cambridge.

Wolff, L., 1994, *Inventing Eastern Europe: The Map of Civilization on the Mind of the Enlightenment*, Stanford, CA.

Wolff, L., 2001, *Venice and the Slavs: The Discovery of Dalmatia in the Age of Enlightenment*, Stanford, CA.

HABSBURG MONARCHY

Agnew, H.L., 2003, 'Czechs, Germans, Bohemians? Images of Self and Other in Bohemia to 1848', in N.M. Wingfield (ed.), *Creating the Other: Ethnic Conflict and Nationalism in Habsburg Central Europe*, New York and Oxford, 56–77.

Auty, R., 1970, 'Changing Views on the Role of Dobrovský in the Czech National Revival', in P. Brock and H.G. Skilling (eds), *The Czech Renascence of the Nineteenth Century: Essays Presented to Otakar Odložilík in Honour of his Seventieth Birthday*, Toronto and Buffalo, NY, 14–25.

Barany, G., 1966, 'The Awakening of Hungarian Nationalism before 1848', *Austrian History Yearbook*, II, 19–50.

Barany, G., 1967, 'Hungary: The Uncompromising Compromise', *Austrian History Yearbook*, III, Pt 1, 234–59.

Barany, G., 1968, *Stephen Széchenyi and the Awakening of Hungarian Nationalism 1791–1841*, Princeton, NJ.

Beller, S., 1996, *Francis Joseph*, Harlow.

Beneš, V.L., 1967, 'The Slovaks in the Habsburg Empire: A Struggle for Existence', *Austrian History Yearbook*, III, Pt 2, 335–64.

Blanning, T.C.W., 1970, *Joseph II and Enlightened Despotism*, London.

Blanning, T.C.W., 1994, *Joseph II*, London and New York.

Bridge, F.R., 1972, *From Sadowa to Sarajevo: The Foreign Policy of Austria–Hungary 1866–1914*, London.

Bridge, F.R., 1990, *The Habsburg Monarchy Among the Great Powers 1815–1918*, New York and Oxford.

Bridge, F.R., 2002, 'The Foreign Policy of the Monarchy', in M. Cornwall (ed.), *The Last Years of Austria–Hungary: A Multinational Experiment in Twentieth-Century Europe*, revised and expanded edn, Exeter, 13–45.

Brock, P., 1976, *The Slovak National Awakening: An Essay in the Intellectual History of East Central Europe*, Toronto.

Cornwall, M., 2000, *The Undermining of Austria–Hungary: The Battle for Hearts and Minds*, Basingstoke and London.

Cushing, G.F., 1960, 'The Birth of National Literature in Hungary', *Slavonic and East European Review*, XXXVIII, no. 91, June, 459–75.

Deak, I., 1979, *The Lawful Revolution: Louis Kossuth and the Hungarians 1848–1849*, New York.

Despalatović, E.M., 1975, *Ljudevit Gaj and the Illyrian Movement*, Boulder, CO.

Dickson, P.G.M., 1987, *Finance and Government Under Maria Theresia*, vol. II: *Finance and Credit*, Oxford.

Djordjević, D., 1967, 'The Serbs as an Integrating and Disintegrating Factor', *Austrian History Yearbook*, III, Pt 2, 48–82.

Eisenmann, L., 1971 [1904], *Le compromise austro-hongrois de 1867: Étude sur le dualisme*, Hattiesburg, MS.

Evans, R.J.W., 1979, *The Making of the Habsburg Monarchy 1550–1700: An Interpretation*, Oxford.

Evans, R.J.W., 2000, '1848–49 in the Habsburg Monarchy', in R.J.W. Evans and H. Pogge von Strandmann (eds), *The Revolutions in Europe 1848–1849: From Reform to Reaction*, Oxford, 181–206.

Evans, R.J.W., 2001, 'Der ungarische Nationalismus im internationalen Vergleich', in U. von Hirschhausen and J. Leonhard (eds), *Nationalismen in Europa: West- und Osteuropa im Vergleich*, Göttingen, 291–305.

Evans, R., 2003, 'Kossuth and Štúr: Two National Heroes', in L. Péter, M. Rady and P. Sherwood (eds), *Lajos Kossuth Sent Word ... Papers Delivered on the Occasion of the Bicentenary of Kossuth's Birth*, London, 119–33.

Gerschenkron, A., 1977, *An Economic Spurt That Failed: Four Lectures in Austrian History*, Princeton, NJ.

Good, D., 1984, *The Economic Rise of the Habsburg Empire 1750–1914*, Berkeley and Los Angeles, CA.

Holotík, L., 1967, 'The Slovaks: An Integrating or a Disintegrating Force?', *Austrian History Yearbook*, III, Pt 2, 365–93.

Ingrao, C., 1994, *The Habsburg Monarchy 1618–1815*, Cambridge.

Isaievich, I., 1994, 'Galicia and Problems of National Identity', in R. Robertson and E. Timms (eds), *The Habsburg Legacy: National Identity in Historical Perspective*, Edinburgh, 37–45.

Janos, A.C., 1982, *The Politics of Backwardness in Hungary 1825–1945*, Princeton, NJ.

Jászi, O., 1929, *The Dissolution of the Habsburg Monarchy*, Chicago, IL and London.

Jelavich, C., 1967, 'The Croatian Problem in the Habsburg Empire in the Nineteenth Century', *Austrian History Yearbook*, III, Pt 2, 83–115.

Jenks, W.A., 1974 [1950], *The Austrian Electoral Reform of 1907*, New York.

Kann, R.A., 1974, *A History of the Habsburg Empire 1526–1918*, Berkeley, Los Angeles, CA and London.

Kimball, S.B., 1970, 'The Matica Česká, 1831–1861: The First Thirty Years of a Literary Foundation', in P. Brock and H.G. Skilling (eds), *The Czech Renascence of the*

Nineteenth Century: Essays Presented to Otakar Odložilík in Honour of his Seventieth Birthday, Toronto and Buffalo, NY, 53–73.

Király, B.K., 1969, *Hungary in the Late Eighteenth Century: The Decline of Enlightened Despotism*, New York.

Komlos, J., 1983, *The Habsburg Monarchy as a Customs Union: Economic Development in Austria–Hungary in the Nineteenth Century*, Princeton, NJ.

Kozik, J., 1986, *The Ukrainian National Movement in Galicia 1815–1849*, edited and with an introduction by L.D. Orton, Edmonton.

Macartney, C.A., 1962, *Hungary: A Short History*, Edinburgh.

Macartney, C.A., 1969, *The Habsburg Empire 1790–1918*, London.

Magocsi, P.R., 1982, 'The Language Question as a Factor in the National Movement', in A.S. Markovits and F.E. Sysyn (eds), *Nationbuilding and the Politics of Nationalism: Essays on Austrian Galicia*, Cambridge, MA, 220–38.

May, A.J., 1968 [1951], *The Hapsburg Monarchy 1867–1914*, New York.

Milne, A., 1975, *Metternich*, London.

Okey, R., 2001, *The Habsburg Monarchy c. 1765–1918: From Enlightenment to Eclipse*, Basingstoke and London.

Orton, L.D., 1978, *The Prague Slav Congress of 1848*, New York.

Padover, S.K., 1967, *The Revolutionary Emperor: Joseph II of Austria*, London.

Palairet, M., 1993, 'The Habsburg Industrial Achievement in Bosnia–Hercegovina 1878–1914: An Economic Spurt that Succeeded?', *Austrian History Yearbook*, XXIV, 133–52.

Remak, J., 1959, *Sarajevo: The Story of a Political Murder*, London.

Rothenberg, G.E., 1966, *The Military Border in Croatia 1740–1881: The Study of an Imperial Institution*, Chicago, IL.

Rudnytsky, I.L., 1967, 'The Ukrainians in Galicia under Austrian Rule', *Austrian History Yearbook*, III, Pt 2, 394–429.

Sayer, D., 1998, *The Coasts of Bohemia: A Czech History*, Princeton, NJ.

Schorske, C.E., 1980, 'Politics in a New Key: An Austrian Trio', in C.E. Schorske, *Fin-de-Siècle Vienna: Politics and Culture*, London, 116–80.

Scott, H.M., 1990, 'Reform in the Habsburg Monarchy 1740–90', in H.M. Scott (ed.), *Enlightened Absolutism: Reform and Reformers in Later Eighteenth-Century Europe*, Ann Arbor, MI, 145–87.

Seton-Watson, R.W., 1972 [1908], *Racial Problems in Hungary*, New York.

Sked, A., 2001, *The Decline and Fall of the Habsburg Empire 1815–1918*, 2nd edn, Harlow.

Spira, T., 1973, 'Aspects of the Magyar Linguistic and Literary Renaissance during the Vormärz', *East European Quarterly*, VII, no. 2, Summer, 101–24.

Stourzh, G., 1992, 'The Multinational Empire Revisited: Reflections on Late Imperial Austria', *Austrian History Yearbook*, XXIII, 1–22.

Sugar, P.F., 1958, 'The Influence of the Enlightenment and the French Revolution in Eighteenth Century Hungary', *Journal of Central European Affairs*, XVII, no. 4, January, 331–55.

Sugar, P.F., 1963, *Industrialization of Bosnia–Hercegovina, 1878–1918*, Seattle.

Sugar, P.F., 1999, 'Government and Minorities in Austria–Hungary – Different Policies with the Same Result', in P.F. Sugar, *East European Nationalism, Politics and Religion*, Aldershot, 7–12.

Szabo, F.A.J., 1994, *Kaunitz and Enlightened Absolutism 1753–1780*, Cambridge.

Taylor, A.J.P., 1964 [1948], *The Habsburg Monarchy 1809–1918: A History of the Austrian Empire and Austria–Hungary*, Harmondsworth.

Thomson, S.H., 1967, 'The Czechs as Integrating and Disintegrating Factors in the Habsburg Empire', *Austrian History Yearbook*, III, Pt 2, 203–22.

Vucinich, W.S., 1967, 'The Serbs in Austria–Hungary', *Austrian History Yearbook*, III, Pt 2, 3–47.

Vucinich, W.S., 1975, 'Croatian Illyrism: Its Background and Genesis', in S.B. Winters and J. Held (eds), *Intellectual and Social Developments in the Habsburg Empire from Maria Theresa to World War I: Essays Dedicated to Robert A. Kann*, Boulder, CO, 51–73.

Wandycz, P.S., 1967, 'The Poles in the Habsburg Monarchy', *Austrian History Yearbook*, III, Pt. 2, 261–86.

Williamson, Jr., S.R., 1991, *Austria–Hungary and the Origins of the First World War*, Basingstoke and London.

Zeman, Z.A.B., 1977 [1961], *The Break-up of the Habsburg Empire 1914–1918: A Study in National and Social Revolution*, New York.

Zwitter, F., 1967, 'The Slovenes and the Habsburg Monarchy', *Austrian History Yearbook*, III, Pt 2, 157–88.

POLAND–LITHUANIA

Davies, N., 1981, *God's Playground: A History of Poland*, vol. I: *The Origins to 1795*, Oxford.

Gierowski, J.A., 1982, 'The International Position of Poland in the Seventeenth and Eighteenth Centuries', in J.K. Fedorowicz *et al.* (eds), *A Republic of Nobles: Studies in Polish History to 1864*, Cambridge, 218–38.

Grochulska, B., 1982, 'The Place of the Enlightenment in Polish Social History', in J.K. Fedorowicz *et al.* (eds), *A Republic of Nobles: Studies in Polish History to 1864*, Cambridge, 239–57.

Halecki, O., 1963, 'Why Was Poland Partitioned?', *Slavic Review*, XXII, no. 3, September, 432–41.

Konczacki, J.M., 1986, 'Stanislaw August Poniatowski's "Thursday Dinners" and Cultural Change in Late Eighteenth Century Poland', *Canadian Journal of History*, XXI, April, 25–36.

Lukowksi, J., 1991, *Liberty's Folly: The Polish–Lithuanian Commonwealth in the Eighteenth Century 1697–1795*, London and New York.

Lukowski, J., 1999, *The Partitions of Poland: 1772, 1793, 1795*, London and New York.

Lukowski, J. and Zawadzki, H., 2001, *A Concise History of Poland*, Cambridge.

Nieuwazny, A., 2000, 'The Polish Kingdom (1815–1830): Continuity or Change?', in D. Laven and L. Riall (eds), *Napoleon's Legacy: Problems of Government in Restoration Europe*, Oxford and New York, 115–28.

Porter, B.A., 2000, *When Nationalism Began to Hate: Imagining Modern Politics in Nineteenth-Century Poland*, London and New York.

Rostworowski, E., 1982, 'War and Society in the Noble Republic of Poland–Lithuania in the Eighteenth Century', in G.E. Rothenberg *et al.* (eds), *East Central European Society and War in the Pre-Revolutionary Eighteenth Century*, New York, 165–82.

Wandycz, P.S., 1974, *The Lands of Partitioned Poland 1795–1918*, Seattle and London.

Zamoyski, A., 1987, *The Polish Way: A Thousand-Year History of the Poles and their Culture*, London.

Zamoyski, A., 1992, *The Last King of Poland*, London.

OTTOMAN EMPIRE AND THE BALKANS

Anderson, M.S., 1966, *The Eastern Question 1774–1923: A Study in International Relations*, London and Basingstoke.

Banac, I., 1984, *The National Question in Yugoslavia: Origins, History, Politics*, Ithaca, NY and London.

Bataković, D.T., 1994, 'Ilija Garašanin's Načertanije: A Reassessment', *Balcanica*, XXV, no. 1, 156–73.

Black, C.E., 1943, 'The Influence of Western Political Thought in Bulgaria 1850–1885', *American Historical Review*, XLVIII, no. 3, April, 507–20.

Campbell, J.C., 1944, 'The Influence of Western Political Thought in the Rumanian Principalities 1821–1848', *Journal of Central European Affairs*, IV, no. 3, October, 262–73.

Carnegie Endowment for International Peace, 1914, *Report of the International Commission to Inquire into the Causes and Conduct of the Balkan Wars*, Washington, DC, republished in 1993 in facsimile reprint by George F. Kennan, as *The Other Balkan Wars: A 1913 Carnegie Endowment Inquiry in Retrospect with a New Introduction and Reflections on the Present Conflict*, Washington, DC.

Clogg, R. (ed.), 1973, *The Struggle for Greek Independence: Essays to Mark the 150th Anniversary of the Greek War of Independence*, London and Basingstoke.

Clogg, R. (ed.), 1977, *The Movement for Greek Independence 1770–1821*, London and Basingstoke.

Clogg, R. (ed.), 1981, *Balkan Society in the Age of Greek Independence*, London and Basingstoke.

Clogg, R., 1982, 'The Greek Orthodox Millet in the Ottoman Empire', in B. Braude and B. Lewis (eds), *Christians and Jews in the Ottoman Empire: The Functioning of a Plural Society*, vol. I: *The Central Lands*, New York and London, 185–207.

Clogg R., 1992, *A Concise History of Greece*, Cambridge.

Cornwall, M., 1995, 'Serbia', in K. Wilson (ed.), *Decisions for War, 1914*, London, 55–96.

Crampton, R.J., 1987, *A Short History of Modern Bulgaria*, Cambridge.

Deletant, D., 1981, 'Romanian Society in the Danubian Principalities in the Early 19th Century', in R. Clogg (ed.), *Balkan Society in the Age of Greek Independence*, London and Basingstoke, 229–48.

Ferguson, A., 1981, 'Montenegrin Society 1800–1830', in R. Clogg (ed.), *Balkan Society in the Age of Greek Independence*, London and Basingstoke, 205–28.

Frangos, G.D., 1973, 'The *Philiki Etairia*: A Premature National Coalition', in R. Clogg (ed.), *The Struggle for Greek Independence: Essays to Mark the 150th Anniversary of the Greek War of Independence*, London and Basingstoke, 87–103.

Georgescu, V., 1973, 'The Romanian Boyars in the 18th Century: Their Political Ideology', *East European Quarterly*, VII, no. 1, Spring, 31–40.

Hitchins, K., 1969, *The Rumanian National Movement in Transylvania 1780–1849*, Cambridge, MA.

Hitchins, K., 1977, *Orthodoxy and Nationality: Andreiu Şaguna and the Rumanians of Transylvania, 1846–1873*, Cambridge, MA.

Hitchins, K., 1979, 'Religion and Rumanian National Consciousness in Eighteenth-Century Transylvania', *Slavonic and East European Review*, LVII, no. 2, April, 214–39.

Hitchins, K., 1994, *Rumania 1866–1947*, Oxford.

Jelavich, B., 1983, *History of the Balkans*, vol. I: *Eighteenth and Nineteenth Centuries*, Cambridge.

Jelavich, B., 1984, *Russia and the Formation of the Romanian National State 1821–1878*, Cambridge.

Jelavich, C. and Jelavich, B., 1977, *The Establishment of the Balkan National States 1804–1920*, Seattle.

Kushner, D., 1976, *The Rise of Turkish Nationalism 1876–1908*, London.

Lewis, B., 1968, *The Emergence of Modern Turkey*, 2nd edn, London, Oxford and New York.

MacKenzie, D., 1985, *Ilija Garašanin: Balkan Bismarck*, New York.

Mackridge, P., 1981, 'The Greek Intelligentsia 1780–1830: A Balkan Perspective', in R. Clogg (ed.), *Balkan Society in the Age of Greek Independence*, London and Basingstoke, 63–84.

Malcolm, N., 1994, *Bosnia: A Short History*, London and Basingstoke.

Malcolm, N., 1998, *Kosovo: A Short History*, London and Basingstoke.

Mango, C., 1973, 'The Phanariots and the Byzantine Tradition', in R. Clogg (ed.), *The Struggle for Greek Independence: Essays to Mark the 150th Anniversary of the Greek War of Independence*, London and Basingstoke, 41–66.

Mardin, Ş., 1962, *The Genesis of Young Ottoman Thought: A Study in the Modernization of Turkish Political Ideas*, Princeton, NJ.

Mazower, M., 2000, *The Balkans*, London.

McCarthy, J., 1997, *The Ottoman Turks: An Introductory History to 1923*, Harlow.

McCarthy, J., 2001, *The Ottoman Peoples and the End of Empire*, London.

McGrew, W.W., 1985, *Land and Revolution in Modern Greece 1800–1881: The Transition in the Tenure and Exploitation of Land from Ottoman Rule to Independence*, Kent, OH.

Miller, W., 1966 [1927], *The Ottoman Empire and its Successors 1801–1927*, 3rd edn, London.

Palairet, M., 1997, *The Balkan Economies c. 1800–1914: Evolution without Development*, Cambridge.

Pavlowitch, S., 1981, 'Society in Serbia 1791–1830', in R. Clogg (ed.), *Balkan Society in the Age of Greek Independence*, London and Basingstoke, 137–56.

Pavlowitch, S.K., 1999, *A History of the Balkans 1804–1945*, London and New York.

Pech, S.Z., 1969, *The Czech Revolution of 1848*, Chapel Hill, NC.

Petrovich, M.B., 1976, *A History of Modern Serbia 1804–1918*, vol. I, New York and London.

Poulton, H., 1997, *Top Hat, Grey Wolf and Crescent: Turkish Nationalism and the Turkish Republic*, London.

Psomiades, H.P., 1976, 'The Character of the New Greek State', in N.P. Diamandouros *et al.* (eds), *Hellenism and the First Greek War of Liberation (1821–1830): Continuity and Change*, Thessaloniki, 147–55.

Quataert, D., 2000, *The Ottoman Empire 1700–1922*, Cambridge.

Ramsaur, Jr., E.E., 1957, *The Young Turks: Prelude to the Revolution of 1908*, Princeton, NJ.

Shaw, S.J., 1963, 'The Ottoman View of the Balkans', in C. Jelavich and B. Jelavich (eds), *The Balkans in Transition: Essays on the Development of Balkan Life and Politics since the 18th Century*, Berkeley and Los Angeles, CA, 56–80.

Shaw, S.J., 1971, *Between the Old and the New: The Ottoman Empire under Selim III 1789–1807*, Cambridge, MA.

Shaw, S.J., 1976, *History of the Ottoman Empire and Modern Turkey*, vol. I: *Empire of the Gazis: The Rise and Decline of the Ottoman Empire 1280–1808*, Cambridge, London, New York and Melbourne.

Shaw, S.J. and Shaw, E.K., 1977, *History of the Ottoman Empire and Modern Turkey*, vol. II: *Reform, Revolution and Republic: The Rise of Modern Turkey 1808–1975*, Cambridge.

Singleton, F., 1985, *Short History of the Yugoslav Peoples*, Cambridge.

Skiotis, D.N., 1976, 'The Greek Revolution: Ali Pasha's Last Gamble', in N.P. Diamandouros *et al.* (eds), *Hellenism and the First Greek War of Liberation (1821–1830): Continuity and Change*, Thessaloniki, 97–109.

Stoianovich, T., 1960, 'The Conquering Balkan Orthodox Merchant', *Journal of Economic History*, XX, June, 234–313.

Stoianovich, T., 1962, 'Factors in the Decline of Ottoman Society in the Balkans', *Slavic Review*, XXI, no. 4, December, 623–32.

Stokes, G., 1975, *Legitimacy Through Liberalism: Vladimir Jovanović and the Transformation of Serbian Politics*, Seattle and London.

Stokes, G., 1990, *Politics as Development: The Emergence of Political Parties in Nineteenth-Century Serbia*, Durham, NC and London.

Sugar, P.F., 1977, *Southeastern Europe under Ottoman Rule 1354–1804*, Seattle and London.

Tappe, E.D., 1973, 'The 1821 Revolution in the Rumanian Principalities', in R. Clogg (ed.), *The Struggle for Greek Independence: Essays to Mark the 150th Anniversary of the Greek War of Independence*, London and Basingstoke, 135–55.

Todorova, M., 1997, *Imagining the Balkans*, New York and Oxford.

Vickers, M., 1995, *The Albanians: A Modern History*, London and New York.

Vucinich, W.S., 1962, 'The Nature of Balkan Society under Ottoman Rule', *Slavic Review*, XXI, no. 4, December, 597–616.

Wilson, D., 1970, *The Life and Times of Vuk Stefanović Karadžić 1787–1864: Literacy, Literature and National Independence in Serbia*, Oxford.

Woodhouse, C.M., 1981, "The 'Untoward Event": The Battle of Navarino 20 October 1827', in R. Clogg (ed.), *Balkan Society in the Age of Greek Independence*, London and Basingstoke, 1–17.

Xydis, S.G., 1994 [1969], 'Modern Greek Nationalism', in P.F. Sugar and I.J. Lederer (eds), *Nationalism in Eastern Europe*, Seattle and London, 207–58.

Zeman, Z.A.B., 1988, 'The Balkans and the Coming of the War', in R.J.W. Evans and H. Pogge von Strandmann (eds), *The Coming of the First World War*, Oxford, 19–32.

RUSSIA

Falkus, M.E., 1972, *The Industrialisation of Russia 1700–1914*, Basingstoke.

Geyer, D., 1987, *Russian Imperialism: The Interaction of Domestic and Foreign Policy 1860–1914*, translated from the German by Bruce Little, Leamington Spa, Hamburg and New York.

Gooding, J., 1986, 'The Liberalism of Michael Speransky', *Slavonic and East European Review*, LXIV, no. 3, July, 401–24.

Hartley, J.M., 1994, *Alexander I*, London and New York.

Hartley, J.M., 1996, 'The "Constitutions" of Finland and Poland in the Reign of Alexander I: Blueprints for Reform in Russia?', in M. Branch, J.M. Hartley and A. Mączak (eds), *Finland and Poland in the Russian Empire: A Comparative Study*, London, 41–59.

Hosking, G., 1998, 'Empire and Nation-Building in Late Imperial Russia', in G. Hosking and R. Service (eds), *Russian Nationalism, Past and Present*, Basingstoke and London, 19–34.

Hosking, G., 1998, *Russia: People and Empire 1557–1917*, London.

Jelavich, B., 1991, *Russia's Balkan Entanglements 1806–1914*, Cambridge.

Kappeler, A., 2001, *The Russian Empire: A Multiethnic History*, Harlow.

Kochan, L. and Keep, J., 1997, *The Making of Modern Russia from Kiev Rus' to the Collapse of the Soviet Union*, new edn, Harmondsworth.

Kohut, Z.E., 1983, 'The Ukrainian Elite in the Eighteenth Century and its Integration into the Russian Nobility', in I. Banac and P. Bushkovitch (eds), *The Nobility of Russia and Eastern Europe*, New Haven, CT, 65–96.

Kohut, Z.E., 1986, 'The Development of a Little Russian Identity and Ukrainian Nation-building', *Harvard Ukrainian Studies*, X, no. 1–2, June, 559–76.

Laue, T.H. von, 1963, *Sergei Witte and the Industrialization of Russia*, New York and London.

Lieven, D.C.B., 1983, *Russia and the Origins of the First World War*, Basingstoke and London.

Magocsi, P.R., 1996, *A History of Ukraine*, Toronto.

McCauley, M. (ed.), 1984, assisted by P. Waldron, *Octobrists to Bolsheviks: Imperial Russia 1905–1917*, London.

Moon, D., 1992, *Russian Peasants and Tsarist Legislation on the Eve of Reform: Interaction between Peasants and Officialdom 1825–1855*, London and Basingstoke.

Mühlen, H. von zur, 1994, 'Das Ostbaltikum unter Herrschaft und Einfluß der Nachbarmächte (1561–1710/1795)', in G. von Pistohlkors (ed.), *Deutsche Geschichte im Osten Europas: Baltische Länder*, Berlin, 173–264.

Petrovich, M.B., 1956, *The Emergence of Russian Panslavism 1856–1870*, New York and London.

Raeff, M. (ed.), 1966, *Plans for Political Reform in Imperial Russia 1730–1905*, Englewood Cliffs, NJ.

Raeff, M., 1966, *Origins of the Russian Intelligentsia: The Eighteenth-Century Nobility*, New York.

Raeff, M., 1970, 'Pugachev's Rebellion', in R. Forster and J.P. Greene (eds), *Preconditions of Revolution in Early Modern Europe*, Baltimore and London, 161–202.

Raeff, M., 1992, 'Ukraine and Imperial Russia: Intellectual and Political Encounters from the Seventeenth to the Nineteenth Century', in P.J. Potichnyj, M. Raeff, J. Pelenski and G.N. Žekulin (eds), *Ukraine and Russia in Their Historical Encounter*, Edmonton, 69–75.

Riasanovsky, N.V., 1959, *Nicholas I and Official Nationality in Russia 1825–1855*, Berkeley and Los Angeles, CA.

Riasanovsky, N.V., 1993, *A History of Russia*, 5th edn, Oxford.

Rogger, H., 1962, 'Nationalism and the State: A Russian Dilemma', *Comparative Studies in Society and History*, IV, no. 3, April, 253–64.

Rogger, H., 1983, *Russia in the Age of Modernisation and Revolution 1881–1917*, London and New York.

Saunders, D., 1992, *Russia in the Age of Reaction and Reform 1801–1881*, London and New York.

Saunders, D., 1995, 'Russia and Ukraine under Alexander II: The Valuev Edict of 1863', *International History Review*, XVII, no. 1, February, 23–50.

Saunders, D., 1995, 'Russia's Ukrainian Policy (1847–1905): A Demographic Approach', *European History Quarterly*, XXV, no. 2, April, 181–208.

Seton-Watson, H., 1967, *The Russian Empire 1801–1917*, Oxford.

Slezkine, Y., 1997, 'Naturalists versus Nations: Eighteenth-Century Russian Scholars Confront Ethnic Diversity', in D.R. Brower and E.J. Lazzerini (eds), *Russia's Orient: Imperial Borderlands and Peoples 1700–1917*, Bloomington and Indianapolis, IN, 27–57.

Stockdale, M.K., 1996, *Paul Miliukov and the Quest for a Liberal Russia 1880–1918*, Ithaca, NY and London.

Thaden, E.C., 1964, *Conservative Nationalism in Nineteenth-Century Russia*, Seattle.

Thaden, E.C., 1984, *Russia's Western Borderlands 1710–1870*, Princeton, NJ.

Thaden, E.C., 1996, 'Traditional Elites, Religion and Nation-Building in Finland, the Baltic Provinces and Lithuania 1700–1914', in M. Branch, J.M. Hartley and A. Mączak (eds), *Finland and Poland in the Russian Empire: A Comparative Study*, London, 1–15.

Tolz, V., 1997, *Russia*, London.

Vucinich, W.S., 1962, 'The Nature of Balkan Society under Ottoman Rule', *Slavic Review*, XXI, no. 4, December, 597–616.

Weeks, T.R., 1996, *Nation and State in Late Imperial Russia: Nationalism and Russification on the Western Frontier 1863–1914*, DeKalb.

Weeks, T.R., 2001, 'Official and Popular Nationalisms: Imperial Russia 1863–1914', in U. von Hirschhausen and J. Leonhard (eds), *Nationalismen in Europa: West- und Osteuropa im Vergleich*, Göttingen, 411–32.

Wittram, R., 1973 [1954], *Baltische Geschichte: Die Ostseelande Livland, Estland, Kurland 1180–1918*, Darmstadt.

PRUSSIA/GERMANY

Blanning, T.C.W., 1990, 'Frederick the Great and Enlightened Absolutism', in H.M. Scott (ed.), *Enlightened Absolutism: Reform and Reformers in Later Eighteenth-Century Europe*, Ann Arbor, MI, 245–88.

Carr, W., 1991, *A History of Germany 1815–1990*, 4th edn, London.

Dwyer, P.G. (ed.), 2000, *The Rise of Prussia 1700–1830*, Harlow.

Friedrich, K., 1997, 'Facing Both Ways: New Works on Prussia and Polish–Prussian Relations', *German History*, XV, no. 2, 256–67.

Friedrich, K., 2000, 'The Development of the Prussian Town 1720–1815', in P.G. Dwyer (ed.), *The Rise of Prussia 1700–1830*, Harlow, 129–50.

Gothelf, R., 2000, 'Frederick William I and the Beginnings of Prussian Absolutism 1713–1740', in P.G. Dwyer (ed.), *The Rise of Prussia 1700–1830*, Harlow, 47–67.

Hagen, W.W., 1980, *Germans, Poles, and Jews: The Nationality Conflict in the Prussian East, 1772–1914*, Chicago, IL and London.

Hagen, W.W., 1986, 'The Junkers' Faithless Servants: Peasant Insubordination and the Breakdown of Serfdom in Brandenburg-Prussia 1763–1811', in R.J. Evans and W.R. Lee (eds), *The German Peasantry: Conflict and Community in Rural Society from the Eighteenth to the Twentieth Centuries*, London, 71–101.

Hewitson, M., 2004, *Germany and the Causes of the First World War*, Oxford and New York.

Ingrao, C., 1990, 'The Smaller German States', in H.M. Scott (ed.), *Enlightened Absolutism: Reform and Reformers in Later Eighteenth-Century Europe*, Ann Arbor, MI, 221–43.

Melton, E., 2000, 'The Transformation of the Rural Economy in East Elbian Prussia 1750–1830', in P.G. Dwyer (ed.), *The Rise of Prussia 1700–1830*, Harlow, 111–28.

Pogge von Strandmann, H., 1988, 'Germany and the Coming of the War', in R.J.W. Evans and H. Pogge von Strandmann (eds), *The Coming of the First World War*, Oxford, 87–123.

Porter, I. and Armour, I.D., 1991, *Imperial Germany 1890–1918*, London and New York.

Schieder, T., 2000 [1983], *Frederick the Great*, edited and translated by S. Berkeley and H.M. Scott, London and New York.

Scott, H.M., 2000, 'Prussia's Emergence as a Great Power 1740–1763', in P.G. Dwyer (ed.), *The Rise of Prussia 1700–1830*, Harlow, 153–76.

Scott, H.M., 2000, '1763–1786: The Second Reign of Frederick the Great', in P.G. Dwyer (ed.), *The Rise of Prussia 1700–1830*, Harlow, 177–200.

Smith, W.D., 1986, *The Ideological Origins of Nazi Imperialism*, New York and Oxford.

Wehler, H.-U., 1985, *The German Empire 1871–1918*, Leamington Spa and Dover, NH.

INDEX

Index